COLLECTIVE JUDGING IN COMPARATIVE PERSPECTIVE

COLLECTIVE JUDGING IN COMPARATIVE PERSPECTIVE

Counting Votes and Weighing Opinions

Edited by
Birke Häcker
Wolfgang Ernst

INTERSENTIA
Cambridge – Antwerp – Chicago

Intersentia Ltd
8 Wellington Mews
Wellington Street | Cambridge
CB1 1HW | United Kingdom
Tel: +44 1223 736 170
Email: mail@intersentia.co.uk
www.intersentia.com | www.intersentia.co.uk

Distribution for the UK and
Rest of the World (incl. Eastern Europe)
NBN International
1 Deltic Avenue, Rooksley
Milton Keynes MK13 8LD
United Kingdom
Tel: +44 1752 202 301 | Fax: +44 1752 202 331
Email: orders@nbninternational.com

Distribution for Europe
Intersentia Publishing nv
Groenstraat 31
2640 Mortsel
Belgium
Tel: +32 3 680 15 50
Email: mail@intersentia.be

Distribution for the USA and Canada
Independent Publishers Group
Order Department
814 North Franklin Street
Chicago, IL 60610
USA
Tel: +1 800 888 4741 (toll free) | Fax: +1 312 337 5985
Email: orders@ipgbook.com

Collective Judging in Comparative Perspective. Counting Votes and Weighing Opinions

ISBN 978-1-78068-624-0
D/2020/7849/73
NUR 820

British Library Cataloguing in Publication Data. A catalogue record for this book is available from the British Library.

PREFACE

This collection is the product of a conference entitled 'Counting Votes and Weighing Opinions – Collective Judging in Comparative Perspective', held at All Souls College, Oxford, on 20 and 21 July 2017. The event was co-organised by the editors (both University of Oxford) together with Professor Beate Gsell (Ludwig-Maximilians-Universität München) and Professor Thomas Rüfner (Universität Trier). Our co-organisers regularly sit on cases heard by Higher Regional Courts of Appeal in Germany (Oberlandesgericht München and Koblenz, respectively).

The aim of the conference was to bring together distinguished judges and academics from around the world to discuss the mechanisms, processes and challenges of collective decision-making by judicial bodies. Participants came from a mix of civil law and common law jurisdictions. Judges from national, supranational and international courts reported on their respective practices and experiences, leading to an exchange of views on the pros and cons of various different approaches. Lord Neuberger of Abbotsbury, who was at the time of the conference about to step down as President of the UK Supreme Court, in a closing speech elegantly pulled together all the various red threads that had emerged over two days of intense debate.

Most of contributions contained in this book are updated, amended and in a few cases significantly expanded versions of the papers delivered at the conference. For the purposes of this publication, we have ordered them by the type of jurisdiction they pertain to. The book commences with an 'impulse paper' prepared by Wolfgang Ernst that also initiated the conference itself. The chapters include two (by Professor Gertrude Lübbe-Wolff and by Judge Theodor Meron, co-authored by Christos Ravanides) which would have been given at the conference had not circumstances beyond the speakers' control prevented them from attending. Towards the end of the book, we have added a part containing 'voices from the audience'. It encompasses contributions by conference attendees who kindly agreed to provide insight into their own experience of collective judging in other bodies, or who offered reflections and comments on the conference topic from an academic perspective. The book concludes with some remarks by the organisers, flagging aspects we found particularly interesting and which we think could inform future 'court design'.

As editors, we would like to thank, first and foremost, our co-organisers Beate and Thomas who helped conceive the conference and whose substantive input and financial contribution towards travel costs was invaluable. The conference itself was hosted and generously funded by All Souls College, Oxford. We are sure to be speaking for everybody involved in thanking the Warden and Fellows of the College for their magnificent hospitality. We are also very grateful to the participants for their various contributions and to the authors for bearing with us over a somewhat protracted editing process. Finally, we are indebted to Ann-Christin Maak-Scherpe and her team at Intersentia Publishing, particularly Rebecca Moffat, for producing such an elegant volume.

Birke Häcker
Wolfgang Ernst

CONTENTS

LIST OF CASES

INTERNATIONAL CRIMINAL TRIBUNALS

EUROPEAN COURT OF HUMAN RIGHTS

EUROPEAN COURT OF JUSTICE

AUSTRALIA

GERMANY

FEDERAL CONSTITUTIONAL COURT

FEDERAL SUPREME COURT

FEDERAL ADMINISTRATIVE COURT

FEDERAL LABOUR LAW COURT

SWITZERLAND

UNITED KINGDOM

UNITED STATES OF AMERICA

LIST OF CONTRIBUTORS

Sir Jack Beatson
Former Lord Justice of Appeal at the Court of Appeal of England and Wales; Visiting Professor, University of Oxford

Thomas von Danwitz
Judge of the Court of Justice of the European Union; Professor of Public Law and European Union Law at the University of Cologne (on leave)

Matthew Dyson
Associate Professor of Law, University of Oxford, and Fellow of Corpus Christi College, Oxford

Harry T Edwards
Senior Circuit Judge and Chief Judge Emeritus of the United States Court of Appeals for the DC Circuit, Washington DC; Professor of Law, New York University School of Law

Wolfgang Ernst
Regius Professor of Civil Law, University of Oxford, and Fellow of All Souls College, Oxford

Kevin Garnett QC
Former Member of the Boards of Appeal of the European Patent Office

Msgr Markus Graulich
Undersecretary of the Pontifical Council for Legislative Text; former Prelate Auditor of the Tribunal of the Roman Rota (*Tribunal Rotæ Romanæ*)

Beate Gsell
Professor of Private Law, Civil Procedure and European Private Law and Procedure, Ludwig-Maximilians-Universität (LMU) München; Judge at the Higher Regional Court of Appeal in Munich (*Oberlandesgericht München*)

Birke Häcker
Professor of Comparative Law and Director of the Institute of European and Comparative Law, University of Oxford, and Fellow of Brasenose College, Oxford

Dominique Hascher
Judge of the Supreme Judicial Court of France (*Cour de cassation*), Paris

Sir Launcelot Henderson
Lord Justice of Appeal at the Court of Appeal of England and Wales; Fellow of All Souls College, Oxford

Richard Hyland
Distinguished Professor of Law, Rutgers Law School, Camden, New Jersey

Susan Kiefel AC
Chief Justice of Australia

Georg Kodek
Judge of the Austrian Supreme Court (*Oberster Gerichtshof*); Professor of Civil and Commercial Law at Wirtschaftsuniversität (WU), Vienna

James Lee
Reader in English Law, The Dickson Poon School of Law, King's College London

Sir Keith Lindblom
Lord Justice of Appeal at the Court of Appeal of England and Wales

Gertrude Lübbe-Wolff
Former Judge at the German Federal Constitutional Court; Professor (em.) of Public Law at the University of Bielefeld

Theodor Meron
Judge of the International Residual Mechanism for Criminal Tribunals; Visiting Professor, University of Oxford, and Fellow of Trinity College, Oxford

Angelika Nussberger
Professor of Constitutional Law, Public International Law and Comparative Law at the University of Cologne; former Vice-President of the European Court of Human Rights

Akira Ojima
Chief Judicial Research Official at the Supreme Court of Japan; former Presiding Judge of the Tokyo High Court

Naoki Onishi
Presiding Judge of the Otsu District Court (Head of the Criminal Division); former Judge of the Tokyo High Court

Christos Ravanides
Legal Officer at the Office of Legal Affairs of the United Nations; former deputy *chef de cabinet* to Judge Theodor Meron, then-President of the International Criminal Tribunal for the former Yugoslavia (ICTY)

Lord Reed of Allermuir
President of the Supreme Court of the United Kingdom

Thomas Rüfner
Professor of Private Law, Roman Law, Legal History and Civil Procedure, the University of Trier; Judge at the Higher Regional Court of Appeal in Koblenz (*Oberlandesgericht Koblenz*)

Johanna Schmidt-Räntsch
Deputy Presiding Judge of the Vth Civil Senate of the German Federal Court of Justice (*Bundesgerichtshof*); Honorary Professor, Humboldt-Universität (HU) Berlin

Thomas Stadelmann
Judge at the Swiss Supreme Court (*Bundesgericht*)

PART I

DESIGNING COLLEGIATE COURTS' DECISION-MAKING PROCESSES

CHAPTER 1

THE FINE-MECHANICS OF JUDICIAL MAJORITARIANISM

Wolfgang ERNST*

I. JUDICIAL MAJORITARIANISM AS A 'GROUP CHOICE' ISSUE

This chapter tries to identify key issues of judicial majoritarianism as a basis for discussion. Rather than promoting an ultimate master plan, it focusses on asking questions and reporting practical models, which are in use or have been proposed. The issues and model solutions set out here are extracted from a comparative survey of legal history, published in 2016.[1] Participants in

* Regius Professor of Civil Law, University of Oxford, and Fellow of All Souls College, Oxford.

1 W Ernst, *Rechtserkenntnis durch Richtermehrheiten: "group choice" in europäischen Justiztraditionen* (Tübingen, Mohr Siebeck, 2016). An English edition is being prepared

the 2017 'Collective Judging' Conference were given this chapter for inspiration; it is published here with only a few alterations.

Collegiate courts must overcome disagreement between judges in order to see a pending case decided. One can look at the decision-making process from various perspectives, for example that of collective choice theory or that of psychological group dynamics. For the lawyer, a more obvious aspect lies in the procedural rules pertaining to the collegiate decision-making exercise. While the legal aspect may not be easily separable from potential other aspects, it suggests itself as the focus for a comparative survey. There is a great variety of approaches to what seems to be the core problem of collegiate courts: How to arrive at a decision in spite of judges' disagreement? Insofar as judicial majority-seeking takes place in a conference of judges, the competences and procedures of such conferences are pertinent issues. Similar problems exist for tribunals of arbiters, although in terms of group psychology they may differ considerably from permanent courts since the latter can operate, at least for a while, with a stable composition of judges.

The method by which several judges' opinions are 'fused' in deciding the case at hand, and also in shaping the law of the land, is a decisive moment in the exercise of judicial power. It deserves no less attention than the doctrine of statutory interpretation. The intellectual operations needed in this respect are not at all self-evident.

II. THE JUDGES' CONFERENCE FROM A COMPARATIVE PERSPECTIVE

From a comparative perspective, we find the majority requirement applied in two very different modes. In Anglo-American judicial systems, the case at hand is decided by the majority of opinions, the order made by the court being determined by looking at the constituent individual judges' end results only. The unitary order made by the court may thus be accompanied by multiple reasoning, each opinion developed independently by any judge who finds he[2] must express his individual view of the case. While the specific case is decided in a way which, regarding the result, satisfies a majority of judges, it is another matter whether divergent reasoning developed by these judges allow the extraction of a *ratio decidendi* further down the line. By contrast, in the typical continental/civilian system, decision-making power lies with

for 2021. For an English language review of the original book, see R Hyland, 'Book Review' (2018) 47 *Quaderni Fiorentini* 560–71.

2 In this chapter, the meaning of the words 'he', 'his' or 'him' should be read to encompass the female 'she' or (as may be appropriate) 'her'/'hers'.

the conference of judges alone. Here, every judge – as a member of the conference – can just do his best to influence the collective decision. If he feels that reaching an agreement would unduly compromise his individual view of the case, he cannot fall back on an individual decision. The judges' conference in the civilian tradition establishes – if necessary by taking votes – a common view of the evidentiary aspect as well, so that chambers pronounce with one voice not only on the legal arguments, but also on the assumed facts of the case. From the author's perspective, the difference between an aggregate of individual judgments, occasionally capable of being fused into a judgment of the court (or not), and a unitary judgment coming, by necessity, from the conference of judges, is not a matter of degree only. It is an issue of allocation of judicial competence and – like all matters of competence – not of an easily gradable nature.

From a comparative perspective, one may also note that the typical civilian/continental court is subdivided into fixed chambers (going under different names) to which judges are appointed for fixed terms, and that the courts typically regulate the assignment of incoming cases in an abstract manner, which they are indeed required by law to do. When the members of such a chamber come together, they constitute a properly constituted judicial body to which the inner-court organisational scheme has assigned a specific competence of its own.

Different systems provide widely different platforms for the exchange of judicial views within the collegiate court. In the typical continental system, the judicial power is vested in and exercised by the conference itself: You cannot get to a judgment unless the judges have come together in a formal conference, or have arrived at an agreement in a round-robin circulation of a draft judgment. A pre-hearing conference may be convened as well, so that the *rapporteur*, as the lead judge, can induct his colleagues into the case and suggest an outcome. These conferences are subject to detailed regulation, partly by way of legislation, partly by way of the courts' internal rules of procedure ('Local Rules of Practice').

A few aspects of the controlling rules will be set out in the following sections. One odd feature of most continental systems can be pointed out right away: Even where judges' conferences are regulated in quite a detailed manner, one cannot normally tell whether the respective regulations are adhered to, since the proceedings within the judges' conference (with the notable exception of the Swiss Federal Court)[3] are confidential. Breaches of this confidentiality can qualify as a criminal offence.

3 On the Swiss position, see T Stadelmann's contribution in chapter 9 of the present collection (at pp 185–192).

Where the decision stems from the judges' formal conference, the steering of this conference becomes a crucial element of the overall decision-making process. In this process, the presiding judge is not merely the *primus inter pares*. By virtue of his steering powers, he can, if this is his ambition, become the prime mover – much more so than a Chief Justice in the traditional Anglo-American system: The more conference-oriented the decision-making process, the more power is exercised by the presiding judge, typically at the expense of the lower-ranked members of his conference.

Paradoxical as it may seem, if the decision-making is to emerge from a truly joint exercise, the lead judge, the *rapporteur*, becomes another central figure. Any sensible judicial discussion needs a thorough and detailed analysis as a starting point. Such an analysis best comes from one person working in solitude; the later discussion will bring out the strengths and weaknesses of the lead judge's draft analysis. The lead judge inevitably has a much better insight into the case than the other members of the conference. From the point of view of cost-efficiency, it is tempting to let the lead judge also act as the case-manager, in control of all 'paperwork', including the ultimate copy-editing of the judgment: 'That is the advantage of the draftsman: he can concede points without conceding substance, and he can also draft the concessions' (John Kenneth Galbraith).[4] The lead judge and the presiding judge can make a powerful team. In these circumstances, the system can in effect revert to a covert single-judge system; the other judges of the conference letting the lead judge have his way, as long as he has the backing of the presiding judge. The collegiate character of the decision can become illusory. In order not to lose the advantages of free collective deliberations, counter-measures have been brought into play, for example the appointment of a second *rapporteur*. In the French *Cour de cassation*, the *doyen* of each chamber is co-responsible for the case-management, which may perhaps countermand excessive influence of the *rapporteur*. The ideal, of course, is a system, which compels every judge to give a substantial opinion of his own; but scarcity of time and resources may force courts to compromise.

Anglo-American systems did not evolve around judges' conferences, but rather let each judge take his own independent decision, including the evaluation of evidence. If there is the wish to see one's own views prevail as the majority view, a judge can seek bilateral negotiations and arrangements, but these are not controlled by specific rules. One can single out one's discussion partners, bypassing those with whom one thinks one will not find enough common ground anyway. It may turn out that one or the other judge is not involved in any exchange, while others try to form alliances and – in doing so – together go over some of the legal arguments, thus enjoying the benefit of

---

4 JK Galbraith, *A Life in Our Times: Memoirs* (Boston, Houghton Mifflin, 1981) 94.

an intellectual exchange. From a continental observer's perspective, this 'free market' process of judges coming together in pairs or groups makes for a process very different from the proceedings of a continental-style judges' conference. It may also be seen as lacking accountability. Looking for a best practice, it may not be possible to crowd out altogether informal coalition-building in the corridors or at the coffee machine, but offering a joint platform with every judge in attendance may shift at least some of the judges' exchanges into a more transparent arena. Here, all views, however unlikely to become views of the court's majority, could equally be given a fair hearing.

Establishing an open-minded intellectual exchange of judges' views has long been hindered by the idea that a judge, even when working in a collegiate court, expresses his opinion in a once-and-for-all exercise of his judicial power, which by this very act is exhausted. The opinion once formally voiced was thought to become his irreversible contribution to the decision of the case. This traditional model is not amenable to the tentative tabling of arguments, testing the waters, so to speak. Historically, the traditional continental conferences of the civilian tradition also started in a rigid sequence of individual judges' speeches, each already representing the judge's definitive contribution to the court's overall decision. Later, one introduced second rounds of voting, so that views subsequently expressed by other judges could be taken into account when it came to the ultimate vote. From a modern perspective, a favourable design of a conference seems to lie in the separation of two different stages. In a first stage, the judges come together for an argumentative exchange of views, with no view expressed here committing the judge to a specific vote. It is preferable, I think, to compel every judge to offer his views at this stage. If voicing one's opinion is optional, the conference may degenerate into a monologue of the lead judge (*rapporteur*). In the second stage, a formal voting process is arranged which alone makes for the actual exercise of the judicial power. Here voting issues arise which will be addressed later on in this chapter.

In the older system, where judges spoke only in an actual exercise of their judicial power and therefore once and for all, the speaking order was of considerable importance. If there is only one final round (not preceded by a conference), judges further down the voting order can take into account the views expressed in the earlier votes (including the option of simply joining one of them), while judges who have already voted cannot revise their declared decision. Courts traditionally tended to have fixed systems determining who voted first. Should the highest-ranking judge come first or the lowest-ranked judge, so as to be encouraged to take an independent stance? Whenever a *rapporteur* is appointed, he is usually assigned a preferred place in the voting order, regardless of his rank. In systems where the conference is split into two parts (deliberation and voting), the order of contributions loses much of its earlier importance: Should a lazy judge feel inclined to follow his heavyweight colleagues or the presumable majority view, the preceding discussion should have given him sufficient information.

Collegiate decision-making is expensive, and it gets the more expensive the more judges are involved. For the sake of judicial efficiency, collegiate courts tend to single out cases which can be disposed of by a bench of a smaller size (the court sitting *in quorum*) – or even by a single member of the court – and to reserve the operation of the full court for cases which seem to deserve the extra effort (sitting *in banco*). The distinction between cases which deserve a hearing of the full court from cases of somehow lesser importance can be handled in a discretionary manner or it can be predetermined by abstract rules. Obviously, the sensitivity concerning the statutory predetermination of the competent judge(s), as developed in the civilian tradition, will also play a role here.

III. FORMAL ISSUES OF INTRA-COURT COLLECTIVE DECISION-MAKING

1. MAJORITY REQUIREMENTS

While collective judicial decisions are usually taken by a simple majority, judicial supermajorities (qualified majorities) have come into play as well. With respect to cases involving judicial review, the Polish Parliament recently passed a law requiring the country's Constitutional Court to find a 2/3-majority for striking down Acts of Parliaments as unconstitutional. The measure met with harsh criticism.[5] In the 1930s, the Roosevelt administration had toyed with a similar concept to break the US Supreme Court's blockade of some of the New Deal legislation.[6] In favour of such regulation, it has been argued that an Act passed by a Parliamentary majority could only be undone by a 'better' majority ruling taken in another branch of the state, so that decisions involving judicial review – where recognized – should require a supermajority. In meting out the death penalty, a majority of one was considered insufficient in many jurisdictions; this two-vote-majority requirement does not seem to be in play anymore.

Civilian systems not infrequently require a 2/3-majority for the criminal sentence or for the guilty verdict implied in such a sentence. This oddity is the remnant of a transplantation of the English jury into civilian

5 'Poland: Lech Wałęsa warns against "undemocratic" curbs on court', *The Guardian*, 23 December 2015.

6 J Shesol, *Supreme Power. Franklin Roosevelt vs. The Supreme Court* (New York, Norton & Co, 2010), 170–72, 252.

criminal justice systems, which started around 1800. Afraid that the English unanimity requirement for the jury verdict would hamper criminal law enforcement, legislators settled for supermajority requirements, of which the 2/3 variant proved the most popular. When enlightenment authors discussed the merits and downsides of the jury-system, they employed mathematical models to determine to which degree upping the supermajority requirement promised a greater likelihood of a 'correct' judgment. Among others, Nicolas de Condorcet[7] and Pierre Simon Laplace[8] contributed to this debate, which is continuing to this day.[9]

Civilian systems sometime combine the jury with their traditional colleges of justices, so that one 'group choice' decision (regarding the sentencing) follows the other (regarding the guilt). This allows combinations of two different majority requirements. Although many countries have by now abolished the jury (or severely curtailed its field of application), the qualified majority for criminal sentencing seems to have survived. Where the 2/3 majority requirement is applied to a college of justices, which operates without a jury, an odd distinction occurs in that the same chamber has to come to a finding of guilt, for which a 2/3 majority is required, whereas all other decisions, especially on the sentencing, are taken by simple majority. Any supermajority requirement causes additional problems when applied to the reasons given for a judgment.[10]

As cases travel up through the judicial system, fresh majority decisions are called for at each instance. It is possible that the final decision fails to muster a majority among all the judges which have given their opinion along the way.[11] No one seems to have taken an interest in the exotic proposal, made in the early 19th century,[12] calling for a proportionate influence of all the judges' opinions, regardless of their position in the court hierarchy, on the ultimate outcome.

We establish judicial majorities by counting heads. Medieval societies, built on a stratified system of orders, had little difficulty when such hierarchies were mirrored in a gradation of voting powers in a judicial college. These times are

---

7 N de Condorcet, *Essai sur l'application de l'analyse à la probabilité des décisions rendues à la pluralité des voix* (Paris, Imprimerie Royale, 1785).

8 A chapter of his 'Theorie analytiques des probabilités' is entitled 'De la probabilité des jugements des tribunaux', PS Laplace, *Œuvre comlètes*, vol 7 (Paris, Académie des Sciences, 1866), XCIV et seq.

9 For example: LA Kornhauser and LG Sager, 'The many as one – Integrity and Group Choice in Paradoxical Cases' (2004) 32 *Philosophy and Public Affairs* 249; C List and P Pettit, 'On the many as one – a reply to Kornhauser and Sager' *Philosophy and Public Affairs* (2005) 377; D Landa and J R Lax, 'Legal Doctrine on Collegiate Courts' (2009) 71 *The Journal of Politics* 946.

10 *Cf* n 19 below.

11 M Berlins and C Dyer, *The Law Machine* 4th edn (London, Penguin, 1994) 29.

12 J von Sonnenfels, *Über die Stimmenmehrheit bei Criminalurteilen* (Wien, Camesina, 1801).

over and we now universally subscribe to 'one judge, one vote'. Every now and then, there is a complaint that it would be preferable if one could weigh the different sides by the quality of their supporting arguments. This proposal is fuelled by a longstanding reservation against all kind of majority-based decision-making. However, as no method seems available to gauge the quality of legal arguments, engaging in a quarrel about qualities of arguments would only shift the controversy onto another level, making it more – not less – acrimonious. It could also undermine the court's authority.

Judges are not allowed to abstain. Systems differ as to the latitude with which they allow judges to recuse themselves. Some common law courts seem to allow judges of the court to join in the decision-making at will, so judges could stay away from a case at their discretion, as long as a sufficient number of judges are willing to sit on the case. Once the specific bench has been put together, a formal recusation becomes necessary. The civilian idea that the judges who will ultimately decide the case at hand need to be predetermined by statutory provisions (the so-called 'statutory judge'), will require subjecting applications for recusal to a fairly rigorous vetting process on the basis of precise regulations.

2. THE JUDICIAL TIE

Some judiciaries are set up so as to allow only uneven numbers to operate as the respective chamber, making sure that exiting judges are always replaced. No tied vote can thus occur. Where systems allow decisions to come from an even-numbered panel, one method to avoid a judicial tie is the addition of another judge to the bench. This mechanism, for a long time used in arbitration as well (here the term is the 'super-arbiter'), comes in two variants: Either the additional judge is confronted with the opinions of both sides from which he then has to pick one, or – less efficiently – hearings and deliberations start anew before and in a now uneven-numbered court/tribunal.

Few court rules positively grant the presiding judge a *casting vote*, traditionally called the '*calculus Minervae*'.[13] The statutes of the International Court of Justice may be a notable exception. Modern arbitration rules, which try to avoid even-numbered tribunals in the first place, provide that in the case of a tied vote the ultimate decision-making power falls to the presiding arbiter: If no majority award can be issued, the award will come not from the tribunal, but from the president as a single-arbiter.[14] He is not restricted to

13 Based on Minerva's intervention in the proceedings against Orest: Aischylos, Eumenides 742/3.

14 Article 32(1) ICC 2017 Arbitration Rules.

choosing between the contradictory opinions of his (former) co-arbiters, but can come up with a fresh opinion of his own.

In an even-numbered court, a frequently used maxim for getting to grips with the judicial tie is *in dubio pro reo*, with *reus* here meaning the defendant in civil cases as well as the accused in criminal cases.[15] In civil cases, the rule works in a role-dependent manner: If a potential defendant takes the initiative and brings a claim for a declaratory judgment negating the potential claimant's right, a judicial tie means he loses; had he waited for the other party to come forward as claimant, the other party would have lost.

On an appellate level, the tie-breaker rule *semper praesumitur pro negante* works against the appellant, as the decision of the lower court is upheld. Where the appellate court is equally divided, the case finds its final decision on the lower court's level. For systems where judgments work as precedents, the question arises whether the reasoning of that half of the court which prevailed in dismissing the appeal on the strength of *semper praesumitur pro negante* can become the 'law of the land'. The US Supreme Court in such instances issues a *pro curiam* decision, consisting in the bare statement 'The judgment is affirmed by an equally divided court'. As far as the English doctrine of precedent is concerned, one may ask whether a *ratio decidendi* can be extracted from the reasoning of that half of the court which prevailed in dismissing the appeal, and whether the precedential value retains the rank as coming from the lower court or is elevated to the rank of the divided court that dismissed the appeal.[16]

Historically, the preference given to the defendant was supplemented by several other rules on specific issues, which, in the case of a judicial tie, gave preference to one outcome over the other, and did so for substantive reasons (*favor causae*). For example, if the validity of a last will was challenged, an evenly divided court was considered to uphold rather than avoid the will (*favor testamenti*). In church courts, a *favor matrimonii* was observed. Such rules, which work role-independently, hardly seem to be in play anymore today.

3. CHOOSING BETWEEN MORE THAN TWO SOLUTIONS

a) *Reducing the Number of Solutions Step-by-Step*

Most judicial decision-making is of a binary nature. This holds especially true on the appellate level, where appeals are either granted or dismissed.

15 The rule is usually taken to be of an evidentiary nature, but has emerged, in Roman law, as a means to resolve judicial ties: Ernst (n 1) 27–31.

16 R Cross and JW Harris, *Precedent in English Law*, 4th edn (Oxford, Oxford University Press, 1991) 86–88.

However, there are also instances where choices of a non-binary nature have to be made, for example in the determination of sums, be it years of a prison sentence or monetary sums to be awarded as damages. If judges of a collegiate court split up between three or more options, it is possible that no option commands a simple majority (> ½). Different mechanisms promise to overcome this kind of deadlock. A model developed in the history of the French judiciary aims to uphold the majority requirement by gradually eliminating minority positions: Those who advocate the choice least popular in the conference are compelled to choose, in a second round of voting, between the remaining options; the process is repeated until a majority is built for one choice.[17] The method does not work smoothly in all cases. If there are two least attractive options, the question arises which camp has to give. To establish this, one could have an intermediate vote of the whole court showing which of these two choices has the overall least support. There are also other methods, some of which are tailored to the specific problems of quantitative divergences (b) while others are geared at qualitative divergences (c).

b) Special Approaches for Quantitative Divergences

A Roman law rule held that in case of disagreement over sums, the overall judgment should be for the lowest sum (D. 42,1,38,1; Paul). In its original context, this rule was not as awkward as it may appear today. For a decision to be taken by more than one judge, the Romans subscribed to the concept of multiple judgments, rather than that of a unitary judgment, coming from a collegiate judicial body. There simply was no unitary decision with a blank which could be 'filled' by a new number, resulting by some algorithm into which all individual proposals are fed. To avoid a no-decision outcome, the Roman jurists opted for the lowest sum, which could be seen as having a quasi-unanimous support. It also coincided with the maxim *in dubio pro reo*.

Where a unitary judgment of the court can be dissociated from the opinions of the individual judges, there can – and indeed must – be a 'new' number as the court's decision. This sum must somehow be arrived at from the plurality of proposed sums. Various methods have been suggested and are, in fact, used in practice.

- Going for the arithmetic average can result in a sum that has not been positively proposed by any judge and is as such not formally supported by a majority of judges' votes.

---

17 On Article 117 of the 1806 *Code de Procedure Civil* see Ernst (n 1) 153–57.

- The median is the sum proposed by the judge 'in the middle'. It is a value actually supported by at least one judge, and it probably can be seen as most 'agreeable' for the court as a whole, since it minimises the overall divergence of judges from the final result. If an even number of judges decides, one can take the arithmetic average of the lower and the upper median, but the result is not a sum actually proposed by one of the judges.
- Applying the general majority rule leads to acceptance of the sum agreed by a simple majority (> ½). In case no sum meets this majority requirement, one takes the vote(s) for the highest sum to be votes for the next-lower sum, and that step is repeated until a sum musters the majority requirement. The result is a sum in fact proposed by one of the judges and supported by a majority of judges, if only on the strength of the presumption that in a vote for a specific sum implies a vote for any lower sum. In an uneven-numbered court, the result will be the median, because in a three judges court the 'highest sum'-vote goes to the 'middle one', which then commands a majority. The resulting sum, however, can diverge from the arithmetic average in a random way. If, for example, five judges advocate a compensation of 500, 500, 500, 2,000, and 2,500 respectively, there is a majority for 500, while the arithmetic average would be 1,200. This result stays the same, whatever extreme sums the minority judges should advocate; the two outvoted judges could for example go into 5-digit figures without any effect. If, however, one of the three judges who voted for 500 were to change her vote to 700, then 700 would become the court's result, while the arithmetic average would move up to 1,240.

c) *Special Approaches for Qualitative Divergences*

The academic discussion of judicial decision-making culminated in a problem that has perhaps the least practical relevance. The archetypical case used since the Roman antiquity to illustrate and discuss the problem is that of a seven judges' court, with two judges advocating exile, two others a monetary fine, and three the death penalty.[18] Should one let the relative majority carry the day (death penalty)? Or is it more appropriate to join the votes for a monetary fine and for exile to a regular majority, on the basis that these two choices, as a matter of substance, seem to be closer together than each does in relation to the death penalty? But which of the two should then prevail? Should the less harsh penalty be preferred? Or does the law suit end without judgment? Another approach allows for a second round of voting, along the lines set out above, under (a), and this may indeed promise a more rational outcome.

---

18 Gellius, *Noctes Atticae* 9, 15.

4. ARRIVING AT JOINT REASONING

a) *Integral or Sequential Voting*

We expect judgments to be supported by reasoning. Judges may agree on the result but not on the reasoning. In the Anglo-American model of collective decision-making, each judge may fall back on his preferred reason. This in a way postpones the difficulties of merging divergent reasoning until another court in the future has to extract a common *ratio decidendi* from the multiple judgments.

The traditional civilian concept expects the collegiate court to arrive at a reasoned judgment that in its entirety is supported by a majority of judges.[19] Around 1800, the theoretical view emerged that for reasons of legal logic, a collegiate court needed to have separate votes for each and every controversial element of its decision.[20] The reason for the court's unitary judgment would follow automatically as the aggregate of all majority-supported sub-decisions. Some authors assumed that the ultimate vote on the end-result would thereby become superfluous and indeed unseemly: once all sub-questions had been decided, the overall result was already a given. In this manner alone, the argument ran, collegiate courts could produce judgments that were logically as consistent as judgments issued and 'motivated' by a single judge.

Compared to 'one integral voting on the end result' – which incidentally coincides with the result arrived at in the Anglo-American systems – the 'sequential voting on each element' can produce substantially different results. Take a case such as *Re A (conjoined twins)*,[21] where each of the three judges gave a different reason for why doctors should be allowed to separate Siamese twins, namely self-defence, necessity, and lack of intent, respectively. If one had subjected each of these reasons to a separate majority vote, it would have been possible for none of the reasons to command a majority. The resulting outcome, though accompanied by majority-based reasoning, would have been the exact opposite of what each of the three judges in effect really wanted.

In complex cases depending on a number of disputed issues, the above-mentioned method becomes more questionable still: breaking up the

---

19 If the decision requires a supermajority, an odd question ensues. Does the supermajority requirement pertain to the reasoning as well? In a criminal procedure with a qualified majority requirement for a conviction (see the paragraph ending in fn 10), abstract legal arguments made in favour of the accused would prevail on the basis of 1/3 of the bench, whereas arguments running against the accused would need the support of at least 2/3 of the judges.

20 W Ernst, 'Modalités de vote dans les tribunaux collégiaux. La diffusion des idées des Lumières en Europe au 19ème siècle' (2018) 15 *GLOSSAE. European Journal of Legal History* 81–98.

21 *Re A (conjoined twins)* [2001] 2 WLR 480 (CA).

decision-making process into ever more minute elements might actually reverse the result. And who is to say how miniscule the steps should be, into which the granular decision-making process ought to be broken down? The advocates of step-by-step voting argued that it was impossible to reach a consistent 'motivation' if the decision had in fact been reached for wildly divergent reasons. Occasionally continental European legislators, when remodelling procedural laws, felt compelled to address the issue, in which case they tended to opt for step-by-step voting processes.

b) *Forcing a Judge to Stay in Play* Stante Conluso

A distinctive feature of a judicial decision-making process in the sequentialist manner is the duty of every judge to proceed on the basis of the majority decision(s) already taken, even if she had been outvoted at a previous vote. Beginning in the late 18th century, one indeed finds express directives to continue voting *stante concluso*. It remains an issue, however, whether the outvoted judge must continue on an 'as if' basis, or whether he can maintain his reservations and let them guide his voting conduct in the next stages of the decision-making process. For example, can a judge who had voted 'not guilty' then vote for a more lenient sentence since he had held (and as an individual continues to hold) the accused to be innocent, or does he have to join the sentencing process on the assumption that the accused was guilty as found by the majority? For criminal law proceedings, the Austrian law allows a judge to excuse himself in such a situation; his 'missing' vote is construed as having been given for the most lenient punishment advocated among the remaining judges.[22] In any case, a judge who continues to participate due to the *stante concluso*-principle is compelled to contribute his legal expertise to what – from his perspective – may be issues of a hypothetical nature, since according to his own opinion regarding the case at hand he would not have to address the specific point on the decision-path at all. From his point of view, he has to act as a legal expert, not as a judge deciding the case at hand. His continued voting input, however, counts just as much as that of every judge of the majority who had outvoted him in an earlier step.

c) *Presenting the Court with a Number of Preconceived Judgments*

As regards the handling of sub-questions to be taken 'along the way' to reaching the ultimate decision, the modern French *Cour de cassation* is said to use a procedure which differs from that of other countries. According to German theory, the judges in their conference should arrive at their ultimate

[22] §42(3) of the Austrian Code of Criminal Procedure.

decision step-by-step. The decision emerges by developing a decision-path unbeknown at the beginning: When the first steps are taken, it is still unclear which ultimate result they will lead to, since the outcome of the votes to follow is still open. (In practice, however, the proposal of the *rapporteur* is likely to be followed and the preceding debate will have shown where the judges are heading). By contrast, the *rapporteur* of a Chamber of the French *Cour de cassation* has to offer his colleagues a choice of complete paths, making it transparent from the outset what the overall shape of the judgment is going to be if one or the other option were to be chosen. One could say that, in theory, the German system aims for an open-ended sequence of decision modules rather like individual dishes on a menu: It picks the next course only after the last has been eaten, while the French system lets the court choose from a variety of menus, each of which consists in an already well-composed sequence of courses.

Yet another method seems to be employed by the International Court of Justice (ICJ). A table of all disputed issues is drawn up, and every judge is asked to vote on each of them. The overall result is then taken to structure and draft the judgment of the court. When the overall result of the returned questionnaires is established, it may turn out that, in retrospect, one would not have needed to ask certain questions, since the majority result on other questions, which for reasons of legal logic take priority, makes them moot. When giving his answers, a judge therefore cannot know for sure whether his answer to a specific question will be decisive or turn out to be of a merely hypothetical nature.

If a collegiate court is faced with a variety of well-described pathways, each representing a different and differently undergirded judgment, it is tempting to see this as a group choice between more than two solutions. The court must decide whether it wants to dissolve this 'choice'-situation into a sequence of single binary decisions, or to apply a method appropriate for choosing between two or more options, seeing each of these pre-fabricated judgments as one 'option'.[23]

d) *How Much Should the Public Know?*

In the European civilian tradition, all collegiate judgments are issued as unitary judgments of the chamber, not revealing that the judgment was arrived at by virtue of only a majority decision. Civilian systems typically show an unwillingness to let the public (or at least the parties) see any disagreement among the judges.[24] Civilian judgments do not divulge to what extent disagreement in the judges' conference had to be overcome, on which topics votes were taken

---

[23] *Cf* above, section III.3 a) of the present chapter.

[24] The exception of the Swiss Federal Court has already been mentioned: see text to n 3 above.

and with what specific results. The individual judge's contributions to the judgment of the court remains under a veil of secrecy. A cloak of anonymity makes it impossible for the public to attribute a specific argument to the individual judge who introduced it into the debate.

For half a century or so, the topic of dissenting opinions has been intensely discussed throughout most if not all of the civilian systems. The dissenting opinion, as now occasionally recognised in civilian systems, nevertheless remains an odd creature. It allows the individual judge to set out his own view of the law insofar as it diverges from the court's majority. These dissenting opinions do not pertain to different assumptions as to the facts of the case. The respective document is not in itself a judgment, nor is it a part of the courts' disposition. It is a memorandum of sorts. Allowing individual judges to set out, in such a separate document, their individual view as to the state of the law does not excuse a judge who exercises this option from taking part in the judges' conference until the very end. The judge will therefore stay involved in a process of adjudication, which for him is of an abstract manner due to his disagreement with regard to a specific legal argument.

The bureaucratic manner of civilian courts, producing a unitary judgment while at the same time concealing even persistent disagreement among the judges, is no model for our time. This model does not do justice to what James Lee has aptly called the 'inherent controversiality of the law'.[25] Freedom of Information Acts allow us to look into the inner workings of the administrative branch of government, and it seems odd that the workings of the judiciary should be able to avoid a similar degree of transparency.

[25] J Lee, 'A Defence of Concurring Speeches' [2009] *Public Law* 305, 327.

PART II

COLLEGIATE COURTS IN THE COMMON LAW TRADITION

CHAPTER 2

COLLECTIVE JUDGING IN THE UK SUPREME COURT

Robert Reed*

From the perspective of a lawyer from one of Europe's civilian jurisdictions, the United Kingdom Supreme Court (UKSC) must appear rather curious. No formal rules govern the size of constitutions of the Court or their composition. The deliberative procedure is not laid down anywhere. There is not even any official explanation of how it is decided how many judgments will be written in a particular case, or who will write them. A German lawyer might be unsurprised to learn that there is no equivalent in English of the concept of the *gesetzlicher Richter*.[1]

Like much in Britain, the Supreme Court is largely regulated by conventions and established practices rather than rules. It has to be understood in the light of history. It is the successor of the Appellate Committee of the House of Lords, and it has inherited much from its Parliamentary predecessor. But, as

---

* The Rt Hon Lord Reed of Allermuir is the President of the Supreme Court of the United Kingdom and was at the time of the conference (and when this chapter was written) a Justice there. He was previously a judge of the Court of Session in Scotland, and is also a non-permanent judge of the Hong Kong Court of Final Appeal and an ad hoc judge of the European Court of Human Rights.

1 Literally, a 'lawful judge'.

its creation provided an opportunity for change, the Supreme Court also exhibits some innovations.

I. THE HOUSE OF LORDS

A little history to begin with. From about the twelfth century, the High Court of Parliament exercised both legislative and judicial functions.[2] Although separate common law courts later developed, Parliament remained the highest court of Royal justice. Its judicial functions came to be exercised by the House of Lords, after it emerged as a separate House in the late fourteenth century. Over time, it limited its jurisdiction to appeals from the lower courts,[3] and the convention became established that only those members of the House with judicial experience would participate. In Victorian times, the procedures were reformed, and in 1876 legislation was enacted which allowed for the appointment to the House of professional salaried judges, often referred to as 'Law Lords', specifically in order to deal with the final appeals in our legal system. They continued to hear appeals in the Chamber of the House of Lords until 1948, when noise caused by workmen repairing bomb damage to the Palace of Westminster forced the Law Lords to move to a committee room and form themselves into an Appellate Committee.

The Appellate Committee is what lawyers usually refer to when they speak of the 'House of Lords' as a court. It numbered twelve members, who normally sat in panels of five. The same judges also sat, usually in panels of the same number, as the Judicial Committee of the Privy Council (JCPC), which from the nineteenth century exercised the function of the Privy Council – a body which advises the Monarch – to hear appeals from British colonies and other jurisdictions outside the United Kingdom. Uniquely, the Law Lords were not members of the judiciary of England and Wales, or of Scotland or Northern Ireland, but lay outside the ordinary institutional and governance arrangements for the courts.

It is important to remember that the Appellate Committee, although functionally a court, was formally a Parliamentary committee. So it did not sit in a courtroom, but in one of the committee rooms in the Palace of Westminster.[4] Like other committees, the Committee entered the room

2 The position was broadly similar in Scotland.

3 Subject to some exceptions. The last criminal trial to be heard in the House of Lords was in 1935, and its criminal trial jurisdiction was abolished in 1948.

4 It also sat from time to time (particularly during the Parliamentary recess) in the Chamber itself. I once appeared there as counsel. You stood at a small lectern, where there was scarcely room to place your papers. Senior counsel, as I was, were required to wear long-bottomed wigs. I felt as if I was appearing in *Iolanthe*.

first, preceded by a clerk who called out 'their Lordships' to counsel lined up respectfully beyond the public entrance into the room. Once their Lordships were ready, counsel were admitted in order of seniority, followed by their instructing solicitors. As they were sitting as members of a Parliamentary committee, the Law Lords did not wear robes, but were dressed in ordinary clothes. They did not sit at a raised bench, but at a table at the same level as counsel, and only a few feet away. The table was horseshoe-shaped, as in other committee rooms, so that the members of the Committee could see each other and deliberate together. Like the members of other Parliamentary committees (and, indeed, like other British courts, but to a greater degree), they did not sit in respectful silence and listen to perorations, but frequently interrupted counsel with questions, often directed as much at other members of the Committee as at the counsel who was their ostensible target, and often steered the discussion into directions which counsel might not have anticipated or welcomed. At the end of the hearing, their clerk called out 'Clear the Bar', and counsel and their solicitors quickly gathered up their books and papers and left the room, leaving the Committee to its deliberations.

Thus, what was, in function, the final court of appeal, was in form a Parliamentary committee. That had a profound effect on its decision-making procedures. As a committee of the House of Lords, it had to report back to the House in order for its decisions to be given effect. There were essentially two ways in which it could report. One, which was used only occasionally, was for the Committee to prepare a joint report, which was then laid before the House and voted upon (the members of the Committee being the only members to take part in the vote). The other method, which was almost always used, was for each member of the Committee to prepare a speech. That is why it is a solecism to refer to the 'judgments' of a member of the House of Lords: they are correctly described as 'speeches'. They had to be speeches, because that is how a member of the House conveys his views to its other members. And each member of the Committee had to deliver his own speech: there could not be joint speeches, let alone a single speech by all the members of the Committee, since members of the House speak one at a time rather than in unison. Of course, if one member of the Committee agreed with the speech of another, then that was all he need say. Hence the most common form of decision: one speech discussing the case at length and coming to a conclusion, and four other speeches amounting to little more than 'I agree'. The decision was then taken by means of a vote in the House, the members of the Committee being the only persons voting.

The members of the Committee worked on their speeches largely independently of one another, and then circulated them in draft. The degree to which members commented on each other's speeches, and responded to comments on their own draft, was variable, but more limited than in current practice. The fact that drafts and comments were generally circulated in hard copy did not encourage a more collaborative approach. The fact that members of the Committee, and their judicial assistants, did not have their offices located together, and did not have their own separate dining facilities, also affected the degree of collegiality.

II. CROSSING THE SQUARE

When, in 2009, the Appellate Committee of the House of Lords was abolished, and its members (with two exceptions)[5] crossed Parliament Square to become Justices of the Supreme Court, they brought some of their old practices with them, but left others behind. The Justices of the Supreme Court are judges, not members of a Parliamentary committee.[6] They sit in courtrooms, not in committee rooms. But they do not look like other judges, and their courtrooms do not look like other courts. They continue to wear ordinary clothes.[7] They continue to sit at a table at the same level as counsel, only a few feet away. The table remains horseshoe shaped, so that the Justices can easily communicate and watch each other's reactions. They continue to interrupt counsel and to steer the discussion into the areas which they consider important. The Court continues to be constituted usually by five Justices. This enables it to hear two appeals simultaneously, or to hear one appeal in the Supreme Court and another in the JCPC, which has its courtroom in the same building.[8] The Justices remain outside the judiciaries of the separate jurisdictions of the United Kingdom, and their institutional and governance arrangements. They are almost the only judges who are United Kingdom judges, and the Court is directly accountable to Parliament.[9] Unlike the judges of

---

5 Lord Scott of Foscote retired the day before the Supreme Court began business. Lord Neuberger resigned to become Master of the Rolls, the head of civil justice in England and Wales. He subsequently joined the Supreme Court, as its second President, in 2012.

6 They continue to be given the title 'Lord' by Royal Warrant, but those appointed since 2009 have not been members of the House of Lords, with the exception of myself: I was granted a peerage on my appointment as President of the Supreme Court.

7 They have robes (against the wishes of some of the original Justices), but they only wear them on ceremonial occasions.

8 This remains the final court of appeal for 28 jurisdictions with links to the United Kingdom. As they include a number of jurisdictions which are important centres for financial services (such as the Cayman Islands and the British Virgin Islands), and others which generate a large volume of criminal, civil and constitutional appeals (such as Jamaica and Mauritius), the JCPC has a significant amount of work. The appeals are normally heard by five Justices of the Supreme Court, sitting as members of the JCPC.

9 The Court's annual report is presented to Parliament in accordance with section 54 of the Constitutional Reform Act 2005, and the President and Deputy President of the Court give evidence annually to the House of Lords Constitution Committee. The Chief Executive is also the Court's Accounting Officer, and can be (and has been) required to give evidence to the House of Commons Public Accounts Committee.

many other European countries, they come to the job with long experience of independent decision-making as practising lawyers and as trial judges sitting alone, as well as experience on lower appellate courts.[10]

Since the Justices are judges, they prepare judgments, not speeches. That change has made it possible for there to be joint judgments, or single judgments of the Court. In addition, the Court has from the outset embraced the use of new technology. So draft judgments are circulated by email, and comments on them are circulated in the same way. Each draft judgment prompts a lively discussion via email, and results in the preparation of a revised draft, which is then circulated, prompting further discussion, and further revision. And so the preparation of a judgment becomes an iterative process, in which every member of the Court participates. I shall return to this.

The physical layout of the building, and the facilities available, encourage a collaborative approach. Our offices are next to one another, occupying part of the second floor and most of the third floor of the building. The offices of our judicial assistants are adjacent. We each have a spacious room, with a table and several chairs, where colleagues can drop in to discuss matters. Most of us work with our doors open, encouraging discussion to take place. We have a dining room, where all of us normally have lunch together every day we are sitting.

III. OTHER INHERITED CHARACTERISTICS

Two other basic aspects of the Supreme Court, inherited from the House of Lords, also have to be understood. First, there is no right of appeal to the Supreme Court.[11] The only right is to apply for permission to appeal. Such applications are referred to Appeal Panels, each comprising three members of the Court, at regular intervals. The Appeal Panels are chaired by the four senior members of the Court. The other Justices are rotated among the panels

---

10 This is true even of those Justices who have been appointed from less traditional backgrounds. Lady Hale, a former academic lawyer, was a trial judge prior to her appointment to the Court of Appeal. Lord Sumption, who was appointed to the Supreme Court directly from the Bar, had long experience as an independent practitioner and also as a Deputy (ie part-time) High Court judge, as well as experience as an appellate judge in the Channel Islands.

11 In Scottish appeals, it is quite common for the court below to have granted leave, applying a similar test to that applied by the Supreme Court. Listing directions as to the time estimate, the number of Justices who should sit and any other appropriate directions (eg as to the composition of the court) are sought from the Appeal Panel. Where leave has been granted by the court below, or where (in the JCPC) an appeal lies as of right, the President will decide the time estimate, the number of Justices, who should sit and (in the JCPC) whether hearing by video link is appropriate, and will give any other appropriate directions.

as much as possible in order to ensure that the same panels are not used for each round of applications. Applications are assigned to panels principally on the basis of the Justices' expertise. They are usually determined on paper, although a small number are determined after an oral hearing, and in some cases a decision in respect of a particular ground of appeal may be left to be decided at the hearing of the appeal. As provided in the relevant Practice Direction,

> 'Permission to appeal is granted for applications that, in the opinion of the Appeal Panel, raise an arguable point of law of general public importance which ought to be considered by the Supreme Court at that time, bearing in mind that the matter will already have been the subject of judicial decision and may have already been reviewed on appeal.'[12]

In cases raising a point of EU law, the criterion is as set out in article 267 TFEU and the case of *CILFIT*.[13] In practice, about 75 cases are granted permission each year: around a third of the applications.[14] The Appeal Panels estimate the time required for the hearing and advise on the number of members of the Court who should sit.

Secondly, every appeal receives an oral hearing. This is regarded as having great benefits, in enabling points to be explored with counsel in depth, usually beyond the scope of their written arguments, as well as in ensuring the transparency of the proceedings. The Justices raise what is on their minds, and sometimes engage in debate with each other.

IV. CONSTITUTIONS FOR APPEALS

The Court's Registrar prepares draft constitutions of the Court a few months before a term begins. The four senior members of the Court preside in the Supreme Court or chair the Board in the JCPC. The Appeal Panel will have given directions as to the size of the court. In some cases, the President, the Deputy President or the chair of an Appeal Panel will have directed that a particular Justice should sit on an appeal. In the absence of particular

---

12 Practice Direction 3.3.3. The procedure is set out in the Supreme Court Rules 2009, SI 2009/1603, and in Practice Direction 3. A similar criterion applies in relation to Scottish appeals, under section 40A of the Court of Session Act 1988 (as amended).

13 On the preliminary reference or ruling procedure under Article 267 of the Treaty on the Functioning of the European Union (TFEU), see also the contribution by T von Danwitz in chapter 13 of the present collection (esp at pp 255, 258–259). For details of the *CILFIT* criteria and especially the so-called 'acte clair' doctrine, see the case of *CILFIT and Lanificio di Gavardo SpA v Ministero della Sanità* (6 October 1982), C-283/81, EU:C:1982:335.

14 A further 40 or so cases are heard each year in the JCPC.

directions, the Registrar seeks to ensure that there are at least two members of the court with relevant expertise and, for example, that the Northern Irish Justice sits on a Northern Irish appeal and at least one of the Scottish Justices sits on a Scottish appeal.[15] Whenever feasible, the court will contain a mix of genders.[16] In addition, consideration is given to the number of days on which each Justice is scheduled to sit,[17] and whether extra reading time or judgment writing time should be given to the Justice who it is anticipated will give the lead judgment. The Registrar also tries to ensure that all Justices sit in both the Supreme Court and the JCPC during a term wherever possible. Attention is also paid to family ties or other factors which might give rise to a potential perception of bias.[18]

The draft constitutions are submitted to the President and Deputy President for their approval before being circulated to the other members of the Court. The Registrar's draft may be amended at either stage for a variety of reasons. For example, it may be felt by the President and Deputy President that an appeal merits a larger or smaller court than it has been allocated.[19] Or it may be felt that a particular Justice needs to be given time to produce a judgment in another case, and should therefore have fewer sitting days. Or it may be felt that a fairer distribution of cases of particular interest, or of cases of interest to particular

15 It is also regarded as important to include in the court hearing each appeal at least one Justice who does not have particular expertise in the area in question. This reflects in part a degree of scepticism about the value or significance of legal specialisation. It also reflects the importance of questioning attitudes which may have developed as a matter of habit, and of ensuring that, as a former Chief Justice of Australia has put it, the law does not evolve into a kind of archipelago of islands of expertise. Most Justices also prefer to sit in cases concerning a variety of subjects.

16 This has become more difficult since Lady Hale's retirement, and the reduction in the number of female Justices to two, since they cannot cover every appeal between them unless they sit more frequently than their male colleagues. It is also considered appropriate to have both female Justices sit on appeals where female participation is especially important (eg equal pay cases), although the consequence is that other appeals will have all-male courts.

17 An attempt is made to ensure that Justices sit for approximately equal amounts of time. This is monitored, and statistics are provided to the Justices. An attempt is also made to ensure that each Justice has one week clear of sitting each term, so as to provide an opportunity to write the more difficult judgments. An attempt is also made to ensure that the Justices have an equal opportunity to sit on the more interesting and important cases.

18 For example, Lord Mance did not sit on appeals against decisions of the Court of Appeal in which Arden LJ sat, as they are married. For the same reason, Lady Black does not sit on appeals in cases in which McCombe LJ sat.

19 Courts comprising seven Justices are used where appeals are felt to be of particular importance, especially if they involve a reconsideration of previous decisions of the Supreme Court or the House of Lords. In exceptionally difficult or important cases, a court comprising nine Justices has occasionally been used. A court comprising eleven Justices has been used twice, in the Brexit appeals (*R (Miller) v Secretary of State for Exiting the European Union* [2017] UKSC 5, [2018] AC 61, and *R (Miller) v Prime Minister* [2019] UKSC 41, [2020] AC 373), in order to forestall criticism, in the event that a smaller court had sat, that a different decision might have been taken if the court had been differently composed.

Justices, can be achieved. Or it may emerge that Justices are unavailable on dates when they have been scheduled to sit.[20] Changes in composition can occur after the constitutions have been approved, for example because of sudden illness. Most Justices sit in less than half of the cases heard by the Supreme Court.[21]

A court constituted by five Justices is used in about 90% of cases.[22] The published criteria to be used when considering whether more than five Justices should sit are set out on the Court's website:

- If the court is being asked to depart, or may decide to depart from a previous decision.
- A case of high constitutional importance.
- A case of great public importance.
- A case where a conflict between decisions in the House of Lords, the JCPC and/or the Supreme Court has to be reconciled.
- A case raising an important point in relation to the European Convention on Human Rights.

The use of odd numbers of judges to hear appeals is required by legislation[23] and is intended to avoid the possibility of the court's being equally divided. I can recollect one case, in which there were more than two possible outcomes, in which a court comprising seven Justices was unable to reach a majority decision agreeing on a single outcome. The appeal was then re-heard before a court of nine, and a majority eventually emerged.[24]

V. PREPARATION FOR THE HEARING

As explained earlier, all appeals are heard orally, following the common law tradition. The Appeal Panel normally decides the length of the hearing, as explained earlier, and then leaves it to counsel to agree how the allocated

---

20 Justices may be unavailable for a variety of reasons. For example, I sit occasionally on the European Court of Human Rights, and may be absent for that reason. Other Justices have other commitments. They may also be unavailable from time to time for personal reasons.

21 In 2015–16, only the President, Lord Neuberger, the Deputy President, Lady Hale, and Lord Toulson sat in the majority of appeals. I came next, sitting in 49% of appeals. When Justices are not sitting in the Supreme Court, they are often sitting in the JCPC.

22 The proportion has steadily increased over time, from around 75% of hearings during the presidency of Lord Phillips to 88% during that of Lord Neuberger and over 90% during that of Lady Hale.

23 Section 42(1)(a) of the Constitutional Reform Act 2005.

24 *R v Waya* [2012] UKSC 51, [2013] 1 AC 294.

time should be divided amongst themselves. If they were unable to agree, the presiding Justice would determine the matter, but that has never been necessary in my experience. Most appeals are allocated one day, and the great majority of appeals fall within a range of half a day to two days.

The members of the Court who are to hear an appeal are provided with the papers about a week in advance. They will read, as a minimum, the judgments of the courts below, an agreed statement of facts and issues, and written arguments for the parties and any interveners. That is usually a substantial amount of reading.[25]

The Court has considered, and rejected, the adoption of a *juge rapporteur* system.[26] I have observed the system in operation on the European Court of Human Rights, where I have sat on an occasional basis for many years as an ad hoc judge, and also on the French *Cour de cassation*, where I spent two weeks on an exchange some years ago. I understand the value of such a system in a court with a very heavy caseload. On the Supreme Court, however, the fact that only a small number of appeals are given permission enables every Justice hearing an appeal to read the papers and to be fully engaged.

On the morning of the hearing, the members of the court to hear an appeal gather in the room of the member who will preside at the hearing – usually either the President or the Deputy President, but sometimes one of the next two most senior Justices – fifteen minutes before the hearing is due to start. There will be a short discussion of the case.[27] At that stage, any views expressed are understood to be of a preliminary nature. The purpose of the meeting is to consider how the hearing ought to be handled. It may be, for example, that five arguments are being run, and that the appellant has to win on every one of them in order for the appeal to succeed. In that case, if it is felt that the fifth argument is the weakest, the court may want to hear the appellant on that argument first. If it fails, the hearing may come to an end at that point, possibly without the respondent even being called on to reply. At the least, in a situation of that kind, the court will want to discuss whether to hear the appellant on all five points and then to hear the respondent's reply, or to hear the opposing arguments on each individual point in turn. It sometimes emerges at these meetings that a member of the court thinks that there is a way of looking at the case, or a precedent, which has not been mentioned by counsel in their written arguments, and discussion will then focus on how, and at what stage of the hearing, the point should be raised.

---

25 Taking as random examples the two cases I am working on as I write this chapter, it amounts to 187 pages in one case and 315 pages in the other.

26 Literally, a reporting judge, who prepares a report on the case for the court.

27 Most of the Justices will also have discussed the case with their judicial assistants.

VI. DURING THE HEARING

During the hearing, the members of the court commonly have a brief word about the case when they adjourn at lunchtime or at the end of the day, and when they gather for the resumption of the hearing after an adjournment. Discussion again focuses primarily on the conduct of the hearing, but views may be expressed about the cogency of the arguments heard so far. Some Justices may also get together at the end of the day, sometimes with their judicial assistants, to discuss where their thinking about the case has got to, and the points which might be explored before the continuation of the hearing the following day.[28]

VII. THE CONFERENCE

At the end of the hearing, the members of the court normally meet in the conference room or the Justices' lounge to discuss the case. Sometimes, this discussion may be postponed to allow Justices more time to gather their thoughts.[29]

The discussion has a structured character. Each of the Justices in turn gives his or her analysis of the case, in reverse order of seniority. The analysis is expected to be comprehensive and considered, although it takes a fairly summary form, and the views expressed are understood to be of a provisional character. Each Justice will normally have prepared written notes, typically in my own case of about two pages of A4. The most junior Justice will speak first, usually for about ten minutes, but sometimes for considerably longer, depending on the complexity of the case. The other Justices then follow in reverse order of seniority, the presiding member of the court[30] having the last word. If different views have been expressed, there is then likely to be an open discussion. The presiding member of the court will guide the discussion, with a view to a good-humoured and rational argument. A consensus may be reached, or differences may be crystallised.

---

28 For example, during a hearing concerned with the interpretation of a judgment of the Court of Justice of the European Union, a colleague and I agreed that counsel were focusing excessively on the meaning of the language used in the English language version, and agreed that I would consider the language used in the French text and he would consider the German version. I will also discuss with my judicial assistant how our thoughts about the case are evolving, and any research which might be undertaken.

29 For example, in the first Brexit case mentioned in n 19 above (*R (Miller) v Secretary of State for Exiting the European Union* [2017] UKSC 5, [2018] AC 61), discussion was postponed for several days, on the basis that, in the meantime, each member of the court would circulate a written summary of his or her views.

30 Usually either the President or the Deputy President.

At the end of the discussion, the presiding member of the court will ask one of the others to write a judgment, or will volunteer to do so himself or herself. If the court is divided, the member who is asked to write will obviously be a member of the majority. The minority are generally expected, as a matter of courtesy, to await the circulation of the draft judgment before circulating their own draft.[31] Nevertheless, a dissenter will sometimes issue a judgment very quickly, hoping to persuade the other members of the court.

The decision as to who is asked to write the judgment is a matter of particular importance in a common law system, where judgments are very fully reasoned and are an essential source of law. Who is asked is a matter for the judgement of the presiding member of the court, and depends on weighing a number of factors. Experience can be important: for example, a contentious judgment in an area of the law where the court has a recognised expert may be best received if that person writes it. Sensitivities can be relevant: for example, I have been asked to write judgments in Scottish appeals concerned with family law, notwithstanding my relative inexperience in that field when compared with other members of the court. It was felt that, if criticisms had to be made of the judgments or the procedures of the courts below, they would come better from a judge who had held a senior position in the Scottish courts. Fairness is also important: it would be resented if the most interesting and important judgments were hogged by a few members of the court. Workload also matters: in order to ensure that judgments are produced reasonably quickly, and that individuals do not become stressed by overwork, an effort is made to keep an eye on how much outstanding work each member of the court has. The post-hearing discussion is also important: if a member of the court has produced a particularly clear and compelling analysis of the case, he or she may well be the best person to write the judgment.

It has become increasingly common in recent years for Justices to produce joint judgments. This can be a good solution where more than one Justice would like to write, and their views of the case are broadly aligned. It works particularly well where the case raises a number of distinct issues, which the Justices can divide between them.[32] As Deputy President and President, I have supported the idea of having two Justices work on the most important and difficult judgments, so as to ensure that more than one person has been thinking really hard about the problem before the Court.

31 It may, however, be provided at an earlier stage to the Justice writing the majority judgment, so as to assist in focussing the issues dividing the court at the earliest opportunity.

32 As, for example, in *Littlewoods Ltd v Commissioners for Her Majesty's Revenue and Customs* [2017] UKSC 70, [2018] AC 869.

VIII. AFTER THE CONFERENCE

After the conference, the Justice who has been asked to write will produce a draft judgment, bearing his or her own name. It is circulated to the other members of the court by email, and usually also in hard copy. There then begins the next phase of the consideration of the case: interchanges and debate, mostly conducted by email. Depending on the case, and in particular on whether the members of the court are in agreement or not, this phase can last only a few weeks, or several months.

By the time the draft judgment is circulated, the members of the court are at some distance from the post-hearing discussion, and their positions may have altered, especially after reading the analysis in the draft judgment. They may agree with the outcome but not with all aspects of the reasoning, or they may disagree with the outcome.[33] They normally respond by circulating comments on the draft, which may be more or less critical. Depending on their nature, the author of the judgment may be able and willing to accommodate them. The comments which are offered and accepted are normally of relatively minor significance. If there is a more profound disagreement, a concurring judgment (a judgment agreeing with the result, but disagreeing with the reasoning), or a dissenting judgment (one disagreeing with the result) is likely to be drafted and circulated. Where, however, there are strong reasons for issuing a single judgment (for example, in criminal appeals, or in other cases where it is important to give lower courts clear and unequivocal guidance), compromises may be reached on more significant aspects of the reasoning, or the Court may 'go small', by deciding the case on a narrow basis and avoiding wider and more controversial issues. As in other courts,[34] compromise can result in greater indeterminacy, but where the court is divided on an important aspect of doctrine, that is not necessarily a bad thing. It is a question of judgement whether the best solution in a particular case is to acknowledge the division on the court by issuing majority and concurring or dissenting judgments, or to issue a judgment which is more vaguely expressed and leaves the contested issue open for further argument in another case.

Current practice (differing from that of the House of Lords) is generally to favour a single majority judgment, so that the reasoning of the majority is expressed in a unitary way.[35] This assists legal practitioners and lower courts, although it has been criticised by legal academics. The collegiality of the Supreme Court enables this practice to work. Concurring judgments may be

---

[33] The importance of appeals to the Supreme Court generally lies in their legal reasoning, rather than the outcome on the facts.

[34] For example, in the Court of Justice of the European Union (CJEU).

[35] In the legal year 2015–16, 75 cases were decided by the Supreme Court, of which 47 (63%) involved a single judgment. The proportion has been similar or greater in subsequent years.

unavoidable where judges arrive at the same outcome by different processes of reasoning, but it is important that the differences in reasoning should be made plain. Multiple reasoning is favoured only where the Court is working in a developing area of the law and wishes to indicate a number of possible paths for future development. This has been a feature, for example, of some recent cases concerned with unjust enrichment,[36] although a single judgment was issued where the Court wished to give authoritative guidance to lower courts.[37]

IX. COMPARISON WITH OTHER COURTS

I shall finish by making a few points of comparison between decision-making in the Supreme Court and in some other courts.[38] I am conscious of the limited experience on the basis of which I make these points. Nevertheless, the impressions of a judge from a different legal tradition may be of some interest.

1. On the Supreme Court, the most important stage in collective decision-making is not the conference after the hearing, where the views expressed are provisional, but the hearing itself, where interventions by members of the court can be persuasive, and more especially the process of drafting judgments, when interchanges between the members of the court are particularly important. The strength of the judgments arises partly from the interplay of different viewpoints at that stage. By comparison, on the European Court of Human Rights, and on the French *Cour de cassation*, the deliberation is of central importance, and the subsequent process of drafting the judgment has historically been relatively formal.
2. Consequently, conferences in the Supreme Court have a less formal character than those in the European Court of Human Rights and the *Cour de cassation*. That said, I have been conscious, when sitting on the European Court of Human Rights, that the very formality of the *délibéré*[39] can result in important discussions taking place informally, for example during tea breaks.

---

36 For example, *Benedetti v Sawiris* [2013] UKSC 50, [2014] AC 938, and *Menelaou v Bank of Cyprus Plc* [2015] UKSC 66, [2016] AC 176.

37 *Investment Trust Companies v Revenue and Customs Commissioners* [2017] UKSC 29, [2018] AC 275.

38 I have in mind particularly the European Court of Human Rights and the French *Cour de cassation*. These courts are specifically considered by A Nussberger (chapter 12) and by Dominique Hascher (chapter 6) in their respective contributions to the present collection.

39 The deliberations on the case.

3. On the Supreme Court, every judge is equally engaged in the case: all members of the court have read the same papers, and all make a significant contribution to the decision-making process. Every member of the court is expected, at the conference, to give a substantial opinion on the case. The fact that the Court hears only a small number of appeals each year, each of which has been assessed as raising an arguable point of law of general public importance, enables this level of engagement to exist. By comparison, my experience on the European Court of Human Rights has been that not all of the judges contribute significantly to the deliberation. The most significant contributions to the discussion are usually made by the *juge rapporteur* and the national judge. If they are in agreement, some if not most of the other judges may have little to add. My impression on the *Cour de cassation* was that the *juge rapporteur* and the *doyen*[40] were the leading figures in the discussion.
4. The culture of judgment-writing on the Supreme Court, and in the common law tradition more generally, is utterly unlike that on the European Court of Human Rights or, to an even greater degree, that on the *Cour de cassation*. On the European Court of Human Rights, the judgment is designed to give effect to the decision reached at the *délibéré*. It is principally drafted by the Registry, rather than by the judges.[41] The result is often boilerplate drafting, with stock formulae appearing in one judgment after another. When the judgment returns to the court for approval, attention tends to focus on the correctness of the French. On the *Cour de cassation*, the judgment is extremely formalised.[42] The style is impersonal and magisterial, and there can be no dissent: the State is telling its citizens what the law is. On the UK Supreme Court, on the other hand, a judgment is written by an individual judge in his or her own personal style. It may include humour, or references to literature or history. It may be written in a narrative style, or more analytically. Where a judge has a particularly individual style of writing, the identity of the author may be obvious to informed readers even without looking at the name at the top of the page. The judge's reasoning is set out transparently. It may

40 The longest-serving member of the court.

41 There is a drafting committee, but in my experience its practical involvement is limited. A notable feature of the committee is that, in my experience, it has always been chaired by the *juge rapporteur*, even if he or she was a member of the minority on the court. That created difficulties in one case in which I took part. When the draft judgment is placed before the court for approval, alternative drafts can then be put forward. The final text is then determined by a vote, sentence by sentence, following discussion.

42 If I remember correctly, when judgments were delivered, the parties, if they attended the hand-down, would all leave the court as soon as they heard the word '*vu*': that was the signal that the appeal had succeeded. From 1 October 2019 the *Cour de cassation* adopted a change in the style of its judgments, known as 'style direct', so as to provide clearer reasoning.

include the expression of his doubts, hesitations, and reservations. The text is of the utmost importance. The reasoning is the focus of intense attention and discussion by the other members of the court. Ultimately, if one judge's concerns about the text cannot be met by concessions on the part of the draftsman, a concurring or dissenting judgment will be drafted.

CHAPTER 3

COLLECTIVE JUDGING IN THE COURT OF APPEAL OF ENGLAND AND WALES

Jack BEATSON, Launcelot HENDERSON and Keith LINDBLOM*

I. INTRODUCTION

The Court of Appeal of England and Wales consists of 38 Lord and Lady Justices of Appeal ('LJs') as well as the Lord Chief Justice, the Master of the Rolls, the President of the Queen's Bench Division, the President of the Family Division, and the Chancellor of the High Court. The Master of the Rolls is the President of the Court, and one of the members of the Court holds the office of Vice-President. Since 2007, one member of the Court has held the office of Senior President of Tribunals. The three words which characterise its work are 'flexibility', 'informality', and 'collegiality'. Each has advantages and disadvantages. In our experience, collegiality is generally present even when there are sharp differences which cannot be resolved. It is achieved in a similar way to that described by Judge Harry T Edwards in the US Court of Appeals for the DC Circuit,[1] but without rules and with few guidelines.

---

* Sir Jack Beatson was formerly Lord Justice of Appeal at the Court of Appeal of England and Wales, and is Visiting Professor at the University of Oxford; Sir Launcelot Henderson and Sir Keith Lindblom are Lord Justices of Appeal at the Court of Appeal of England and Wales. Lord Justice Henderson is also Distinguished Fellow of All Souls College, Oxford. This chapter is a lightly revised version of three ten-minute presentations by the three Lord Justices at the 'Collective Judging' conference on 20 July 2017. Unless otherwise stated, any views expressed reflect their individual, personal views.

1 See chapter 5 of the present collection.

The majority of the members of the Court of Appeal sit in two appellate jurisdictions, the Court of Appeal Civil Division and the Court of Appeal Criminal Division. The Lord Chief Justice has overall responsibility for the entire Court and sits in both Divisions, but is primarily the head of the Criminal Division. The head of the Civil Division is the Master of the Rolls. Members of the Court also sit in a third jurisdiction, the Divisional Court, which hears important judicial reviews and public law cases, such as the first *Miller* case concerning article 50 of the Treaty on European Union,[2] and challenges to and statutory appeals from the decisions of inferior courts, including appeals in extradition and professional discipline cases.

Some LJs do not sit in crime; and some sit predominantly in crime. All LJs are assisted by a 'clerk' for administrative but not legal work, and most have a Judicial Assistant, a young lawyer who prepares bench memos on a case, sorts out the papers in cases where what the parties have presented is not well arranged (perhaps because they are unrepresented lay people), and researches particular questions on which we consider the skeleton arguments are unclear, unsatisfactory, or incomplete. They provide valuable assistance, but our impression is that at present their role and contribution is very different to that of a judicial clerk in United States Federal courts.

II. THE COURT OF APPEAL CIVIL DIVISION

As to civil appeals, there are about 1,200 substantive or full appeals heard each year, and in 2015–2016 there were also 4,385 applications for permission to appeal, considered first on the papers, with the possibility, if permission was refused, of renewing the application to an oral hearing. The number of applications for permission has risen in recent years, principally in immigration cases. In 2011 there were 3,058 such applications. Including applications for permission, there has been an increase of over 50% in the workload of the Court in the period between 2010 and 2016. Since October 2016, the right to renew an application to an oral hearing has been removed. Such a hearing will only occur in cases where applications for permission to appeal were made after 3 October 2016 if the judge considering the case on the papers so directs. Normally oral hearings of applications for permission are heard by a single LJ, at a hearing lasting about half an hour. Sometimes, they are heard by two LJs, and they can take up to three hours.

Most civil appeals are heard by three members of the Court of Appeal, although sometimes one member of the court will be a first instance judge,

2 *R (Miller) v Secretary of State for Exiting the European Union* [2016] EWHC 2768 (Admin); aff'd [2017] UKSC 5, [2018] AC 61. The Lord Chief Justice, the Master of the Rolls and Sales LJ sat in the Divisional Court.

normally from the Chancery or Family Divisions of the High Court. In cases considered to be straightforward, in particular appeals from county courts rather than from the High Court, the appeal may be heard by a two-judge Court of Appeal. In 2015, pressure of work led to consideration being given to increasing the use of two-judge courts for such cases. We deal with the advantages and disadvantages of such courts below. Traditionally, the same panel of three would sit together for a period of three weeks. We discuss this further below. At this stage, it suffices to say that this enabled the work to be allocated fairly and reflecting the particular expertise of members of the panel and, because the group was together for a period, it also facilitated good working relationships. Over the last few years, however, there have been more changes in the composition of panels. The reasons are complex. In part, the changes in constitutions reflect the pressures of the increased caseload and the demand for a judge with a particular expertise that is in short supply. In part, they reflect the increased administrative and out-of-court responsibilities of many members of the Court. A time and motion study in 2015 showed that a significant percentage of the time of Court of Appeal judges is being spent on administrative and management tasks.[3]

The constitution of panels is decided well in advance, three times a year. The presiding judge in each panel is the senior judge of the three, and he or she will deal with (or ask one of the other members of the panel to deal with) any procedural matters that arise before the hearing of the cases allocated to the panel, as well as presiding at the hearing itself. The constitution of the panels is a judicial function, performed by the two 'Masters' of the Court of Appeal (who are second-tier judges with particular expertise in procedural matters: despite their title, both the current Masters are women), subject to the supervision of the Master of the Rolls or his deputy, the Vice President of the Civil Division. In general terms, the aim is to ensure that all members of the court sit with each other at regular intervals, and hear cases which lie outside, as well as within, their respective areas of expertise. This promotes collegiality, and also the potential advantages of 'cross-fertilisation' of skills and perspective which may result from having a non-specialist judge on the panel for a particular appeal. Judges self-certify their level of expertise in the areas of the Court's work, in a table which the listing officers will be able to consult (if need be) when allocating cases to be heard by each panel. In practice, the main areas of expertise of individual judges will of course be well known to the Masters, the listing officers and the judge's colleagues. The system is informal and pragmatic, but in our experience generally works well in practice.

---

3 Lord Justice Briggs, Civil Courts Structure Review: Final Report (July 2016), para [1.19] and pp 150–53 of Annex 4, available online via https://www.judiciary.uk/wp-content/uploads/2016/07/civil-courts-structure-review-final-report-jul-16-final-1.pdf (last accessed 27 March 2020).

In full or substantive appeals, our practice is to allocate the responsibility for preparing the first or 'lead' judgment, in advance of the hearing, to a single judge (or, occasionally, to two or even all three members of the Court, if the case is a heavy one involving many different issues). The aim is to allocate according to expertise and to ensure a fair distribution of the load of 'lead' judgments and applications for permission between the panel. It is more difficult to do this where the same panel only sits together for a week, or occasionally for a single case. The allocation is the prerogative of the presiding judge, who will usually circulate his or her suggestions to the other members of the panel about two or three weeks before the hearing. Although such allocations used to be made 'ex cathedra' by certain presiders, the modern style is to reach a decision by discussion and consensus, albeit subject to an informal expectation that you will comply with the provisional allocation put forward by the presider unless you have a good reason to question it.

When reading into the case to prepare for the hearing, members of the panel may exchange e-mails, for example where one has raised points about matters such as the state of the papers before the Court or a case or statutory provision which has not been cited in the written submissions so that the attention of the parties can be drawn to the matter in advance of the hearing. There will generally be a discussion before the hearing of a full appeal either in the presiding judge's room or outside the Court (particularly if one member of the panel has been hearing an application for permission). The panel will discuss their provisional views of the strengths and weaknesses of an appeal, based on their pre-reading of the papers, in particular the judgment below, the skeleton arguments, the authorities, and any material the parties have highlighted. The meeting may last for about half an hour. In our experience, these exchanges are very useful. They identify points on which members of the Court would like clarification from the advocates. They do not lead to views crystallising before the oral submissions have been heard. Where the Court rises during the hearing (for example, for the lunch adjournment, or at the end of the first day), the judges are likely to have a brief exchange of views on where they are.

After the end of the hearing, there is generally a further discussion. The panel will consider the outcome, and, where there is agreement, discuss in broad terms the route to that outcome. Where there is no agreement either as to outcome or as to the route to an agreed outcome, there will be a fuller discussion so that each member of the panel understands the position of his or her colleagues. Since it is the experience of at least one of us that it is the process of actually writing the judgment which tends to clarify one's thoughts, and may in some cases lead to a change of mind about the conclusion one is ultimately going to reach, it is generally understood that the lead judge is not bound to adhere to any provisional conclusion reached in discussions after the hearing, and matters are sometimes left on the footing that he or she will see how the issues emerge from the process of writing before circulating the draft to the other members of the panel for their consideration. We should also add that, in some cases, the panel is so clear about the result by the end of the hearing that the Court announces its decision immediately, with written reasons to follow in due course. In such cases, it is obviously no longer open to the Court to change its mind, and the purpose of the written judgment or judgments is simply to explain the reasons which led the Court to its decision.

III. JUDGMENTS

The next stage is to write the judgments. In the case of oral applications for permission to appeal, *ex tempore* judgments are almost invariably given. In the vast majority of full appeals, judgment is reserved, but *ex tempore* judgments are occasionally given. *Ex tempore* judgments are far less common in full appeals than they were 25 years ago. This is partly because hearings used to be longer, leaving more time for preliminary views to be formed, and for some work to be done on parts of the judgment before and after the hearing each day. When one of us became a member of the Court of Appeal five years ago, some of the senior judges regularly gave *ex tempore* judgments in what they saw as simple cases. This is no longer the position and such judgments are now seldom given in full appeals in civil cases, although they are occasionally.

In a full appeal, each judge is free to write a judgment. We have referred to the practice of assigning responsibility for the 'lead' judgment in every full appeal to one member of the panel. The 'lead' judgment is the one which is produced first and distributed to the members of the constitution. Some judges who are going to lead on a given appeal find it helpful to write out – at least in note form – the facts found in the court below, and to summarise what they consider to be the important issues, and what difficulties each party appears to face before the hearing. After a draft is circulated, there is further discussion. The other members of the panel will make suggestions, ranging from identifying typos and points of style, to more substantive matters. In many cases, the judge who has written the lead judgment is content to take in the suggestions. If so, the other judges are likely to agree rather than to write concurring judgments. Where there is no agreement either as to the result or as to the reasoning, there may be further discussion, either in a meeting or by e-mail exchanges. If the differences are not resolved, the judge in question will write either a dissenting judgment or one concurring in the result but setting out his or her reasoning and route to that conclusion.

In the last 20 years, there has been increased use of the notion of 'judgments of the court', either prepared by one, but which all sign up to, or with different members of the Court contributing different sections or parts. Such judgments may be convenient, for example, where one member of the

Court is a judge with a leadership role and administrative and other duties, or where the case involves discrete and self-contained points on very different areas, or simply where there are multiple issues and a division of labour is appropriate. For instance, this was done in an appeal concerning a challenge by tobacco companies to regulations requiring tobacco products to be in plain packaging, which involved issues of intellectual property law and several distinct questions of domestic and EU public law.[4] In cases of this type, the usual practice is for the judgment to be handed down by the presiding judge, and for it to be prefaced by a statement that it is the judgment of the court to which all its members have contributed. Other kinds of case where a judgment of the court will often be appropriate are cases which involve an issue of major public importance, or where the Court has to criticise the personal conduct of the judge below. Although, as a matter of precedent, a judgment of the Court carries no extra authority, it is in practice likely to carry more weight, or at least be perceived to do so, in cases of unusual sensitivity or public significance.

In recent years, attempts have been made by the Master of the Rolls to encourage 'short-form' judgments, similar to (although fuller than) the 'memo' judgments in some other jurisdictions. A well-publicised example of such a judgment in an immigration case is provided by the February 2017 decision in *BS (Congo) v The Secretary of State for the Home Department*, in which the Secretary of State's appeal was dismissed.[5] It is thought that such a judgment may be appropriate in cases which raise no issue of law, principle, or wider general significance, and where all the relevant facts are set out in the judgment of the court below, and are not disputed in the appeal. A spokesman from the Judicial Office stated that 'in such cases, it may be possible to avoid reciting all the facts, the course of the proceedings and the judgments below, and proceed, after a brief introduction, to a statement of the decision on the principal arguments on the appeal and the outcome of the appeal'.[6] The idea is that the judgment will only be of interest to the parties, so the fact that it is not self-contained and it is necessary to read the judgment below to understand it will not matter. Although such judgments have also been advocated on the ground of efficiency and clarity, they may not always be conducive to efficiency because, adapting Blaise Pascal's famous statement,

4 *R (British American Tobacco and others) v Secretary of State for Health* [2016] EWCA Civ 1182, [2017] 3 WLR 225.

5 *BS (Congo) v The Secretary of State for the Home Department* [2017] EWCA Civ 53, [2017] 4 WLR 45.

6 'Keep it snappy: judges get to the point in fewer words', *The Times*, 9 February 2017. The idea is not new: see the model short-form judgment by Lord Wilberforce in *Brumby (Inspector of Taxes) v Milner* [1976] 1 WLR 1096 (HL) 1099.

writing a short but accurate judgment may well take longer than writing a longer one.[7]

One point which we would emphasise is that our judgments are all our own work. No parts of them are written for us, even in draft. Our 'clerks', most of whom are not legally qualified, do not draft our judgments. If we are fortunate, one of our judicial assistants will have produced a bench memo on the case, and they may have helped with research on points of law, but it is no part of their function to provide first drafts of even the factual parts of our judgments. This means that the writing of judgments is an exacting and time-consuming task, and different judges approach it in different ways and with different personal styles; but it does at least mean that, although perfection is unattainable, the product of our labour should generally be of high quality. We are certainly all very conscious that it is on the quality of our judgments that the reputation of the Court ultimately rests.

IV. TWO-JUDGE COURTS

In recent years – largely with a view to accelerating the output of determined appeals in a Court under very severe pressure – increasing use has been made of two-judge, rather than three-judge, constitutions in civil appeals. There is a growing proportion of appeals now being dealt with in this way. Previously, the practice had generally been to use three-judge constitutions for most civil appeals, sometimes composed of two Lord or Lady Justices of Appeal and a High Court judge.[8]

There are some obvious advantages in the use of two-judge constitutions, and also some disadvantages, not all of which perhaps are immediately obvious. The two most obvious advantages are, first, that the use of two-judge constitutions enables a more efficient and flexible use of the Court's resources, and secondly, therefore, that many appeals will reach a hearing, and will be decided, sooner than they otherwise would have been. In view of the delays to hearings in the Court because of the high volume of its workload – which gave rise to this reform – those are significant advantages.

There are, of course, some potential disadvantages. These can be avoided only if care is taken to ensure that appeals raising sufficiently complex issues of law, or issues of general public importance, or issues with unusually significant personal or financial consequences for the litigants, and perhaps for others as well, are heard by three-judge constitutions.

---

7 *Cf* B Pascal, *Lettres Provinciales* (1657), no XVI: 'Je n'ai fait celle-ci plus longue que parce que je n'ai pas eu le loisir de la faire plus courte.'

8 Section 54 Senior Courts Act 1981, as amended by the Access to Justice Act 1999.

First, there is the risk of disagreement on the outcome. This is not the same thing as disagreement as to the correct path to the same conclusion. Two judges may sometimes agree that an appeal should be allowed or dismissed, but be divided as to the correct route to that conclusion. This presents no difficulty in principle, because in those circumstances each judge can give a judgment, agreeing as to the outcome, explaining how he or she has arrived at that conclusion and why he differs from the analysis of the other judge. If there is disagreement on the outcome, the appeal will have to be heard afresh, by a constitution of three. This problem seldom arises, because two-judge constitutions have rarely disagreed. This is also true of the Divisional Court, in which two-judge constitutions are normal, and disagreements are uncommon, indeed rare. In three-judge constitutions the rate of dissent is also very low – measured in single-figure percentages.

A second potential disadvantage, less obvious than the first, goes to the deliberative dynamic itself. There will be cases where the likelihood of disagreement emerges before the hearing, and it is possible to add a third judge to a two-judge constitution in good time. This can happen, for example, when the appeal turns on a disputed question of statutory construction or the reconciliation of two previous judgments in the Court of Appeal or the Supreme Court. But there are cases where the Court's provisional consensus on the outcome is broken by oral advocacy at the hearing – in itself a valuable feature of our system. If an impasse emerges in the deliberations of a two-judge court during or after the hearing, the tenor of the discussion between the judges may be quite different from that in a three-judge court, where dissent is possible and a dissenting judgment may itself be of some value in any subsequent appeal to the Supreme Court. The freedom to dissent in a three-judge court encourages each member of the Court to express both his or her views and his or her doubts – which, in our view, is a significant merit.

V. THE COURT OF APPEAL CRIMINAL DIVISION

We turn to the Court of Appeal Criminal Division. In 2015–2016 there were 1,417 applications for permission to appeal against conviction, 82 of which were granted and 160 of which were referred to the full Court; and 4,072 applications for permission to appeal against sentence, 647 of which were granted and 273 of which were referred to the full Court. Most applications are considered initially by a single High Court judge on the papers. The role of the High Court judges in filtering the applications is vital and saves the full Court considerable time. The full Court heard 260 appeals against conviction, 94 of which were allowed; and 1,294 appeals against sentence, 924 of which were allowed. Of the applications for permission which were refused, 302 applications for permission to appeal against conviction and 498 applications for permission to appeal against sentence were renewed to the full Court.

In the Court of Appeal Criminal Division, a member of the Court of Appeal will normally preside over the hearing but, save in the most important cases, he or she will sit with two first instance judges. One of the first instance judges may be a senior circuit judge rather than a High Court judge. His or her role is to bring front line criminal trial experience to the deliberations of the Court of Appeal Criminal Division. The typical week in criminal appeals is one and a half days reading, and three and a half days in court. In cases where the issue is the sentence rather than the conviction, the Court may consist of two judges, either one LJ and one High Court or Circuit judge, two High Court judges, or one High Court and one Circuit judge.

While hearings for complicated criminal appeals may last for over a day and in some cases for several days, in general the Court of Appeal Criminal Division will often hear seven or eight cases a day. Unlike in civil appeals, it always gives a judgment of the Court. There is no provision for separate judgments, although there is provision for the presiding judge to certify a point of law. The Criminal Appeal Office assigns the task of writing the judgment but the members of the constitution can, in discussion, reallocate. Secondly, no doubt because of the work load, the majority of its judgments are *ex tempore.*

While pre-reading and pre-preparation is a feature of both the Court of Appeal Civil Division and the Court of Appeal Criminal Division, there are differences as a result of the number of cases that have to be dealt with in the Court of Appeal Criminal Division. On the day of the hearing, there is a full pre-court meeting to go through each case and express provisional views. Because the pace of work means that most judgments are *ex tempore*, the judge giving the judgment will prepare a draft (sometimes with two conclusions, as he or she may not know the views of the others until the pre-court meeting). Increasingly, drafts, or summaries, are exchanged by e-mail on the day before the hearing.

CHAPTER 4

AN AUSTRALIAN PERSPECTIVE ON COLLECTIVE JUDGING

Susan KIEFEL*

I. BACKGROUND

The High Court of Australia is the final appellate and constitutional court in Australia. It comprises seven justices. An appeal brought in its appellate jurisdiction requires a grant of special leave. Some 400–500 applications for special leave are determined each year and about 60 cases proceed to full oral hearing.[1] Judgments are currently delivered within six months from the date of hearing[2] and often earlier.

Argument on an appeal is usually heard by five justices. It may be increased to all seven justices, for example where it is sought to have a previous decision of the Court overruled. In matters in the original jurisdiction of the Court, such as constitutional matters, it is usual for all justices to sit.

The time taken for hearings, generally speaking, ranges from a half-day to two days. Estimates of time are provided by the parties and considered by

* The Hon Susan Kiefel AC is Chief Justice of Australia.

1 High Court of Australia, *Annual Report 2015–2016* (Kingston ACT, 2016) 20, Table A, available online via http://www.hcourt.gov.au/publications/annual-reports/annual-reports (last accessed 29 February 2020).

2 Ibid 19.

the Court. The Court provides an allocation of time for the hearing and the lawyers are expected to divide that time amongst themselves. It is not usual for a matter to exceed the time allocated, but the Court will extend time if it considers it to be necessary. This circumstance does not often arise.

Some time prior to a sitting, a document is circulated amongst the justices identifying the matters to be heard, those matters which require all available justices to hear them, and otherwise the justices who will constitute a panel of five. The document is in the nature of a proposal about which other views may be stated. For obvious reasons the Court tries to avoid sitting in even numbers, but there are statutory mechanisms for resolving a matter where the opinion as to the outcome is equally divided.[3]

The ways in which the justices of the High Court deliberate and decide matters necessarily reflects a balance drawn between institutional values and competing external pressures. The judgments of the High Court in more recent times reflect a shift away from individualism in favour of a more collegiate approach that places greater weight on the timely delivery of judgments and provision of guidance for lower courts. That is not to say that the Court prizes unanimity or that an obligation is felt to strive to achieve it in the same way as may be the case in civilian courts. However, greater acceptance of the benefits of collegiate discussion appears to have contributed to an increase in unanimous or joint judgments.

II. PREPARATION

The process leading to deliberation in the Court starts with preparation for the oral hearing. Effective deliberation requires each justice to understand the issues and have some familiarity with the relevant materials. Each justice is expected to prepare for all matters on which he or she will sit in advance of the oral hearing. Individual preparation enables each justice to engage with the argument during the hearing and participate on an equal footing in subsequent deliberations.

The justices' preparation is facilitated by comprehensive written submissions that the parties are required to file before the hearing. These submissions are made publicly available after the parties certify that they are in a form suitable for publication on the internet. Preparation may involve not just an understanding of the shape and content of the arguments contained in the submissions and where issue is joined, but also an understanding of relevant legislation and key cases. The level of preparation will obviously vary according to the nature of the case, the time allowed for it and the individual justice.

---

[3] Judiciary Act 1903 (Cth), section 23.

It is generally understood that judges may have different ideas about how much preparation they should, and can, undertake. With a few exceptions, I think that most High Court justices would prepare as much as time allows and as much as they consider necessary to the particular case. Much depends on how up-to-date one is with outstanding judgments and where one draws the line between continuing to write them and preparing for the next sittings. Nevertheless, there is something of an expectation on the part of one's colleagues that everyone will be prepared to a reasonable level. It can be obvious during a hearing if a justice is not.

Justices may allocate tasks to their legal associates,[4] such as providing a summary of the factual background, the curial history of the matter, and the issues raised and how they have been dealt with in the courts below. They may ask them to carry out discrete research tasks on legal points. However, a justice will read all the essential materials – judgments, written submissions and leading cases – for himself or herself. There is no equivalent of 'briefing' by law clerks, as in some courts in the United States, and no preliminary report or draft opinion is prepared as in superior civilian courts and transnational courts such as the European Court of Justice. Of course much will depend upon the workload of a court. It may well be that the workloads of some civilian courts make it impracticable for judges to review the materials as thoroughly in each case.[5]

It would generally be considered that good preparation enables better engagement with the argument during the hearing and shortens the time taken for it. It is also essential to meaningful discussion with colleagues in conference before or after the hearing.

III. CONFERENCES

The justices of the High Court of Australia generally do not engage in substantial discussion of the issues until after the hearing, although they may have informal discussions with particular colleagues.

The Court has adopted the practice of holding a short meeting at the beginning of each sitting week, preparatory to hearings. Its principal purpose is to identify any procedural issues or matters to which the parties' attention needs to be directed before the hearing, although points of possible importance might be flagged or preliminary views offered. Detailed discussion is generally left until the end of the hearing. An exception might be when a matter

4 Law graduates who work principally as researchers and proofers.

5 M Cohen, 'Ex Ante Versus Ex Post Deliberations: Two Models of Judicial Deliberation in Courts of Law Resort' (2014) 62 *American Journal of Comparative Law* 951, 965.

requires an urgent decision. Such a circumstance may require a higher level of preparedness, including fuller preliminary discussion. No justice is appointed before the hearing as the 'reporting judge'.

It is well known that the oral hearing of an appeal in common law courts involves the bench engaging in a dialogue with counsel. I believe it also to be well accepted that judges communicate with each other through that dialogue. Questions asked of counsel and comments made by judges can be as much for their colleagues to hear as they are to provide an opportunity for counsel to respond.[6]

It is difficult to pinpoint when the practice of having a post-hearing conference commenced. It may be said with certainty that they have been held for about the last 20 years. Correspondence between an outgoing Chief Justice and an incoming Chief Justice in February 1981 reveals that it was not then the practice,[7] although it was thought that it would be profitable to adopt that practice as well as the practice of the preparation of a first draft by one justice.

The post-hearing conference can be substantial. Whilst the pre-hearing conference at which two to four matters are discussed usually takes about half an hour, a post-hearing conference on an individual matter will often take about an hour and will sometimes take much longer.

The structure of deliberation at the post-hearing conference does not follow that of any other court of which I am aware. The justices do not speak in descending order of seniority, as do the justices of the Supreme Court of the United States,[8] or in inverse order, with the most junior justice offering his or her view first, as has traditionally been the case in England and Canada.[9] The position in Australia is rather more informal. It suggests little concern about the possibility of deference. There is a free exchange of views, in no particular order, with the Chief Justice, or the justice who has presided,

6 See A Paterson, *Final Judgment: The Last Law Lords and the Supreme Court* (Oxford and Portland/Oregon, Hart Publishing, 2013) 77.

7 National Archives of Australia: High Court of Australia; M1827, Folders of correspondence, minutes, invitations, speeches and publications relating to the administration of, and Sir Harry Gibbs' association with, the High Court of Australia, 1961–1987; 97, Correspondence – Justices of the High Court, 1932–1986 (A letter from Sir Garfield Barwick CJ to Sir Harry Gibbs). I am indebted to Professor John Williams for this reference.

8 United States Courts, 'Supreme Court Procedures', available online via http://www.uscourts.gov/about-federal-courts/educational-resources/about-educational-outreach/activity-resources/supreme-1 (last accessed 29 February 2020).

9 Lord Neuberger, 'Sausages and the Judicial Process: the Limits of Transparency' (Speech delivered at the Annual Conference of the Supreme Court of New South Wales, Sydney, 1 August 2014) [14]–[15], available online via https://www.supremecourt.uk/docs/speech-140801.pdf (last accessed 29 February 2020); E Macfarlane, *Governing from the Bench: The Supreme Court of Canada and the Judicial Role* (Vancouver, UBC Press, 2013) 103.

steering the meeting. There is opportunity for persuasion, for criticism, and for debate. If a justice states a view, he or she will be expected to explain it and to defend it.

The purpose of conferring is not to secure a single collective decision, nor are the justices required to strive to achieve unanimity. The aim is to provide a forum for deliberation, to allow areas of disagreement to be identified, to test different views and to ascertain whether there is a clear majority. Votes are not taken, as is the case in other courts. That said, in more recent years there has been a concerted effort to find common ground and reduce the number of individual judgments where justices are largely in agreement.

Until quite recently there was rarely more than one meeting held post-hearing, largely because once the process of writing a judgment commences, views tend to become entrenched. We have now found that if views are divergent or there is no clear majority, so long as another meeting is arranged within a short period of time, that problem may be overcome. We are also finding that further meetings, where we can concentrate on the 'sticking points', tend to be quite fruitful. By way of example, on one occasion four of the five justices who had heard the appeal were agreed as to the outcome, but reached it by two different routes in two separate judgments. There was no clear majority opinion. This was of particular importance given the area of law concerned, where trial judges require certainty. The justices involved met a number of times to discuss divergences and the correctness of the views stated. In the end result, one justice was persuaded to the contrary of the justice's initial view and three of the four were able to produce one majority judgment.

There has been a clear willingness on the part of the justices to participate in more extensive discussion than before and to work through difficult questions together. The outcome may not always be one majority judgment, although it often is, but the process of discussion is considered to be of benefit in any event.

IV. THE FIRST DRAFT

If there is a clear majority at the end of the meeting, one justice is usually assigned the task of producing a first draft. The first draft may be allocated on the basis of the issues being of particular interest to a justice, but there are no strict rules for the assignment of cases. The first draft may simply be allocated to a particular justice in order to achieve an equitable allocation of work. If there is not a clear majority, sometimes a justice volunteers to produce a first draft, perhaps hoping to bring colleagues to his or her point of view.

There may be occasions when, even though there is general agreement as to the resolution of the issues and as to the outcome of an appeal, it is decided not to allocate a first draft. This may occur where it is considered that the state of the law in a particular area needs to be developed and that more than one judgment might promote that development. In such circumstances, the view might be taken that it is not necessary for the Court to speak only with one voice, by way of example, where there is a novel question of constitutional law. It may also be observed from decisions in the area of constitutional law that there are more likely to be more nuanced approaches to issues, even if the same conclusion is reached. A first draft might not be allocated in this kind of situation. These are matters for discussion amongst the justices at the post-hearing meeting.

Another circumstance where a first draft may not be allocated is where the justices need to work their way through the problem and writing a judgment is the only way to do it. In this event no allocation is usually made, but there may be further, better informed discussions later and an exchange of views between justices who share a particular point of view. They might then agree amongst themselves who should write the judgment or they might write separately. Where there is no allocation at the post-hearing conference (and this is increasingly rare), the result may be multiple judgments employing different reasoning.

Those who are not assigned a first draft will usually make further detailed notes after the meeting, have further research undertaken, and prepare an outline, or even a draft of their own, in preparation for the receipt of the first draft from their colleague.

The principal purpose of a first draft is to enable those who are of the same view to agree with it and thus to avoid unnecessary judgments. By 'unnecessary' I mean judgments which add nothing of substance to what has already been written.

This is not to suggest that there may not be perfectly valid reasons why another justice may find it appropriate to write a separate judgment. Even if that be so, a first draft is a valuable resource. It should not be necessary for other justices to set out the facts again, at least not completely if they do write separately. The first draft will also identify the relevant legislative provisions and place them in context, identify the parties' arguments, and discuss the authorities which bear upon the issues.

There is a method to writing first drafts. It is said that in the German Federal Constitutional Court, a *rapporteur* who drafts an opinion 'broadly reflective of a wide common denominator of agreement, often representing a compromise' is more likely to secure agreement at the conference.[10] The justices of the High Court are probably less inclined to aim for a compromise position, at least

10 D Kommers and R Miller, *The Constitutional Jurisprudence of the Federal Republic of Germany*, 3rd edn (Durham, Duke University Press, 2012) 28.

in any substantial sense. Nevertheless, a draft opinion needs to be succinct and should not be composed in the idiosyncratic style of the author. A long judgment which says more than is necessary is less likely to attract agreement.

V. CONCURRENCE AND DISSENT

The first draft judgment is circulated to the other justices in order to ascertain if those of like view will agree with it. Other justices may, having read the draft, request changes to be made. Suggested changes are usually contained in a memorandum in which an explanation is given for the changes. It would not be usual to suggest a change in its essential reasoning or a substantial rewriting of it, although suggestions may nevertheless be of significance. The author of the first draft is not obliged to accept any proposed changes, but usually will if he or she agrees with them and they are consistent with his or her reasoning, in order to have the justice making the suggestions concur.

Agreement is expressed by the circulation of a judgment which states no more than the fact of agreement with the reasons and the orders proposed by the author of the first draft. That justice is then usually 'joined in' to the first draft, with his or her consent. The justice's name appears on the judgment together with that of the author. I am not aware of such a practice in other common law courts. In Australia intermediate appellate courts do not use it. It is uniquely a practice which has been adopted by the High Court. It is difficult to pinpoint when it was first utilised; there is no record of any discussion about it so far as I am aware.

The effect of the High Court's practice of 'joining in' is to render the author largely anonymous. The aim is to avoid encouraging justices to write separately simply to show that they have understood the issues. Some might argue that a reader should know who the author is, although it is difficult to see what the benefit of that knowledge could be.

Most justices will 'join in' if they agree with the reasoning and there is no other obstacle to agreement. They will agree although they may have wished to write themselves. They may even think they might have expressed it somewhat better than their colleague's draft. Indeed, they may have written a draft, which they now effectively shelve. They appreciate that there is every good reason to reduce the number of individual judgments published in a matter.

As recognised in jurisdictions that have adopted the reporting judge system, it is not possible to produce judgments in a timely manner if each judge produces a separate judgment in every matter. More importantly, single majority judgments can instil confidence in the Court's decision and are more likely to provide a clear ratio and guidance to courts below. They provide greater certainty of the law, which would generally be regarded as an institutional aim.

This is particularly important in some areas of the law, such as criminal trial procedure. Additional judgments which concur in the result, but seek to add something, may detract from this certainty and can affect the clarity of the ratio.

It is also recognised that nowadays judges in the courts below do not have the time to wade through a number of individual judgments in order to find the point on which the majority reasons turn. These things said, there is a limit to how far justices will compromise their fundamental position. This aspect of the common law tradition is still strongly felt, although I would suggest that justices strive to appreciate other viewpoints and to discern weaknesses in their own. However, in the end a justice will not join in another's judgment unless he or she is truly persuaded of the correctness of its reasoning and approves of the way in which it is expressed.

It may be apparent from the discussion of 'joined in' judgments that they are not truly 'joint' in the sense of being a collaborative product between two or more justices. In my experience judgments of this kind are rare on the High Court, although there are occasions when different aspects of a single judgment are written by different justices. The process of editing to produce a homogeneous style in the one judgment can be difficult and time consuming. Judgments of this kind may often resemble a committee decision which is less directly stated than would be the case in an individual judgment. The effort involved in collaboration may be more than would be the case had one justice simply written the whole judgment alone. That said, in large, complex cases joint judgments have their place.

I earlier observed that there may be valid reasons for a justice to write separately even when he or she agrees with the result. Most obviously, this is necessary when a justice employs a different method of reasoning in arriving at the same result. Alternatively, there may be something that he or she considered necessary to be added to what has been written, which was not accommodated within the first draft. An important qualification may be thought necessary. It may contain a statement of principle, or even a footnote, which a justice does not wish to be taken to approve but which the author has declined to remove. A justice may consider that the judgment has not been expressed clearly enough, or it may be written in a style which they do not wish to be seen to adopt.

Generally speaking, if an appellate judge cannot agree with the view of the majority, it is his or her duty to dissent. Common law courts tend to view dissent as an important means of ensuring transparency by revealing the true composition of the Court. Although there is an increasing trend towards publication of dissenting judgments in some civil law jurisdictions, dissent does not appear to be viewed through the same lens. It is said that, where civilian courts such as the German Federal Constitutional Court permit publication of dissenting opinions, there may be a tendency to forgo publishing a dissent 'at least partly out of a sense of institutional loyalty' unless 'prompted by deep personal convictions'.[11] While that is not true of the High Court of Australia, it would nevertheless be expected that a justice who is considering dissenting will first endeavour to understand the majority view and consider whether he or she can accept it as a possible view, not the least because if a number of one's colleagues are persuaded to a point of view, it could just be that one is wrong.

A justice who finds it necessary to write a dissenting judgment will have greater liberty to write in his or her individualistic style. However, a dissent must be more than a well-written 'angry tirade'; it must 'show convincingly how wrong the majority is'.[12] It is sometimes those dissents that are written with least 'zeal' or 'rhetoric' that prove most influential in future.[13]

VI. PROFESSOR WOLFGANG ERNST'S QUESTION

At the outset of these proceedings, Professor Wolfgang Ernst posed the question whether the aims of the courts could be achieved by public exposure of the process of deliberation, such as occurs in Switzerland from time to time.[14]

The answer to that question, from the Australian perspective, is in the negative. The free exchange of ideas which is central to our process of decision-making is unlikely to occur in such an environment.

In any event, public exposure of decision-making processes is not necessary. Any interested person is able to access the written arguments of the parties. The discussion which ensues at the hearing in Court can be observed by attending the Court or viewing the audio-visual recordings provided on the Court's website. The reasons for judgment are detailed.

VII. CONCLUSION

The approach of the High Court to its decision-making in more recent times might be thought to have developed somewhat differently from the traditional common law model. Discussion in conference is now considered to be very important to decision-making and justices are willing participants in longer,

11 Kommers and Miller (n 10) 29.

12 A Lynch, 'Introduction – What Makes a Dissent "Great"?' in A Lynch (ed), *Great Australian Dissents* (Cambridge, Cambridge University Press, 2016) 1, 8, citing M Urofsky, *Dissent and the Supreme Court: Its Role in the Court's History and the Nation's Constitutional Dialogue* (New York, Pantheon Books, 2015) 407.

13 Lynch (n 12) 12.

14 See W Ernst's contribution in chapter 1 of the present collection (at pp 5, 16–17).

and sometimes multiple, conferences. There is a well understood aim to reduce the number of individual judgments of the majority.

This reflects an acceptance that it is more important for the purposes of certainty and clarity, and for confidence in the judgments of the Court, that there be one judgment if possible and as few as possible otherwise. This requires a judge to think institutionally rather than individualistically. That said, the common law ideal of independence of thought is still strongly felt. A justice will only 'join in' if he or she is persuaded to that view. There is no sense of obligation felt to achieve a collective decision in every case.

CHAPTER 5

COLLEGIAL DECISION-MAKING IN THE US COURTS OF APPEALS

Harry T Edwards*

* The Hon Harry T Edwards is Senior Circuit Judge and Chief Judge Emeritus of the United States Court of Appeals for the DC Circuit, Washington DC. He is also Professor of Law at New York University School of Law.

I. INTRODUCTION

1. EXPLORING THE INTERNAL DECISION-MAKING PROCESSES OF COLLEGIAL COURTS

In advance of the conference for which this chapter was written, Professor Wolfgang Ernst prepared a very thoughtful essay on 'Designing Collegiate Courts' Decision Making Processes – The Fine-Mechanics of Judicial Majoritarianism',[1] in which he offered his view of the core problem of collegiate courts:

> 'In all collegiate courts disagreement between judges must, at least to some degree, be overcome in order to see the pending case decided .... There is a great variety of approaches to what seems to be the core problem of collegiate courts: How to come to a decision in spite of judges' disagreement? Insofar as judicial majority-seeking takes place in a conference of judges, the competences and procedures of such conferences are pertinent issues ....
>
> The method by which several judges' opinions are fused in deciding the case at hand, and also in shaping the law of the land, is a decisive moment in the exercise of judicial power.'

Professor Ernst's essay reflects on some of the perceived differences between 'Anglo-American judicial systems' and typical 'continental/civilian judicial system[s]'. He says that in Anglo-American judicial systems,

> 'the case at hand is decided by the majority of opinions, the order of the court being established by looking at the constituent individual judges' conclusions and end results. The unitary order of the court may be accompanied by multiple reasoning, each opinion developed independently by any judge who finds he must express his individual view of the case.'

In contrast, Professor Ernst explains that in continental/civilian judicial systems,

> 'decision making power [typically] lies with the conference of judges alone. Here, every judge – as a member of the conference – can just do his best to influence the collective decision. However, [the judge] cannot fall back on an individual decision, if he feels that reaching an agreement would unduly compromise his individual view of the case.'

1 An amended version of W Ernst's stimulus paper is published as chapter 1 of the present collection.

Professor Ernst's description of the Anglo-American judicial system raises some interesting questions, at least insofar as it alludes to collegial decision-making in federal appellate courts in the United States. I will have more to say about this below. As a preview, however, my starting point is that the decision-making practices of the US Courts of Appeals cannot be usefully equated with those of the US Supreme Court because the organisational structures and judicial responsibilities of the courts are strikingly different. Furthermore, as I explain below, during the past five years, only 1.3% of the decisions issued by the Courts of Appeals included a dissent; whereas, during the same period, 56% of the decisions issued by the Supreme Court included a dissent. The extraordinarily high number of unanimous decisions issued by the Courts of Appeals says a lot about our decision-making. This will be a focal point of this paper.

2. THIS PAPER CONCERNS THE US COURTS OF APPEALS

This paper examines the work of the federal Courts of Appeals in the United States. I will not address federal District Courts, because they are strictly trial, not appellate, tribunals. And I will not discuss state courts, because they are too numerous and varied in their approaches to decision-making. In addition, some state court judges are elected to office, and this raises issues regarding judicial independence that are different from what is seen in the federal courts.

This paper will not attempt to assess collegial decision-making in the US Supreme Court. The Supreme Court is the highest court in the United States, so the importance of its work cannot be understated. The Supreme Court operates very differently from the Courts of Appeals, however.

a) *The US Courts of Appeals Cannot Be Usefully Equated with the US Supreme Court*

Article III, Section 1 of the United States Constitution states that '[t]he judicial Power of the United States, shall be vested in one supreme Court, and in such inferior Courts as the Congress may from time to time ordain and establish.' Although the Constitution establishes the Supreme Court, Congress is given the power to decide how to organise the high Court. Over the years, various Acts of Congress have altered the number of seats on the Supreme Court, from a low of five to a high of ten. Shortly after the Civil War, the number of seats on the Court was fixed at nine. Today, one Chief Justice and eight Associate Justices serve on the Supreme Court. Like all federal judges, Justices are appointed by the President and are confirmed by the Senate. They typically hold office for life. The salaries of the Justices cannot be decreased during their term of office. These limits are meant to protect the independence of the judiciary from the political branches of government.

Article III, Section 2 of the Constitution establishes the jurisdiction of the Supreme Court. The Court has original jurisdiction over certain cases, eg suits between two or more states and/or cases involving ambassadors and other public ministers. The Court has appellate jurisdiction over almost any other case that involves a point of constitutional and/or federal law, or that falls within the federal courts' diversity jurisdiction.[2]

The web site of the Supreme Court Historical Society offers some useful insights on how the Court works:

> 'Supreme Court cases come in three varieties. Least numerous are the "original jurisdiction" actions, brought by one state against another, or between states and the federal government. The Constitution also empowers the Court to hear "all Cases affecting Ambassadors, other public Ministers and Consuls." In these the Court sits as a trial body from which there is no appeal.
>
> Few original jurisdiction cases are filed – usually one to five a term – but sheer bulk makes many of these difficult ....
>
> More numerous, but mercifully shorter, are cases from state courts. If any state tribunal decides a federal question and the litigant has no further remedy within the state, the Supreme Court may consider it.
>
> Most common – roughly two-thirds of the total – are requests for review of decisions of federal appellate or district courts. The great majority of cases reach the Supreme Court through its granting of petitions for writs of certiorari, from the Latin *certiorari volumnus*, "we wish to be informed."
>
> Normally the "writ of cert" says in effect to an appellate court, "Send us the record in this case you decided recently." In very rare instances a writ of certiorari before appellate judgment says, "Send us the record in this case you haven't reviewed yet." It enables the Court to act with maximum speed in unusual cases of great public importance.
>
> With some 7,000 petitions annually, deciding which case to decide is a load in itself. According to a court historian, "it is arguably the most important stage in the entire Supreme Court process." ...
>
> Each Justice determines how he or she will vote to accept or reject each certiorari petition, usually calling for a law clerk's memorandum analyzing the petition ....
>
> [Most] of the petitions end at this point, with a vote not to accept the case. The Justices may be satisfied that the decision of the lower court was correct, or that

---

2 See http://www.uscourts.gov/about-federal-courts/educational-resources/about-educational-outreach/activity-resources/about (last accessed 17 February 2020).

the case has no national significance, or, in some instances, that the Supreme Court lacks jurisdiction. Whatever the reason for denial, the effect is to allow the decision of the lower court to stand.'[3]

Too often scholars, members of the media, and other interested persons mistakenly think that the work of the Courts of Appeals can be measured by reference to the decision-making practices of the Supreme Court. It is sometimes assumed that because the Supreme Court and the Courts of Appeals are appellate tribunals within the federal judicial system, and that most of the Supreme Court's docket includes review of decisions issued by the Courts of Appeals, the Justices and judges must operate in a similar fashion in resolving cases before them. Nothing could be further from the truth. The collegial operations and internal decision-making processes of the Supreme Court and the Courts of Appeals are strikingly different. And these differences must be understood in order to comprehend decision-making in the Courts of Appeals.

In 'Pitfalls of Empirical Studies that Attempt to Understand the Factors Affecting Appellate Decisionmaking', my co-author and I pointed out that,

> 'because of the Court's unique status and operating procedures, it is difficult to draw broad conclusions about decisionmaking in the federal courts of appeals from studies of the Supreme Court. The Court, which is seen by many to play a major role in American political life, controls the evolution of federal constitutional law, fixes constructions of disputed federal statutes and regulations, gives content to federal common law, and has great discretion in choosing which cases to hear and resolve. The Court hears only a limited number of cases each year, and many of those involve high profile, controversial, and difficult legal issues. In contrast, the intermediate courts of appeals only occasionally deal with very high profile issues. The courts of appeals also hear far more cases each year than does the Supreme Court, have only very limited control over their dockets, and normally sit in panels of three (not en banc).'[4]

And in 'The Effects of Collegiality on Judicial Decision Making', I explained that

> 'the Supreme Court's docket consists of many more "very hard" cases than do those of the lower appellate courts. The majority of the cases in the circuit courts admit of a right or a best answer and do not require the exercise of discretion. Lower appellate

---

3 The Supreme Court Historical Society, 'How the Court Works – Types of Cases the Court Hears', available online via http://supremecourthistory.org/htcw_casesthecourthears.html (last accessed 17 February 2020).

4 HT Edwards and MA Livermore, 'Pitfalls of Empirical Studies that Attempt to Understand the Factors Affecting Appellate Decisionmaking' (2009) 58 *Duke Law Journal* 1895, 1904. A Court of Appeals sitting *en banc* ('in bench') typically consists of all active judges on the court.

> courts are thus constrained far more than the Supreme Court. As a result, in the eyes of the public, the media, judges, and the legal profession, the Supreme Court is seen as more of a "political" institution than are the lower appellate courts. The Supreme Court also faces the burden of having to sit en banc in every case. This may mean that collegiality on the Court operates very differently from the collegial process at work in the lower appellate courts, where judges only rarely sit en banc.'[5]

As can be seen from the charts in the Appendices,[6] during the five terms from 2011–12 through 2015–16, the Supreme Court issued an average of 67 decisions each term. The Courts of Appeals (excluding the Federal Circuit, for which no data was available), *published* an average of 4,182 decisions each term. And the Courts of Appeals issued an average of 34,536 decisions on the merits (both published and unpublished) each term. During this same five-term period, the lowest number of *published* decisions issued by a Court of Appeals during one term was 152 and the highest number was 635.

The Supreme Court routinely sits *en banc* to resolve decisions on the merits. The Courts of Appeals almost always decide cases with three-judge panels. As the Appendices show, during the five terms from 2011–12 through 2015–16, only 228 cases were heard *en banc* in the Courts of Appeals, i.e., an average of only 46 per term, or four per circuit per term. If the Ninth Circuit is excluded, then there were only 134 cases heard *en banc* during this period, an average of 27 per term, or two per circuit per term.

In the Supreme Court, oral arguments are heard in almost every case in which a decision is rendered on the merits. Oral arguments are usually 30 minutes per side. And a full, published opinion usually accompanies every decision. In the Courts of Appeals, however, most cases are decided without oral argument; oral arguments are typically limited to 15 minutes per side; and most decisions are not 'published'.[7]

Another highly noteworthy difference between the Supreme Court and the Courts of Appeals is the number of separate dissenting and concurring opinions that accompany decisions on the merits. The data in the attached Appendices show that very few dissenting and concurring opinions accompany the decisions issued by the Courts of Appeals. For the terms between October 2011 and September 2016, here is what the data show about the work of the Courts of Appeals:

- The Courts of Appeals routinely rendered decisions without a dissent about 90% of the time in their 'published' decisions.

---

5 HT Edwards, 'The Effects of Collegiality on Judicial Decision Making' (2003) 151 *University of Pennsylvania Law Review* 1639, 1644.

6 For this and the following, see tables C.1.–D. on pp 117–126 below.

7 An explanation of 'published decisions' appears in the Appendix (at p 108 below).

- There are no data for the numbers of dissenting and concurring statements accompanying 'unpublished' decisions. There are undoubtedly a few such decisions, but it is generally agreed that the number is miniscule. I have assumed that the Courts of Appeals rendered decisions without a dissent or a concurrence 100% of the time in their 'unpublished' decisions.
- The Courts of Appeals issued 172,680 total decisions on the merits (ie published and unpublished) between 2011 and 2016. Only 2,220 of those decisions included a dissenting opinion. In other words, only 1.3% of all decisions issued by the Courts of Appeals included a dissenting opinion.
- The Courts of Appeals issued 20,909 published decisions between 2011 and 2016. Only 2,220 of those decisions included a dissenting opinion. In other words, only about 10.6% of the published decisions included a dissent.
- The Courts of Appeals issued 151,771 unpublished decisions on the merits between 2011 and 2016. Thus, 'unpublished' decisions made up 87.89% of all such dispositions issued by the Courts of Appeals during those five years. As noted above, these decisions almost always reflect unanimous judgments of the court.
- Less than 1% (.73%) of the total decisions (i.e., published and non-published) issued between 2011 and 2016 included a concurring opinion.
- Approximately 6% of the published decisions issued between 2011 and 2016 included a concurring opinion.

The picture is very different for the Supreme Court. The data in the attached Appendices show that dissenting and concurring opinions routinely accompanied the decisions issued by the Supreme Court between 2011 and 2016:

- 56% of the signed decisions on the merits included an opinion dissenting at least in part.
- 41% of the signed decisions on the merits included a concurring opinion.
- Only 46% of the signed decisions on the merits reflected unanimous judgments.

The simple point here, which I will amplify in the coming pages, is that the decision-making processes of the Courts of Appeals – including the number of cases heard and decided each term, the complexity of the cases, oral arguments, composition of judicial panels, published decisions, separate opinions accompanying decisions, authority to decline to review certain cases, etc – cannot meaningfully be equated with the work of the Supreme Court. The Supreme Court sets the course for decision-making in both federal and state courts on matters having to do with the United States Constitution and federal statutes. Moreover, the real impact of Supreme Court opinions is probably greater than the actual authority granted to the Court under the Constitution. The nine Justices of the Court are national figures, who are well known to large segments of the American population. And their opinions are reported, studied, and debated as a matter of course. Therefore, it cannot be doubted that the Supreme Court is the most important judicial body in the United States. Nor can it be doubted that Supreme Court decisions often have a great impact on important matters of public policy.

b) *The Work of the US Courts of Appeals Offers a Compelling Example of Collegial Decision-Making*

Even though inferior to the Supreme Court, the Courts of Appeals are extremely important judicial tribunals. The Courts' influence is considerable because each court is authorised to establish legal precedent in significant regions of the country and to decide actions involving Congress, the executive branch, and major federal agencies. In addition, because the Supreme Court only rarely grants *certiorari* in petitions for review, the Courts of Appeals have the final word on most cases that are within their jurisdiction. Year in and year out, simply by dint of the huge volume of cases decided, most of the 'law-making' done by the federal judiciary comes from the Courts of Appeals, not the Supreme Court. In light of these considerations, I have decided to focus on the federal Courts of Appeals in reflecting on collegial decision-making in the United States. In my view, the work of these courts offers a rich source of material for our consideration.

In his essay on designing collegiate courts' decision-making processes,[8] Professor Ernst paints a bleak picture of how appellate courts function in Anglo-American judicial systems. He says that

> 'each judge take[s] his own independent decision, including the evaluation of evidence. If there is the wish to see one's own views prevail as the majority view, bilateral negotiations and arrangements can be sought, but these are not controlled by specific regulations. One can thus single out one's discussion partners, bypassing those with whom one thinks one will not find enough common ground anyway. It may turn out that one or the other judge is not involved in any exchange, while others try to form alliances and – in doing so – together go over some of the legal arguments, thus enjoying the benefit of an argumentative exchange. From a continental observer's perspective this "free market" process of judges coming together in pairs or groups (or not) seems fairly un-bureaucratic and unregulated.'

I cannot easily square this view of appellate decision-making with my experiences as a Court of Appeals judge. When I first read this critique, it seemed more consistent with the general public perception of decision-making at the US Supreme Court.

---

8 See n 1 above and the accompanying text.

It is somewhat ironic that Professor Ernst's suggestion of a 'sensible design' for appellate decision-making *does* ring true to me. He says that,

> '[i]f one asks for a sensible design, it might be a good idea to have something like a formal judges' conference where all views, however unlikely to become views of the court's majority, are equally given a fair hearing. It may not be possible to crowd out coalition building on the corridor or at the coffee machine altogether, but offering a joint platform with every judge in attendance may shift at least some of the judges' exchanges into a more transparent arena.'

In the discussion that follows, I will suggest that the model to which Professor Ernst subscribes – 'formal judges' conference[s] where all views … are equally given a fair hearing' – is the decision-making model that is typically followed by the Courts of Appeals in most circuits. I will also contend that *collegial* decision-making can be greatly facilitated by *collegiality*, which I take to mean that the judges on a court respect the work and abilities of their colleagues with whom they share equal authority and a common commitment to 'getting the law right'.[9] When a Court of Appeals' operation is infused with collegiality – ie the judges' personal politics and ideological preferences do not play a significant role in judicial deliberations – decision-making invariably improves.[10]

II. COLLEGIAL DECISION-MAKING IN THE US COURTS OF APPEALS[11]

1. A BRIEF HISTORY OF THE US COURTS OF APPEALS

The Constitution of the United States vests federal judicial power in the US Supreme Court and 'in such inferior Courts as the Congress may from time to time ordain and establish.' US CONST. art. III, §1. In the Judiciary Act of 1789, Congress ordained and established such inferior courts: one federal district court per state, primarily for admiralty and maritime cases, and circuit courts, which at the time served primarily as trial courts with limited appellate jurisdiction.

---

9 Edwards (n 5) 1679.

10 In my discussion of collegial decision-making and collegiality, I will readily draw on my prior writings in Edwards and Livermore (n 4) and Edwards (n 5). And, to avoid weighting this paper with cumbersome citations, I will frequently rely on these two law review articles without attribution when the words are mine alone.

11 Sources for materials in the next two subsections have been drawn from:

- Act of 13 February 1801, ch IV ('Judiciary Act'), 2 Stat 89 (1801).
- Act of 1866, ch 2010 ('Judicial Circuits Act'), 14 Stat 209 (1866).

Each of the three circuit courts consisted of two Supreme Court Justices and a local district judge. Geography dictated which members of the Supreme Court sat on a circuit: each Justice was assigned to a circuit, and travelled to the districts within that circuit to meet with the local district judge, sometimes as many as 27 times a year for a single Justice. This practice became known as 'circuit riding'. Circuit riding continued, with variation, until 1911.

In the Judiciary Act of 1801, Congress increased the number of circuits to six, expanded their jurisdiction to 'all cases in law or equity, arising under the constitution and laws of the United States', and authorised 16 judgeships specifically for the circuit courts.[12] The following year, with a different political party in power, Congress repealed the judgeships and expanded jurisdiction, but kept the increased number of circuits.

In 1807, a seventh circuit was added, along with a Supreme Court Justice. The Justices now each rode a single circuit. Between 1812 and 1837, an eighth and ninth circuit, and two more Supreme Court Justices, were added.

In 1855, Congress established a circuit specifically for California, with its own circuit judgeship. This 'California Circuit' was abolished in 1863 and incorporated with Oregon into a tenth circuit, and a corresponding tenth Justice was added to the Supreme Court.

After the Civil War, in the Act of 1866, Congress abolished the tenth circuit, rearranged which states constituted which circuit, and reduced the seats on the Supreme Court from ten to seven.[13] The same act reestablished independent circuit judgeships and reduced circuit riding for Supreme Court justices to once every two years. In 1869, Congress increased the seats on the Supreme Court to nine, as it remains today.

In the Judiciary Act of 1891, Congress left the circuit courts largely intact but created nine US circuit courts of appeals (now US Courts of Appeals for 12 geographic circuits) and transferred the appellate jurisdiction of the former circuit courts to the Courts of Appeals. The Act also created

---

- Federal Judicial Center, 'The Structure of the Federal Courts', available online via https://www.fjc.gov/history/timeline/8276 (last accessed 17 February 2020).
- United States Constitution.
- United States Courts, 'Authorized Judgeships', available online via https://www.uscourts.gov/judges-judgeships/authorized-judgeships (last accessed 17 February 2020).
- United States Courts, 'Judicial Vacancies', available online via http://www.uscourts.gov/judges-judgeships/judicial-vacancies (last accessed 17 February 2020).
- United States Courts, 'Court Website Links', available online via http://www.uscourts.gov/about-federal-courts/federal-courts-public/court-website-links (last accessed 17 February 2020).
- US Code, Title 28 (Judiciary and Judicial Procedure), hereinafter '28 USC', §§45, 371, 1291, 1331.

12 Act of Feb 13, 1801, ch IV, 2 Stat 89, 92.

13 14 Stat 209 (1866).

corresponding judgeships for 'circuit justices'. Each appeal was heard by a panel of three: one existing circuit judge, one district judge, and one of the newly authorised circuit justices. The appellate jurisdiction of the US Courts of Appeals continues to today, primarily to consider appeals from 'all final decisions of the district courts'.[14]

In 1891, Congress established the 'Court of Appeals of the District of Columbia', now the US Court of Appeals for the District of Columbia Circuit, better known simply as the 'DC Circuit'.

In 1912, Congress abolished the circuit courts and transferred their remaining trial court jurisdiction to the district courts. Today, district courts primarily hear cases between citizens of different states and 'civil actions arising under the Constitution, laws, or treaties of the United States',[15] and have supplemental jurisdiction over state law claims. Also in 1912, Congress split the Eighth Circuit into two geographic regions, creating a new Tenth Circuit. In 1981, Congress split the Fifth Circuit into two geographic regions, creating a new Eleventh Circuit. No new geographical circuit has been established since.

In 1982, Congress created the US Court of Appeals for the Federal Circuit to hear appeals from a number of existing federal courts and boards.

2. THE COMPOSITION OF THE US COURTS OF APPEALS TODAY

Congress passed the most recent bill expanding federal judgeships in 1990, which created 11 new circuit judgeships, totaling 179 authorised seats. However, as of April 2017, there were 20 federal appellate vacancies. The duties of the 159 active judges are shared with 98 additional 'senior judges', judges who have retired their seats but still remain on the court and participate in decision-making.

- In the **First Circuit** – which covers Maine, Massachusetts, New Hampshire, Puerto Rico, and Rhode Island – there are six active judges and five senior judges.
- In both the **Second Circuit** – which covers Connecticut, New York, and Vermont – and the **Third Circuit** – which covers the states of Delaware, New Jersey, and Pennsylvania, as well as the US territory of the Virgin Islands – there are 11 active judges and 11 senior judges each.

---

14 28 USC §1291.
15 28 USC §1331.

- In the **Fourth Circuit** – which covers Maryland, North and South Carolina, Virginia, and West Virginia – there are 15 active judges and four senior judges.
- In the **Fifth Circuit** – which now covers Louisiana, Mississippi, and Texas – there are 14 active judges and eight senior judges.
- In the **Sixth Circuit** – which covers Kentucky, Michigan, Ohio, and Tennessee – there are 14 active judges and 11 senior judges.
- In the **Seventh Circuit** – which covers Illinois, Indiana, and Wisconsin – there are nine active judges and three senior judges.
- In the **Eighth Circuit** – which covers Arkansas, Iowa, Minnesota, Missouri, Nebraska, and both North and South Dakota – there are nine active judges and six senior judges.
- In the **Ninth Circuit** – which is by far the largest geographic circuit, covering the states of Alaska, Arizona, California, Hawaii, Idaho, Montana, Nevada, Oregon, and Washington, as well as the US territories of Guam and the Mariana Islands – there are 25 active judges and 19 senior judges.
- In the **Tenth Circuit** – which covers Colorado, Kansas, New Mexico, Oklahoma, Utah, and Wyoming – there are 12 active judges and nine senior judges.
- In the **Eleventh Circuit** – which covers Alabama, Florida, and Georgia – there are ten active judges and four senior judges.
- In the **DC Circuit** – which is located in Washington, DC – there are 11 active judges and six senior judges.
- In the **Federal Circuit** – which is located in Washington, DC – there are 12 active judges and six senior judges.

The **12 geographic circuits** hear appeals from the district courts in 94 federal judicial districts. However, Congress has enacted some authorising statutes that vest exclusive jurisdiction over challenges to final agency actions in Courts of Appeals. In such situations, petitions for review are filed directly with the appropriate Court of Appeals, not the district court.

The **DC Circuit** covers the smallest geographic area of any circuit – the Court's jurisdiction extends only to Washington, DC. The Court reviews a large number rulemakings, enforcement actions, and other decisions of federal executive and independent agencies that are based in the nation's capital. Many of these actions arise pursuant to causes of action under the Administrative Procedure Act (1946). As a result, the Court receives a uniquely large number of petitions for review in cases involving administrative law and plays a central role in reviewing actions of federal agencies – such as the Federal Communications Commission, National Labor Relations Board, Environmental Protection Agency, Federal Energy Regulatory Commission, Federal Aviation Administration, Department of Energy, and Department of Homeland Security – that establish and enforce national policies in the substantive areas over which the agencies have authority.

The **Federal Circuit** is unique among the 13 circuit Courts of Appeals. It has nationwide jurisdiction in a variety of subject areas, including international trade, government contracts, patents, trademarks, certain money claims against the US government, federal personnel, veterans' benefits, and public safety officers' benefits claims. Appeals to the Court come from all federal district courts, the US Court of Federal Claims, the US Court of International Trade, and the US Court of Appeals for Veterans Claims. The Court also takes appeals of certain administrative agencies' decisions, including the US Merit Systems Protection Board, the Boards of Contract Appeals, the Patent Trial and Appeal Board, and the Trademark Trial and Appeal Board. Decisions of the US International Trade Commission; the Office of Compliance, an independent agency in the legislative branch; the Government Accountability Office Personnel Appeals Board; and the Department of Justice Bureau of Justice Assistance also are reviewed by the Federal Circuit. The Court's jurisdiction consists of administrative law cases, intellectual property cases, and cases involving money damages against the US government. The administrative law cases consist of personnel and veterans claims. Nearly all of the intellectual property cases involve patents. Suits for money damages against the US government include government contract cases, tax refund appeals, unlawful takings, and civilian and military pay cases.

Over the years, a number of Court of Appeals judges have been appointed to serve on the Supreme Court. From 1891 (when the US Courts of Appeals were established) to the present, 26 of 62, or 42%, of the Supreme Court Justices who served during that time first served as judges on a circuit Court of Appeals. Three Justices who retired from the Supreme Court continued to serve on a Court of Appeals. Of the nine Justices currently serving on the Supreme Court, all but one served as a Court of Appeals judge.

Federal appellate judges are appointed for life subject to 'good [b]ehaviour'.[16] The Chief Judges of the circuit Courts of Appeals are appointed by succession based on the order of seniority of the active judges on the Court who are under 65 years of age, have served for one year or more as a judge, and have not previously served as Chief Judge.[17] Absent special circumstances, a Chief Judge cannot serve longer than seven years and cannot continue to serve after the age of 70.[18]

Court of Appeals judges may retire after reaching the age of 65 and having served for 15 years.[19] If a judge is older than 65, the service requirements

16 US CONST art III, §1.
17 28 USC §45(a)(1).
18 28 USC §45(a)(3).
19 28 USC §371(a), (c).

diminish each year by a corresponding year until the judge reaches the age of 70: for example, a judge may retire at the age of 70 after having served ten years. Upon retirement, the judge continues to receive, for life, the same salary that he or she received in his or her last year of service.[20] As an alternative to retirement, subject to the same service requirements, a judge may take 'senior status', that is, 'retain the office but retire from regular active service'.[21] So long as a senior judge continues to carry a caseload which is at least 25% of that of an active judge, the senior judge continues to receive regular compensation, including any annual salary increases.[22] The salary of a federal judge may not be reduced: The Constitution requires that so long as a judge holds office 'during good [b]ehaviour', the judge's compensation 'shall not be diminished'.[23]

3. THE METHODS AND QUALITY OF COLLEGIAL DECISION-MAKING

In assessing the decision-making of the Courts of Appeals, I will address three important questions: (a) What procedures are used to facilitate decision-making? (b) Do decision-making procedures facilitate genuine and effective efforts by the judges to reach unanimous decisions? (c) How should we measure the quality of the decisions rendered by the Courts of Appeals?

a) What Procedures and Policies are Followed to Facilitate Decision-Making?

Most cases that come before the Courts of Appeals are resolved by three-judge panels. And, typically, judges sit on different panels during each sitting period. For example, 'Judge A' may be assigned to sit with 'Judge B' and 'Judge C' in September, and then be assigned to sit with 'Judge D' and 'Judge E' in October. Cases are randomly assigned to panels during each sitting period to avoid any appearances of impropriety.

In almost all cases, the parties submit written briefs, but the three-judge panels hear oral argument in only a small percentage of the cases before the court. As the data in the Appendices show,[24] most cases are resolved pursuant to *unpublished* decisions. An unpublished disposition might be reflected in a judgment that includes a brief explanation of the court's order,

---

20 28 USC §371(a).
21 28 USC §371(b).
22 28 USC §371(e)(1).
23 US CONST art III, §1.
24 See p 110 below.

a judgment with an accompanying memorandum explaining the court's decision, or a short opinion.

Oral arguments and *published* decisions are reserved for the most significant cases on the court's docket. Rule 34 of the Federal Rules of Appellate Procedure[25] says that: 'Oral argument must be allowed in every case unless a panel of three judges who have examined the briefs and record unanimously agrees that oral argument is unnecessary for any of the following reasons: (A) the appeal is frivolous; (B) the dispositive issue or issues have been authoritatively decided; or (C) the facts and legal arguments are adequately presented in the briefs and record, and the decisional process would not be significantly aided by oral argument.' Although the Rule might be construed to suggest that oral argument is the norm, it is not. As the figures in the attached Appendices show, a large majority of the decisions by the Courts of Appeals are issued without oral argument.

Rule 36 of the Federal Rules of Appellate Procedure indicates that a court's judgment in a case may be rendered 'without an opinion'. In other words, the Federal Rules do not require the Courts of Appeals to 'publish' their decisions or to include an opinion explaining the court's judgment. The Courts of Appeals have adopted circuit rules to determine when the court's disposition of a case will be 'published'. For example, Circuit Rule 36 for the DC Circuit[26] provides:

> 'Published Opinions. An opinion, memorandum, or other statement explaining the basis for the court's action in issuing an order or judgment will be published if it meets one or more of the following criteria:
>
> (A) with regard to a substantial issue it resolves, it is a case of first impression or the first case to present the issue in this court;
> (B) it alters, modifies, or significantly clarifies a rule of law previously announced by the court;
> (C) it calls attention to an existing rule of law that appears to have been generally overlooked;
> (D) it criticizes or questions existing law;
> (E) it resolves an apparent conflict in decisions within the circuit or creates a conflict with another circuit;
> (F) it reverses a published agency or district court decision, or affirms a decision of the district court upon grounds different from those set forth in the district court's published opinion;
> (G) it warrants publication in light of other factors that give it general public interest.

25 The Federal Rules of Appellate Procedure are available online via https://www.law.cornell.edu/rules/frap (last accessed 17 February 2020).

26 The DC Circuit Rules are available online via https://www.cadc.uscourts.gov/internet/home.nsf/Content/VL%20-%20RPP%20-%20Circuit%20Rules/$FILE/RulesFRAP20191201a.pdf (last accessed 17 February 2020).

> All published opinions of the court, prior to issuance, will be circulated to all judges on the court; printed prior to release, unless otherwise ordered; and rendered by being filed with the clerk.'

Other circuits have similar rules, but in practice the judges on a panel have wide discretion to determine whether or not to publish a decision.

Each circuit follows slightly different procedures in disposing of appeals. For example, some circuits may adopt special procedures to handle high volume appeals, say, for example, in *pro se* (where the litigant represents him- or herself, without an attorney) or immigration cases.[27] But all circuits follow the same general approach: Briefs are filed in every appeal, as is the record from the trial court or the agency whose decision is under review. After the judges review the briefs and the record, consider the applicable law, and hear oral arguments (if they are held in the case), they deliberate over the decision.

Many judges assign their law clerks to draft 'bench memoranda' to prepare for oral arguments and deliberations with other judges. Bench memoranda may summarise the case record, analyse the parties' respective positions, and discuss applicable precedent, according to the needs and preferences of the judge. The judges' preparations before deliberations are crucially important to the success of their decision-making. It is generally accepted that each judge on a panel will carefully read the parties' briefs, the record, and the relevant legal materials before the judges meet to weigh the merits of a case. It does not matter whether the case is scheduled for oral argument or whether it is destined to be decided by unpublished judgment. What matters is that the judges should be equally well prepared when the time comes to confer over the disposition of an appeal.

Oral arguments can be immensely helpful in refining the issues in a case, especially complex and difficult ones. The judges, however, count on the lawyers carefully and effectively to lay out their parties' positions in written briefs that are submitted well before oral argument. Appellate cases are framed by the written briefs, so the lawyers must structure and limit their oral arguments in line with the matters properly raised in those briefs. Oral arguments allow the advocates to clarify critical facts that are in the record, amplify their principal arguments, and explain why the arguments from opposing counsel cannot carry the day. Because oral arguments are tightly focused on the written briefs, it is not unusual for judges to be aggressive in questioning the lawyers, both to clarify the parties' respective positions on the matters at issue and to alert their judicial colleagues to any concerns they may have about a case. If the time allotted for oral argument appears to be

---

27 See L Hooper, D Miletich and A Levy, *Case Management Procedures in the Federal Courts of Appeals*, 2nd edn (Federal Judicial Center, 2011, available online via https://www.fjc.gov/sites/default/files/2012/CaseMan2.pdf, last accessed 17 February 2020) 29–30, 38–40.

too short, the presiding judge may allow each side to take additional time to respond to the judges' questions.

This process only works well if all judges are equally well prepared in advance of oral arguments. Individual judges who are not well prepared cannot thoughtfully engage with the advocates during oral arguments, and they cannot usefully deliberate with their colleagues when cases are discussed after oral arguments. The judges do not use oral arguments to discern the parties' arguments – we expect to know their arguments after having read the briefs. Therefore, oral arguments are typically used to afford the attorneys an appropriate amount of time to address the judges' concerns about the arguments that have already been presented to the court in the briefs. Given this model of decision-making, in most cases it makes no sense to allow attorneys to present oral arguments that last many hours, let alone many days, as is done in some other countries.

Deliberations among the judges are always confidential, to ensure full and open consideration of cases before a panel. Private deliberations allow the judges honestly to air their views with one another as they strive for consensus. Posturing is thus minimised in favour of fruitful conversations about the merits of pending cases. During deliberations, the judges determine whether to issue an unpublished judgment or a full published decision.[28] The presiding judge assigns the case to a panel member who assumes responsibility for preparing the judgment or writing the opinion for the panel. If the writing judge runs into problems, she or he may pursue further deliberations with the other panel members to clarify the disposition of the case. Normally, however, the panel counts on the judge who has the writing assignment to put together a strong opinion that reflects the panel's determination of how the case should be decided. And writing judges have every incentive to produce strong opinions because, at least with respect to published dispositions, the judge who writes for the panel normally signs the opinion – ie, the disposition reflects the panel's considered judgment, but the opinion reflects the written work of the assigned judge.

When the proposed judgment or opinion is completed, the writing judge circulates the draft to the other two judges on the panel for their review and suggested edits. After the panel agrees on the disposition, the judgment or opinion is released by the court. Throughout this process, the judges are assisted in their legal research and drafting – as they prefer – by their own

28 The decision whether or not to issue a published or unpublished decision may occur at any of a number of stages once an appeal has been filed. Different circuits use different approaches with regard whether to issue a published decision: See Hooper, Miletich and Levy (n 27) 30–34; S Wasby, 'Unpublished Court of Appeals Decisions: A Hard Look at the Process' (2004) 14 *Southern California Interdisciplinary Law Journal* 67.

law clerks or by staff attorneys employed by the court to help handle certain categories of unpublished dispositions.

In deciding cases, the judges who serve on a panel are not obliged to agree on the rationale supporting a judgment. Nor is every judge required to endorse any majority opinion that accompanies a decision. And individual judges are free to write separate concurring or dissenting opinions, as they see fit. *Nonetheless, judges on the courts of appeals are tightly constrained in their decision-making.* When Court of Appeals judges decide a case, they focus on legal materials to reach their result, including the case record compiled in the trial court or agency; the judgment, decision, or verdict under review from the trial court or agency; the precise issues that have been raised and preserved by the litigants; the parties' arguments as reflected in written briefs and oral arguments; the constitutional, treaty, statutory, rules, or contractual provisions at issue; the applicable standards of review; and case precedent where applicable. Crucially, Court of Appeals judges understand that, save when the court sits *en banc*, a panel is bound by established circuit precedent. And, of course, the judges are always bound by Supreme Court precedent in deciding cases. In assessing the work of the Courts of Appeals, it is crucially important to account for these constraints.

b) Do Decision-Making Practices Facilitate Genuine and Effective Efforts by the Judges to Reach Unanimous Decisions?

Three-judge panel decisions are the end product of decision-making. And the decision in such a case is a byproduct of the collective effort of those three judges. Viewed in this way, one might reasonably assume that the decision produced by the panel is more important than any variations in the views of the individual judges who produced it. It is not quite this simple, however. Decisions are the result of collective effort, but individual judges continue to have distinct voices in the decision-making process.

Court of Appeals judges are often very independent thinkers, quite confident in their own views. Most are used to making decisions on their own, or at least advocating very aggressively for their positions. A number of appellate judges have served as trial judges and are accustomed to deciding cases more or less on their own. Furthermore, judges serve for life and judicial independence protects individual judges from improper influence from other branches of government.

No judge can be compelled to adopt a view of a case that he or she rejects. Although the majority of a panel must agree on the judgment in a case, most published decisions are signed by the judge who wrote the opinion for the panel. As a result, a number of opinions, especially those that attract public attention, are attributed to the judge who wrote for the panel. And individual judges are free to append concurring or dissenting opinions to any decision. In highly controversial cases, these separate opinions may draw attention and single out the judges who wrote the opinions.

Individual judges also receive attention in other ways. Federal judges, who are appointed by the President and must be confirmed by the Senate, sometimes face highly public confirmation proceedings. Scholars who aim to study the work of the Courts of Appeals routinely identify individual judges in an effort to discern whether panel decisions have been influenced by the perceived personal politics or ideological leanings of the judges who issued the decision. Individual judges are usually well known to the lawyers who routinely appear before the court. Because Court of Appeals judges are seen to be in prestigious positions, they receive numerous opportunities to teach part-time at law schools, give public speeches, write law review articles, and participate in important public endeavours both in the United States and abroad. High-achieving law school graduates apply to individual judges to serve as their law clerks. And, although the judges on a Court of Appeals routinely sit together to hear cases, judicial chambers are relatively independent operations that are typically located in different cities within the circuit. Court of Appeals judges are not as well known as Supreme Court Justices. But they are hardly silent or anonymous contributors to public life in the United States. Many judges are fairly well known to the public, especially in their circuits. And a number have well-established reputations for the published opinions that they author.

Given the status and independence of Courts of Appeals judges, it is not unreasonable to wonder whether individual judges can genuinely participate in panel deliberations with a common goal to reach unanimous decisions, and with the understanding that a decision produced by a panel is more important than the individual judges who produced it. In other words, are individual judges willing to temper strongly held personal views in service of collegial decision-making, which is fundamentally a group enterprise? I believe that, as a general matter, the answer to that question is 'yes'.

Most Court of Appeals judges quickly come to understand that judicial authority below the Supreme Court is tightly constrained. As noted above, when Court of Appeals judges decide a case, they are obliged to focus on legal materials to reach their result. Judges do not have free reign to decide cases as they think best, without regard to the record, the issues properly before the court, the applicable standards of review, and precedent. If precedent controls the disposition of a pending case, the judges on the panel must follow it. It does not matter whether a judge agrees with established precedent; we are bound to apply the law of the circuit in deciding cases before us. And this is what most Court of Appeals judges faithfully do in exercising their responsibilities on the bench. Why? Because professional responsibility, integrity, and the rule of law require it. Judicial independence does not supersede these obligations.

In April 2016, Judge Pamela Harris, who was appointed to the US Court of Appeals for the Fourth Circuit in 2014, spoke on 'Collegiality and Appellate Decisionmaking' at the University of Chicago Law School. Judge Harris had a distinguished record in private practice, government service, and law teaching before joining the court. I was fortunate to have her as one of my law clerks during the 1990–91 term, and we have remained good friends ever since. She was gracious enough to share her unpublished speech with me and I will reference it here and elsewhere in this paper. What Judge Harris had to say about her first three years on the bench is illuminating:

> 'What I had not been prepared for or been able to anticipate in any real way [when I first joined the court], is just how *collective* th[e] decision-making process is for federal appellate judges – how little of it is about what I think in isolation, and how much of it is about what I think in relation to what two other judges think …. Here is the central truth of my work as a judge: I can't do anything unless I can persuade at least one other judge to go along with me …. Deciding how a case comes out and on what grounds is fundamentally a group enterprise. And a recognition of that fact is at the heart of what most judges mean when we talk about judicial collegiality.'

It is interesting that Judge Harris readily acknowledges that the reality of collegial decision-making came as a bit of a surprise to her. This does not surprise me, however, because I do not think that most members of the public, including legal scholars and members of the media, really understand 'just how *collective* th[e] decision making process is for federal appellate judges'. What is most significant about Judge Harris' comment is that she makes it clear that, although the practices and requirements of collegial decision-making came as a surprise to her, she readily accepted her new responsibilities:

> 'For me, collegiality means embracing, not chafing at, the collective nature of appellate decision-making. It's "leaning in" to making decisions in active engagement with your colleagues: Knowing each other; really listening to and respecting each other's views; being willing to be persuaded and also to persuade, to be part of that dialogue. This is a genuine choice, as an appellate judge …. [In my view, collegial decision making is a] very substantive conception of the role of an appellate judge, in which reaching decisions through interaction is central to the job.'

Judge Harris' conception of the role of an appellate judge corresponds with what I have seen in my work and heard from many judicial colleagues across the country during my 37 years as a Court of Appeals judge. It is the prevailing norm among Court of Appeals judges.

What confuses some people who observe and comment on the work of the Courts of Appeals is that judges sometimes disagree, even sharply, over the proper resolution of some cases. This causes some commentators to claim that our decision-making is unduly influenced by the personal political and ideological leanings of the individual judges. The available data refute these claims. Here is what the data in the Appendices show for the five terms from 2011–2012 through 2015–2016:

- Most decisions on the merits issued by the Courts of Appeals were unanimous.
- Counting both 'published' and 'unpublished' decisions, the Courts issued a total of 172,680 decisions on the merits. Only 2,220 of these decisions (1.3%) included a dissent.
- 'Unpublished' decisions constituted nearly 90% of all dispositions by Courts of Appeals between 2011 and 2016. There were 151,771 unpublished decisions out of 172,680 total dispositions (87.89%).
- The Courts issued a total of 20,909 'published' decisions. Only 2,220 of these decisions (10.6%) included a dissent.

As the data indicate, the judges on the Courts of Appeals rarely disagree in their dispositions on the merits. Think about it. In 172,680 decisions issued on the merits, only 1.3% included a dissent. Any judge understands what this means: we routinely deliberate carefully over the cases before us and aim to get the law right. And in an astonishingly high number of our decisions – 98.7% – we reach unanimous judgments.

The data also show that there are very few *en banc* dispositions in the Courts of Appeals. Most decisions on the merits are issued by three-judge panels. Only the Ninth Circuit decided a relatively large number of cases pursuant to *en banc* review, and even in that circuit the number is not unduly high. During the 2015–2016 term, the Ninth Circuit issued 6,709 decisions on the merits, 516 of which were published decisions, but only 21 came after *en banc* review. Overall, the data show that the circuits routinely trust their three-judge panels to get the law right and rarely resort to *en banc* review to second-guess panel decisions.

Some commentators try to discount the data by suggesting that 'unpublished' decisions should not count for much because these dispositions involve relatively easy cases. There are three responses to this claim: First, every decision on the merits issued by a Court of Appeals requires the judges to apply the applicable law. It does not matter whether some cases are less difficult than others. Judges can disagree on impermissible grounds in both easy and hard cases. It is significant that the cases that should not admit of disagreement do not. Second, even if only 'published' decisions are counted, there are very few dissents in the decisions issued by the Courts of Appeals. As indicated above, the Courts issued a total of 20,909 'published' decisions during the five terms between 2011 and 2016, and only 2,220 of these decisions

(10.6% of the total) included a dissent. Third, in cases in which there is a dissenting opinion, the judges do not invariably vote along presumed political party lines.

With respect to the last point above, I studied the judgments of the DC Circuit reviewing administrative agency actions between 2000 and 2008. Here is what I found:[29]

> 'I selected this eight-year period because a Republican president, George W. Bush, was in the White House, Congress was controlled by Republicans for a majority of the eight years, and a clear majority of the judges on the D.C. Circuit was appointed by Republican presidents. I selected administrative agency actions because it is well understood that this large category of cases includes some of the most difficult and controversial appeals heard by the D.C. Circuit. If judges' personal political and ideological predilections played a significant role in their decisions during this period, a place to look for its effect would be the court's decisions to support or overturn agency actions (in support of or against the Republican administration) and/or sharp divisions among judges along political lines. That is not what our case dispositions indicate ....
>
> During the eight years, from September 2000 through July 2008, there were only forty-one instances [in 913 dispositions] in which dissenting opinions issued in cases involving review of administrative agency action ....
>
> The data also show that judges routinely crossed presumed political party lines when they dissented .... These data indicate that in almost 60 percent of the cases in which a dissent was filed, the judges did not vote along presumed political party lines.
>
> [The data also offer] some examples of hard and very hard cases, involving mixed panels in which the decision of the court is unanimous. These opinions ... show how the judges of the court carefully consider the record, construe the law, and apply precedent to reach a consensus in difficult and important cases. All of the cases cited involved meaningful judicial deliberations, as do most hard and very hard cases. It is no answer for an empirical legal scholar to tell us that the judges who joined the decision really did not mean what is said in the opinion or that some judges concurred in the result even though they disagreed with the outcome. Empirical legal scholars make such claims, but they are specious. We mean what we say in our opinions and our judgments constitute the law of the case and the law of the circuit. We take this seriously.'

There is another important point that should not be lost in this discussion: Dissenting opinions are not invariably evidence of dysfunction in a Court

---

29 Edwards and Livermore (n 4) 1956–57 (portion of article written solely by Judge Edwards).

of Appeals, nor are dissents necessarily an indication that decision-making has been inappropriately influenced by the ideological or political views of individual judges. Some cases are simply very hard and the judges on the panel reasonably disagree. The matter under review may present an issue of first impression; or the issue before the court is highly complicated or controversial; or there may be no clearly controlling precedent. In these circumstances, deliberations among appellate judges are more difficult and there is more room for discretion in the exercise of appellate decision-making.

Appellate cases are idiosyncratic; it is therefore hard to generalise meaningfully about their susceptibility to determinate resolution. Based on what I have seen during the course of my 37 years on the bench, however, I have estimated that approximately 50–60% of the cases decided by the Courts of Appeals are relatively 'easy'; in other words, the pertinent legal rules seem unambiguous and their application to the facts appears clear. A dispute falling into this category, I believe, admits of only one creditable answer. Were I to vote to decide an easy case in any other way, I would expect to be accused of having made an error, not merely of having voted or ruled unwisely. Again, using rough estimates, I have estimated that in only 5–15% of the disputes that come before me in any given term do I conclude, after reviewing the record and all of the pertinent legal materials, that the competing arguments drawn from those sources are equally strong. Put differently, only in those few cases do I feel that a fair application of the law to the facts leaves me in equipoise and that to dispose of the appeal I must rely on some significant measure of discretion. I view these cases as 'very hard'. I have found that the remaining cases are neither 'easy' nor 'very hard'. I view them as 'hard'. Some of my colleagues might disagree with these estimates, but our quibbles would be insignificant. I think that most judges would agree that at least half of our cases are relatively straightforward; and most would agree, I think, that the percentage of 'very hard' cases is not unduly large.

The appeals falling into the middle category – 'hard' – are the critical core of Court of Appeals work. In these cases, each party is able to make at least one legal argument that the judges find colourable; however, after research, reflection, and deliberations, the judges conclude that the argument(s) advanced by one party seem demonstrably stronger than the argument(s) advanced by the other. In such circumstances, the judges feel constrained to render judgment in favour of the party who has made the more compelling claims. And, in my view, it is quite impressive that the judges of the Courts of Appeals issue decisions in these cases that rarely include a dissent.

Actually, the small number of dissents is not hard to explain in light of how most Court of Appeals judges work: Most judges are well-prepared before oral argument and deliberations; most judges are respectful of their colleagues and prepared to deliberate seriously over hard issues, and most judges generally prefer to reach unanimous decisions. As Judge Harris observed, a manifestation of robust collegial decision-making occurs

> 'when a panel works its way together through a tricky case, and may find its way to mutual agreement on a ground that is different – often narrower – than where some of the judges may have started. This again feels to me like an extremely productive and beneficial process. Most judges, I think, have a very understandable sense that if we can identify a point of decision on which all three judges agree, that decision is more likely to be correct than one that is not unanimous. Based on my discussions with my colleagues, this is true even for judges much more experienced than I am; even for them, there's a welcome confidence and reassurance in a unanimous decision. [I] [t]hink this is especially true – and especially justified – with respect to unanimous decisions that are reached only after some initial disagreement, and an open exchange of different views that leads to a more fully considered and carefully refined decision and opinion. Again … when I think back on the opinions I've written that are the result of this kind of sustained engagement and give-and-take among the judges on a panel, I am convinced that they are an improvement on what I would have produced if left to my own devices …. I am convinced that … decisions and opinions are better – more fully reasoned, sounder and stronger – when they've been refined in this crucible of active engagement and debate.'

I have always been distressed by unbridled statements from scholars and commentators who claim that, because some cases admit of discretion in the exercise of appellate decision-making, these decision outcomes have been tainted by the personal political or ideological predilections of individual judges. But any assessment of appellate decision-making that fails to discriminate between forms of moral/political reasoning intrinsic to law and those that are extrinsic to law is flawed. Legal reasoning involves moral judgment (not in the form of personal whim or preference, but rather in the situated and disciplined elaboration of the conventional norms of the American political community) in cases in which judges exercise delegated or common-law-making authority. Therefore, the mere assertion that judges are sometimes influenced by political or ideological considerations in their decision-making is unilluminating. There may be occasions when some judges inappropriately resort to moral/political reasoning that is extrinsic to law, but there is no evidence that these lapses are frequent or that they have corrupted decision-making in the Courts of Appeals.

Legal scholars try to use empirical methods – most notably the statistical analysis of case outcomes – to understand the effect of extra-legal factors on appellate decision-making. The principal problem with such empirical legal analyses is that they cannot distinguish between legal and extra-legal factors without considering and accurately accounting for the most important determinants of appellate decision-making: (1) the case records on appeal, (2) the applicable law, (3) controlling precedent, and (4) judicial deliberations.

By failing to account for these core determinants – in part, perhaps, because they cannot be easily or accurately measured – the field of empirical legal studies fails to provide a nuanced understanding of how legal and extra-legal factors interact to generate judicial decisions, and likely over-emphasises extra-legal factors. It is noteworthy, however, that even on their own limited terms, empirical studies predict very little about the effects of extra-legal factors on appellate decision-making.[30]

Finally, it almost goes without saying that judges are bound to disagree at times on the applicability of precedent. And we are bound to disagree at times on the proper rationale or disposition of some cases, especially in 'very hard' cases that admit of no straightforward answer. A good, well-functioning collegial court leaves space for constructive disagreement and well-placed dissenting decisions. Strong dissents may give rise to *en banc* consideration by the entire court or review by the Supreme Court; it may cause a party to reconsider some contestable actions even after it has prevailed before the Court of Appeals; and it may cause Congress or a government agency to reform undesirable policies. So long as separate opinions are not seen to be the norm in appellate decision-making, they are neither surprising nor concerning.

c) *How Should We Measure the Quality of the Decisions Rendered by the Courts of Appeals?*

The decision-making procedures followed by a court mean very little if the judges' decisions are unworthy of respect. But how should we measure the quality of judicial decision-making? What are the hallmarks of distinguished work by a Court of Appeals? What does the public expect of its courts? What do the judges expect of themselves?

It is not enough in my view simply to examine the decision-making methods of the circuits without questioning whether the decisions and accompanying opinions issued by the Courts of Appeals are creditable. This is a hard question to address because the answer may depend in part upon whether the courts' judgments are *qualitatively* sound, not just whether the decisions are unanimous. Thus, for example, we might want to consider whether the decisions faithfully adhere to legal requirements? Or whether the decisions are well written and clear? Or whether the opinions accompanying the decisions adequately address the parties' claims? Reasonable people might disagree on the answers to these questions.

There are standards, however, pursuant to which we can generally assess the work of Court of Appeals judges. I do not mean that we can do this in

---

30 See F Cross, 'Collegial Ideology in the Courts' (2009) 103 *Northwestern University Law Review* 1399, 1402.

precise quantitative terms, but we surely can subscribe to a set of criteria that Court of Appeals judges ought to follow in attending to their responsibilities. Based on my nearly four decades as a member of the US Court of Appeals for the DC Circuit – which have included seven years as Chief Judge, membership on the Judicial Conference of the United States, countless interactions with my own colleagues, judges from other circuits, and members of the Supreme Court, and untold hours studying and writing about appellate decision-making – I would offer the following list of criteria:

- First and foremost, the Courts of Appeals judges must adhere to the constraints implicit in our mission. We decide cases only within our jurisdiction; our judgments are based on the record before us, and the relevant constitutional, statutory, and regulatory provisions at issue; we follow the Supreme Court's commands and adhere to the law of the circuit; we aim to write decisions narrowly to address only the issues before us that have been properly raised and preserved by the parties; and we decide cases pursuant to the controlling standards of review.
- Second, judges must faithfully follow the law of the circuit and avoid writing decisions that inappropriately rely on the personal predilections of individual judges.
- Third, judges should strive to avoid writing dissenting opinions. Justice Brandeis appropriately recognised that dissents should be 'saved for major matters if the Court is not to appear indecisive and quarrelsome,' the appearance of which 'are drains on the energy of the [Judiciary]'.[31] I agree. In my view, decisions are likely to be sounder and stronger when they have been refined in the crucible of active engagement and debate among three judges who are determined to reach common ground in the panel's judgment. I also believe that unanimous decisions enhance the credibility of courts.
- Fourth, the members of the court should minimise *en banc* review of panel decisions. *En banc* review is consuming, often inefficient, sometimes unduly contentious, and, some judges would say, rarely worth the effort. *En banc* review should be reserved for only singularly important issues, or situations when the law of the circuit is in disarray and needs to be clarified. The members of three-judge panels should have a sense that their work is respected and not routinely subject to *en banc* review. This, in my view, encourages the members of three-judge panels to produce high quality opinions that adhere to the constraints implicit in our mission.
- Finally, in reaching decisions, members of three-judge panels should work to reach common ground on the rationale supporting the judgment. This makes

[31] J Frank, 'Book Review' (1958) 10 *Journal of Legal Education* 401, 404, reviewing A Bickel, *The Unpublished Opinions of Mr. Justice Brandeis: the Supreme Court at Work* (Harvard, The Belknap Press of Harvard University Press, 1957).

it easier for the parties and others who read the courts' opinions to understand the law of the circuit. It also avoids distortions in case precedent.

I am sure that there are other considerations that might come into play in any assessment of appellate decision-making. But, at least with respect to the work of the US Courts of Appeals, the foregoing list reflects my best effort to state the principal criteria.

I should add that, unlike decisions issued by the Supreme Court on constitutional issues, most decisions of the Courts of Appeals are not inviolate. Our judgments may be modified by Supreme Court review, congressional legislation, agency actions modifying contested regulations, and settlements by the parties who come before the court. In other words, if our decisions are perceived to be misguided, there are processes pursuant to which our actions can be altered. The stakes are not the same in the Courts of Appeals and the Supreme Court. I have always thought that this helps the judges to stay within the constraints implicit in our mission and do our utmost to reach the correct judgment in each case.

4. THE EFFECTS OF COLLEGIALITY ON COLLEGIAL DECISION-MAKING

In his exhaustive study of collegial decision-making,[32] Professor Frank Cross shows how the Courts of Appeals have had a profound impact on the law in the United States. He tellingly demonstrates that while the judges on these appellate courts are sometimes influenced by their personal predilections and by the views of the political party of their appointing President, judicial decision-making is principally influenced by legal requirements. Or, in Professor Cross' words, '[t]here is some rigorous evidence that the law matters.'[33] For example, '[a] study of seminal circuit court decisions in the areas of antitrust, environmental law, and search and seizure found that [changes in Supreme Court precedent] appeared to influence subsequent [circuit court] rulings, independent of ideology.'[34] He also shows that the Courts of Appeals have remained independent of the other branches of government and free from undue influence of interested parties.[35] In a later piece, Professor Cross says that although collegiality among judges has not been the subject of many useful empirical studies, there is research that suggests that collegiality

32 F Cross, *Decision Making in the U.S. Courts of Appeals* (Stanford, Stanford University Press, 2007).
33 Ibid 46.
34 Ibid.
35 See, eg, ibid 56–57 (executive branch); 123–47 (litigants).

can produce significant effects on judicial decisions.[36] These are important starting points to my discussion of the effects of collegiality.

I have already indicated my views on the empirical studies that purport to assess the work of judges on the Courts of Appeals, so I will not repeat them here. Suffice it to say that these empirical studies are largely misguided and, more importantly, they offer no useful views on normative practices that appellate judges should follow in their decision-making. The main point here is that we know from Professor Cross' work and the other available data that the ideological preferences of individual judges have only a very limited effect on decision-making in the Courts of Appeals.

What is at issue in the ongoing collegiality-ideology debate is not whether judges have well-defined political beliefs or other strongly held views about particular subjects; surely they do, and this, in and of itself, is of little moment. Instead, the real issue is the degree to which individual judges' personal views ordain the outcomes of the cases that come before the appellate courts. Collegiality helps ensure that results are not preordained. The more collegial the court, the more likely it is that the cases that come before it will be determined on their legal merits.

a) *The Need for Collegiality*

One might ask, what is collegiality? In my view, it is a process that helps to create the conditions for principled agreement, by allowing all points of view to be aired and considered. It allows judges of differing perspectives and philosophies to communicate with, listen to, and ultimately influence one another in constructive and law-abiding ways. And collegiality mitigates judges' ideological preferences and enables us to find common ground and reach better decisions. Collegiality thus facilitates collegial decision-making.

In an uncollegial environment, divergent views among members of a court often end up as dissenting opinions. Why? Because judges tend to follow a 'party line' and adopt unalterable positions on the issues before them. This is especially true in hard and very hard cases that involve highly controversial issues. Judges who initially hold different views tend not to think hard about the quality of the arguments made by those with whom they disagree, so no serious attempt is made to find common ground. Judicial divisions are sharp and firm. And sharp divisions on hard and very hard issues give rise to 'ideological camps' among judges, which in turn beget divisions even in some cases that are not very hard. It is not a good situation.

In my 37 years on the DC Circuit, I have learned that fruitful deliberations can fail when a court is 'broken' for want of collegiality. I saw this first hand when I joined the DC Circuit in 1980. During my first day as a member

36 Cross, 'Collegial Ideology in the Courts' (n 30) 1408.

of the court, I was greeted by one of the senior members of the court who, after saying 'hello', asked, 'Can I count on your vote?' I was floored by the question. I responded that he could count on my vote only on those occasions when we agreed on how a case should be decided. I came to understand, however, that – in those days – the DC Circuit was ideologically divided on many issues. If two or three so-called 'liberal' or 'conservative' judges were randomly assigned to sit together, they might use the occasion to tilt their opinions pursuant to their partisan preferences. Judges of similar political persuasions too often sided with one another (say, on petitions for *en banc* review) largely out of partisan loyalty. We dissented more, and we were more inclined to rehear cases *en banc*.

What I saw was that when a court is bereft of collegiality, judges become distrustful of one another's motivations; they are less receptive to ideas about pending cases and to comments on circulating opinions; and they stubbornly cling to their first impressions of an issue, often readily dismissing suggestions that would produce a stronger opinion or a better result.

b) How Does a Court Instill and Maintain Collegiality?

After some difficult times, the DC Circuit started to change when the court adopted several internal operating rules to facilitate cooperation among judges and infuse ordinary interactions with a sense of shared purpose. For example, we agreed that every judge must sit with every other active judge on the court at least four times in a term. This rule prevented any one group of judges from sitting together too often and promoted familiarity and good working relationships among all judges on the court. We also agreed that, absent a grave emergency, the court would not use visiting judges from other circuits to serve on three-judge panels on our court. This rule implied no disrespect for our judicial colleagues from other courts. Rather, the members of the court decided that, to ensure expeditious issuance of our decisions, balanced work assignments among our judges, and coherence in the law of the circuit, only the judges of the court should do the work of our court. In other words, we adopted a policy that took into account the culture and needs of our court and facilitated decision-making.

We also adopted rules governing the circulation of opinions. For example, judges must respond to draft opinions from other judges within five days. This is a vitally important rule because any judge who has completed work on an assigned opinion wants to hear from the other two judges on the panel as promptly as possible while the opinion is still fresh on the mind of the writing judge. If a judge wants to write a separate opinion, she or he must do so within thirty days after the third judge has concurred in the majority opinion. This rule also prevents individual judges from unduly holding up the court's work. Once a panel agrees on a disposition, the proposed judgment or opinion must be circulated to the entire court for seven days so that all members of the court keep abreast of the court's work. We also publish statistics each month indicating how many opinions each judge has pending. And a judge who has three or more assigned opinions pending on 15 August is not allowed to sit on any new cases in the new court term until the backlog is cleared. These and other case management rules had a tremendous effect on improving interactions among the members of the court.

I do not suggest that every court should have the same rules. Circuits are like families, so we should operate in ways that best accommodate our situations. Appropriate rules are important, however, because they structure the paths by which judges collaborate on opinions. And they protect against maverick behaviour that might run counter to the court's mission. In my research for this paper, I sent a questionnaire to the Chief Judges of the 13 US Courts of Appeals inquiring about the decision-making processes in each circuit. The results of the survey (shown in the Appendices) are noteworthy in confirming that different circuits have adopted internal operating procedures to facilitate collegiality in decision-making:

- The answers to survey question number 3 indicate that most circuits follow a practice of having the junior judge speak first at conferences. The answer for 'Circuit B' says that 'conferences are informal', even though the junior judge speaks first. This is likely true for most circuits. In my circuit, for example, even though the junior judge speaks first, the judges often engage in fruitful discussions to amplify their views and to get a better understanding of their colleagues' views. And, on occasions, the judges may engage in an extended conversation to see if they can close the gaps in their positions.
- The answers to survey question number 5, regarding the assignment of opinions, are illuminating. The presiding judge normally has the authority to assign opinions. But the survey answers show that many circuits find ways to accommodate their judges. The answer for 'Circuit C' – 'don't be greedy … try to give one of the "good" cases to each judge' – is emblematic. 'Circuit G' generally allows senior judges the first pick. This is gracious and respectful of senior judges, but an unusual approach.
- In response to survey question number 6, all circuits have rules regarding when judges are expected to respond to a colleague's proposed opinion.
- The answers to survey question 7 show that most circuits have policies covering when judges are expected to complete their writing assignments, but the rules vary from circuit to circuit.
- In the open-ended question on the survey, the Chief Judge from 'Circuit I' said:

  > '[We sometimes follow] a practice by which a panel engages in some (and often substantial) dialog concerning cases listed for a sitting. These discussions

ultimately lead to decisions concerning which listed cases will be argued (although [Internal Operating Procedures] require argument when only one judge requests it[)]. These preliminary discussions also permit panel members to: (1) resolve threshold issues; (2) hone other issues; (3) determine how much argument time should be accorded each side; (4) discuss what is or may be worthy of precedential treatment; and (5) share specific concerns in advance of the sitting.'

- Judge Jon Newman, the former Chief Judge of the Second Circuit, who was aware of my work on this project, wrote to me to explain his court's use of sequential voting:

  'For all our immigration cases (petitions to review [Board of Immigration Appeals] decisions), we place them in a non-argument calendar and send the papers to a judge designated Judge No. 1, who has a week to mark a ballot and send it to Judge No. 2, who votes within a week and sends the ballot to Judge No. 3, who votes with[in] a week. These are not permanent panels. I learned this technique from the 11th Circuit, which I think uses it for many motions. If one judge wants oral argument, the case is sent to an argument calendar.'

The particular practices of the various circuits are less important than the fact that each circuit has adopted internal operating procedures to facilitate collegial decision-making.[37] And those procedures have been tailored to each circuit's unique cultures and needs. Institutional rules and norms motivate judges to behave in ways that further the institutional mission and influence how they do their jobs. Collegiality plays a very important role in 'institutionalising' judges into the shared mission of getting the law right. Internal operating procedures are promulgated by the members of a court, so the judges have a real stake in their enforcement. The consequence is a cross-fertilising effect between collegiality and internal rules.

Deliberation is one of the most important components of collegiality. Rules that structure our deliberations ensure that we deal with substantive ideas effectively as a group. For example, as noted above, in most circuits, the senior active judge on a panel presides during conferences, and judges speak in inverse order of seniority. And the senior judge in the majority typically assigns opinions. Although simple, these rules help keep our conferences professional, respectful, and orderly. Collegiality does not consist of spontaneous conversations by the water cooler. It consists primarily of ordered deliberation in which all views are aired and considered to every judge's satisfaction.

Judge Richard Posner has written that judges 'don't deliberate very much' and that '[j]udicial deliberation is overrated.'[38] My experience does not support

37 For details see Hooper, Miletich and Levy (n 27).

38 R Posner, 'The Role of the Judge in the Twenty-First Century' (2006) 86 *Boston University Law Review* 1049, 1051.

this view. I have found that, on a collegial court, judicial deliberations are pervasive and fruitful. Judicial colleagues who have worked together over time and come to know perspectives and views of one another can anticipate a colleague's initial 'takes' on certain cases without ever having to discuss the case in detail. This facilitates the judges' questioning of advocates during oral arguments, and it also enhances deliberations in conference. Indeed, I have found that a judge's cognition during preparations for oral argument can be moderated in anticipation of a colleague's views – a kind of tacit deliberation.

Judges deliberate when they raise questions during oral argument to alert their colleagues to their concerns. Judges deliberate in conference and continue to deliberate after conference when they raise issues uncovered in their research. Judges deliberate when they circulate draft opinions, receive their colleagues' responses, and negotiate resolutions to any differences. And during all of these occasions, judges on a court blessed with collegiality keep an open mind about the correct result pending the conclusion of deliberations.

Collegiality can have positive effects on decision-making even when a court is sitting *en banc*. A good example of this occurred when the DC Circuit heard and decided the case of *United States v Microsoft Corporation*.[39] The issues in that case were as difficult as any that I have seen in my 37 years on the bench, and, at least when measured by public attention, the case was one of the most important ever heard by the DC Circuit. Months before the court heard argument, *The Washington Post* had published an article on the likely outcome of any appeal in the DC Circuit. The headline read, 'A Game of Judicial Roulette: Microsoft's Fate Could Hinge on Which Judges Hear Appeal', and the article predicted that the court's decision would be a matter of 'dumb luck', 'judicial lotto', and 'blue-bucket bingo', clearly implying that the political leanings of the judges would outweigh any other considerations in the court's ruling.[40] Yet, after many months of deliberations, the court sitting *en banc* issued a unanimous, unsigned, 125-page opinion. The press had been wrong.

The *Microsoft* decision was forged as much out of productive disagreement as out of agreement. The judges found that through careful, collective exploration and consideration of the different views of each judge, a product that reflected consensus emerged. The freedom to disagree with one's colleagues, which is fostered by collegiality, enabled the judges accurately and honestly, and without hesitation, to identify what was common ground and what was not, all the while remaining open to revising their views. Instead of asking

---

39 *United States v Microsoft Corporation* 253 F.3d 34 (DC Circuit 2001) (*en banc, per curiam*). *Per curiam* ('by the court') decisions do not identify any one judge as the author.

40 D Segal, 'A Game of Judicial Roulette: Microsoft's Fate Could Hinge on Which Judges Hear Appeal', *Washington Post*, 20 November 1998, D1.

each other 'What is your vote?', the judges asked 'What makes sense to you?' It was a stunning achievement in collegial decision-making.

The dynamics of collegial decision-making are also influenced by a variety of intangible factors. For example, if a colleague has a special expertise in a particular area or a reputation for thoughtfulness and strong preparation, that judge may be credited by other judges during the deliberation process. On a court that has the benefit of collegiality the judges adjust to their colleagues' personal idiosyncrasies, talents, and limitations, and look for ways to draw strength from the best that each judge has to offer.

Unsurprisingly, the judges in a number of circuits arrange events that allow members of the court to engage with one another in settings outside of the courtroom. Judge Pamela Harris reported that, in the Fourth Circuit, the judges

> 'follow every conference with lunch; the three judges who sat together [g]o out together for a purely social lunch, no business discussed. I balked a bit ... at first; time right after conference is when I want to sit down alone and process everything that's just happened. But [I came] to see that lunch is a key ritual of collegiality, making manifest what my colleagues also were telling me more directly: that our disagreements about cases don't have consequences for our personal relationships.'

In the DC Circuit, luminaries from other professional fields are often invited to have lunch with the judges to discuss their work. The sessions are relaxed and informative, and they afford the judges time to discuss matters other than case work. At the beginning of each term, a dinner is arranged for the judges and their spouses to allow us to 'kick off' the new term in good spirits. At the end of each term, the Chief Judge hosts a gathering of the judges at which we drink champagne to toast the completion of another year of work, tell tales about one another, and laugh about the trying moments of the year that just ended. Most circuits have gatherings of these sorts to bring together members of the court. What the courts have found is that judges behave more collegially on the bench when they have opportunities to enjoy social gatherings outside the courtroom and the conference room.

The Chief Judge of the circuit is uniquely placed to both oversee the court's operations and take steps to bolster collegiality. Most Court of Appeals judges 'live' relatively privately in their chambers, with their law clerks and assistants. Save for motions conferences, oral arguments, post-hearing conferences, and judges' meetings, the judges work alone in chambers with their staff and have only limited occasions to reflect on court operations. The Chief Judge of the circuit is the person who brings together the various parts of the circuit. The Chief oversees the work of the clerk's office and the circuit executive; approves budget expenditures and automation initiatives; presides over the Judicial Council which sets policies for the Court of Appeals and the district courts; serves on the Judicial Conference of the United States, which sets policies for all of the circuits; interacts with the Administrative Office of the US Courts, which serves the needs of the courts with respect to personnel, automation, and budget functions; and works with various bar committees that interact with the courts. Most members of the court have no interest in these responsibilities, in part because they trust the Chief Judge to attend to the needs of the circuit. During my seven years as Chief Judge of the DC Circuit, I learned that it is imperative for the Chief to be very active in addressing the needs of the court, to help create and maintain a collegial environment. This cannot be left to the court's managers, because they do not have the standing with the judges to press for collegiality.

The Chief Judge position is filled according to the seniority of the judges on the court. The most senior active judge on the court of appeals who is under 65 years old is designated Chief; and that person may serve for seven years or until she or he reaches the age of 70, whichever comes first. This means that not all members of the court will have occasion to serve as Chief Judge. And not all judges are equally interested in serving as Chief. It is my impression, however, that the judges who accept the position work very hard to fulfil the responsibilities of the job. And the Chief Judges have good networks through the Judicial Conference of the United States, the Administrative Office of the Courts, the Federal Judicial Center, and their circuit executives and clerks of the courts, so they have good support systems in pursuing their administrative and managerial responsibilities.

c) *The Potential Threats to Collegiality*

Although there is little doubt that collegiality facilitates collegial decision-making, collegiality is not a given. There are a number of things that can threaten judicial collegiality. For example, the size of the court may make it more difficult to maintain collegiality. It stands to reason that the larger the court, the less frequently any two judges sit together and interact with each other. I have always assumed that it is easier to achieve and maintain collegiality on a court with 12 members than on one with 20 or 30. Smaller groups have the potential to interact more efficiently, making close and continual collaboration more likely.

Another threat is the location of the judges' chambers. When judges are spread apart, they may interact less because they sit in distant locations. Having all the circuit's judges in the same building, as with the DC Circuit and the Federal Circuit, can be immensely helpful. The ease of face-to-face interactions outside the context of oral arguments, conferences, and judges' meetings can make a difference, especially for a Chief Judge who is trying hard to hear, understand, and address the needs of her or his colleagues.

However, history tells us that collegiality can be lost in a single location like the DC Circuit, and it can be effectively maintained in circuits whose judges are based in diverse locations. I have always believed that the number of judges on a circuit is a more important variable than the location of the judges' chambers.

The nature and number of a circuit's cases can certainly affect collegial decision-making. For example, circuits that have large numbers of *pro se* and immigration cases face difficult case management problems.[41] Cases of these sorts, especially when they come in high volume, can test the patience of judges and ask more of them than it sometimes seems possible to deliver.

The addition of new judges to a court can also affect collegiality. Joining a Court of Appeals can be a challenge for a new judge because the demands of *collegial* decision-making are different from the demands of many of the positions from which new judges come when they join the court. The problem is particularly challenging when new judges join a court that includes a large number of judges who have worked together for many years.

However, the good thing about a court that is blessed with collegiality is that new judges are able to join the court and find their way relatively easily. Getting the law right is the mission of a truly collegial court. New members of a collegial court should quickly surmise that they have no good incentive to pursue individual ideological goals. And a single new judge has no real standing or authority to undo the norms of collegiality. In due course, new judges should come to appreciate that all judges have a common interest, as members of the institution of the judiciary, in getting the law right, and that, as a result, we are willing to listen, persuade, and be persuaded, all in an atmosphere of civility and respect.

Finally, individual personalities can pose threats to collegiality on a court. There are two principal issues. The first concerns the personal qualities and talents of the persons who are appointed to a court. It is fair to assume that a collegial court is invariably better if all the judges possess great integrity, intelligence, and diligence. This comes only if the judicial appointment process is consistently good. A court, however, has no control over judicial appointments. And, in any event, it is hard to know how much better a court might have been with different appointments.

The second consideration has to do with 'irascible personalities' who sometimes distract from a court's mission. There are two things that can ameliorate unpleasant situations caused by difficult personalities. First, if the circuit has clear rules in place governing internal operating procedures, this helps to ward off potentially disruptive situations. Second, the Chief Judge has the responsibility to maintain civil discourse among the judges. Therefore, there may be times when a Chief Judge will be required to talk

---

41 See Hooper, Miletich and Levy (n 27) 15 et seq, 29 et seq, 38 et seq.

privately with an offending colleague and, with diplomacy and respect, press for courtesy, civility, adherence to circuit rules, or whatever else is required to restore collegiality on the court. Fortunately, it is my impression that most Court of Appeals judges are sufficiently strong, independent, and smart, and thus able to withstand any potential threats to collegiality that might be the byproduct of individual personalities. It is also my impression that most judges try hard not to offend the norms of collegiality.

d) The Lessons Learned

In reflecting on these matters over the years, I have come to understand that there are a number of factors that may affect appellate decision-making, some that should and some that should not. These factors include: the requirements of positive law; precedent; leadership; internal court rules; whether the judges are equally committed to prepare cases carefully and deliberate seriously; how cases are framed and argued by the litigants; judicial appointments; the relative intelligence of the court's judges; the judges' personalities and ideological leanings; diversity on the bench; and whether a court has a core group of well-seasoned judges who have worked together for a good period of time. These are elusive considerations that cannot be easily determined and weighed. They matter, however.

Precedent may be the linchpin:

> 'All judges are bound by precedent, and almost all judges recognize this fact. Therefore, arguments about the meaning of precedent, and the legitimate readings that can be given to governing precedent, are crucially significant in every case. Because precedent can be read according to rules that are broadly shared and understood, even if not objective or universal, judges who might agree about little else can come to a common reading of governing law. Consensus typically fails only when the governing precedent is read in divergent and irreconcilable ways, and judges disagree in how they would exercise any discretion that is given to the court by a lack of clarity in the governing law. Before judges admit to that failure, however, they have ample opportunity to persuade and look for a reasonable resolution on legal grounds.'[42]

I strongly believe that the work of the courts is substantially enhanced if the factors that may affect decision-making are 'filtered' by collegiality. There are cross-fertilising effects between collegiality and certain of these factors. So, for example, collegiality fosters the promulgation of institutional rules, and the presence of these rules promotes collegiality. In the end, collegiality mitigates

[42] Edwards and Livermore (n 4) 1965.

judges' personal predilections and enables us to find common ground and reach better decisions. If politics and ideology significantly affected our decision-making, the courts would issue more dissenting and concurring opinions. The fact that a vast majority of our decisions are unanimous speaks volumes about the positive effects of collegiality on collegial decision-making in the various Courts of Appeals.

III. CONCLUSION

The model of decision-making followed by the US Courts of Appeals largely works because, subject to constitutional limitations, our decision-making processes have been adapted to accommodate the various cultures in each circuit. And, for the most part, the judges appointed to the courts understand and adhere to the constraints implicit in our mission.

I do not mean to sound Pollyannaish, however. Our judicial system is not perfect, and judges have frailties that sometimes adversely affect decision-making. My colleagues and I are constantly tested. We know, for example, that when the executive branch changes following a presidential election, the courts invariably will face important and contentious issues. And collegial decision-making also may be tested when new judges are appointed to the courts. These challenges are not insurmountable, however. As long as we stay within the constraints implicit in our mission, we will retain the capacity to serve justice as we should. And our efforts always will be enhanced if we can maintain collegiality in our collegial decision-making.

APPENDICES

A. Survey of the Chief Judges of the United States Courts of Appeals Regarding Their Courts' Decision-Making Processes

In January 2017, I sent a questionnaire to the Chief Judges of the 13 US Courts of Appeals inquiring about the decision-making processes in their courts. Each Chief Judge was asked to answer the following 11 questions:

1. **When do the Judges on your court conference after oral argument?**
2. **Do the Judges always meet in person to conference after oral arguments?**
3. **In what order do the Judges speak at conference?**
4. **When a panel agrees on the disposition of a case, is the disposition recorded in writing? By whom? Is it posted electronically?**
5. **Do you have any rules or customs regarding the assignment of opinions?**
6. **When a proposed opinion is circulated to the panel, do you have any rules regarding when panel members must respond?**
7. **Do you have any rules or customs regarding when Judges must complete their writing assignments?**
8. **How many sitting days does an active judge have during a court term?**
9. **About how many cases are heard during a single sitting day?**
10. **What is the average amount of time that you allow per side in oral arguments?**
11. **About how many opinions does an active judge write each term? (An average number is fine. Do not include dissenting or concurring opinions.)**

Every Chief Judge completed the questionnaire. Their responses to each question are tabulated on the following pages.

The circuits are labeled *anonymously* and listed *randomly* on the charts showing the tabulations of the questionnaires submitted by the Chief Judges. No Chief Judge is identified by name on the charts.

1. **When do the judges confer after oral argument?**	
Circuits	**Answers**
A	Immediately after oral argument
B	Immediately after oral argument
C	Immediately after oral argument
D	Immediately after oral argument
E	Immediately after oral argument. Three judge panels listen to arguments in 4–8 cases a day (the number depending on case complexity), immediately followed by a conference on all the cases. En banc panels conference immediately after oral argument.
F	Immediately after oral argument. No sharing of information or bench memos occurs prior to oral argument. We meet immediately afterwards and discuss all 6 cases (a typical day's calendar, though sometimes the number is 9).
G	Immediately after oral argument
H	Immediately after oral argument
I	Immediately after oral argument. Our practice is to repair to the chambers of the presiding judge immediately upon completion of the final scheduled argument. Occasionally, a panel member's schedule or return travel plans require later deliberation.
J	Immediately after oral argument. Immediately after the last case is argued in the morning or early afternoon.
K	Immediately after oral argument
L	Immediately after oral argument
M	Immediately after oral argument. At the conclusion of hearing our case arguments, the panel goes immediately to a conference room to discuss and decide the cases.

2. **Do the judges always meet in person to confer after oral argument?**	
Circuits	**Answers**
A	Yes
B	Yes, except for the very rare occa[s]ions when a judge attends the oral argument and conference by video.
C	Yes
D	Yes
E	Yes, with the caveat that, in some cases, some judges participate by video or telephonic conference. (For example, … circumstances, such as weather or illness, force remote participation by judges in conferences. And, in some emergency situations … a judge will listen to the argument later and cast a vote. However, our general rule is that judges are expected to attend in person.) In addition, in extraordinary circumstances when all judges participate in argument via video (such as emergency, last minute oral arguments when an execution is pending), the judges will also confer by video conference.
F	With rare exceptions, yes. [If a] colleague … [has] to appear by video … that judge conferences with the other two by telephone.
G	Yes
H	Yes
I	Occasionally, a judge whose resident chambers are not located in [headquarters] will participate in oral argument by video (or even telephone). On those occasions, conference must also involve video or audio participation.
J	Yes, except on rare occasions when a judge participates by video conference due to weather or disability preventing the judge from attending in person.
K	Yes
L	Yes
M	Yes

3. In what order do the judges speak at conference?	
Circuits	**Answers**
A	Junior Judge speaks first.
B	Usually the junior judge speaks first, but our conferences are informal. Judges speak up freely, thus frequently departing from the usual order. At en banc conferences, the practice has been to start at the junior end with one case and at the senior end with the next.
C	Other. The presiding judge has the discretion to set the order. Many rotate who goes first.
D	Other: The presiding judge manages the conference. Some presiding judges go by seniority, others by reverse seniority, others clockwise starting with the judge who happens to be sitting on the presiding judge's left, others vary the order.
E	Other. 1. In en banc conferences, the junior judge speaks first and each judge then speaks in rising order of seniority, with the Chief Judge speaking last. 2. On three-judge panels, the practice has varied. Generally, the most junior judge speaks first. However, some presiding judges use a system whereby the judge whose chambers has prepared the pre-argument bench memo speaks first.
F	Junior Judge speaks first.
G	Other: There is no protocol as to who speaks first.
H	Junior Judge speaks first.
I	Junior Judge speaks first. "Junior" includes [those] who are on senior status. The presider speaks last.
J	Junior Judge speaks first. This is the order for the first case; thereafter, the speakers are rotated, e.g., in the second case, the second junior judge speaks, then the presiding judge, then the most junior judge, and in the third case the presiding judge speaks first, etc.
K	Junior Judge speaks first.
L	Judge with most seniority speaks first.
M	Junior Judge speaks first. For a panel of three judges, the least senior judge on this Court will speak first. It is the same procedure after an en banc hearing. If a senior judge or a district court judge sitting by designation is on the panel, he/she will speak first.

4. When a panel agrees on the disposition of a case, is the disposition recorded in writing? By whom? Is it posted electronically?	
Circuits	**Answers**
A	Each judge takes written notes during the conference about each case discussed. The notes will conclude with the disposition and the writing assignment.
B	One judge is always assigned as the writing judge for each case. That judge files the opinion electronically with the Clerk of Court. The opinion is posted electronically and is accessible by the public.
C	No, each judges keeps his own notes. We probably should … hav[e] the presiding judge prepare a conference memo.
D	Each judge keeps her own written record
E	The presiding judge, or his or her designate, prepares conference notes detailing the discussion and outcome and circulates the conference notes electronically. The notes are not 'posted' electronically in a manner that off-panel judges or others can access.
F	We have small bench cards, on which each judge records the essence of the discussion and the tentative vote. This usually reflects the final outcome, but occasionally the assigned judge will let the panel know of additional complications or reflections.
G	The panel presider after argument circulates the tentative disposition to the other panel members. Only after the order or opinion is ready for filing is it posted electronically by the clerk's office.
H	Yes. By the senior-most judge. It is posted electronically, internally.
I	All members of the panel usually take notes in conference. The presider circulates to the full court: the names of the cases[;] whether the dispositions will be by Precedential or Non-Precedential opinion; the name of the authoring judge; and if the opinion will be Precedential, a very brief parenthetical describing the issues to be resolved.
J	Nothing is recorded at conference, other than in the individual judges' personal notes. When a final agreement is reached and an order or opinion is drafted, that order or opinion is released by the clerk's office. Yes, all opinions and orders are posted electronically.
K	The disposition is recorded in writing by the presiding judge. The presiding judge then sends a printed panel report to the judges on the panel and the Clerk's Office listing the author and if the opinion is precedential or nonprecedential. The information is not posted electronically.
L	A panel report is prepared by the authoring judge within a week of the conference and circulated to all judges on the court.
M	Yes. The lead judge will send a memorandum to the Chief Judge of the Court on the same day giving the proposed dispositions of the cases and recommendations for case assignments.

5. Do you have any rules or customs regarding the assignment of opinions?	
Circuits	**Answers**
A	The senior active judge on the panel makes the writing assignments after collegial discussion of all the cases and deference to any particular choices of a panel member. The goal is to equalize the writing load.
B	The senior active judge is responsible for assigning the writing judge for each case.
C	No, don't be greedy. [Some of us] try to give one of the "good" cases to each judge.
D	Our practice is that the presiding judge makes the assignments, unless that judge is preliminarily dissenting. Much is done by agreement. If there is a division, often we seek to ask the least committed judge to take a fresh look and take on the writing.
E	The presiding judge, or the most senior judge in the majority, assigns the opinion. Our general custom, as to three judge panels, is that the judge whose chambers prepared the pre-argument memo is assigned the opinion if he or she is in the majority. However, that is custom only, and the presiding judge retains assignment authority.
F	The presiding judge on the panel must be an active circuit judge. The presiding judge is either the Chief Judge, if [he or she] is sitting that day, or the active judge most senior in commission. Either way, the presiding judge assigns all cases, even if he or she will probably dissent.
G	Generally, we try to give Senior Judges first pick as to writing assignment.
H	Although the senior-most judge has authority to assign, generally opinions are chosen in seniority order and/or colleagues indicate which opinions they want to write.
I	By custom, the presider assigns argued cases. Prior to argument, the presider proposes to the panel a three-way assignment of all cases, to then be applicable to all cases that are not argued. The default assumption is that these cases will result in non-precedential opinions, although sometimes a submitted case presents an issue suggesting precedential treatment.
J	The presiding judge assigns all opinions, unless that judge is dissenting, in which case the most senior judge in the majority assigns the opinion drafting. The presiding judge attempts to assign the cases evenly, based on number and difficulty, with any extra case or more difficult case being assigned to the presiding judge. Our custom is a judge does not lobby for or against any particular assignment and always accepts the presiding judge's assignments.
K	Yes, the most senior active judge in the majority assigns.
L	No
M	The Chief Judge of the Court will make the official assignment of the authoring judge for each case. However, the recommendations of the panel are usually followed by the Chief. The memorandum will also indicate the level of difficulty of the writing assignment. If a district court judge is sitting, we try to avoid assigning him/her to author an opinion that reverses a district court judge.

6. When a proposed opinion is circulated to the panel, do you have any rules regarding when panel members must respond?	
Circuits	**Answers**
A	Yes. Judges should give priority to acting on the opinions of fellow judges. Any dissent or special concurrence shall be circulated within 30 days from the date of circulation of the proposed majority opinion. After 30 days, the majority opinion may be filed with a notation reserving the right to file a further opinion.
B	The practice among judges is to give priority to … a proposed opinion from a colleague, and the informal goal is to concur or indicate otherwise within 30 days. With respect to cases on the non-argument calendar, the court's informal goal is … for the second and third judges to act within 21 days [of circulation of the opinion by the writing judge].
C	We have a 10 day rule by custom. You should let a judge know if you can't comply.
D	Most of us have a practice of responding within 24 hours for an average case or 48 hours for a heavier case. If a judge needs to take longer, most judges will send a courtesy memo so stating.
E	1. As to three-judge panels … judges should respond as soon as convenient, and notify the transmitting judge if it cannot be accomplished in 7 days. [We] allow[] the filing of a disposition if two judges have concurred and the third judge has not responded within 60 days. 2. In en banc cases, the Chief sets the timetable, but judges who plan to write separately notify the other members of the panel within 14 days after circulation of the majority opinion.
F	The … Circuit's Internal Operating Procedures address this …. A panel member is supposed to give the circulating opinion top priority and to respond within 14 days. If the response indicates that the other judge wishes to write separately, the dissent or concurrence is supposed to be circulated within 28 days. These rules are not closely followed.
G	The norm is to stop whatever you are doing and comment on the draft.
H	Each judge must try to respond to drafts within five calendar days. If a good reason prevents this, a judge must contact the writing judge to explain and then try to respond as promptly as possible.
I	Our IOP [Internal Operating Procedure] setting forth a time by which non-authoring judges shall respond to the author of the opinion has no method for "enforcement" and is, in practice, merely exhortational.
J	Circulated opinions take first priority. We have an informal custom of responding within 24 hours or asking for more time, which is usually followed.
K	Our procedures say "voting should be given a priority."
L	Yes. We have advisory rules on when panel members must respond, with different time periods for unpublished and published opinions.
M	There is no rule as to when the panel members must respond. In respect for our long tradition of collegiality, panel members will promptly respond by submitting their comments, indicating their concurrence, or stating their intent to write separately.

7. Do you have any rules or customs regarding when Judges must complete their writing assignments?	
Circuits	**Answers**
A	Yes. In civil cases, the decision must issue within 75 days from submission in summary calendar cases and within 90 days from the date of oral argument. In criminal cases, 45 days and 60 days respectively.
B	Our judges understand that prompt disposition is desirable. As an aid to judges in this regard, the court has an informal goal that after oral argument, a substantial percentage of a judge's cases should be circulated to the panel within 60 days .... With respect to cases on the non-argument calendar, the court's informal goal is for the writing judge to circulate an opinion within 60 days ....
C	No. Most have a 6 month from oral argument alarm that goes off.
D	Our practice is that judges are expected to circulate draft opinions within 60 days of argument. Some of our judges find that requirement unrealistic.
E	As to three-judge panels, there are no deadlines. However, at our quarterly court meetings, judges who have not circulated wan opinion within 6 months of submission are required to provide a status report and projected completion date. As to en banc panels, the majority opinion is to be circulated with[in] 45 days after argument, and dissents or separate writings within 30 days after circulation of the majority opinion.
F	Yes, [the] IOP [Internal Operating Procedure] ... addresses this subject in detail.
G	We try to have the opinions filed within 60 days.
H	Judges should make every effort to circulate an opinion within 90 days of assignment. Any judge with three or more assigned opinions pending that are not in circulation to the panel on August 15 will not be assigned to sit on new cases until the backlog is cleared.
I	No
J	We have 60 days and 90 day reports to the chief judge, but nor rules or customs otherwise. The chief judge in an extraordinary situation may speak to a judge who falls behind to determine if that judge needs some assistance.
K	No rules on majority opinions. However, our monthly statistics report lists cases that are over 180 days. Dissents must be circulated within 30 days after the majority opinion is circulated.
L	Yes. We follow the same advisory rules of when judges must circulate an opinion.
M	We have a rule requiring any opinion that has not been circulated and filed within 75[ ] days of its assignment be recorded on a 75-day list, which is distributed to the entire Court. We use this system to encourage promptness in circulating majority opinions, concurrences, and dissents.

8. How many sitting days does an active judge have during a court term?	
Circuits	**Answers**
A	Each active judge has seven sittings of four days each. [28 days]
B	Recently an active judge has had 20 days of oral arguments during a court year. Oral argument cases comprise approximately 15% of the Circuit's caseload. Cases on the non-argument calendar – where the panel has unanimously agreed that oral argument is unnecessary because the issues have been authoritatively decided and/or the decisional process would not be significantly aided by oral argument – are circulated to the writing judge, who prepares an opinion based on the briefs and the record, circulates same to the second judge, and then to the third judge. Each active judge acts as writing judge, second judge, and third judge on a pro-rata share of cases on the non-argument calendar.
C	15–17
D	In the past decade, sitting days have ranged from 20 to 30 per judge per term (September through August). In the last few years, declining dockets have led to an average in the low 20s, but filings are on the increase again. Judges fill the vacuum by writing opinions in submitted cases.
E	Currently, 32 … three-judge argument days, plus additional assigned days of motions, screening, and comeback cases. We generally have 25 en banc hearings in which a limited panel is randomly drawn.
F	Around 30. These are individual days, not a sitting "week."
G	37
H	About 23, depending upon filings.
I	We have no "terms," but each active judge has 5 ½–6 ½ sittings/year. As our caseload has declined, so have the number of sitting days.
J	32 to 38 days
K	Approximately 40
L	28 days, excluding en banc and death-penalty arguments.
M	18–24

9. About how many cases are heard during a single sitting day?	
Circuits	**Answers**
A	A maximum of five cases are heard in one day.
B	The number of cases per day on the oral argument calendar is adjusted depending upon the case load of oral argument cases. In recent years, it has averaged approximately four.
C	6
D	6
E	4–8, depending on complexity. On intake, the Clerk's office assigns a complexity weight from 3 to 10 (and assigning a 24 weight to capital cases). A day's oral argument calendar consists of a total of 24 points.
F	Six normally, except for our "short argument" days (several per judge each year), where there will be nine.
G	5–7
H	Usually 3, sometimes 4, depending upon filings.
I	This number has become too varied to be able to state an average. Customarily, we attempt to avoid more than 4 oral arguments / day.
J	Five, although we have had six or, on a rare occasion, seven when the docket is heavy.
K	Approximately 4
L	It vari[e]s from panel to panel and sitting to sitting. The average is probably four, but there are as many or more cases on the same calendar that are submitted on the briefs and are to be considered and discussed at conference.
M	Four cases

10. What is the average amount of time that you allow per side in oral arguments?	
Circuits	**Answers**
A	Each case is allocated twenty minutes per side. In complex civil or criminal cases and death penalty cases, thirty minutes per side is allowed.
B	The published calendars sets the time per side. The usual time per side is 15 minutes, although some are set for 20 minutes or longer. A motion can request additional time.
C	15 minutes per side. Death penalty is 20 minutes.
D	15 minutes.
E	10 minutes for 3-weight; 15 minutes for 5-weight; 20 minutes for cases above a 5-weight; 30 minutes for capital and en banc cases.
F	Depending on difficulty, 20 minutes/side, 15 minutes/side, or 10 minutes/side. For exceptional cases, such as those involving the death penalty, it will be 30 minutes/side, extendable by the presiding judge.
G	10 minutes
H	The average time granted to a litigant is 15 minutes, but panel questioning usually goes on considerably longer.
I	Fifteen minutes/side in the mine-run case. Longer where cases are complex and/or present multiple substantial issues. Panels agree on this in advance.
J	15 minutes – some others have 10, 20, or 30; but 15 is the most common.
K	15 minutes per side
L	15 minutes. More time for en banc and death-penalty cases.
M	20 minutes

11. About how many opinions does an active judge write each term (not including dissenting or concurring opinions)?[43]

Circuits	Answers
A	163. Our court uses several processes for disposing of cases on the merits. The 163 number is a composite number of the average opinion output for each active judge who participated in disposing of cases on the merits on either a summary calendar, oral argument, or conference calendar. More often than not, these dispositions will not be "published"/precedential opinions. The conference calendar for example focuses principally on large numbers of prisoner and *pro se* appeals that are controlled by settled circuit precedent. As you know, each circuit's volume and makeup varies considerably and affects the processes that each uses. I know that some circuits use "judgments and orders" as part of their processes and the screening mechanisms differ also, so trying to compare the numbers can be a bit nuanced!! [The] states [in our circuit] are death penalty states for example, and those appeals are part of our overall numbers.
B	About 16
C	30–34
D	50–60
E	[Approximate estimate]: 20–30 precedential opinions and 200 non-precedent dispositions. (That figure does not include cases decided on screening panels.)
F	[Approximately] 75 or 80. We hear oral argument in every case in which there is a lawyer on both sides, and we presumptively publish everything from orally argued cases.
G	The vast number of our dispositions are by summary orders, prepared mostly by the panel presider. In terms of full opinions, ... somewhere between 12–20 opinions are written by actives.
H	About 16–20, depending upon the year.
I	One to three POs [Precedential Opinions] per sitting. About 1/3 of the NPOs [Non-Precedential Opinions] resulting from the sitting schedule.
J	50
K	45–50
L	70–75 approx.
M	24–30

43 The figures on this chart are complicated and possibly confusing. Some answers refer to the number of 'published' decisions written by each judge, and some (as for 'Circuit A') refer to both published and unpublished dispositions.

Additional comments to amplify any of your answers to the questions posed above:	
Circuits	**Answers**
A	
B	
C	
D	
E	
F	
G	
H	
I	[We sometimes follow] a practice by which a panel engages in some (and often substantial) dialog concerning cases listed for a sitting. These discussions ultimately lead to decisions concerning which listed cases will be argued (although IOPs require argument when only one judge requests it[)]. These preliminary discussions also permit panel members to: (1) resolve threshold issues; (2) hone other issues; (3) determine how much argument time should be accorded each side; (4) discuss what is or may be worthy of precedential treatment; and (5) share specific concerns in advance of the sitting.
J	
K	
L	
M	

B. Case Processing Statistics for the US Courts of Appeals During the Five Terms from 2011–2012 Through 2015–2016

B.1. Explanation of the Data

The tables on the following pages contain case data for the US Courts of Appeals in every circuit except the Federal Circuit. What follows is a brief explanation of the data and how it was collected:

Total Number of Decisions on the Merits: The Administrative Office of the United States Courts ('AO') tracks how many decisions on the merits are issued each year by each circuit. (A 'year' starts on 1 October and ends the following 30 September. For example: 1 October 2011 through 30 September 2012.)

Published Decisions: The AO tracks how many 'published' decisions on the merits are issued each year by each circuit.

Unpublished Decisions: The number of 'unpublished' decisions on the merits is calculated by subtracting the number of published decisions from the total number of dispositions in a year.

Number and Percentage of Decisions with at Least One Concurring Opinion: Westlaw searches captured nearly all published decisions for each circuit in a given year. Within that group of decisions, Boolean searches captured the universe of decisions with concurring opinions. To determine percentages, the number of decisions with concurring opinions were divided by either the number of published decisions or the total all decisions on the merits for that year.

Number and Percentage of Decisions with at Least One Dissenting Opinion: This category includes both decisions with a dissent, and decisions with a separate opinion concurring in part and dissenting in part. Westlaw searches captured all published decisions in a given year with dissenting opinions and/or with opinions concurring in part and dissenting in part. To determine percentages, the number of decisions with dissenting opinions were divided by either the number of published decisions or the total all decisions on the merits for that year.

Decisions with Multiple Concurring and Dissenting Opinions: If a decision included two concurrences, it was counted only once. If a decision had both a dissenting opinion *and* an opinion concurring in part and dissenting in part, it was counted only once in the dissenting opinions category. If a decision had both a separate dissenting opinion and a separate concurring opinion, however, it was counted once for each category.

Number of Active and Senior Judges: These data were collected from the database available at the Federal Judicial Center, 'History of the Federal Judiciary', http://www.fjc.gov/history/home.nsf/page/research_categories.html. These data are current through 6 March 2017.

B.2. 'Unpublished' Decisions

Federal Rule of Appellate Procedure 32.1 gives guidance to the courts of appeals on 'unpublished' decisions. The Rule provides, as follows:

> 'Rule 32.1 – Citing Judicial Dispositions
>
> (a) Citation Permitted. A court may not prohibit or restrict the citation of federal judicial opinions, orders, judgments, or other written dispositions that have been:
>   (i) designated as "unpublished," "not for publication," "non-precedential," "not precedent," or the like; and
>   (ii) issued on or after January 1, 2007.
>
> (b) Copies Required. If a party cites a federal judicial opinion, order, judgment, or other written disposition that is not available in a publicly accessible electronic database, the party must file and serve a copy of that opinion, order, judgment, or disposition with the brief or other paper in which it is cited.'

A good discussion of 'unpublished' decisions is available in David R Cleveland's article, 'Local Rules in the Wake of Federal Rule of Appellate Procedure 32.1'.[44] Professor Cleveland usefully explains that:

> 'Publication, citation, and precedent are three different aspects of common law opinions. They are related, but not necessarily dependent upon one another. The degree to which common law opinions have possessed these characteristics has varied throughout the history of the common law. Early decisions were rarely published, and were precedent only in the aggregate, but were always citable to the court. Later, as decisions became more commonly published, the power of precedent increased, and, of course, litigants remained free to urge upon the court an action it had previously taken by citing past decisions. This trend of increasingly common publication and increasingly strong precedent was a feature of both colonial America and England in that period. By the end of the nineteenth century, the entrepreneur John West had created a system of comprehensive publication of all federal appellate opinions, an effort that was of great interest to the bench and bar.[13] While other, less comprehensive, reporters and even summaries of the law like the early Restatements existed, "[l]awyers chose the comprehensive style of reporting, preferring that all precedent be available." From the dawn of the twentieth century until the mid-1970s, that was the state of the federal judiciary as a whole: full publication, strong precedent, and unfettered citation.'[45]

[44] DR Cleveland, 'Local Rules in the Wake of Federal Rule of Appellate Procedure 32.1' (2010) 11 *Journal of Appellate Practice & Process* 19; see also Wasby (n 28).

[45] Ibid 21–22 (footnotes omitted).

Times have changed, however, and Professor Cleveland argues that the reference to 'unpublished' decisions is now a misnomer:

> '[The] tripartite system has largely fallen apart – crushed under the inexorable turn of the wheels' progress, which themselves are driven by the inherent demand for readily accessible precedent among lawyers, litigants, and judges. The restrictions on publication have been undone by changes in technology and by persistent practices of the federal bar and federal judiciary. Though still labeled "unpublished opinions," these opinions are published, not only online but also in printed volumes such as the West's Federal Appendix. This is in large part due to the continuous use of these opinions by practitioners and judges--despite the opinions' citation or precedential status. Second, new Rule 32.1 allows citations of all opinions presently being issued by the federal courts of appeals. This was good news for the large number of judges and lawyers already using these opinions despite the citation ban. These opinions are now effectively published and plainly citable. What remains is the same ambiguity inherent in the system since the first local rules on the subject following the 1973 Committee's recommendation: What is the precedential value of these opinions? New Rule 32.1 did not resolve this issue, and the local rules in its wake have continued to come to different answers in different circuits.'[46]

Professor Cleveland's principal findings regarding the Courts of Appeals' regulation of 'unpublished' decisions in recent years are noteworthy:[47]

- What makes a decision suitable for non-publication is still subject to different rules in different circuits. The generally accepted characteristic of unpublished opinions is that they apply settled law to facts so unremarkable that the case does not expand or contract the law.
- The citability of unpublished opinions issued before January 1, 2007, remains in flux; local rules vary from completely permissive to completely restrictive to unclear. This undercuts the uniformity that the new federal rule was supposed to bring to the federal justice system regarding the use of unpublished opinions.
- [T]he precedential status of unpublished opinions ... remains an issue of particular disagreement among the circuits' local rules .... While the majority of circuits do not view unpublished opinions as precedential, there is a significant minority that take a different, if less unequivocally stated, position.

---

46 Ibid 23–24 (footnotes omitted).

47 Ibid 27–28, 48, 49, 55 (footnotes omitted).

B.3. The Vast Majority Of The Decisions Issued By The Courts Of Appeals Are Unanimous

The data on the pages below confirm that very few dissenting and concurring opinions accompany the decisions issued by the Courts of Appeals in the United States. Data has been collected for 12 of the 13 circuits – the First through the Eleventh Circuits, and the DC Circuit. No information was available for the Federal Circuit.

'Unpublished' decisions constituted nearly 90 percent of all dispositions by Courts of Appeals between 2011 and 2016. There were 151,771 unpublished decisions out of 172,680 total dispositions (87.89% of the total). I have assumed that dissents rarely, if ever, accompany unpublished decisions.

Between 2011 and 2016, counting both 'published' and 'unpublished' decisions, the courts of appeals issued a total of 172,680 decisions on the merits. Only 2,220 of these decisions (or 1.3% of the total) included a dissent.

Between 2011 and 2016, the Courts of Appeals issued a total of 20,909 'published' decisions. Only 2,220 of these decisions (10.6% of the total) included a dissent.

B.4. First Circuit

	2011–2012	2012–2013	2013–2014	2014–2015	2015–2016
Total Dispositions on the Merits	972	936	870	914	941
Published	357	325	313	351	326
Unpublished	615	611	557	563	615
Number of decisions with at least one Concurrence	13	6	4	10	10
Decisions with at least one Concurrence as a % of Published Dispositions	3.6%	1.8%	1.3%	2.8%	3.1%
Decisions with at least one Concurrence as a % of Total Dispositions	1.3%	0.6%	0.5%	1.1%	1.1%
Number of decisions with at least one Dissent	14	14	13	17	12
Decisions with at least one Dissent as a % of Published Dispositions	3.9%	4.3%	4.2%	4.8%	3.7%
Decisions with at least one Dissent as a % of Total Dispositions	1.4%	1.5%	1.5%	1.9%	1.3%

Number of Active Judges as of 6 March 2017: 6.
Number of Senior Judges as of 6 March 2017: 5.

B.5. Second Circuit

	2011–2012	2012–2013	2013–2014	2014–2015	2015–2016
Total Dispositions on the Merits	3448	3085	2825	2628	2622
Published	286	359	275	281	251
Unpublished	3162	2726	2550	2347	2371
Number of decisions with at least one Concurrence	15	20	11	14	15
Decisions with at least one Concurrence as a % of Published Dispositions	5.2%	5.6%	4%	5%	6%
Decisions with at least one Concurrence as a % of Total Dispositions	0.4%	0.6%	0.4%	0.5%	0.6%
Number of decisions with at least one Dissent	19	22	30	18	21
Decisions with at least one Dissent as a % of Published Dispositions	6.6%	6.1%	10.9%	6.4%	8.4%
Decisions with at least one Dissent as a % of Total Dispositions	0.6%	0.7%	1.1%	0.7%	0.8%

Number of Active Judges as of 6 March 2017: 11.
Number of Senior Judges as of 6 March 2017: 11.

B.6. Third Circuit

	2011–2012	2012–2013	2013–2014	2014–2015	2015–2016
Total Dispositions on the Merits	2493	2715	2402	2118	2246
Published	239	169	184	152	158
Unpublished	2254	2546	2218	1966	2088
Number of decisions with at least one Concurrence	12	10	4	10	11
Decisions with at least one Concurrence as a % of Published Dispositions	5%	5.9%	2.2%	6.6%	7%
Decisions with at least one Concurrence as a % of Total Dispositions	0.5%	0.4%	0.2%	0.5%	0.5%
Number of decisions with at least one Dissent	19	25	22	21	25
Decisions with at least one Dissent as a % of Published Dispositions	7.9%	14.8%	12%	13.8%	15.8%
Decisions with at least one Dissent as a % of Total Dispositions	0.8%	0.9%	0.9%	1%	1.1%

Number of Active Judges as of 6 March 2017: 11.
Number of Senior Judges as of 6 March 2017: 11.

B.7. Fourth Circuit

	2011–2012	2012–2013	2013–2014	2014–2015	2015–2016
Total Dispositions on the Merits	3808	3828	3603	3194	4874
Published	238	233	224	198	178
Unpublished	3570	3595	3379	2996	4696
Number of decisions with at least one Concurrence	20	26	23	18	14
Decisions with at least one Concurrence as a % of Published Dispositions	8.4%	11.2%	10.3%	9.1%	7.9%
Decisions with at least one Concurrence as a % of Total Dispositions	0.5%	0.7%	0.6%	0.6%	0.3%
Number of decisions with at least one Dissent	48	37	44	38	27
Decisions with at least one Dissent as a % of Published Dispositions	20.1%	15.9%	19.6%	19.2%	15.2%
Decisions with at least one Dissent as a % of Total Dispositions	1.3%	1%	1.2%	1.2%	0.6%

Number of Active Judges as of 6 March 2017: 15.
Number of Senior Judges as of 6 March 2017: 4.

B.8. Fifth Circuit

	2011–2012	2012–2013	2013–2014	2014–2015	2015–2016
Total Dispositions on the Merits	4027	4176	4267	4045	4484
Published	353	358	402	332	430
Unpublished	3674	3818	3865	3713	4054
Number of decisions with at least one Concurrence	20	29	28	18	13
Decisions with at least one Concurrence as a % of Published Dispositions	5.7%	8.1%	7%	5.4%	3%
Decisions with at least one Concurrence as a % of Total Dispositions	0.5%	0.7%	0.7%	0.4%	0.3%
Number of decisions with at least one Dissent	46	39	47	38	44
Decisions with at least one Dissent as a % of Published Dispositions	13%	10.9%	11.7%	11.4%	10.2%
Decisions with at least one Dissent as a % of Total Dispositions	1.1%	0.9%	1.1%	0.9%	1%

Number of Active Judges as of 6 March 2017: 14.
Number of Senior Judges as of 6 March 2017: 8.

B.9. Sixth Circuit

	2011-2012	2012-2013	2013-2014	2014-2015	2015-2016
Total Dispositions on the Merits	3297	3588	3238	3147	3250
Published	403	340	261	313	304
Unpublished	2894	3248	2977	2834	2946
Number of decisions with at least one Concurrence	26	25	32	25	28
Decisions with at least one Concurrence as a % of Published Dispositions	6.5%	7.4%	12.3%	8%	9.2%
Decisions with at least one Concurrence as a % of Total Dispositions	0.8%	0.7%	1%	0.8%	0.9%
Number of decisions with at least one Dissent	51	57	56	46	53
Decisions with at least one Dissent as a % of Published Dispositions	12.7%	16.8%	21.5%	14.7%	17.4%
Decisions with at least one Dissent as a % of Total Dispositions	1.5%	1.6%	1.7%	1.5%	1.6%

Number of Active Judges as of 6 March 2017: 14.
Number of Senior Judges as of 6 March 2017: 11.

B.10. Seventh Circuit

	2011-2012	2012-2013	2013-2014	2014-2015	2015-2016
Total Dispositions on the Merits	1470	1702	1737	1588	2098
Published	571	570	635	590	634
Unpublished	899	1132	1102	998	1464
Number of decisions with at least one Concurrence	11	19	14	20	19
Decisions with at least one Concurrence as a % of Published Dispositions	1.9%	3.3%	2.2%	3.4%	3%
Decisions with at least one Concurrence as a % of Total Dispositions	0.7%	1.1%	0.8%	1.3%	0.9%
Number of decisions with at least one Dissent	28	20	23	25	32
Decisions with at least one Dissent as a % of Published Dispositions	4.9%	3.5%	3.6%	4.2%	5%
Decisions with at least one Dissent as a % of Total Dispositions	1.9%	1.2%	1.3%	1.6%	1.5%

Number of Active Judges as of 6 March 2017: 9.
Number of Senior Judges as of 6 March 2017: 3.

B.11. Eighth Circuit

	2011–2012	2012–2013	2013–2014	2014–2015	2015–2016
Total Dispositions on the Merits	2175	2161	2238	2276	2419
Published	575	519	554	574	604
Unpublished	1600	1642	1684	1702	1815
Number of decisions with at least one Concurrence	19	25	30	25	24
Decisions with at least one Concurrence as a % of Published Dispositions	3.3%	4.8%	5.4%	4.4%	4%
Decisions with at least one Concurrence as a % of Total Dispositions	0.9%	1.2%	1.3%	1.1%	1%
Number of decisions with at least one Dissent	55	50	51	46	59
Decisions with at least one Dissent as a % of Published Dispositions	9.6%	9.6%	9.2%	8%	9.8%
Decisions with at least one Dissent as a % of Total Dispositions	2.5%	2.3%	2.3%	2%	2.4%

Number of Active Judges as of 6 March 2017: 9.
Number of Senior Judges as of 6 March 2017: 6.

B.12. Ninth Circuit

	2011–2012	2012–2013	2013–2014	2014–2015	2015–2016
Total Dispositions on the Merits	7938	7247	7222	6551	6709
Published	605	589	565	557	516
Unpublished	7333	6658	6657	5994	6193
Number of decisions with at least one Concurrence	34	51	51	44	46
Decisions with at least one Concurrence as a % of Published Dispositions	5.6%	8.7%	9%	7.9%	8.9%
Decisions with at least one Concurrence as a % of Total Dispositions	0.4%	0.7%	0.7%	0.7%	0.7%
Number of decisions with at least one Dissent	120	106	126	91	101
Decisions with at least one Dissent as a % of Published Dispositions	19.8%	18%	22.3%	16.3%	19.6%
Decisions with at least one Dissent as a % of Total Dispositions	1.5%	1.5%	1.7%	1.4%	1.5%

Number of Active Judges as of 6 March 2017: 25.
Number of Senior Judges as of 6 March 2017: 19.

B.13. Tenth Circuit

	2011–2012	2012–2013	2013–2014	2014–2015	2015–2016
Total Dispositions on the Merits	1315	1460	1424	1267	1571
Published	240	264	298	256	234
Unpublished	1075	1196	1126	1011	1337
Number of decisions with at least one Concurrence	18	17	17	16	15
Decisions with at least one Concurrence as a % of Published Dispositions	7.5%	6.4%	5.7%	6.3%	6.4%
Decisions with at least one Concurrence as a % of Total Dispositions	1.4%	1.2%	1.2%	1.3%	1%
Number of decisions with at least one Dissent	18	11	18	20	30
Decisions with at least one Dissent as a % of Published Dispositions	7.5%	4.2%	6%	7.8%	12.8%
Decisions with at least one Dissent as a % of Total Dispositions	1.4%	0.8%	1.3%	1.6%	1.9%

Number of Active Judges as of 6 March 2017: 12.
Number of Senior Judges as of 6 March 2017: 9.

B.14. Eleventh Circuit

	2011–2012	2012–2013	2013–2014	2014–2015	2015–2016
Total Dispositions on the Merits	3664	3965	3807	3383	4763
Published	247	237	274	257	259
Unpublished	3417	3728	3533	3126	4504
Number of decisions with at least one Concurrence	16	27	34	15	29
Decisions with at least one Concurrence as a % of Published Dispositions	6.5%	11.4%	12.4%	5.8%	11.2%
Decisions with at least one Concurrence as a % of Total Dispositions	0.4%	0.7%	0.9%	0.4%	0.6%
Number of decisions with at least one Dissent	17	26	27	18	26
Decisions with at least one Dissent as a % of Published Dispositions	6.9%	11%	9.9%	7%	10%
Decisions with at least one Dissent as a % of Total Dispositions	.5%	.7%	.7%	.5%	.5%

Number of Active Judges as of 6 March 2017: 10.
Number of Senior Judges as of 6 March 2017: 4.

B.15. DC Circuit

	2011–2012	2012–2013	2013–2014	2014–2015	2015–2016
Total Dispositions on the Merits	488	439	481	511	570
Published	198	202	221	253	218
Unpublished	290	237	260	258	352
Number of decisions with at least one Concurrence	24	29	19	28	19
Decisions with at least one Concurrence as a % of Published Dispositions	12.1%	14.4%	8.6%	11.1%	8.7%
Decisions with at least one Concurrence as a % of Total Dispositions	4.9%	6.6%	4%	5.5%	3.3%
Number of decisions with at least one Dissent	26	14	24	24	25
Decisions with at least one Dissent as a % of Published Dispositions	13.1%	6.9%	10.9%	9.5%	11.5%
Decisions with at least one Dissent as a % of Total Dispositions	5.3%	3.2%	5%	4.7%	4.4%

Number of Active Judges as of 6 March 2017: 11.
Number of Senior Judges as of 6 March 2017: 7.

B.16. Totals for All Circuits

Total dissents: 2,220

Total concurrences: 1,265

Total published: 20,909

Total decisions on the merits: 172,680

Percentage of total decisions on the merits with at least one concurrence: 0.73%

Percentage of total decisions on the merits with at least one dissent: 1.3%

C. Additional Data on the Work of the US Courts of Appeals from 2011–2012 Through 2015–2016

C.1. Number of *En Banc* Dispositions in each Circuit

US Courts of Appeals
Cases Terminated on the Merits After Oral Hearing or Submission
En Banc, by Circuit, During the 12-Month Period Ending 30* September

	2012	2013	2014	2015	2016
DC	1	0	1	2	0
1st	2	1	0	1	2
2nd	0	0	1	0	0
3rd	11	2	1	2	4
4th	2	2	1	3	1
5th	5	11	5	5	4
6th	3	5	1	2	4
7th	4	4	4	3	4
8th	3	2	7	2	1
9th	22	14	17	20	21
10th	4	0	0	1	0
11th	2	4	1	2	0
TOTAL	**59**	**45**	**40**	**43**	**41**

*Includes Initial Hearings or Rehearings *En Banc*
Source: Administrative Office of the United States Courts, Washington, DC, Statistical Tables for the Federal Judiciary, tbl.B-10, US Courts of Appeals—Cases Terminated on the Merits after Oral Arguments or Submission on Briefs, by Circuit, During the 12-Month Period Ending 30 September (formerly Table S-1).

C.2. Total Decisions on the Merits (both Published and Unpublished) Issued by Each Circuit

US Courts of Appeals
Cases Terminated on the Merits, by Circuit,
During the 12-Month Period Ending 30 September

(These totals are for 'lead case' dispositions. In other words, the numbers do not include cases that were consolidated with the lead case.)

	2012	2013	2014	2015	2016
DC	488	439	481	511	570
1st	972	936	870	914	941
2nd	3,448	3,085	2,825	2,628	2,622
3rd	2,493	2,715	2,402	2,118	2,246
4th	3,808	3,828	3,603	3,194	4,874
5th	4,027	4,176	4,267	4,045	4,484
6th	3,297	3,588	3,238	3,147	3,250
7th	1,470	1,702	1,737	1,588	2,098
8th	2,175	2,161	2,238	2,276	2,419
9th	7,938	7,247	7,222	6,551	6,709
10th	1,315	1,460	1,424	1,267	1,571
11th	3,664	3,965	3,807	3,383	4,763
TOTAL	**35,095**	**35,302**	**34,114**	**31,622**	**36,547**

Source: Administrative Office of the United States Courts, Washington, DC, Statistical Tables for the Federal Judiciary, tbl.B-10, US Courts of Appeals—Cases Terminated on the Merits after Oral Arguments or Submission on Briefs, by Circuit, During the 12-Month Period Ending 30 September (formerly Table S-1).

C.3. Published Decisions on the Merits Issued by Each Circuit

US Courts of Appeals
Published Decisions in Cases Terminated on the Merits, by Circuit, During the 12-Month Period Ending 30 September 30

	2012	2013	2014	2015	2016
DC	198	202	221	253	218
1st	357	325	313	351	326
2nd	286	359	275	281	251
3rd	239	169	184	152	158
4th	238	233	224	198	178
5th	353	358	402	332	430
6th	403	340	261	313	304
7th	571	570	635	590	634
8th	575	519	554	574	604
9th	605	589	565	557	516
10th	240	264	298	256	234
11th	247	237	274	257	259
TOTAL	**4,312**	**4,165**	**4,206**	**4,114**	**4,112**

Source: Administrative Office of the United States Courts, Washington, DC, Statistical Tables for the Federal Judiciary, tbl.B-10, US Courts of Appeals—Type of Opinion or Order Filed in Cases Terminated on the Merits, by Circuit, During the 12-Month Period Ending 30 September (formerly Table S-3).

C.4. The Average Time per Appeal from the Date of Filing to the Date of Disposition

US Courts of Appeals
Median Time Interval in Months from Filing of Notice of Appeal or Docket Date to Last Opinion or Final Order for Cases Terminated on the Merits, by Circuit, During the 12-Month Period Ending 30 September

	2012	2013	2014	2015	2016
DC	10.4	12.6	13.4	13.8	11.7
1st	11.1	11.2	11.5	13.0	10.8
2nd	12.2	10.4	10.6	10.2	10.8
3rd	7.7	6.3	6.4	8.4	6.7
4th	5.7	5.0	5.2	5.3	4.0
5th	9.0	9.3	8.9	9.4	8.8
6th	14.7	10.1	9.1	8.6	8.3
7th	8.3	8.0	7.1	7.2	5.8
8th	5.5	5.8	6.0	5.3	5.3
9th	15.3	13.3	12.4	14.1	15.2
10th	8.3	8.2	8.3	7.8	6.7
11th	7.2	7.6	7.1	7.4	4.4
TOTAL	**9.8**	**9.0**	**8.5**	**8.5**	**7.4**

Source: Administrative Office of the United States Courts, Washington, DC, Statistical Tables for the Federal Judiciary, tbl.B-10, US Courts of Appeals—Median Time Intervals in Months for Cases Terminated on the Merits, by Circuit, During the 12-Month Period Ending 30 September.

C.5. The Average Time per Case from the Date of Oral Argument to the Date of Disposition

US Courts of Appeals
Median Time Interval in Months from Oral Argument to Last Opinion or Final Order for Cases Terminated on the Merits, by Circuit, During the 12-Month Period Ending 30 September

	2012	2013	2014	2015	2016
DC	2.4	2.7	3.0	3.7	3.1
1st	3.2	2.7	3.1	3.0	2.4
2nd	0.7	0.8	0.9	0.5	0.6
3rd	3.1	3.0	3.4	3.4	3.9
4th	2.1	2.2	2.0	2.4	2.2
5th	1.3	1.3	1.4	1.2	1.3
6th	2.8	2.7	2.3	2.7	2.5
7th	3.2	3.2	2.8	2.9	2.8
8th	3.6	3.6	3.6	3.5	3.9
9th	1.1	1.2	1.1	1.3	1.1
10th	3.7	4.3	3.9	3.7	3.0
11th	1.9	1.6	1.7	2.1	1.8
TOTAL	**2.1**	**2.1**	**2.1**	**2.1**	**2.0**

Source: Administrative Office of the United States Courts, Washington, DC, Statistical Tables for the Federal Judiciary, tbl.B-10, US Courts of Appeals—Median Time Intervals in Months for Cases Terminated on the Merits, by Circuit, During the 12-Month Period Ending 30 September.

C.6. Number of Cases Decided on the Merits after Oral Argument

See: http://www.uscourts.gov/data-table-numbers/b-10

The percentages shown in these charts are deceptive because 'total cases' includes all consolidated cases. In other words, a decision on the merits may dispose of a number of cases – the 'lead case' and any cases that were consolidated with the lead case. However, there is only one oral argument and one decision for all of the consolidated cases.

US Courts of Appeals—Appeals Terminated on the Merits after Oral Arguments During the 12-Month Period Ending 30 September 2012

Circuit	Total Cases Disposed of on the Merits	Number of Cases Disposed of after Oral Arguments	Percentage of Cases in Which Oral Argument Was Heard
TOTAL	37,806	7,115	18.8
DC	712	220	30.9
First	1,052	302	28.7
Second	3,729	871	23.4
Third	2,581	313	12.1
Fourth	4,020	423	10.5
Fifth	4,630	828	17.9
Sixth	3,532	772	21.9
Seventh	1,613	617	38.3
Eighth	2,306	429	18.6
Ninth	8,372	1,562	18.7
Tenth	1,351	325	24.1
Eleventh	3,908	453	11.6

NOTE: This table does not include data for the US Court of Appeals for the Federal Circuit.

US Courts of Appeals—Appeals Terminated on the Merits after Oral Arguments During the 12-Month Period Ending 30 September 2013

Circuit	Total Cases Disposed of on the Merits	Number of Cases Disposed of after Oral Arguments	Percentage of Cases in Which Oral Argument Was Heard
TOTAL	**37,820**	**6,914**	**19.6**
DC	537	233	53.1
First	997	259	27.7
Second	3,399	958	31.1
Third	2,845	225	8.3
Fourth	4,023	432	11.3
Fifth	4,789	796	19.1
Sixth	3,798	655	18.3
Seventh	1,868	644	37.8
Eighth	2,296	396	18.3
Ninth	7,582	1,512	20.9
Tenth	1,490	354	24.2
Eleventh	4,196	450	11.3

NOTE: This table does not include data for the US Court of Appeals for the Federal Circuit.

US Courts of Appeals—Appeals Terminated on the Merits after Oral Arguments During the 12-Month Period Ending 30 September 2014

Circuit	Total Cases Disposed of on the Merits	Number of Cases Disposed of after Oral Arguments	Percentage of Cases in Which Oral Argument Was Heard
TOTAL	**36,851**	**6,646**	**19.5**
DC	634	240	49.9
First	942	248	28.5
Second	3,111	825	29.2
Third	2,493	238	9.9
Fourth	3,787	350	9.7
Fifth	5,203	805	18.9
Sixth	3,460	478	14.8
Seventh	1,902	681	39.2
Eighth	2,348	407	18.2
Ninth	7,515	1,530	21.2
Tenth	1,457	397	27.9
Eleventh	3,999	447	11.7

NOTE: This table does not include data for the US Court of Appeals for the Federal Circuit.

US Courts of Appeals—Appeals Terminated on the Merits after Oral Arguments During the 12-Month Period Ending 30 September 2015

Circuit	Total Cases Disposed of on the Merits	Number of Cases Disposed of after Oral Arguments	Percentage of Cases in Which Oral Argument Was Heard
TOTAL	**34,244**	**6,496**	**20.5**
DC	797	288	56.4
First	993	289	31.6
Second	2,914	786	29.9
Third	2,185	221	10.4
Fourth	3,363	293	9.2
Fifth	4,743	801	19.8
Sixth	3,305	526	16.7
Seventh	1,739	613	38.6
Eighth	2,394	427	18.8
Ninth	6,898	1,507	23.0
Tenth	1,301	347	27.4
Eleventh	3,612	398	11.8

NOTE: This table does not include data for the US Court of Appeals for the Federal Circuit.

US Courts of Appeals—Appeals Terminated on the Merits after Oral Arguments During the 12-Month Period Ending 30 September 2016

Circuit	Total Cases Disposed of on the Merits	Number of Cases Disposed of after Oral Arguments	Percentage of Cases in Which Oral Argument Was Heard
TOTAL	**39,252**	**6,392**	**17.5**
DC	786	262	46.0
First	998	260	27.6
Second	2,953	820	31.3
Third	2,323	208	9.3
Fourth	5,175	287	5.9
Fifth	5,028	762	17.0
Sixth	3,448	488	15.0
Seventh	2,214	638	30.4
Eighth	2,551	411	17.0
Ninth	7,056	1,556	23.2
Tenth	1,604	331	21.1
Eleventh	5,116	369	7.7

NOTE: This table does not include data for the US Court of Appeals for the Federal Circuit.

D. The US Supreme Court

Supreme Court Case Data October Terms 2011–2015

Category/Term	2011–12	2012–13	2013–14	2014–15	2015–16
Decisions on the merits (signed opinions following argument)	65	73	67	66	63
Summary Reversals	11	5	6	8	13
Number of merits opinions with unanimous judgments (Excluding summary reversals) (Percentage of total merits decisions)	26 (40%)	33 (45.2%)	42 (62.7%)	23 (34.8%)	29 (46%)
Number of merits decisions with at least one dissent (Percentage of same)*	40 (61.5%)	41 (56.2%)	27 (40.3%)	43 (65.2%)	35 (56%)
Number of merits decisions with at least one concurrence (Percentage of same)	26 (40%)	33 (45.2%)	26 (38.8%)	28 (42.4%)	25 (39.7%)
Number of merits decisions with multiple separate opinions (Percentage of same)	21 (32.3%)	27 (37%)	20 (29.9%)	37 (56.1%)	26 (41.3%)

* This category includes decisions concurring in part and dissenting in part.

Total decisions with dissents (including opinions concurring in part/dissenting in part): 186 (55.7%)

Total decisions with concurrences: 138 (41.3%)

Total decisions with unanimous judgments: 153 (45.8%)

Total signed decisions: 334 (This number includes a small number of *per curiam* decisions decided after oral argument).

Notes Regarding Data on the Work of the Supreme Court

- The 'dissents' category includes opinions with separate opinions concurring in part and dissenting in part.
- The 'Decisions on the merits' category does not count consolidated cases separately. Thus, if two cases were consolidated, they are counted as one.
- The 'dissents' and 'concurrences' categories do not include any dissents or concurrences in summary reversals issued by the Court.

- Data was compiled from the following sources:[48]
  - SCOTUSblog. E.g.: http://www.scotusblog.com/wp-content/uploads/2016/06/SB_stat_pack_OT15.pdf
  - Wikipedia. E.g., https://en.wikipedia.org/wiki/2011_term_opinions_of_the_Supreme_Court_of_the_United_States
  - https://www.supremecourt.gov

Additional Information Regarding Work of the Supreme Court

Number of arguments heard by the Court on a sitting day:

From Supremecourt.gov: '[T]he Court generally hears two one-hour arguments a day, at 10 a.m. and 11 a.m., with occasional afternoon sessions scheduled as necessary'.[49]

It is not infrequent for the Court to hear one or three arguments per day, but the most common number of arguments heard is two.

Time allotted for oral arguments:

From Supremecourt.gov: 'With rare exceptions, each side is allowed 30 minutes argument …'[50]

Number of sitting days per term:

The Court schedules 37–40 argument days per term.

Source: The Supreme Court calendars for the 2011–2016 October Terms.

48 All websites last accessed 17 February 2020.

49 https://www.supremecourt.gov/visiting/visitorsguidetooralargument.aspx.

50 https://www.supremecourt.gov/about/procedures.aspx.

PART III

COLLEGIATE COURTS IN THE EUROPEAN CIVIL LAW TRADITION

CHAPTER 6

COLLECTIVE JUDGING IN THE FRENCH *COUR DE CASSATION*

Dominique HASCHER*

I. INTRODUCTION

The expression of collegiality in the decision-making process is as diverse as there are types of jurisdictional organisations. At any rate, collegiality cannot be reduced to decision by bare majority.

Because of a particular distrust of the judiciary in France, originating in the Revolutionary period, the judicial function has historically been split among countless small-sized courts which assume their role collegially in a manner that leaves no room in the making of the judgment to the personal individuality of judges.[1] The judiciary is regarded as a branch of the civil service, where collegiality is traditionally perceived as a safeguard against the passions and arbitrariness of those who should not have been awarded a judicial position in the first place as well as a tool to counterbalance the lower level of experience of the most junior judicial panel members.[2]

The function of a supreme court has repercussions on its internal organisation and on the rules of procedure which, in turn, influence the collegial decision-making process.

---

* Dominique Hascher is Judge of the Supreme Judicial Court of France (*Cour de cassation*) and President of the *Société de législation comparée*, Paris.

1 J-L Halpérin, 'Le juge et le jugement en France à l'époque révolutionnaire' in R Jacob (ed), *Le juge et le jugement dans les traditions juridiques européennes* (Paris, LGDJ, 1996) 233.

2 J-M Coulon, M-N Teiller and E Serrand, *Réflexions et propositions sur la procédure civile* (Paris, La documentation française, 1997).

The *Cour de cassation*, which is the apex court of the general court system, was created in 1790 as a body attached to the National Assembly without power to interpret statute law. It was not before 1837 that the *Cour de cassation*, sitting in plenary session, could impose its decisions on the lower courts without referring questions of interpretation to the legislative branch of government.[3]

In the context of an absence of an independent constitutional power, the *Cour de cassation*'s role, although not that of an agent of the legislature today, is confined to applying statutes to the disputed cases, if need be, in interpreting statutory law, but – in doing so – only legal arguments can be made.[4]

The so-called 'motivation' of the judgment is necessarily brief, as is the statutory provision to be interpreted and applied.[5] The *Cour de cassation* cannot modify, add or subtract anything to written law, nor even does the Court have to explain the interpretative method it uses.[6] An appeal to the *Cour de cassation* lies only in questions of law, and the judgment only answers those questions of law which have been raised by the appeal. A judgment of the *Cour de cassation* contains no recitals of the particulars of the case, of the factual story, of the past proceedings, and no summary of the parties' respective contentions.

Although there has been a filtering process of appeals since 2001,[7] the Court does not select its cases. Because the role of the *Cour de cassation* is to correct – by way of review – erroneous judgments of lower courts, it has to hand down a judgment in every appeal raising allegations of illegality in connection with the judgment of a lower court.[8]

---

3 P Hébraud, 'Le juge et la jurisprudence' in *Mélanges offerts à Paul Couzinet* (Toulouse, Université des sciences sociales de Toulouse, 1974) 329; J Krynen, *L'Etat de Justice France, XIIIe-XXe siècle*, vol 2 (Paris, Gallimard, 2012).

4 The syllogistic form of judgments is ill adapted to other forms of reasoning beyond the deductive approach, such as the proportionality and subsidiarity techniques employed by European courts, and to the consideration of policy arguments in addition to legal arguments. See the contributions in *Juges et jugements: l'Europe plurielle* (Paris, Société de Législation Comparée, 1998).

5 A Plantey, 'L'esprit du Code', Académie des Sciences morales et politiques, session of 15 March 2004, available online via https://academiesciencesmoralesetpolitiques.files.wordpress.com/2019/01/code_civilplantey.pdf (last accessed 29 February 2020).

6 M Bobek, *Comparative Reasoning in European Supreme Courts* (Oxford, Oxford University Press, 2013) 97.

7 The Law of 25 June 2001 (Article 1014 Code of Civil Procedure) creates a procedure for non-admission, which is – however – not a screening process based on the financial interest at stake or importance of the question raised for the development of the law, because all appeals are examined by the Court. It only allows for a negative mode of control when the appeal is based on non-meritorious grounds. This dispenses the Court from giving a formal judgment.

8 J Boré, 'L'avenir du contrôle normatif face aux fluctuations du contrôle de cassation' in *Le Tribunal et la Cour de cassation 1790–1990: Volume jubilaire* (Paris, Litec, 1990) 193. 20,398 new appeals (civil and criminal) were filed in 2016: see Cour de cassation, *Rapport annuel* (Paris, La documentation française, 2017) 323.

II. COLLEGIAL WORK AND THE DECISION-MAKING PROCESS

Within different court systems, collegial work starts at very different stages of the proceedings and varies according to the degree of preparation of the case.[9] The style of proceedings will necessarily influence that moment. In common law systems, where orality of the procedure is regarded as a condition of fair trial and of an impartial process, collegial work does not really begin until after the hearing. In my experience, when a panel of common law judges assembles for the hearing, each of them has prepared individually. The members of the panel may briefly have exchanged views before entering the courtroom, and they each have individual dialogues with the parties' lawyers during the hearing.[10]

Before the *Cour de cassation*, after the expiry of time limits for the parties to file in their briefs, the case is assigned to a judge[11] of one of the six Chambers of the Court to which the case has been referred ('orientated').[12] The reporting judge, the so-called '*rapporteur*', drafts a report on the case summarising

9 The moment also varies according to the source of the decision-makers' power. In arbitration, where the legitimacy of the members of an Arbitral Tribunal derives from the will of the parties, collegial work should begin as early as possible. This is explicable against the backdrop of co-arbitrators who are close to the parties by their nomination process, the diversity of origin of the members of the Arbitral Tribunal, considering their nationality, legal education, culture and languages. In such a context, collegiality serves to create unity of the Arbitral Tribunal and to build confidence in the process. Co-arbitrators appointed by the parties are seen as fully participating in the conduct of the arbitration: see D Hascher, 'Principes et pratique de procédure dans l'arbitrage commercial international' in *Collected Courses of the Hague Academy of International Law*, vol 279 (The Hague/Boston/London, Martinus Nijhoff Publishers, 1999) 51. By comparison, judges – who are members of permanent judicial bodies – do not need to recreate a collegial environment for each case. On arbitration specifically, see SM Schwebel, 'The Majority Vote of an International Arbitral Tribunal' in *Etudes Lalive* (Basel/Frankfurt am Main, Helbing & Lichtenhahn, 1993) 671; J-D Bredin, 'Le secret du délibéré arbitral' in *Etudes Bellet* (Paris, Litec, 1991) 71; C Reymond, 'The President of the Arbitral Tribunal' (1994) 9 *ICSID Review – Foreign Investment Law Journal* 1; A Reiner, *ICC Schiedsgerichtsbarkeit: Ein Handbuch für die Praxis* (Wien, Manz, 1989).

10 Lord Carnwath, 'After the Constitutional Reform Act 2005: The Birth of the United Kingdom Supreme Court' in *Les juridictions suprêmes en France et au Royaume Uni: L'apparition de nouveaux modèles?* (Paris, Société de Législation Comparée, 2014) 35.

11 The judge can also be drawn from the ranks of the conseillers-référendaires, a category of judges in their mid-career who are appointed to the Cour de cassation for a ten-year non-renewable period (see Ordonnance n° 58-1270 du 22 December 1958, Article 28-1).

12 Article R 431-2 *Code de l'organisation judiciaire* ('COJ'). By contrast with common law jurisdictions, the *Cour de cassation*, as any other French court, is sub-divided into specialised 'benches' (Article L 421-1 COJ). Each Chamber of the *Cour de cassation* is an independent judicial community. My experience is therefore limited to the practices of the First Chamber, which deals with general private law and international law.

the questions of law raised by the appeal, the relevant precedents and legal authorities.

The report is then communicated to the parties. The *rapporteur* also compiles two other documents, which are not communicated to the parties and are for the Court's internal use only. These two documents are a note summing up the *rapporteur's* position on the case and one or more draft judgments. While freedom of access to some internal working documents of the Court (eg the report or the opinion of the Advocate General) should be seen as affirming that a supreme court is also a public forum, we are still far from a conversational approach to the law.[13]

Although the *rapporteur* may interact with colleagues of the same Chamber or of another Chamber to check a point of law falling within their area of knowledge, collegial work starts with the (electronic) communication of the report, the note and draft judgment(s) to the other members of the Chamber. This should also be considered the starting point of deliberations. If a member of the Chamber disapproves of the *rapporteur's* proposed solutions, an advance notice would be helpful for future discussions at the hearing. Otherwise, lobbying with colleagues and backstage manoeuvring unbeknownst to the *rapporteur* before the hearing entails the danger of perverting the deliberation process. The conditions under which deliberations take place ought to be organised, and certain ethical standards in the deliberating process should be respected.

The senior judge (who is typically also the *doyen*)[14] and the President of the Chamber meet before the hearing to discuss pending cases without the presence of the *rapporteur*. This two-judge court, which is called the '*conférence*', produces a number of observations on the draft judgment drawn up by the *rapporteur*, with whom it can express dissent or concur. The minutes of the Conference meetings are generally communicated two weeks before the hearing to all members of the Chamber and to the *rapporteur*,[15] who is then required to modify the draft judgment according to the suggestions made by the '*conférence*'. This amended draft will be discussed by the appropriate quorum of the Chamber.

Subject to other views of the Conference, the *rapporteur* proposes putting the case before the section panel or a limited panel of three. Each of the six Chambers is divided into sections (composed of a minimum of five judges

13 S Breyer, *Pour une démocratie active (Active Liberty)* (Paris, Odile Jacob, 2005).

14 See comment in n 28 below.

15 The outcome of the *conférence* meeting is also communicated to the Advocate General, but not to the parties. On the issue of fair trial and the status of the Advocate General, see the judgment of the ECHR in the case of *Reinhardt and Slimane-Kaïd v France*, app 21/1997/805/1008 and 22/1997/806/1009, 31 March 1998.

for deliberations)[16] and sub-sections, which are panels of three (composed of the President, the senior judge and the *rapporteur*), to which more than half of the cases are referred for decision.[17]

Orientation before a three-member panel should, as a rule, be reserved for obvious and uncontroversial decisions. In case of substantial disagreement between the *rapporteur* and the Conference, the case should be orientated before a section panel. Other considerations may come into play.[18] At any rate, each Chamber should disclose the relevant criteria for the orientation of the case before a section panel or a three-member panel. These criteria should be known of the parties and applied. Notwithstanding the possibility of calling for a plenary session of all sections of one Chamber, there is a practice according to which more difficult or important cases are deliberated, in addition to the members of one section of the Chamber, by members chosen by the President of the Chamber from amongst the members of another section. It should of course not be possible to adjust the composition of the Court in order to make up for a majority. Convening a special court in order to achieve a particular result cannot be allowed. This raises the issue of the 'legal judge' (*gesetzlicher Richter*), a concept well-known in the German judicial organisation.[19]

There are also temporary benches with judges drawn from a minimum of three chambers, namely:

(1) Joint Chambers (minimum of 13 judges) for matters falling within the purview of several Chambers or when it is likely that different solutions would be reached by different Chambers.[20] This mechanism is another opportunity for a second orientation of the appeals following their initial allocation to one of the six Chambers of the Court;
(2) Plenary sessions of the Court (19 judges) for matters of special importance and when the case is appealed a second time before the *Cour de cassation* on grounds of violation of the law.[21] The plenary session provides for a dialogue between three members of the Chamber which issued the first judgment (other than those who delivered the judgment) and their sixteen other colleagues drawn from the other Chambers of the Court.

16 Article R 431-5 COJ.
17 Article L 431-1 COJ.
18 A judgment deliberated by a section panel is, as a rule, systematically reported. On the reporting policy of the Court, see Le club des juristes, H de Castries and N Molfessis (eds), *Rapport sécurité juridique et initiative économique* (Paris, Mare et Martin, 2015) 184, available online via https://www.leclubdesjuristes.com/wp-content/uploads/2015/05/S%C3%A9curit%C3%A9-juridique-WEB.pdf (last accessed 27 March 2020).
19 See F Ferrand, *Droit processuel*, 6th edn (Paris, Dalloz, 2011) 710.
20 Articles L 421-4, L 431-5 and R 431-11 COJ.
21 Articles L 421-5, L 431-6 and R 431-11 COJ.

> The plenary session is a regulatory mechanism of the relations between the lower courts and the *Cour de cassation* as well as among lower courts themselves. In about a third of cases, the plenary session agrees with the first remanding court (the *cour d'appel de renvoi*) when the latter has refused to comply with the application of the law resulting from the judgment of the *Cour de cassation* which remanded the case. If, on the other hand, the plenary agrees with the judgment of the Chamber of the *Cour de cassation* and annuls the judgment of the first remanding court, the second remanding court must comply with the decision of the plenary. The plenary session mechanism is also a means of allowing the 'rebellion' of the lower courts to develop while controlling it by preserving the Court's mission of interpreting the law in a final manner after two turns of judicial debate.[22]

Before the *Cour de cassation*, a hearing is a formal meeting of all members of one relevant Chamber section during which the President of the Chamber invites each *rapporteur* of the cases that are orientated before the entire section to take the floor for an oral summary of the report,[23] followed by an invitation to the Advocate General to state his/her conclusions.[24] It is only in the rare occurrence that the parties inform of their presence at the oral hearing that these will be invited to summarise briefly their written arguments before the Advocate General's opinion is delivered.[25] Thereafter, the Court retires for deliberations in Chambers. These are held without the presence of the public, the parties and the Advocate General.[26] Secrecy of the deliberations has not always been the rule at the *Cour de cassation*, where the non-controversial appeals were in fact publicly deliberated until the early 20th century.[27] The post-hearing discussions mark the end of the decision-making process. At the end of the session, the judgment will be adopted without further deliberations.

III. COUNTING VOTES AND WEIGHING OPINIONS

Cases are discussed according to the seniority of each *rapporteur*. Deliberations in Chamber start by an invitation of the President to the *rapporteur* to expose

---

22 There are also informal consultation mechanisms of one Chamber by another (Article 1015-1 Code of Civil Procedure), see G Canivet, 'L'organisation interne de la Cour de cassation favorise-t-elle l'élaboration de sa jurisprudence ?' in N Molfessis (ed), *La Cour de cassation et l'élaboration du droit* (Paris, Economica, 2004) 3.

23 Article 1017 Code of Civil Procedure.

24 Article 1019 Code of Civil Procedure.

25 Article 1018 Code of Civil Procedure.

26 Article 448 Code of Civil Procedure.

27 E Faye, *La Cour de cassation* (Paris, A Chevalier-Marescq, 1903, reprinted 1999 in the *Editions la mémoire du droit*), 256. See, however, G Canivet, 'Comprendre le délibéré? Ou « Le Mystère de la chambre du Conseil »' in *Mélanges Guinchard* (Paris, Dalloz, 2010) 205.

his/her views on the case. The *rapporteur* may at that moment express disagreement with the proposals of the Conference. When the case has been orientated before the entire section, the other judges are invited next by the President to express their opinion in order of seniority. Subsequently the *référendaires* are also invited, in order of seniority, to take the floor. The views expressed by the *référendaires*, with the exception of the *rapporteur* if it happens to be a *référendaire*, are not counted for the purposes of the votes. The group of *référendaires* is therefore only consulted.

Last, the President of the Chamber gives his opinion. The President's opinion in the deliberation session is therefore the least influential, as each member of the deliberating panel has already expressed an opinion beforehand. However, in practice the proposals of the *conférence* may already reflect the joint opinion of the President and of the senior judge (although there is no rule to this effect, since it largely depends on the degree of self-confidence of the President and on how he/she gets along with the senior judge[28]). Otherwise, the proposals will primarily reflect the opinion of the senior judge, whose task it is to prepare the meetings of the *conférence*.

The senior judge and the President are not formally tied to their opinion as expressed in the proposals of the *conférence*. However, there is a strong presumption that they will cast their votes accordingly. When the case is assigned to a three-judge court, the President and the senior judge may therefore already have majority votes. This works well if cases orientated before a three-judge court are those where there is no substantive disagreement between the members of the panel. The other members of the section, aside from the three-judge court, are often present in the deliberating room during the discussion. They can make remarks on the draft judgment, but this is not formally taken into account for cases which have been orientated before a three-member panel.

Abstentions are not allowed, as this would be a breach of judicial duty tantamount to a denial of justice under Article 4 of the *Code civil*, which prohibits judges from declining to rule on a case simply because of the silence, obscurity or inadequacy of statute law.[29] Where there is a tie in the votes of one section, the case must be referred to a plenary session of the Chamber combining all sections, and if a tie again occurs there, the matter is heard before a Joint Chambers session. In practice, this seldom happens because

28 Since 2019, the role of '*doyen*' is no longer automatically assigned to the senior judge, but the *doyen* is instead chosen by the President of the Chamber from among the judges who have put themselves forward (Article R 421-6 COJ). The new nomination system impacts the status of the *doyen* in the deliberations.

29 P Bellet, 'Servitudes et libertés du juge: les articles 4 et 5 du code civil français' in P Vassart, G Haarscher, L Ingber and R Vander Elst (eds), *Arguments d'autorité et arguments de raison en droit* (Bruxelles, Nemesis, 1988) 145.

one or more members of the deliberating panel would recast their vote to end the tie.

In light of the above, the deliberating process is made up of a succession of monologues by each member, but hardly of a general discussion. Whenever a point raised by a member of the panel was unknown to the *rapporteur*, especially where the other members of the section have already discussed the matter before the hearing, the *rapporteur* should be given an opportunity to reply once all panel members have expressed their views. Most of the time however, the *rapporteur* has only one go. Persuasion of the other deliberating members of the Chamber in post-hearing deliberations without the possibility of a dialogue does not allow the *rapporteur* to engage much in a frank and open debate on the points of nicety of his/her position, as this would happen at the expense of the proposed solution being adopted.

Not all judges are equally engaged in the case. Individual interventions may even be reduced to a minimum, with an opining judge agreeing with the amended draft judgment proposed by the *conférence*, or with a previous speaker. One's personal attitude during the deliberations generally depends on the amount of work put into the preparation of the court session and/or one's interest in the subject matter of the case. But because members of the Court have no assistance in the preparation of cases, the discussions will as a rule not extend beyond the contents of the report tabled by the *rapporteur*, unless individual members have engaged in independent personal research and collected further information. In-depth discussions rarely happen.[30]

A member of the panel who disproves of the views of the *rapporteur* should not only say so, but should demonstrate that the contrary solution is preferable. Collegiality cannot be reduced to a vote. The juxtaposition of different solutions, allowing for a modification of the majority's opinion and for a compromise to be reached with the minority, requires the possibility of exchanging views.[31] Without proper debate and a right to replicate, the differences of opinions tend to be antagonised to the detriment of the final solution, and valuable opportunities of improving upon the proposed solution are lost.

---

30 As a frequent *rapporteur* of international and arbitration law matters, which essentially amount to judge-made law, I (like many of my predecessors in the bench) often have general discussions with academics in the field and practitioners about the possibility of changing of the law or overruling. This dialogue, which could be described as a form of 'enlarged deliberation', is often more precious in developing the law than the result of interactions with the other members of my Chamber in the *Cour de cassation*. See also G Canivet, 'La Cour de cassation et la doctrine' in *Mélanges Aubert* (Paris, Dalloz, 2005) 373.

31 L Husson, 'Les trois dimensions de la motivation judiciaire' in C Perelman and P Forier (eds), *La motivation des décisions de justice: Travaux du Centre national de recherches de logique* (Bruxelles, Bruylant, 1978) 69.

I would now like to return to the influence of the *rapporteur* in the deliberations. Cases are assigned to a particular judge for report depending on the legal questions raised in the appeal.[32] In judicial systems where judges are by and large assimilated to civil servants, raising the quality of a collective judging body by allowing its members to specialise in particular areas of the law, is one way of maintaining public confidence in the judicial service. This prompts a question: Might fears not therefore arise in respect of the *Cour de cassation* that a specialised judge could shape particular areas of the law without much control? Yet an affirmative answer would fail to take into consideration that an assembly vote may always result in an unforeseen outcome because the members who know best on a substantive level are not always those who are the most convincing to their colleagues.

Judgments of the *Cour de cassation* are produced by anonymous benches. The Court hands out one single and unitary judgment, without concurring or dissenting opinions.[33] A former English judge has noted the inferiority of single judgments for the development of the law: 'A single judgment must get the agreement of at least all in the majority so it tends to be no more than the highest common factor in their views'.[34] As regards the *Cour de cassation*, the single judgment must be viewed in the context of the absence of any independent power to create law, the Court's mission being confined to uncovering the meaning of written, ie statutory law. In light of the task with which the *Cour de cassation* has historically been entrusted, a single sentence judgment is best deemed to express the legislator's will under a syllogistic format.[35] The *Cour de cassation* is confined to this structure of reasoning, and it would be beyond its remit to give justifications for statute law.[36] Judgments consequently remain silent on the reasons for the decision.[37] While they enunciate the conclusion of the Court's deliberations, the discussions which

32 Article 1012 Code of Civil Procedure.

33 Dissents are not even possible under a 'sealed envelope' procedure, as permitted before the Italian *Corte di cassazione* since the enactment of the law on judges' civil liability (Article 16 of Law no 117 of 13 April 1988).

34 Lord Reid, 'The Judge as Law Maker' (1972–73) 12 *Journal of the Society of Public Teachers of Law* 22.

35 For better intellegibility of the Court's judgments, the *Rapport de la Commission de reflexion sur la réforme de la Cour de cassation* (April 2017) recommended the introduction of 'direct speech' style and the sequential numbering of paragraphs. Yet this will not amount to a break with the deductive style reasoning inherent to the traditional mission of the *Cour de cassation*, see P Bellet, 'La Cour de cassation' (1978) 30 *Revue internationale de droit comparé* 193.

36 Halpérin (n 1) 233.

37 T Bingham, 'Reasons and Reasons for Reasons: Differences Between a Court Judgment and an Arbitration Award' (1988) 4 *Arbitration International* 141.

happen during the deliberations and which motivate the judgment are not reproduced.[38]

A single judgment is further justified by a system which negates the individuality of judges and instead emphasises that the judiciary is an anonymous collective body. As remarked by Guy Canivet, former *premier président* of the *Cour de cassation*, the collegial courts exist, but judges have no individual existence.[39] Single anonymous judgments go hand-in-hand with a hierarchical career service judiciary. This may seem somewhat paradoxical, as individual authority plays an important role in assembly discussions. Deliberations in the *Cour de cassation* give rise to a diversity of opinions, but they do so in a largely unorganised manner. There is world of nuances between collegiality and collective judging considered as an interactive process among individuals.

Dissenting opinions strengthen judge-made systems of law, where collegiality is a reflection of individualism.[40] Lord Bingham once suggested that dissenting opinions should reflect five dialogues: (1) with the parties' counsels, (2) with fellow judges who disagree with the dissenter, (3) with judges who have decided precedents with which the dissenter disagrees, (4) with future generations of litigants, and (5) with foreign colleagues.[41] By contrast, members of the *Cour de cassation* would in all likelihood be incapable of writing a dissenting opinion. This is due not only to judicial culture, but also down to the fact that the role and task of judges depends in large parts on their legitimacy, which is mainly based on the mode of their selection and nomination. Before the *Cour de cassation*, individual opinions would be devoid of much significance in the making of French law. In legal systems such as those of in the common law sphere, where the judiciary better reflects society generally and where judges are chosen according to their merits and experience, individual opinions can contribute to the development of the law precisely on account of the authority of those who express them.[42]

Under the influence of European law and the European Convention for Human Rights, a number of changes have already occurred in the working methods of the *Cour de cassation*, such as the possibility of involving an *amicus curiae*, of 'impact assessment' processes, and allowing for the use of

---

38 A Touffait and A Tunc, 'Pour une motivation plus explicite des décisions de justice, notamment de celles de la Cour de cassation' [1974] *Revue Trimestrielle de Droit civil* 487.

39 Canivet (n 27) 205.

40 H Muir-Watt, 'La motivation des arrêts de la Cour de cassation et l'élaboration de la norme' in N Molfessis (ed), *La Cour de cassation et l'élaboration du droit* (Paris, Economica, 2004) 53.

41 *Fairchild v Glenhaven Funeral Services Ltd* [2002] UKHL 22, [2003] 1 AC 32 [34]–[35]; *JD v East Berkshire Community Health NHS Trust* [2005] UKHL 23, [2005] 2 AC 373, [49]–[50]. See B Markesinis, 'Laudatio for the Rt. Hon. The Lord Bingham of Cornhill, KG, Hon.' (Paris, Institut de France, 2009).

42 RB Ginsburg, 'The Role of Dissenting Opinions' (2010) 95 *Minnesota Law Review* 1.

comparative law by the *juge rapporteur*.[43] As before other supreme courts of European Union countries, there are opportunities of multilevel dialogue with the European Courts that have enhanced the rule of law and the protection of fundamental rights in Member States,[44] thus promoting broader conceptions of justice that go beyond the traditional role of the *Cour de cassation*. Judges of the *Cour de cassation* expressing themselves on societal matters should adopt the methods of the European Courts, including proportionality reasoning and other judicial techniques which would enhance the legitimacy of the *Cour de cassation* in conducting a critical appraisal of national law.

IV. CONCLUSION

Deliberation is both a simple and fragile process. Deliberating methods are crucial because of the significance of the decisions which stand at the end of a largely unorganised process. Judges are law-makers, but they have to posit for themselves rules governing their activities. As stated by a former President of the *Cour de cassation*, the legitimacy of a supreme court rests to a large extent on the adoption of a judicial method in its decision-making processes, and the transparency of the process is as important as the protection of fair trials and the clarity of judgments.[45]

---

43 *Rapport de la Commission de réflexion sur la réforme de la Cour de cassation* (April 2017), available online via https://www.courdecassation.fr/IMG/Rapport%20sur%20la%20r%C3%A9forme%20de%20la%20Cour%20de%20cassation.pdf (last accessed 29 February 2020). See also G Canivet, 'The Practice of Comparative Law by the Supreme Courts: Brief Reflection on the Dialogue between the Judges in French and European Experience' in B Markesinis and J Fedtke (eds), *Judicial Recourse to Foreign Law: A New Source of Inspiration?* (London, UCL Press, 2006), also available via (2006) 80 *Tulane Law Review* 1377; M Rolland, 'La magistrature française devant le droit comparé' in *Livre du centenaire de la SLC* (Paris, LGDJ, 1969) 341.

44 G Canivet, 'Les relations entre les cours suprêmes et la Cour de Justice des Communautés européennes', speech delivered at the University of Münster on 23 October 2006; idem, 'Activisme judiciaire et prudence interprétative' (2007) 50 *Archives de philosophie du droit* 7, also available online via https://www.courdecassation.fr/publications_26/discours_entretiens_2039/archives_2201/prudence_interpretative_9936.html (last accessed 29 February 2020).

45 G Canivet, 'Vision prospective de la Cour de cassation', Conférence à l'Académie des sciences morales et politiques, 13 November 2006, available online via https://www.courdecassation.fr/IMG/File/pdf_2006/13-11-2006_canivet.pdf (last accessed 29 February 2020).

CHAPTER 7

COLLECTIVE JUDGING IN GERMANY

Johanna SCHMIDT-RÄNTSCH*

I. INTRODUCTION

German law is created by the *Bundestag* and the *Bundesrat*, the German legislative bodies. Its essential components are characterised by the great

---

* Johanna Schmidt-Räntsch is Deputy Presiding Judge of the Vth Civil Senate of the German Federal Court of Justice (*Bundesgerichtshof*) and an honorary professor at Humboldt University in Berlin. This contribution uses parts of the author's contribution to K Riesenhuber (ed), *European Legal Methodology*, (Cambridge, Intersentia, 2017), namely 'Chapter 3 National Perspectives, §23 Germany', at 591–681.

codifications of the 19th century – the Civil Code,[1] the Land Register Code,[2] the Code of Civil Procedure,[3] the Act on Forced Sale and Forced Administration,[4] the Penal Code,[5] the Code of Criminal Procedure,[6] and the Courts Constitution Act[7] – as well as the great 20th century works of legislation in the area of public law – the Federal Building Code,[8] the Act on Administrative Procedure,[9] the Social Code,[10] and the Code of Administrative Court Procedure.[11] These codifications and laws determine the structural principles of German civil, criminal and public law, and in particular the essential rights and obligations of citizens, undertakings and public bodies. Their provisions are sometimes very detailed. A classic example of this is Article 961 BGB, which allows a beekeeper to enter the land of a third party on which his bee swarm has settled, in order to recapture the bees and return them to their hive. But the vast majority of provisions confine themselves to setting out general principles which must then be fleshed out by the courts. However, in a world that is becoming more complex, the number of such principles is increasing steadily.

Many legal cases can of course be resolved by a reading of the text of the relevant legislative provisions. In the vast majority of cases, however, the courts must (so to speak) 'translate' – judgment after judgment – the abstract rule of law into concrete real-life rules in order to make the general rule more comprehensible. German courts have thus spun a dense web of case law around numerous provisions. This is why we distinguish the written law from the law as experienced, which consists of the provision of law as well as the case law associated with it. To learn about the legal reality in Germany, it is therefore not sufficient simply to read the relevant legislative provisions.

---

1 *Bürgerliches Gesetzbuch*, abbreviated BGB; the Civil Code came into force on 1 January 1900.

2 *Grundbuchordnung*, abbreviated GBO; the Land Register Code came into force partly on 1 January 1900, partly following the installation of the land register in the German districts, at the latest by 1 January 1910.

3 *Zivilprozessordnung*, abbreviated ZPO; the Code of Civil Procedure came into force on 30 January 1877.

4 *Gesetz über die Zwangsversteigerung und die Zwangsverwaltung*, abbreviated ZVG; the Act on Forced Sale and Forced Administration came into force on 1 January 1900.

5 *Strafgesetzbuch*, abbreviated StGB; the Penal Code came into force on 15 May 1871.

6 *Strafprozessordnung*, abbreviated StPO; the Code of Criminal Procedure came into force on 1 October 1879.

7 *Gerichtsverfassungsgesetz*, abbreviated GVG; the Courts Constitution Act came into force on 1 October 1879.

8 *Baugesetzbuch*, abbreviated BauGB; the Federal Building Code came into force on 23 June 1960.

9 *Verwaltungsverfahrensgesetz*, abbreviated VwVfG; the Act on Administrative Procedure came into force on 1 January 1977.

10 *Sozialgesetzbuch*, abbreviated SGB; the Social Code consists of twelve parts which themselves form special 'Part-Codes'. The first of these Part-Codes, SGB I (Social Code Part I), came into force on 1 January 1976, the last on 1 January 2005.

11 *Verwaltungsgerichtsordnung*, abbreviated VwGO; the Code of Administrative Court Procedure came into force on 1 April 1960.

It is also necessary to study the attendant commentaries, which consist of the case law concerning those provisions. It will sometimes be surprising to find provisions that have not been fine-tuned or 'finished' in this sense by case law and have remained virtually virgin legal territory for decades. In the German Civil Code, untouched provisions of this kind are found mainly in the area of property law. Over the course of the last century, the community of those applying the law in Germany has become so used to the availability of case law individual provisions of legislation that they have a sense of insecurity when they encounter such untouched provisions, and feel fortunate when the Federal Court of Justice or any other of the five Federal Supreme Courts interpret them and begin to weave a web of case law around them.

There are, however, also numerous legal areas in German law lacking codification or any other coherent set of legal provisions to which recourse is available for the resolution of legal cases. The courts cannot escape their obligation to decide such cases and must therefore close the gaps left behind by the legislative bodies. They then look for similar legal situations that have been regulated by statute law and examine whether the solution developed in these cases is also applicable to the case before them. They then apply the legal resolution to the current case by way of analogy. If this is not possible, they develop a new solution for the present case from general legal principles. A particularly good example is labour law, for which statutory arrangements should have been put in place long ago, as envisaged by the German Unification Treaty – something that has still not happened. There are a few special statutes and a number of provisions in the Civil Code, but the latter are not specifically tailored to the employment relationship. All necessary rules have been established through collective agreements and the Federal Labour Court, particularly with respect to the law on industrial action. What we have here is genuine 'case law' as we know it from countries with a common law system.

II. THE GERMAN LEGAL SYSTEM

1. EXTENT OF THE BINDING EFFECT OF LANDMARK JUDGMENTS

The case law developed by the German Federal Supreme Courts differs from the case law of the courts in common law systems in one crucial respect: landmark judgments of the Federal Supreme Courts or other courts have no strictly binding effect. While these landmark judgments, as in countries of different legal families, are designed to provide guidance to the courts of first and second instance and to those applying the law, German law tries to achieve the same result not by the binding effect, but by the persuasiveness of the judgments. The five German Federal Supreme Courts themselves may not simply diverge from each other's landmark judgments. They must go to a 'Joint Senate' (*Gemeinsamer Senat der Obersten Gerichtshöfe des Bundes*), which then decides how a given question is to be answered. The decision of that Joint Senate is binding for all Federal Supreme Courts. A senate within one of the Federal Supreme Courts may furthermore not simply diverge from a landmark judgment of another senate of the same court. They must go to a special senate of that court, which then decides the question with binding effect on all senates of the court. However, all other courts are not bound either by such landmark judgments or the decisions of other courts. The sole exceptions to this are decisions delivered on appeal, which are binding on the lower courts in the case at issue. A local court, for example, may therefore decide a question of law as it holds to be correct, even if the Supreme Court of the relevant branch of the judiciary – in the case of a local court the Federal Court of Justice – has already ruled differently. However, a court that wants to diverge from the decision of a court of the same or a higher instance must, if legally provided, admit an appeal in the case. The parties can then go to the next instance, and ultimately have the competent Federal Supreme Court resolve the issue of whether the previous answer to the question of law should or should not stand. The courts generally only make use of their ability to diverge from the case law of the Federal Supreme Courts where they see an aspect that the relevant Supreme Court has not yet recognised, or where they believe that changed circumstances require a change in the case law. These mechanisms ensure that the answer to a question of law can be re-examined where necessary and can be adapted to changing circumstances.

2. DISTRIBUTION OF LEGISLATIVE POWERS

In Germany, there is no single jurisdiction as regards the enactment of statutes. Legislative powers are instead divided between the Federation and the *Länder*, the German federal states. The criteria by which the legislative competences are divided between the Federation and the federal states are not the same criteria as the ones by which, for instance, the competence of the European Union is determined. While the competence of the European Union is determined in accordance with the relevant market freedoms and the objectives of the European Union, the internal legislative competence of the Federation and its states in Germany is determined according to subject matter. The difference can be illustrated by two examples: The first example is Directive 1999/44/EC on the sale of consumer goods,[12] which was enacted

12 Directive 1999/44/EC of the European Parliament and of the Council of 25 May 1999 on certain aspects of the sale of consumer goods and associated guarantees (OJ L 171, p 12).

by the European Union on the basis of its competence with respect to the European internal market and consumer rights. In Germany, this Directive had to be implemented by a federal law, because the Federation is responsible for enacting legislation in the areas of civil law, competition law and court proceedings. The second example is Directive 2010/13/EU on broadcasting,[13] which was enacted by the European Union on the basis of its competence with respect to the European internal market. In addition to federal provisions, this also required an agreement between the German federal states because they have the basic legislative competence for radio and television broadcasters and had to create uniform national rules.

III. THE GERMAN JUDICIAL SYSTEM

1. ACCESS TO THE COURTS

Unlike other countries, legal disputes, especially in the areas of labour, administrative, social and tax law in Germany, have to be decided by courts, not tribunals, boards or other bodies outside the courts. This is because under the Basic Law, the German Constitution (*Grundgesetz*), every citizen has a fundamental right to go to the courts and may therefore not be referred to non-judicial bodies. The courts of first instance and appellate courts are courts of the German federal states. The Supreme Courts are federal courts. The states have no Supreme Courts, and conversely, the Federation has no courts of first instance and no appellate courts, with three exceptions. These are the Federal Patent Court and two Military Disciplinary Courts for disciplinary matters relating to members of the German armed forces. Another special feature of the German judicial system is constitutional jurisdiction, which exists in all German federal states and in the Federation itself. It has a threefold function: first, it decides disputes among the various constitutional bodies; second, it reviews the constitutionality of both the enactment and the substance of both state and federal law; third, it gives citizens the ability to have judicial decisions reviewed to determine whether or not these have violated procedural and other fundamental rights in the application of the law. All citizens can address such concerns to the Federal Constitutional Court. Irrespective thereof, citizens in some of the states can also appeal to

---

[13] Directive 2010/13/EU of the European Parliament and of the Council of 10 March 2010 on the coordination of certain provisions laid down by law, regulation or administrative action in Member States concerning the provision of audiovisual media services (Audiovisual Media Services Directive) (OJ L 95, p 1).

the constitutional court of the relevant federal state, although only in order to have a potential infringement of rights recognised in the specific state's constitution reviewed. The constitutional courts can reverse the decisions of most other courts, but the decisions of federal courts can only be reversed by the Federal Constitutional Court. This is an option which is also available for the decisions of the Federal Supreme Courts.

2. ORGANISATION OF THE GERMAN COURTS

The German courts do not constitute a single jurisdiction (made up, as in Ireland for instance, of the Circuit Courts, District Court, High Court, Court of Appeal and Supreme Court) responsible for all cases, regardless of the area of law into which they fall. In Germany, courts are instead divided into five branches or jurisdictions, each of which is responsible for specific areas of law. Each of these jurisdictions has courts of first instance and a Federal Supreme Court, and four also have appellate courts. There is the ordinary jurisdiction in civil and criminal matters, exercised by the local courts, regional courts, Higher Regional Courts and the Federal Court of Justice (*Bundesgerichtshof*, abbreviated BGH), labour jurisdiction for employment and labour law matters exercised by local labour courts, the higher labour courts and the Federal Labour Court (*Bundesarbeitsgericht*, abbreviated BAG), administrative jurisdiction for administrative disputes exercised by the administrative courts, the higher administrative courts and the Federal Administrative Court (*Bundesverwaltungsgericht*, abbreviated BVerwG), social jurisdiction for social law matters exercised by the social courts, the higher social courts and the Federal Social Court (*Bundessozialgericht*, abbreviated BSG), and financial jurisdiction for tax disputes, which has only two instances: fiscal courts and the Federal Finance Court (*Bundesfinanzhof*, abbreviated BFH).

3. JUDICIAL BODIES IN THE GERMAN COURTS

The Supreme Courts decide by senates constituted of five judges each, who are not necessarily professional judges. A decision by one single judge is provided for only in a few special cases, such as decisions in costs matters and the arrest warrants issued by the judge in preliminary proceedings before the Federal Court of Justice. All other courts decide either by single judge or by judicial bodies constituted of three or more judges, such as the court of lay assessors at the local courts, the chambers of the regional courts, or the senates at the Higher Regional Court and the Courts of Appeal, or the corresponding courts of the other branches of judiciary. The rules concerning the composition of the judicial bodies of the first instance courts and the Courts of Appeal of the different jurisdictions vary greatly.

IV. CONDITIONS OF DELIBERATION AND DECISION-MAKING

1. COLLECTIVE DECISIONS

When German courts decide constituted as a chamber, a senate or another judicial body composed of several judges, the judges making up the judicial body do not decide each one for him- or herself. They decide collectively. At the end of the litigation there will thus not be individual judgments by each of the judges participating in the judicial body, but one single judgment of the body as a whole. All judges together give a uniform judgment comprising a uniform set of operative provisions and a uniform set of grounds signed by all participants. The parties of the litigation do not receive an original version of the judgment signed by the participating judges, but an official copy sealed with the court's seal. The original version remains in the court's files.

2. PARTICIPANTS IN DELIBERATION AND VOTING

Only the judges who are competent and designated to sit on a given case may participate in the deliberation and the finding of the decision, and they are indeed obliged to do so.[14] From the German point of view, there is no choice because the German Basic Law[15] – our constitution – provides a fundamental constitutional right to the 'lawful judge'.[16] The courts have to establish schedules of responsibilities determining which judge and which chamber or senate is competent to decide which case.[17] If judicial bodies are composed of more judges than provided by law, the relevant chamber or senate, too, has to establish a schedule of responsibilities showing which judge of the chamber or senate has to participate in which case.[18] These rules have to be established by the competent organisational bodies – the so-called 'presiding committee' of a court[19] for the schedule of the court as a whole, and all judges of the relevant

14 See §192(1) and (3) GVG.
15 *Grundgesetz*, abbreviated GG; the Basic Law came into force on 24 May 1949.
16 Article 101 GG.
17 §21e(1) GVG.
18 §21g(1) GVG.
19 It is composed of the court's President and a number of elected judges, depending on the number of the judges at the relevant court. These rules apply to all German courts, from to a local court all the way to a Federal Supreme Court.

chambers or senates for the schedule of their chamber or senate – for each year in advance. These schedules are binding. They may not be altered during the year as a matter of discretion, but only if the workload of the chamber, senate or single judge concerned has become too large or too small, if a judge is permanently prevented from the exercise of his office, or if a judge comes from or changes to another court. If, for instance, a judge plans to give a speech on a day the chamber or senate plans to deliberate or to hold a public hearing, the judge has to apply for leave of absence. Having been granted such leave, the judge legally prevented from the exercise of his office during the time of the leave granted and must be represented by the colleague who is determined as his representative in case of absence in the schedule of responsibilities of the chamber or senate. If the judge does not apply for leave of absence, he or she has to participate in the deliberation or in the public hearing and has to forego the opportunity to give a speech or the participation in a conference or other event.

In Germany, judges of the judicial body other than those determined by the schedule of responsibilities are not allowed to participate in deliberating and voting, even if they are interested in the case or have special experience and expertise. That is true not only for the deliberation and decision-making of other chambers or senates within the court, but also in the case of a chamber or senate which is composed of more judges than legally required. In the latter case, too, the chamber or senate deliberates and decides by the group of judges of the chamber or senate who are responsible for the case according to the applicable schedule of responsibilities. This group of judges may not even let another member of the chamber or senate take part in deliberating, even if there is a colleague with great experience in cases like the one they are sitting on, and even if his or her participation would be very useful.

A difficult challenge to which this system gives rise is how to avoid contradictions between the different groups of judges of a chamber or senate. This task is especially important for the senates of the Supreme Courts, because these courts have to ensure a uniform judicial practice. Statute law does not provide special bodies to resolve such dissents where they occur. Normally the group of judges that first has to deal with the issue decides the legal question; the other group(s) of judges of the senate accept the decision without being legally bound to it. If a major question arises, the senate normally organises an informal plenary debate of all judges of the senate. The judges then agree or – if necessary – vote by majority on how the question should be decided. This agreement or voting does not, however, bind the relevant group of judges that has to decide the case where the question arises. Yet usually the judges follow their informal plenary agreement or voting in order to ensure a uniform practice within the senate.

3. MOMENT OF DELIBERATION AND VOTING

Common lawyers would probably expect judges to take time deliberating and deciding after having heard the case. This is also a common practice in Germany and particularly in the German Supreme Courts. By proceeding this way, the members of the chamber or senate can, on the one hand, form their opinion impartially based on the outcome of the oral hearing. On the other hand, the Presiding Judge can tell the parties during the oral hearing only his or her personal appreciation of the case, but not the provisional opinion of the senate as a whole. The same is true for the other members of the panel, who may ask questions as they think it necessary. The parties in this case are free to focus on the points they themselves believe to be crucial. But they do not know how the panel as a whole tends to decide the case, or which legal questions and arguments it regards as crucial. This is the reason why many chambers and senates of the German courts do not follow the practice of (exclusive) subsequent deliberation, but instead pre-deliberate cases before their oral hearing. One of these senates is 'my' senate, the Vth civil senate of the Federal Court of Justice, of which I am a member.

When we have to give judgment after an oral hearing, we deliberate the case in advance in order to be able to give the parties a provisional assessment of the case. The parties greatly appreciate this procedure because they then know what are, from our point of view, the crucial points of the case and thus which issues they should focus on. After the hearing, we re-enter into our deliberation and see whether the outcome of the oral hearing confirms or throws doubt on the pre-deliberation we had the day before. In many cases the oral hearing confirms the results of the pre-deliberation. The oral hearing may – and not only occasionally does – show aspects which we did not have in mind and which we should address in our judgment. We have also had oral hearings during which the parties' pleadings convinced us that the decision we originally had in mind would not be the best and that we should reach another. Among these cases are a few very famous ones. An example is a case where we had to decide whether or not the special rules concerning the restitution of confiscations in the former GDR prevent recourse to the general rules of private law.[20]

Judges in the common law tradition may perhaps feel uneasy imagining their German colleagues deliberating a case before the oral hearing, having a provisional view of the case, and even telling the parties about it. This astonishing difference stems from the different way in which civil proceedings are conducted in Germany on the one hand and in England, Ireland or other

---

20 BGH (3 April 1992), ref V ZR 83/91, BGHZ 118, 34, 39 et seq.

countries of the Anglo-American legal family on the other hand. Whereas in these countries a judge tends to see the case for the first time during the oral hearing, in Germany each oral hearing will be prepared by written submissions of the parties. In Germany, the oral hearing never starts with the court room filling with people carrying boxes full of documents, files and books for the judges. The judges already know the case well when they start an oral hearing. During the oral hearing in first and second instance courts, the parties therefore like to take the opportunity to amend their written submissions and to discuss primarily the pertinent legal aspects with the judge or the judges. The court may only base its decision on an aspect that a party has evidently overlooked or has deemed to be insignificant if it has given sufficient notice of this fact and has allowed the parties an opportunity to address the matter (unless it concerns merely an ancillary claim). The same applies to any aspect of the case which the court assesses differently from both parties.[21] By law, the judge has a more active role than in common law civil proceedings. In general, the relevant rules also apply to oral hearings before a Supreme Court. Yet there is one decisive difference: The Supreme Courts are bound to the findings of facts of the relevant Court of Appeal. Therefore, in oral hearings before the Supreme Courts, the parties can only discuss the legal aspects of the case as well as defects of the finding of facts by the Courts of Appeal. If the findings of facts are deficient, the Supreme Court will give the case back to the Court of Appeal in order to amend the findings.

4. COURSE OF DELIBERATION

The German Courts Constitution Code (*Gerichtsverfassungsgesetz*, abbreviated GVG) provides rules on the course of deliberation and voting. Somewhat surprisingly, however, it does not contain rules regulating whether the judicial body has to deliberate at all and whether the judges have to hold a meeting, for instance in the office of the Presiding Judge. Because of the absence of such rules, the judges first can decide whether they need a deliberation, or whether they would prefer to decide by circulating the file together with the *rapporteur's* draft from judge to judge, hence voting and deciding by signing the draft. The latter circulating procedure is not provided in the Courts Constitution Code, but is nevertheless a legally permitted option.[22] German courts usually choose this option only for purely formal decisions like the rejection of an admitted appeal or for signing the final version of a judgment or other decision they already have deliberated and voted on. In all other cases, they take time for a joint deliberation. Normally the deliberation and

21 §139(2) ZPO.

22 BGH (28 November 2008) ref LwZR 54/98, NJW-RR 2009, 286 para [8].

voting will take place in a formal meeting of the judges in the office of the Presiding Judge. This option is not always available, however. An example of such situation may be an application for an interim measure which may occur before the local courts as well as before the Higher Regional Courts or even at the Supreme Courts. If in such situations, a decision has to be taken at once, yet not all participating judges are in court, then they are not obliged to meet in person. A deliberation does not necessarily demand a meeting with the personal presence of the participating judges; simultaneous communication of all participating judges under the guidance of the Presiding Judge are sufficient. If such communication is guaranteed by technical means, the judges can also deliberate and vote in accordance with the relevant legal requirements, for instance in a telephone conference.[23]

The course of judicial deliberations in Germany is regulated in quite a detailed manner in the Courts Constitution Code.[24] The Presiding Judge conducts the deliberation; he or she asks the relevant questions and collects the votes.[25] If a dissent arises amongst the judges of the judicial body as regards the subject matter, the wording and sequence of the questions, or concerning the result of the vote, the judges participating in the decision have to resolve this dissent by a joint majority decision.[26] The Courts Constitution Code does not provide rules on the crucial part of the deliberation, which is the debate and discussion amongst the judges. The explanation for the absence of such rules is that the debate and the discussion amongst the judges cannot be regulated. The course of this part of the deliberation depends very much on the personality of the participating judges, on the case to be decided, on the draft of the *rapporteur* and – of course – on the parties' pleadings.

To give you an impression how these rules work out in practice, let me provide you with a brief glimpse behind the curtains of the Vth Senate of the Federal Court of Justice, where I work. This Senate is responsible for decisions on the admission of further appeals against decisions on appeal, and for appeals against the denial of permission to appeal. The judgments of our Senate are in most cases rendered after an oral hearing, whereas the decisions in land registration, forced execution and cases of deportation of asylum seekers and other aliens without residence permit[27] as well as decisions on the admission of the second (further) appeal are given in writing without an

---

23 BGH (29 November 2013), ref BLw 4/12, NJW-RR 2014, 243 para [33]; BAG (14 April 2015), ref 1 AZR 223/14, NJW 2015, 3738 para [12]; BVerwG (13 November 2017), ref 4 B 23/17, accessible via the Juris database, para [18].

24 §§192–197 GVG.

25 See §194(1) GVG.

26 §194(2) GVG.

27 Meanwhile the XIIIth Senate of the Federal Court of Justice is responsible for these special cases.

oral hearing. All of these decisions are taken not by circulating the file from judge to judge, but after deliberation. The basis of the deliberation is a written vote of the *rapporteur*. The *rapporteur* not only proposes how to decide a case; when our Senate has to render a reasoned decision, especially a judgment, also a first draft of the Senate's decision will be presented.

We typically start by deliberating on the (possible) outcome of the case and the operative statutory provisions relevant to the decision. This part of the discussion may be simple. But it can be complicated when we have a choice between different legal approaches. Then we have to discuss and decide not merely the outcome as such, but also the approach. Having achieved consensus on the outcome, we discuss the *rapporteur's* draft of the judgment. We debate the grounds and also the wording of the decision on the basis of the *rapporteur's* draft; this draft we actually discuss from the first to the last page. On the basis of the outcome of our discussion, the *rapporteur* redrafts his or her proposal for the decision which then will circulate amongst the judges, beginning with the Presiding Judge.

5. COURT'S VOTING

Courts generally take their vote on the questions relevant to the decision by an absolute majority.[28] In criminal cases, a majority of two-thirds of the votes is required for any decision against a defendant concerning the question of guilt itself as well as the legal consequences of the offence committed.[29]

In former times, a two-thirds majority was required for a decision of the so-called Higher Lawyers' Courts (*Anwaltsgerichtshöfe*) on the withdrawal of a practitioner's admission to the bar.[30] The Higher Lawyers Courts now apply the same rules as the administrative courts, which decide cases with an absolute majority of votes.

The votes of all judges participating in a decision have the same weight. Lay judges' votes count as much as professional judges' votes. The Presiding Judge or the President of the Court, even the President of a Supreme Court, has no casting vote. There is an exception only for courts which sitting with two professional judges and two lay judges. This occurs in local courts, which may sit on penal cases in an extended bench of two professional judges and two lay judges,[31] as well as occasionally in the so-called Grand Criminal Division (*Große Strafkammer)* of regional Courts, which in smaller

28 §196(1) GVG.

29 §263(1) StPO.

30 See §41(1) of the Federal Lawyers' Act (*Bundesrechtsanwaltsordnung*, abbreviated BRAO) in the version valid until 31 August 2009.

31 §29(2) GVG.

criminal cases can sit in a reduced bench of two professional and two lay judges.[32]

The German Courts Constitution Code determines the sequence of voting as follows: The lay judges have to vote before the professional judges.[33] The judges of each group have to give their votes by seniority, normally starting with the youngest or most junior judge.[34] There is an exception for the voting sequence of the professional judges. If a *rapporteur* is appointed, they start their voting not with the most junior judge, but with the *rapporteur* followed by the most junior.[35] The senates of the Court of Appeal and of the Supreme Courts in Germany normally appoint a *rapporteur*, so that he starts the voting where there are no lay judges participating. The voting concludes with the Presiding Judge giving his or her vote.[36]

The voting procedure will be simple in many cases. At the end of the deliberation, the judges vote one-by-one as provided by the Courts Constitution Code. The voting can also be very complicated, however, as for instance where a case demands deliberating and voting in several steps. For example, if the parties to a sales contract are in dispute over the validity of the contract and also over whether the delivered goods are in line with the contract, the judges first will have to determine and vote on the validity of the contract and afterwards on the question of whether the contractual obligations have been discharged. Theoretically, it may happen that a judge dissenting after an intense debate on the first question subsequently refuses to participate in the further steps of deliberation and voting. This, of course, would be a violation of the judge's duties. Moreover, the court could not decide in its legally required composition if judges were to refuse further participation in the proceedings. The German legislator therefore expressively provided that judges may not deny their participation even if they have dissented in previous steps of deliberation and voting.[37] The consequence of this rule is that every participating judge has to sign the decision or judgment, regardless of whether he or she voted with the majority or the minority on a given issue.

Do these detailed rules determine, one may ask – perhaps with a certain shudder – the judicial day-to-day work? There is, of course, no general answer to this question. How many times and in which cases the statutory rules on deliberation and voting have to be invoked depends on the quality of the working atmosphere in the respective judicial body. My personal impression is that the working atmosphere of the vast majority of judicial bodies in

[32] §76(2), 4th sentence, GVG.
[33] §197, 2nd sentence, GVG.
[34] §197, 1st sentence, GVG.
[35] §197, 3rd sentence, GVG.
[36] §197, 4th sentence, GVG.
[37] §195 GVG.

Germany is so good that they resort to the rules very rarely. Indeed, most have to apply these rules so rarely that they have to consult their collections of legal texts if it really becomes necessity to apply the detailed statutory rules by the book. During my 15 years of service at the Vth Civil Senate of the Federal Court of Justice, I have experienced a formal voting process only three times. In one case, we had to vote question-by-question, and we were very happy when this complicated voting procedure was done. In all other cases, we achieved consent without a formal vote taking place.

6. DYNAMIC OF THE DELIBERATION

The legal rules on deliberation and voting are the same for all German judicial bodies consisting of several judges. However, the dynamic of deliberation and voting differs greatly as between the various bodies. Of course, this dynamic depends very much on the working atmosphere amongst the members of the relevant judicial body. And of course, the depth of the deliberation and its quality also depends on the workload of the courts and the time they can spend on deliberation. An important factor which must not be underestimated is the size of the judicial body. I personally have made the experience that the deliberation in a senate of the Federal Court of Justice composed of five judges normally addresses more aspects of a given case than the deliberation of a similar case in a chamber or senate composed of only three judges. Five judges really do see more than three. This strength of five-judge senates will have the best effect when members of the senate focus on the case and put all their efforts into developing the best solution for the case. Normally, they will achieve consensus and do not need to study the statutory rules on deliberation and formal voting.

7. PRIVACY AND SECRECY OF COURTS' DELIBERATION AND VOTING

The courts' deliberations and their decision-finding and voting processes are not open to the public.[38] Only the designated judges competent to participate in the decision are allowed to join the session. But there are exceptions: junior lawyers undergoing training in the courts, judges serving as assistants of the senates of the Supreme Courts, and foreign judges interested in the work of the courts and keeping absolute secrecy may join the session, though only as spectators. The privacy of courts' deliberation and voting is intended to ensure

[38] §193 GVG.

a free and unfettered debate between the judges participating in the courts' decisions. There are, of course, cases whose outcome does not necessitate an intensive debate amongst the judges. Yet many cases are more complicated. In order to decide such cases, the judges need an intense debate on the appropriate outcome and how to reach it. Supreme Court cases in particular often need an open debate amongst judges and sometimes an actual brainstorming. If such debate and brainstorming had to take place under the eyes of the public, judges would probably restrain themselves and would contribute to the debate what they believe is 'palatable' to the public. The privacy of deliberation and voting, by contrast, creates a protected space for debate and discussion, which encourages free and unrestricted contributions to the debate and voting. This is why the German legislator decided for the privacy of courts' deliberation and voting.

German law not only provides the privacy of deliberations and voting, but also their secrecy.[39] The judges, and of course any other participants in the meeting,[40] have to preserve absolute secrecy about every detail of the deliberation and the voting. They may not reveal these either in public or elsewhere. Even the President of the relevant court has no competence to allow such revelation. The details of the deliberation and voting may only be revealed by the participating judges or other participants as part of a judicial finding of facts by a criminal court in a criminal case against the participating judge for perversion of justice.[41] This strict rule enforces the privacy and secrecy of deliberation and voting.

8. GIVING JUDGMENT

Judgments are handed down either at the end of the oral hearing of the case or in another oral hearing scheduled solely for the pronouncement of judgments. Both hearings are open to the public. This is true also where parts of the main hearing were held under exclusion of the public, for instance where business secrets are at issue. This occurs more often in the lower courts than in higher courts; in the Supreme Courts, these cases are very rare indeed. If we have to decide without an oral hearing, for instance in land registration or forced execution cases, or concerning the permission to appeal to our court, the decision is not given in an oral hearing, but in writing by service.

---

39 §43 of the German Judges' Code (*Deutsche Richtergesetz*, abbreviated DRiG), which came into force on 1 July 1962.

40 See the text following n 38 above.

41 For details, see J Schmidt-Räntsch, *Deutsches Richtergesetz* (Commentary on the German Judges' Code), 6th edn (München, Beck, 2009) §43 para [19].

9. DISSENTING VOTES

The *rapporteur* need not necessarily convince the other members of a judicial panel of his or her proposal. The *rapporteur* or other dissenting members of the panel are allowed to publish dissenting opinions only at the Federal Constitutional Court or at one of the Constitutional Courts of the German federal states. Members of a Senate of the Federal Court of Justice may give dissenting opinions to a special unofficial working file[42] which the Senates of the Court maintain besides the official files.[43] In my experience, this option is very rarely used. I remember one case in which the colleague reflected on giving his dissenting opinion to the working file, but in the end he did not. It is not very attractive to do so since such dissenting opinions are preserved (only) in a special private senate's dossier for the relevant case, which is not open the public. The dissenting vote could therefore only be read once this special dossier is transferred to the Federal Archive, which happens 30 years after the final decision of the Federal Court of Justice is handed down. Other reasons may be that members of the Court's Senates normally reach a consensus and that the parties and the public are normally more interested in the common opinion produced by the Senates than in dissenting votes.

---

42 So called *Senatsheft (*senate's dossier): see §19(2), 2nd sentence, of the Rules of Procedure of the Federal Court of Justice (*Geschäftsordnung des Bundesgerichtshofs*), officially published in Federal Gazette no 83 of 3 March 1952 on the basis of §140 GVG, available online via the website of the Court at http://www.bundesgerichtshof.de/SharedDocs/Downloads/DE/DasGericht/Fundstellen/geschOrdnungBGH1952.pdf?__blob=publicationFile (last accessed 22 February 2020).

43 §10(1), 2nd sentence, of the Rules of Procedure of the Federal Court of Justice.

CHAPTER 8

WHY IS THE GERMAN FEDERAL CONSTITUTIONAL COURT A DELIBERATIVE COURT, AND WHY IS THAT A GOOD THING?

A Comparative Assessment

Gertrude LÜBBE-WOLFF*

Decision-making in the German Federal Constitutional Court (FCC) is a most collegial and collaborative enterprise. A great deal of time is devoted

* Former Judge at the German Federal Constitutional Court; Professor (em.) of Public Law at the University of Bielefeld. The author thanks Birke Häcker for helpful comments and is grateful to *Wissenschaftskolleg zu Berlin*, where she started comparing the workways of constitutional courts as a fellow in 2015/2016.

to discussion in conference. I have never seen a discussion end unless there was agreement that continuing it would not take the Court any further. Even objections by small minorities or by a single panel member are never just passed over as irrelevant. None of the judges, including the President, are immune from having their arguments dismantled and their draft texts rewritten. Much effort is made to find consensus. Where a concern does not prevail, it will at least be taken seriously, not just in conference, but also in the reasons of the resulting decision.[1]

I. VIRTUES OF DELIBERATIVE, CONSENSUS-ORIENTED DECISION-MAKING

The fact that the German FCC works in a deliberative, consensus-oriented way may not universally be regarded as a recommendation for that practice. To the majority of lawyers in some countries, the FCC is a *bête noire* rather than a model: too activist, too talkative, and cultivating an awkward and sometimes opaque language.

As to the language, it must be admitted that reading decisions of the FCC in English can be a torment. But that is mainly a problem of translation by interpreters who, understandably, hardly dare to depart from a literal word-by-word and sentence-by-sentence transposition of the text, thus adding the complications and circumbendibuses of one language to those of the other. In the case of German-to-English translations, the result is often not simply inelegant, but downright repulsive, and sometimes hardly comprehensible.[2] The FCC has been working on improving this situation for some time, but the problem is unlikely to be resolved in a perfectly satisfactory way. German grammar offers tools of elegant compression which make it possible to pack sentences with much more information than would fit into a tolerable English sentence. Untying sentences in apex court judgments will, however, usually require more judgement and self-assurance in the matter than can be expected from anyone but the Justices themselves.

As far as accusations of excessive activism and deficient succinctness are concerned, there is no need, for the purposes of this chapter, to discuss

1 For more detailed accounts, see G Lübbe-Wolff, 'Cultures of Deliberation in Constitutional Courts', in P Maraniello (ed), *Justicia Constitucional, La Justicia constitucional en los diferentes ámbitos del derecho y sus nuevas tendencias*, vol 1 (Resistencia, Chaco, Contexto, 2016) 37, 40 et seq; eadem, *Wie funktioniert das Bundesverfassungsgericht?* (Göttingen, V&R Unipress, 2015), with further references.

2 In fact, I could hardly understand parts of one of my own dissenting opinions when, for the purpose of writing a paper in English, I once looked up the English version on the court's website.

whether there is something to them, because if there was, this would have very little to do with the Court's culture of deliberative, consensus-oriented decision-making. Where – as in Germany – teleological arguments and the balancing of competing interests are important and accepted elements of the legal culture, while strict avoidance of *obiter dicta* is not, and where – as with FCC decisions – it is common to produce detailed and extensive reasons, there may be more material to deliberate on, and more room and scope for compromise, than there is in a culture which is more committed to avoiding judicial discretion and/or judicial reflections that go beyond minimum motivation. It does not follow, however, that a habit of deliberating intensely and trying to find as much consensus as possible will lead to judicial activism. Nor is there a necessary nexus between cooperative, consensus-oriented deliberation and a proliferating style of judgments. So any critic of the role of the FCC in Germany – or in Europe, for that matter – should not *for this reason alone* reject the deliberative, consensus-oriented method of working I have described above.[3]

The advantages of that method by far outweigh any possible drawbacks. Intense communication on the basis of equality helps to avoid mistakes. It helps to understand views and feelings which the majority may not share, but which need to be addressed and acknowledged in order to make a decision acceptable to those who 'lose'. It helps to drop aspirations to infallibility and in promoting mutual respect. Genuine communication and serious efforts to find common ground help to avoid internal polarisation and prevent a bench from splitting into factions.[4] They also help resist temptations to use judicial office as a tool for the promotion of individual star status, and will instead strengthen a sense of community and service. As a result, they help to avoid partisanship and extreme solutions, as well as volatility due to changes in the composition of the bench, and to foster trust in the judicial system (and the political system along with it). The most striking quality to be gained from all

---

3 Nor should the beneficial aspects of that role be neglected, see G Lübbe-Wolff, 'Constitutional Courts and Democracy. Facets of an Ambivalent Relationship' in K Meßerschmidt and AD Oliver-Lalana (eds), *Rational Lawmaking under Review* (Switzerland, Springer International, 2016) 19, 26 et seq.

4 Some authors argue that deliberation is likely to foster polarisation, see C Sunstein, 'Deliberative Trouble? Why Groups Go to Extremes' (2000) 110 *Yale Law Journal* 71; A Paterson, *Final Judgment: The Last Law Lords and the Supreme Court* (Oxford and Portland/Oregon, Hart Publishing, 2013) 96. FCC judges would disagree entirely with this assessment. In discussions of the matter with judges from other national and international courts who describe the culture of communication in their respective courts as deliberative, I have never come across a negative view of such a culture, either. What I have encountered instead are expressions of regret from members of courts or court formations where deliberation does not work (as, for instance, due to overly large size and lack of discipline with respect to length of speeches, in the Grand Chamber of the European Court of Human Rights, ECtHR). On decision-making in the ECtHR, see the contribution by A Nussberger in chapter 12 of the present collection.

of this is the *integrative* quality of the resulting judicature – a quality that is particularly important in constitutional jurisprudence because it meets the primary function of a modern constitution.[5]

In line with this, the FCC has indeed been and still is a remarkably integrative factor in Germany. It is deservedly one of the most trusted institutions in Germany,[6] highly renowned for impartiality and balance. Some, but not many of its decisions come with separate opinions (long term average: about 8%).[7] In spite of the political relevance and controversiality of many of the cases the two senates of the FCC have to decide, they are very rarely split 4:4, and even more rarely along political nomination background lines. Overall, the Court has managed to pacify rather than fuel conflict over controversial issues, not just as far as the parties involved are concerned, but with respect to society as a whole. And, of particular significance in a nation whose underdeveloped sense of the importance of legal institutions once produced aberrations of an unprecedented nature and scale, the Court has brought about exceptional degrees of respect for the German Constitution ('Basic Law' or *Grundgesetz*, GG) and an awareness of its relevance. These are the effects of the Court's culture of deliberation.

One might also look back at the early times when, under Chief Justice Marshall, the US Supreme Court began to build the reputation off which that court lives today without adding to it (to put it mildly). The high rate of decisions showing no split in the court in those days was attained on the basis of far more discussion than the US Justices invest today. In *Talbot v Seeman*, the first case decided by the Marshall Court, public argument lasted four days and was followed by almost a week of deliberations, including a Sunday.[8] The resulting judgment came as an 'opinion of the court', without

---

5 On the integrative function of constitutions, see G Lübbe-Wolff, 'Integration durch Verfassung' (2009) 12 *Zeitschrift des Deutschen Juristinnenbundes* 174, available online via https://www.nomos-elibrary.de/10.5771/1866-377X-2009-4-174/integration-durch-verfassung-jahrgang-12-2009-heft-4 (last accessed 8 March 2020); eadem, 'Homogenes Volk: Über Homogenitätspostulate und Integration' (2007) 27 *Zeitschrift für Ausländerrecht und Ausländerpolitik* 121, available online via http://www.zar.nomos.de/fileadmin/zar/doc/Aufsatz_zar_07_04.pdf (last accessed 8 March 2020).

6 See H Vorländer, 'Die Deutungsmacht des Bundesverfassungsgerichts' in RC van Ooyen, C Möllers and HW Martin (eds), *Das Bundesverfassungsgericht im politischen System*, 2nd edn (Wiesbaden, Springer VS, 2015) 299, 309 et seq.

7 See overview in the statistics for 2017 on the website of the FCC, p 12, available via https://www.bundesverfassungsgericht.de/SharedDocs/Downloads/DE/Statistik/statistik_2017.pdf?__blob=publicationFile&v=3 (last accessed 8 March 2020).

8 JE Smith, *John Marshall. Designer of a Nation* (New York, Henry Holt and Company, 1996), 292. For the very different, largely non-deliberative practice today, see Lübbe-Wolff, 'Cultures of Deliberation' (n 1) 37 et seq; TR Johnson, 'The Supreme Court Decision Making Process' (2016) Oxford Research Encyclopedia, Politics, section entitled 'Decisions on the Merits: Conference Discussions', available online via http://politics.oxfordre.com/view/10.1093/acrefore/9780190228637.001.0001/acrefore-9780190228637-e-98 (last accessed 8 March 2020);

any separate opinions, although the case had been highly controversial along party political lines.[9]

II. SOME RELEVANT PARAMETERS

1. OBJECT OF VOTING AND MAJORITY REQUIREMENTS FOR JUDICIAL DECISIONS

a) *Common Law and Civil Law Traditions*

Common law and civil law systems differ in the way they solve the specific problems of decision-making in multimember courts. Most of the differences can be traced back to the traditions of *seriatim* and *per curiam* decision-making, respectively. Over time, these traditions have partly converged. In the United States, the pure *seriatim* mode of decision-making, with each judge pronouncing a judgment of his own,[10] was abandoned for good in the early 19th century when Chief Justice Marshall made it a rule for the Justices to produce an 'opinion of the court'.[11] Today, even in the mother country of the

---

TR Johnson and MW Sorenson, 'The U.S. Supreme Court's Strategic Decision-Making Process', in R Rogowski and T Gawron (eds), *Constitutional Courts in Comparison. The US Supreme Court and the German Federal Constitutional Court*, 2nd ed (New York/Oxford, Berghahn, 2016) 111, 132; A Ward, 'Junior Varsity Judges? Law Clerks in the Decisional Process of the U.S. Supreme Court', in R Rogowski and T Gawron (eds), ibid, 165, 173.

9 *Talbot v Seaman*, 5 US 1 (1801); Smith (n 8), 291 et seq. Contrary to frequent assumptions in the literature, the absence of separate opinions did not demonstrate that the court had decided unanimously, see C Sunstein, 'Unanimity and Disagreement on the Supreme Court' (2015) 100 *Cornell Law Review* 769, 786 et seq.

10 On – sometimes forgotten – traditions of unanimity that were apparently associated with this model in early times, see C Young, 'The History of Judicial Dissent in England: What Relevance Does it have for Modern Common Law Legal Systems?' (2009) 32 *Australian Bar Review* 96, 101 et seq. For early traditions of inter-court consultations, and of discussing controversial cases among all the common law judges of England in the Exchequer Chamber, see JH Baker, *The Oxford History of the Laws of England*, vol VI, 1483–1558 (Oxford, Oxford University Press, 2003) 41; M Hemmant, 'Introduction' in M Hemmant (ed), *Select Cases in the Exchequer Chamber Before all the Justices of England* (Publications of the Selden Society, vol 51, 1933) xi-xcvii. On the English tradition of orality, with *extempore* judgments at the close of argument, which is closely related to the *seriatim* tradition, but which allowed for exceptions when intermittent deliberation was held necessary ('*curia adversari vult*') see RJ Martineau, *Appellate Justice in England and the United States: A Comparative Analysis* (Buffalo/New York, William S Hein & Co, 1990) 101 et seq; PM Tiersma, 'The Textualization of Precedent' (2007) *Loyola Law School Legal Studies*, Paper No 2007-28, available online via http://ssrn.com/abstract=680901 (last accessed 8 March 2020), 1187, 1189, 1208.

11 On the history of that change, see JR Stoner, 'Heir Apparent. Bushrod Washington and Federal Justice in the Early Republic' in SD Gerber (ed), *Seriatim. The Supreme Court Before John Marshall* (New York and London, New York University Press, 1998) 322, 331 et seq; KM ZoBell, 'Division of Opinion in the Supreme Court. A History of Judicial Disintegration'

common law, the UK Supreme Court not infrequently hands down a 'judgment of the court'.[12] On the other hand, more and more countries in the civil law tradition have departed from the pure *per curiam* mode by allowing their apex courts to publish separate opinions. Common law and civil law traditions thus seem to mingle. But the tendency towards convergence with respect to the incidence of judgments or opinions 'of the court' on the one hand, and publicised individual judicial opinions on the other, should not obfuscate differences that have so far persisted rather unabridged. These differences may be less conspicuous, but they are not necessarily less important than the one which appears to be vanishing.

As far as the specific questions of how to produce *one* solution with *several* judges on the bench are concerned, the most consequential remaining difference between the common law and the civil law tradition relates to majority requirements.[13] The most interesting question here is: What is it that a majority is needed for?

In common law jurisdictions, to this day, a majority of votes is required only for the dispositive part ('outcome') of a decision, not for the reasons. So-called *plurality decisions*, where the majority carrying the outcome is split with respect to the reasons, are possible. In the civil law tradition, the rules with respect to the object of majority requirements – outcome, reasons or both – are often not quite clear, but at least with respect to reasons concerning the law, the dominant view is that all of them need majority support.[14]

(1959) 44 *Cornell Law Review* 186, 192 et seq; Smith (n 8) 292 et seq; G Lübbe-Wolff, 'Cultures of Deliberation' (n 1) 44 et seq.

12 B Hale, 'Judgment Writing in the Supreme Court', UKSC Blog, 25 October 2010, available online via http://ukscblog.com/judgment-writing-in-the-supreme-court-brenda-hale/ (last accessed 29 February 2020); J Mance, 'In a Manner of Speaking: How Do Common, Civil and European Law Compare?' (2014) 78 *Rabels Zeitschrift* 231, 241; R Reed, 'The Supreme Court Ten Years On', 6 March 2019, p 12, available online via https://www.supremecourt.uk/docs/speech-190306.pdf (last accessed 22 May 2020).

13 In both systems, the required majority is usually a simple majority. In some countries, supermajorities are needed for the exercise of certain competences, such as declarations of unconstitutionality of legislation or of political parties: see the cursory overview for Europe in European Commission for Democracy Through Law (Venice Commission), *Opinion on Amendments to the Act of 25 June 2015 on the Constitutional Tribunal of Poland*, Op no 833/2015 CDL-AD(2016)001, paras 76 et seq. For some courts, unanimity requirements are in place for the decisions of very small formations (as for FCC Chambers of three, see n 37 below; similar unanimity requirements apply in, eg, Albania, Austria, Belgium, Korea, Kosovo, Hungary, Peru, Turkey and Slovenia).

14 Some more or less far-reaching exceptions are recognised. In German criminal courts, for instance, lay judges (*Schöffen* or *Geschworene*) do not participate in *writing* reasons. According to Article 34 no 6a, para 2 of the *Reglamento* (rules of court) for the Constitutional Court of Colombia, which is in many respects a Court in the Continental European tradition, the dispositive part of a judgment (*parte resolutiva*) must be approved by an absolute majority of the judges, whereas for the reasons (*parte motiva*) support by a relative majority is sufficient. This is an instance of blending characteristics of Anglo-Saxon/common law and continental European/civil law court design. The same blending has occurred in Kosovo.

In Germany, for instance, the Judicature Act (*Gerichtsverfassungsgesetz*, GVG) does not set out clear rules on whether the reasons of a judicial decision need to be supported by a majority of the judges participating in a decision. The historical legislator deliberately left that controversial question open in the late 19th century.[15] Nowadays, however, it is in practice almost generally answered in the positive as far as questions of law are concerned.[16] For the Federal Constitutional Court, the Rules of Court are framed accordingly.[17]

b) *Effect on the Culture of Deliberation*

The above-mentioned feature of decision-making in civil law jurisdictions is of practical significance because it secures easily identifiable legal guidance.[18] Another effect, less noticeable for external observers, but no less important: A majority requirement with respect to reasons is conducive to a deliberative, consensus-oriented court practice. The need to produce reasons that a majority is willing to support tends to promote discussion and collegiality. This is the case not just because of the greater quantity of text with respect to which majorities have to be identified. Two more factors further increase the need to deliberate and seek convergence.

The first is the problem of *divergent majorities*: Majorities for each of the reasons of a judgment will not necessarily lead to a result which is itself supported by a majority.[19] Contrary to the view that this is a specific problem of a system requiring a majority for the reasons of a judgment, I suggest that it be perceived as a universal problem of collective judicial decision-making

---

The Constitutional Court of this country exhibits most of the characteristics of a court in the Civil Law tradition. The Rules of Procedure, however, permit without any restriction that judges in the majority write concurring opinions (Rule 62, para 1 sentence 3), thus allowing for decisions with reasons that are not supported by a majority. According to information which I owe to Durim Berisha, who clerked for the court, this is because the Rules of Procedure were drafted by a judge from the USA.

15 W Ernst, *Rechtserkenntnis durch Richtermehrheiten: "group choice" in europäischen Rechtstraditionen* (Tübingen, Mohr Siebeck, 2016) 180, 189 et seq.

16 Judges of other German Federal Courts that I have been able to interview on the issue have unanimously confirmed that, as a matter of course, reasons need majority consent. Consensus with respect to this question is also reflected, for instance, in the practice of the Federal Administrative Court (*Bundesverwaltungsgericht*, BVerfG) according to which suggested changes in the drafts of decisions which are, in that court, adopted on the basis of circulating the draft, need to be initialled by three of the five judges in a Senate in order to be accepted.

17 §27, 2nd sentence, FCC Rules of Procedure (*Geschäftsordnung des Bundesverfassungsgerichts*, GO BVerfG).

18 On lack of guidance as a corollary of outcome voting see DG Post and SC Salop, 'Issues and Outcomes, Guidance and Indeterminacy: A Reply to Professor John Rogers and Others' (1996) 49 *Vanderbilt Law Review* 1969, 1070 et seq; S Levmore, 'Ruling Majorities and Reasoning Pluralities' (2002) 3 *Theoretical Inquiries in Law* 87, 97.

19 The problem is also labelled as 'doctrinal paradox', see D Grossi and G Pigozzi, *Judgment Aggregation. A Primer* (California, Morgan & Claypool Publishers, 2014), 8. On historical discussions of the problem in Germany, see Ernst (n 15) 177 et seq.

to which the common law strategy of requiring a majority for the outcome only is just one of the possible solutions. Disregarding possible combinations and fuzzy intersections, the basic possible solutions are the following:

(1) the outcome-oriented solution (requiring a majority for the outcome only);
(2) the reasons-oriented solution (requiring a majority only for the sequence of reasons that will determine an outcome which itself need *not* be supported by a majority);
(3) the indefinite-pressure-to-harmonise-solution (requiring a majority for both reasons and outcome and leaving it to the bench, in the case of divergent majorities as to reasons and outcome, *somehow* – in whichever direction – to overcome the stalemate and to find the necessary double majority);
(4) non-regulation (ie abstention from setting up a general rule on how to proceed in actual cases of divergent majorities; this includes the absence of formal or informal self-imposed court rules).

Common law jurisdictions tend to adopt the first solution, or rather: there was never a definitive departure from the first solution, which has generally been the original one because it is the only one practicable in archaic legal systems with analphabetic judges. This is in line with a generally longer period (or, up to the present, higher degree) of conservation, in common law jurisdictions, of ancient features of adjudication such as orality,[20] heavy reliance on the parties and their pleadings with respect to proof and the scope of arguments to be considered by the court,[21] and a focus on putting an end to the individual controversy rather than on reinforcing and/or clarifying the rules.[22] Civil law jurisdictions, by contrast, have developed different and mostly diffuse strategies of dealing with the problem of divergent majorities. In the practice of apex courts in the *per curiam* tradition, none of the four above-mentioned solutions seems dominant. So far, I have never come across any explicit regulation (unless one counts the rare instances of rules which clearly require

---

20 On the tradition of orality, see Martineau (n 10); M Kirby, 'Judicial Dissent – Common Law and Civil Law Traditions' (2007) 123 *Law Quarterly Review* 379, 384 et seq; on incompatibility of deliberations in backstage conference with the tradition of orality (including publicity), see L Epstein, RA Posner and WM Landes, *The Behavior of the Federal Judges. A Theoretical and Empirical Study of Rational Choice* (Cambridge, Harvard University Press, 2013) 61, 308.

21 Over recent decades, there have been many changes bringing both traditions closer to one another. However, the importance of adversarial elements in common law systems, as opposed to the tendency towards the inquisitorial in civil law systems, continues to be one of the most the most fundamental systemic differences.

22 See Kirby (n 20) 388 et seq.

a majority for both reasons and outcome,[23] as imposing solution 3, which is, however, not an imperative interpretation).

Perhaps the clearest expression of solution 3, implying that *somehow* a compromise must be reached to the effect that both reasons and outcome have majority support, is to be found in the practice of courts which resort to 'integral' voting, ie to submitting decisions to the vote as a whole.[24] This is the practice, for instance, of the French *Conseil constitutionnel*, of the Polish Constitutional Tribunal and, apparently, of the Supreme Court of Japan – a practice which, in complex and controversial cases, may result in the production of numerous drafts until, finally, a version emerges which receives the required majority.[25] From what I have been told in interviews with various Justices, it appears that most courts in the *per curiam* tradition have a tendency towards either the reasons-oriented solution (2) or the pressure-to-harmonise-solution (3), combined with indefinite reservations, ie with a strong element of solution 4. Occasionally, inconsistent practices may be detected.[26] While inconsistencies should of course in principle be avoided, the prevalent strong element of indeterminacy or non-regulation seems quite appropriate, considering that no strict rule will be able to prevent strategic voting, and considering the iterative character of rational legal reasoning, ie the oscillation between judging results by reasons and judging reasons by results.[27] Obviously, the indefinite- pressure-to-harmonise-solution (3) is the one that most clearly requires not only discussion, but also compromise. And each of the solutions 2–4, pure or in more or less diffuse combinations, will require more

---

[23] For the German FCC: §27, 2nd sentence, FCC Rules of Procedure (*Geschäftsordnung des Bundesverfassungsgerichts*, GO BVerfG) in connection with §15(4), 2nd sentence, Federal Constitutional Court Act (*Bundesverfassungsgerichtsgesetz*, BVerfGG) (see already n 17 above); for the Austrian Constitutional Court: §34(2) Rules of Court (*Geschäftsordnung des Verfassungsgerichtshofes*) in connection with §12(1) Jurisdiction Act (*Jurisdiktionsnorm*, JN).

[24] On the difference between integral and sequential voting, see also the contribution by W Ernst in chapter 1 of the present collection (at pp 14–15).

[25] D Schnapper, *Une sociologue au Conseil Constitutionnel* (Paris, Gallimard, 2010) 280, mentions that she was told by the Secretary General of the *Conseil* that former president Robert Badinter had once produced a draft in fourteen successive versions. For the Grand Bench of the Supreme Court of Japan, H Itoh, *The Supreme Court and Benign Elite Democracy in Japan* (Farnham, Ashgate, 2010) 79, reports that, occasionally, more than ten drafts of a decision are produced. As to the Polish Constitutional Tribunal, I am relying on insider information.

[26] In Switzerland, for instance, the Federal Court (*Bundesgericht*) has held that decisions published with reasons need majority votes for the reasons as well as for the dispositive part, Bundesgericht (30.1.1985) BGE 111 Ib 116, 118. According to the Justice who kindly pointed me to this judgment, however, there are panels of that court which do not comply with that rule. It may be that the appearance of non-compliance vanishes if the 1985 judgment is interpreted as leaving room for informal voting (see below, section II.4 of the present chapter).

[27] On judicial reasoning as an iterative process in the sense defined above, see D Neuberger, '"Judge not, that ye be not judged": Judging Judicial Decision-Making' (2015), *The UK Supreme Court Yearbook*, Legal Year 2014–15, 15, 17; M Kriele, *Theorie der Rechtsgewinnung* (Berlin, Duncker & Humblot, 1976) 196 et seq.

deliberation than the outcome-oriented solution adopted in common law jurisdictions (1).

The second factor which increases the need to deliberate in jurisdictions requiring a majority for the reasons of a judgment is the problem of the *missing majority*, ie the problem that voting may fail to yield any majority at all.[28] This problem can arise wherever the choice to be made by voting is between more than two alternatives. If choices A, B and C are available and each gets three out of nine judicial votes, two people will have to change their votes for the required majority to be attained. Contrary to prejudices, this type of institutionalised pressure is not unknown in common law jurisdictions, where lawyers tend to see it as contrary to judicial independence. The problem of a missing majority can arise even where a majority is needed for the outcome only, and even in appellate courts, where outcome options are typically not numerous, but, even in common law jurisdictions, not necessarily reduced to two, either.[29] Obviously, however, occasions for this problem to arise multiply where majorities have to be found not merely for outcomes, but also for reasons; and the increase is not just proportional to the increase in length of text that must be agreed upon by a majority, because the number of alternatives available is less open to in-advance limitations with respect to reasons than it is with respect to outcomes. Accordingly, jurisdictions where majority requirements extend to reasons are much more likely to produce a habit of intense efforts to convince and converge.

2. SUPERMAJORITY REQUIREMENT FOR THE ELECTION OF JUSTICES

FCC Judges must be elected by a two thirds majority.[30] Supermajority requirements of this kind are particularly important in systems where multimember political institutions such as Parliamentary chambers have a decisive say or an important role in the process of selecting and appointing Justices. They counteract the temptation to resort to ever more ideologically committed candidates in order to ensure that they will toe the party line. They will normally keep extremists from the bench and secure the election of judges who are trusted across party lines to be open to arguments.[31]

---

28 On that problem see also the discussion by W Ernst in chapter 1 of the present collection (at pp 11–14).

29 Available options may be to affirm, reverse, or remand the decision under appeal; for these alternatives and further options, see S Levmore, 'Ruling Majorities and Reasoning Pluralities' (2002) 3 *Theoretical Inquiries in Law* 87, 95 et seq.

30 §6(1), 2nd sentence, and §7 BVerfGG.

31 Unless, of course, one single party commands the required supermajority, as is currently the case in Hungary.

Obviously, such a recruitment pattern will be supportive of a constructive culture of deliberation. Supermajority requirements for the election or approbation of Justices are on the rise throughout the world. Two thirds is the supermajority specification I have come across most frequently;[32] however, lower or even higher supermajority thresholds also feature in some countries.[33]

---

32 Beyond the German case (see n 30 above), a two thirds majority is required for the election of Constitutional Court/Supreme Court Justices (generally or, if only a part of them is elected by parliament or by one of the parliamentary chambers) in, eg, Argentina, Belgium, Chile, Croatia, Hungary, and Peru. In Bolivia, a two thirds majority in the legislative assembly is required for nomination as candidate for the *Tribunal Constitucional Plurinacional* in a preselection process. In some countries with mixed appointment systems, two thirds majority requirements are in place only with respect to a part of the Justices. This is the case, for instance, in Chile (for details, see Article 92(1) lit b of the Constitution of the Republic of Chile, and R Carroll and L Tiede, 'Ideological Voting on Chile's Constitutional Tribunal: Dissent Coalitions in the Adjudication of Rights' (2012) 11 *Journal of Human Rights* 85, 89), in Kosovo (Article 114 para 3 of the Constitution of the Republic of Kosovo), in Lebanon (Article 2 of Law no 250 concerning the institution of the Constitutional Council; in this case, the two thirds majority requirement applies to that half of the Justices which is to be nominated by the members of government, while the other half is to be nominated by an absolute majority of the members of parliament), in Italy, where the requirement is, however, lowered to three fifth after three unsuccessful ballots (for details, see the information brochure on the website of the Corte Costituzionale, p 29, available via http://www.cortecostituzionale.it/documenti/download/pdf/Cc_Checosa_2016.pdf, last accessed 29 February 2020), in Morocco (Article 130(1) of the Constitution of the Kingdom of Morocco), in Portugal (for details, see Articles 163h and 222.1 of the Constitution of the Portuguese Republic, and S Amaral-Garcia, N Garoupa and V Grembi, 'Judicial Independence and Party Politics in the Kelsenian Constitutional Courts: The Case of Portugal' (2009) 6 *Journal of Empirical Legal Studies* 381, 386), and in Tunisia (Article 11(3) of Organic Law no 2015-50 concerning the Constitutional Court).

33 In Spain, a three fifth majority is required for of that part of the judicial body which is to be elected by Congress, Senate, and the General Council of the Judiciary, respectively (for details, see the website of the *Tribunal Constitucional* via https://www.tribunalconstitucional.es/en/tribunal/Composicion-Organizacion/composicion/Paginas/default.aspx, last accessed 8 March 2020, and D Toda Castán, 'What is the Situation of Constitutional Jurisdiction in Europe? Worrying News from Spain' *VerfBlog*, 2017/2/02, available via http://verfassungsblog.de/what-is-the-situation-of-constitutional-jurisdiction-in-europe-worrying-news-from-spain/, last accessed 8 March 2020). For the Italian fallback solution, see n 32 above. In the US, until recently, Senate rules permitted a two fifth minority to filibuster the confirmation of a presidential nominee for the Supreme Court. This was changed in 2017 following a democrat threat to filibuster the confirmation of President Trump's nominee Neil Gorsuch, see C Savage, 'The Senate Filibuster Explained', available online via https://www.nytimes.com/2017/04/03/us/politics/filibuster-supreme-court-neil-gorsuch.html (last accessed 8 March 2020), as well as A Liptak and M Flegenheimer, 'Neil Gorsuch Confirmed by Senate as Supreme Court Justice', available online via https://www.nytimes.com/2017/04/07/us/politics/neil-gorsuch-supreme-court.html (last accessed 8 March 2020). In Israel, a majority of seven out of the nine members of the Judicial Selection Committee (or all but two of those who participate, if less than nine), which makes a binding proposal, is necessary for the selection of Supreme Court Justices, *cf* Wikipedia, Article 'Judicial Selection Committee (Israel)', and M Tamir, 'Recent Judicial Appointments to the Israeli Supreme Court: A Victory for Politicians, or Is It?', 25 April 2017, available online via

As with many beneficial institutions, the introduction or maintenance of a supermajority requirement may fail due to vested interests, and often enough due to precisely the type of grievance which it is supposed to remedy. Existing political polarisation is likely to be an obstacle to the setup of a depolarising supermajority requirement, just as corruption is likely to preempt efficient anti-corruption rules, and so forth. That is why beneficial institutional progress takes so much time, to say nothing of the cultural progress that may follow institutional progress only with additional delay. Therefore, as far as a supermajority requirement for the election of Justices is concerned, once the 'cunning of reason' (Hegel)[34] permits its introduction, it makes sense to protect it against regressions by establishing it as a rule of constitutional law.

3. NUMBER OF JUDGES, STABILITY OF PANEL COMPOSITION, AND POLITICAL QUOTA

The vast majority of Constitutional Court or Supreme Court benches are staffed with an uneven number of judges, so as to ensure that normally, with the full bench sitting, any possible split will render a majority. For cases of stalemate, which may nevertheless occur due to absences, a frequent solution is to provide the President with a casting vote.[35] Concerning the German FCC, this is the tie-breaking mechanism only for two exceptional types of decisions, one of them purely internal.[36] Otherwise, a wholly different solution has been adopted which, in combination with an informal political quota for the nomination of judges, yields strong counter-incentives to the formation of internal political factions.

The FCC is composed of two Senates consisting of eight judges each, in steady line-up.[37] That is, the Senates each make up a bench with a kind of

---

https://blog-iacl-aidc.org/test-3/2018/5/26/analysis-recent-judicial-appointments-to-the-israeli-supreme-court-a-victory-for-politicians-or-is-it (last accessed 29 February 2020).

34 'Cunning of reason' (*List der Vernunft*) is Hegel's term for the realisation of what is reasonable via human action which is driven by human passions and interests rather than (immediately) by reason itself (in other words: for the reasonable emerging as a result of the unreasonable).

35 A special version of that solution has been adopted for the Constitutional Court of Austria. Like in the courts of the Holy Roman Empire (Imperial Chamber Court and Aulic Council), the President of the Austrian CC votes *only* when there is a tie; otherwise, the President is a mere chairperson without voting power: see §31, 2nd and 3rd sentence, Constitutional Court Act 1953 (*Verfassungsgerichtshofgesetz 1953*, VfGG).

36 The Presiding Judge has a casting vote in the event of a tie in the committee which decides (internally, without the parties being involved) when it is unclear which of the two Senates of the FCC is competent to decide a case, §14(5), 2nd sentence, BVerfGG, and in the event of a tie in decisions concerning the recusation of a judge, §19(1) BVerfGG.

37 In addition, Chambers of three, which can only decide unanimously, deal with easy cases, §§15a(1), 81, §93d(3), 1st sentence, BVerfGG.

curiate identity. This seems typical of the civil law *per curiam* tradition, as opposed to the tradition in common law countries, where instead of more or less constant combinations of judges in an adjudicating body, continual *re*combinations seem to be more common, or at least rather frequent. Stability of judicial formations is probably in itself a factor that tends to promote open and respectful deliberations, mainly because it generates stable relationships of recurrent cooperation and reciprocity, which are generally more conducive to fair and equitable behaviour than more ephemeral contacts. Of course, where, as in the UK Supreme Court, judges mostly sit in varying combinations of five, seven, nine, or eleven[38] of a total of only twelve, cooperative relations will always be close enough between all members of the court to produce that moderating effect.

To be victorious, applicants before the FCC must, as a rule, win over a majority, ie five of the eight judges on the Senate dealing with their case. This has become culturally relevant in combination with an informal arrangement securing a politically balanced composition of both Senates. The informal arrangement in place for decades was that each of the two major political parties, *CDU* and *SPD* (Christian Democrats and Social Democrats) – or, to be more precise – their groups in the two chambers of the German Parliament (*Bundestag* and *Bundesrat*), have the right to nominate half of the judges on each Senate and will assign a proper share in their nomination rights to possible partners in coalition. Combined with that arrangement, the even number of judges and the way the majority requirement works have exerted a preventive effect on the formation of political voting blocs within the FCC, because they have excluded the possibility of a bloc with a chance to rule by non-dialogic majority rather than try to convince in debate. Under a conservative government, for instance, conservative judges (judges with a conservative party nomination background) might, in theory, vote down any application against acts of the current government without taking pains to engage in serious debate with their colleagues. But such a strategy would not recommend itself, given that governmental majorities can always change and thus put colleagues from 'the other side' into a position to retaliate. In such a framework, strategic faction-building is unlikely even to come to mind.

Yet however beneficial for the court's culture of deliberation, the said arrangement was certainly not flawless. It was never entirely fair, because it disadvantaged smaller parties in the opposition camp. Moreover, it needed to be adapted to changes in the political importance of the parties involved. In 2016, a (partial) adaptation was reportedly agreed upon, according to which in the future,

38 Sitting *en banc* as a full panel. In accordance with section 42(1)(a) of the Constitutional Reform Act 2005, the Supreme Court necessarily 'consists of an uneven number of judges'. Thus there cannot be a panel of 12 Supreme Court Justices.

the Green Party would nominate one in five judges.[39] This new arrangement turned out to be untenable and has meanwhile been replaced by one including the Liberal Party in a 3:3:1:1-allotment of nomination 'rights'.[40] Under the present conditions of political diversification and volatility, stable solutions have become unlikely, but it remains important to preserve an equilibrium or a kind of pluralism on the bench which counteracts the risk of political faction-building.

Many countries have mixed political appointment systems where political equilibrium or sufficient pluralism on the court is difficult to achieve. A judge from one such country told me that in his country, the President has a habit to use his share in the selection power to correct possible imbalances. But that is a matter of individual wisdom and virtue. More reliable institutional safeguards ought to be preferred.

In countries with a (predominantly) professional recruitment system[41] – more typical with respect to Supreme Courts than with respect to specialised Constitutional Courts, and sometimes associated with a habit to appoint career judges only – the need to secure a balance of political inclinations on the bench may seem less salient because in such a system, proximity to political parties or to their values will usually not be among the selection criteria in the first place, and at least initially, they will be less visible to the public. However, the more an apex court has to deal with matters of political interest and importance, the more visible it will become whether or not the case law of that court reflects political bias, and it will be wise to take that into account in the appointment process and to design that process accordingly.

4. INFORMAL VOTING AND THE ROLE OF THE REPORTING JUDGE

A point which has so far not received much attention is that a culture of serious and consensus-oriented deliberation will be enhanced by informalities in

---

39 See the newspaper article by C Rath, 'Neue Formel für die Wahl der Bundesverfassungsrichter', *Die Tageszeitung*, 8 September 2016.

40 The order agreed upon in 2016 would have meant that, in 2018, the Green Party would have been able to nominate the successor of a retiring judge in the First Senate, which would have produced a clear left-liberal dominance in that Senate. Following widespread protest, including concerns voiced by the FCC (not just from the more conservative judges), the order in which the parties involved were to exercise their nomination rights was modified so as to preserve the equilibrium of more conservative and more liberal judges in the Senate. For the new arrangement see C Rath, 'Vier Wahlen für Karlsruhe', *Legal Tribune Online*, 10 March 2020, available online via https://www.lto.de/recht/justiz/j/bverfg-nachfolger-vosskuhle-masing-praesident-vizepraesident-wahlen-neue-richter-karlsruhe/ (last accessed 22 May 2020).

41 This includes election by judicial appointment committees with a preponderance of members from amongst the judiciary.

ascertaining what the opinions of the several judges are – in short: by informal voting –, and by a corresponding flexibility with respect to the disclosure of votes.[42] The practice of the German Federal Constitutional Court is a case in point.

As regards informal voting, the institution of the so-called 'reporting judge' plays an important part. The reporting judge (*rapporteur*) as a typical institution of civil law jurisdictions is not the same as that of the *lead judge* in common law jurisdictions. The term *lead judge* is often applied to the judge who is commissioned to draft the first opinion, with a view to gathering a majority, *after* (first) deliberation and voting in conference.[43] The *rapporteur*, by contrast, has to prepare a text in advance which will serve as the basis for the court's deliberations right from the start.

In the case of the German FCC, the procedure of deliberating on the basis of a text prepared by the *rapporteur* has two stages.

For the first stage, the *rapporteur* has to prepare an extensive report, in Senate cases usually 150–300 pages and often more,[44] which is supposed to summarise the briefs and the history of the case, and – on the basis of existing legislation, case law and jurisprudence – to explore all the legal ramifications, ideally in such a way that, whichever path the majority choose at any of the possible junctions, they will find all the information needed in order to decide how to proceed further. The report usually ends on a suggestion for the so-called *Tenor* (the dispositive part of the judgment) which follows from the reasoning developed by the *rapporteur*. This report is not just a source of information relieving the other judges of the burden of having to do all the research each on their own, nor is it just a necessary device that helps to structure the discussion in conference and to make sure that no legally relevant aspect is forgotten. It also serves as a kind of default option, in the sense that those parts of the reasoning and those conclusions or interim conclusions to which none of the judges raises any objection will be counted as consented. The report thus works as a basis of informal voting by silent acquiescence.

Any objections that have been raised are usually processed in an informal way, too. A controversial issue will normally be discussed at length, up to the point where no new arguments emerge, or where opposition to the

42 On the disclosure of votes, see section II.5 below.

43 See, eg, I Greene, *Final Appeal: Decision-Making in Canadian Courts of Appeal* (Toronto, James Lorimer & Co, 1998) 88 et seq. Alternatively, it is used for the presiding judge, particularly in smaller panels where the most senior judge presides and the term 'President' may appear too pompous; see, eg, M Palmer, 'Compromising Courts and Harmonizing Ideologies: mediation in the administrative chambers of the people's courts of the People's Republic of China' in A Harding and P Nicholson (eds), *New Courts in Asia* (London and New York, Routledge, 2010) 251, 264.

44 For details, see Lübbe-Wolff, 'Cultures of Deliberation' (n 1) 40.

dominant view somehow fades away. The Presiding Justice – ie the President or Vice-President – will then eventually look around and, without having solicited a formal vote, say something like: 'Well, my impression is that we have a consensus on this issue', or '… that we have a majority in favour of …', and if no one objects to this assessment, that is how the issue is considered to have been decided. Such a practice of informal voting spares the proponents of solutions which have not prevailed an explicit backtrack. This is extremely helpful because it neutralises the derationalising effect of certain emotions from which no human is entirely free. Mindful judges know from their own experience as well as from the experience of the behaviour of others that the most difficult of all judicial exercises is getting off a horse once mounted.[45] With the informal practice just described, a judge whose initially voiced opinion on an issue has not succeeded in winning over a majority can leave open – perhaps even in his own mind – whether he has been convinced by a majority or just refrains from writing a dissent.[46] The next case raising the same legal question(s) will as a rule find that same judge on the majority side, where he can always leave it open whether he now sides with the majority on account of existing precedent only, or for additional reasons meanwhile adopted. This particular method of consensus-building[47] is successful, even with respect

45 In Chamber cases, which can only be decided unanimously (see n 37), when a motivated 'reverse'-decision I had proposed as a reporting judge met with objections from one of my colleagues, who instead suggested a non-motivated refusal to decide the case, I found it helpful to let the matter rest for some time. Upon rereading my draft a few weeks later, I sometimes found the suggested alternative more acceptable than I had found it in the days immediately following the weekend I had spent writing the draft. The FCC caseload is such that every judge has to report on several hundred Chamber cases every year. Initial discord in some of them is inevitable. Where there is an insuperable stalemate, transfer of the case to the respective Senate of eight is the only solution. Given the limited processing capacities of the Senates, however, there is institutionalised pressure to find an agreement in the Chamber. In this way, unanimity requirements, which – as a kind of compensation for a smaller number of judges on the bench – are part of the filtering mechanism in many constitutional courts besides the German FCC (also, for instance, in those of Austria, Belgium, Kosovo, Hungary, Korea, Turkey, and Slovenia), can make decisions in minor cases a kind of 'exercise field' for a culture of consensus-seeking in the major cases.

46 One might ask whether this practice, which is common also in other German federal courts, is compatible with the judicial duty to cast a vote (which, in Germany, is implied in various rules of the Judicature Act, GVG, as well as the Law on the Federal Constitutional Court, BVerfGG). For a critical appraisal of non-explicit voting practices, see W Ernst, 'Abstimmen über Rechtserkenntnis' (2012) 67 *JuristenZeitung* 637, 641 et seq. In fact, the FCC practice described above is premised on such a duty in that no judge is ever allowed simply to abstain from voicing his opinion at all and indeed any kind of formal voting, also have their costs.

47 The method is applied in many courts of the *per curiam* tradition, but far from universally. The Constitutional Court of Austria, for instance, relies much more on sequential formal voting. There are, however, limits to the breaking down of questions into sub-questions, and

to 'internalisation', because it builds upon the malleabilities and permeabilites characterising any living system, including systems of individual beliefs.

With all of the functions mentioned above, the report is an indispensable instrument of efficient decision-making in a court with majority requirements in the *per curiam* tradition (see above, section II.2). It is not, however, an institution intended to make the reporting judge more influential than the other judges, and the practice of the FCC aims at preventing any such effect. Reports are as extensive as they are because they are designed to let all members of the bench partake in the expertise acquired by the *rapporteur* in preparing the report.[48] In addition, the report is accompanied by a collection – formerly a paper collection, now an electronic one – of all the materials used in preparing it, including copies of the written submissions of the parties and of all other relevant elements of the file, as well as copies of all the case law and experts' literature cited in the report (except for what each of the judges is supposed to have in his office library, such as the standard collection of FCC decisions). It is up to the judges whether to form their view of the case mainly on the basis of the report, or mainly on the basis of the accompanying materials, or both. As a rule, every single member of the Senate is very well prepared. Objections to the report, sometimes circulated in writing before the conference date, are raised freely, and quite frequently the reporting judge will find his suggestions for the outcome or important parts of the underlying reasoning rejected by a majority of his colleagues.

Collegial interventionism continues at the next stage. Once it becomes clear in the report-based conference(s) what the outcome and the essential reasons of a decision are to be, the judgment text will have to be drafted. As a rule, it is for the *rapporteur* to do this, irrespective of whether or not his report has secured a majority for the proposed outcome. If, however, the *rapporteur* (unwisely) declares himself unable to 'motivate' the outcome decided by the court, a colleague will be found who is willing to take over.[49] The draft will

therefore limits to formal sequential voting, which even a court more committed to formal voting cannot avoid. An alternative is integral voting, as practiced by some courts in the *per curiam* tradition (see above, text accompanying and following n 24). Integral voting, like any other strategy, comes with certain costs: In controversial cases, multiple versions of a draft may have to be produced until a majority is found (see n 24), and as motivating factors to dropping objections, fatigue and – other things being equal – social pressure are likely play a greater part with integral voting than with sequential voting. Integral voting, too, can in theory be accomplished informally, but the cost-benefit-ratio is likely to be much less favourable here.

48 The *rapporteur* is usually not initially an expert in the particular field for which he is reporting. In the FCC, as a rule, reporting competences, which are determined in advance by a schedule of responsibilities, are not allocated according to previous fields of work of the judges.

49 From my twelve years on the FCC, I recall but one case where someone had to step in because a *rapporteur* was so dissatisfied with the Court's findings that he refused to write the judgment.

then be circulated, and all the judges – not just those who agree with the outcome – will suggest changes (using the electronic correction function), often substantial ones, which will then be presented for discussion in another conference or, depending on the number and controversiality of proposed changes, in several further conferences. This second conference stage is called 'reading deliberation' (ie deliberation on the basis of a close reading of the so-called 'consolidated draft' showing the results of the circulation phase).[50] Here again, formal voting is an exception. Passages of the *rapporteur*'s initial draft as well as suggestions for change which he has accepted by incorporating them into the consolidated draft count as accepted in the absence of any challenge. Controversial passages and controversial suggestions for change will be discussed one by one, moving from page to page. It can happen that the objections engendered by a draft are such that someone submits an alternative draft of the decision as a whole or of great parts of it, or that the Senate asks a small number of its members, including the reporting judge, to cooperate in the production of a new version of the draft. And just as in the first stage of deliberations, the discussion of alternatives will usually not end with formal voting. Formal votes by a raising of hands are solicited only when it is unclear from the course of the discussion where the majority lies.

5. POSSIBLE OPACITY OF VOTING BEHAVIOUR

For this practice of informal voting to work in favour of consensus-building in the way just described, the individual judge must be able *not* to communicate publicly how he has voted. Formal and informal rules for the FCC are framed accordingly. Decisions of the Court are signed by *all* the judges sitting in the case,[51] regardless of whether or not they agree with the decision. To common lawyers, this may look like false certification. In the *per curiam* tradition, however, for a judge to sign a decision does not mean that he subscribes to it in a figurative sense. It expresses that he was on the bench sitting in the case, and that the decision is one of that *curia*, not one of the individual judges. The indistinctive signature requirement is a strong symbolic expression of the *per curiam* concept of judicial decision-making. It holds for many apex courts in the *per curiam* tradition, but not for all of them.[52]

---

50 For details of the procedure, which is slightly different in the two Senates, see references in n 1.

51 §30(1), 1st sentence, BVerfGG. If a judge who participated in the decision-making is prevented from signing, this is to be certified by the Presiding Judge, §28(2) GO BVerfG. In the published version of the judgment, signatures are reproduced in typewritten copy.

52 Alternatives in place for some courts are, for instance, signature by the president of the court/the presiding judge of the respective formation (eg, Constitutional Court of Slovenia, with

FCC judges who do not agree with a decision may, but do not have to, add a separate opinion, and the Senates may, but do not have to, disclose the *numerical distribution* of votes in their decisions.[53] This includes the possibility to disclose that a decision was made unanimously, and the possibility to disclose differences with respect to votes on outcome and votes on reasons. It does *not*, however, include the possibility of disclosing names, ie communicating who voted which way. In practice, the Senates will always decide in favour of transparency with respect to how votes were cast if a dissenting member in the minority asks for such disclosure – a courtesy stimulated by the fact that the requesting member might resort to publicising non-unanimity by way of publishing a separate opinion if his motion were rejected.

That leaves the court and its members with an array of nuances in the expression of concord or discord, which not only protects the beneficial informality in ascertaining what the majorities are (see section II.4 above,), but also enhances the consensus-oriented culture of deliberation by providing material which, since its use is discretionary, can be used to find compromise without thereby compromising the law. For instance, if the majority has gone a long way to accommodate a minority concern, eg by narrowing reasons substantially, so that they will have less far-reaching consequences beyond the case at hand, it would be unusual for the judge(s) in the minority not to honour this by renouncing the publication of a dissenting opinion. In turn, the majority would probably have been less inclined to show accommodating behaviour if it had not expected this accommodation to be honoured in such a way.

Interestingly, the US Supreme Court worked with the same opacity at the height of its collegial functioning: There was no general signature requirement, but no requirement that each and every Justice make his vote public, either. From the 'opinion of the court', usually delivered by the Chief Justice, it could not be detected who had supported it. Internal dissent was not necessarily articulated publicly.[54] I would presume that, along with this element of opacity, an associated practice of informal voting similar to the one described above (in section II.4) helped to keep the Supreme Court cohesive in those early times.

exceptions), or by the president/presiding judge and the registrar/secretary/secretary general (eg, Constitutional Court of Austria, European Court of Human Rights). Decisions of the Italian *Corte Costituzionale* are signed by the President (*presidente*), the judge who drafted the decision (*redattore*), and the Secretary General (*cancelliere*). The collective decisions of the French *Conseil constitutionnel* are published without signatures or typewritten copies of signatures. Instead, the last sentence of the decision indicates the judges who took part in the decision ('Jugé par le Conseil constitutionnel dans sa séance du …., où siégeaient ….').

53 §30(2) BVerfGG.

54 Sunstein (n 9). Sunstein, like one of the Justices he quotes as evidence for that practice (and, as far as I can see, in line with general usage in the legal literature), uses the term 'silent acquiescence' to denote non-publication of a judge's objections to the opinion of the court. I am puzzled by that terminology. Would it not be closer to common understanding to

6. PRIVACY OF DELIBERATIONS

Apart from the notable exceptions just mentioned (in section II.5), there is strict *in*transparency in the FCC with respect to the course of deliberations and voting.[55] 'Secrecy of deliberations' is the rule for other German courts, too,[56] and indeed for most courts in the world.[57] There are some countries which depart from the principle of secrecy even for apex courts by providing for public conferencing either generally or in certain parts or circumstances (Brazil, Switzerland, Mexico).[58] Experiences with mandatory deliberation in public do not encourage imitation. In the Swiss Federal Court (*Bundesgericht*), where public deliberation is mandatory inter alia when the Justices are not unanimous, what has come of it is almost omnipresent unanimity[59] (probably in good faith – a nice example of how interest, including the interest in finding one's own behaviour irreprehensible, generates convictions). In Brazil, public deliberations by the Justices of the *Supremo Tribunal Federal* are reported

reserve the term 'silent acquiescence' to internal *con*sent which is not made explicit in public, and to speak of 'silent dissent' or 'silent objections' when internal dissent (or objections with respect to reasons) is what remains undisclosed? Taking non-disclosure of dissent to amount to acquiescence ascribes to the former a meaning which it would only have in a system requiring any dissent from the opinion of the court to be made public. It might even make sense to substitute 'invisible' for 'silent', in order to avoid confusing what is communicated internally with what is communicated in public.

55 §30(1), 1st sentence, BVerfGG.

56 §43 German Law on Judges (*Deutsches Richtergesetz*, DRiG).

57 However, in many common law jurisdictions, including the United Kingdom, formal legal rules prescribing secrecy of deliberations are absent; confidentiality is regarded merely as a convention.

58 For the Mexican *Suprema Corte de Justicia de la Nación* (with a private deliberation following the public one) and for the Brazilian *Supremo Tribunal Federal*, see AR do Vale, *Argumentação constitucional: um estudo sobre a deliberação nos tribunais constitucionais* (Doctoral Thesis, Universidad de Alicante/Universidade de Brasilia, Brasília-Alicante 2015), 107 et seq, available online via https://rua.ua.es/dspace/bitstream/10045/50465/1/tesis_rufino_do_vale.pdf (last accessed 29 February 2020); VA da Silva, 'Deciding without deliberating' (2013), 11 *International Journal of Constitutional Law* 557, 568; F Pou Giménez, 'Changing the Channel. Broadcasting Deliberations in the Mexican Supreme Court' in R David and D Taras (eds), *Justices and Journalists. The Global Perspective* (Cambridge, Cambridge University Press, 2017) 209 et seq; for Switzerland, see short information on the website of the Federal Court (*Bundesgericht*), and H-J Mosimann, M Felber and T Stadelmann, 'Öffentliche Urteilsberatung am Bundesgericht – aktuelle Probleme und Lösungsansätze', *Justice – Justiz – Giustzia* 2014/1; P Eggenberger and C Stöckli, 'Das Volk will wissen, was im Gericht läuft', *plädoyer* 6/0 of 29 November 2010, updated 7 October 2013 (interview with Swiss federal judge M Schubarth and barrister H Heeb), available via https://www.plaedoyer.ch/artikel/d/das-volk-will-wissen-was-im-gericht-laeuft/ (last accessed 8 March 2020).

59 Mosimann/Felber/Stadelmann (n 58). On the Swiss experience, see also the contribution by T Stadelmann in chapter 9 of the present collection.

usually to consist in the Justices just voting *seriatim*, each of them reading their prefabricated opinion.[60] In Mexico, where Supreme Court decisions are extremely fragmented, too, publicly broadcasted deliberations have been identified as a main reason.[61] No wonder: the virtuoso judicial exercise mentioned above[62] is already hard enough to perform in front of just a few colleagues.

7. SEPARATE OPINIONS

An increasing number of countries in the civil law tradition allow at least their apex courts to publish separate opinions. What is the effect of this licence on the culture of decision-making?

It certainly is not a necessary prerequisite for the development of a culture of serious and consensus-oriented deliberation. From conversations with Justices from courts where publication of separate opinions is illicit, I take it that some of these courts work in a fairly deliberative way, with the Justices still listening to one another and trying to convince each other even when majorities are already clear. Several Justices explained this to me as a matter of mutuality: judges in the majority do not cut discussions short and just vote down objections, because they do not want the same to happen to themselves when they are in the minority. This indicates that recruitment patterns preventing bloc dominances (see section II.3 above) are more important than the permissibility of separate opinions.

From my experience on the FCC, however, I would draw the conclusion that in a court with a basically deliberative, consensus-oriented culture, leave to publish separate opinions will further enhance that culture, because it will provide additional motivation for the majority to persuade the minority to join them or at least refrain from publicising objections.[63] For the latter motive to

60 Da Silva (n 58) 568 et seq.

61 Pou Giménez (n 58) 222 et seq; *cf* also M Aragón Reyes, 'La deliberación en los tribunales constitucionales' (2018) 112 *Revista Española de Derecho Constitucional* 377, 378, 384. Pou Giménez, ibid, nevertheless appreciates public deliberations because they help generate trust and improve public knowledge in legal matters.

62 In section II.4, text accompanying n 45.

63 See the example given in section II.5 above (at p 175). *Cf* also do Vale (n 58) 185 et seq; R Lamprecht, *Abweichende Meinungen und ihre Bedeutung für die Rechtskultur* (Baden-Baden, Nomos, 1992) 305, with further references. For the opposite view, see V Ferreres, 'The Consequences of Centralizing Constitutional Review in a Special Court. Some Thoughts on Judicial Activism' (2004) SELA (*Seminario en Latinoamérica de Teoría Constitucional y*

become effective, judges must be allowed to keep objections, and even the mere fact that they do object, to themselves (see section II.5).

III. CULTURE AND INSTITUTIONAL FRAMEWORKS

A productive culture of deliberation does not come into existence because there are nice people on the bench. It comes about as a result of framework conditions and circumstances which act upon behaviour. Humans have the advantage of being able to design and change a great part of the framework conditions affecting their behaviour, ie to create *institutional* frameworks, such as legislation and other types of rules, formal and informal. This capacity is the source of all human progress. As Georg Wilhelm Friedrich Hegel, the great philosopher of institutions, once observed, efficient institutional frameworks often work indirectly.[64] Their efficiency lies in that they produce habits, expectations and corresponding *internalised* norms. Over the sense of autonomy which (rightly) goes with any internalisation of norms, their institutional origin and their need to be institutionally stabilised may easily escape awareness. The institutional frameworks underlying judicial cultures of deliberation are therefore easily overlooked.

IV. CONCLUDING REMARKS

The above passages deal with just those factors which may all too easily escape attention. There are, of course, others. Safeguards of judicial independence and integrity, for instance, are of paramount importance. In the absence of judicial independence, or with corrupt judges, the 'compelling force of the better argument' (as Jürgen Habermas has put it) will not work, and a culture of genuine discussion is unlikely to develop where, due to endemic corruption or governmental control of the judiciary, the outcome of cases is predictable anyway. Caseload, filtering mechanisms, available support by clerks, research departments, etc, determine how much time is available for deliberation. Rules and practices concerning the number of judges on a bench and their selection can be of relevance far beyond the aspects mentioned above. Collegiality will be adversely affected or promoted by factors

---

Política) Paper 39, available online via http://digitalcommons.law.yale.edu/yls_sela/39 (last accessed 29 February 2020) at 21, with further references.

64 For an overview, see G Lübbe-Wolff, 'Die Aktualität der Hegelschen Rechtsphilosophie' in B Sandkaulen and V Gerhardt, *Gestalten des Bewusstseins, Genealogisches Denken im Kontext Hegels* (Hamburg, Felix Meiner Verlag, 2009) 328 et seq (also available online).

generating or preventing internal hierarchies, and so on. Even culture itself works as a framework condition, because it determines expectations and the kind of feedback that people get when they do or do not behave in certain ways. Cultures, however, are never entirely self-supporting. They improve or deteriorate with changing frameworks. That should be kept in mind, whatever the state of satisfaction or dissatisfaction with the culture of deliberation in a given court.

CHAPTER 9

COLLECTIVE JUDGING AT THE SWISS SUPREME COURT

Thomas STADELMANN*

I. PRELIMINARY REMARKS[1]

Switzerland is a Federal Republic consisting of 26 Cantons. The Cantons are sovereign except to the extent that their sovereignty is limited by the Swiss Federal Constitution.[2]

Apart from a few provisions in the Constitution,[3] the Cantons are free in how they organise their courts and how they regulate court proceedings. Thus, there are 27 different systems in Switzerland – 26 for the Cantons and

* Justice Thomas Stadelmann has been a Judge at the Swiss Supreme Court since 2010.

1 The preliminary remarks and specifics regarding the functioning of the Swiss Supreme Court are partly based on an article by T Stadelmann, 'Tax Litigation Before the Swiss Supreme Court' [2016] *Bulletin for International Taxation* 65.

2 Article 3 of the Swiss Constitution.

3 For example Article 30 of the Swiss Constitution provides:

'Judicial proceedings

1 Any person whose case falls to be judicially decided has the right to have their case heard by a legally constituted, competent, independent and impartial court. Ad hoc courts are prohibited.

one for the Federal courts,[4] each with different solutions.[5] The focus of this contribution lies on the rules and regulations applicable to the Swiss Supreme Court (*Bundesgericht*).

II. COGNISANCE

It is important to note that the Swiss Supreme Court cannot, in general, establish or revise the facts of a given case. The facts of a case can only be corrected by the Supreme Court if the Court finds that the facts have been incorrectly established by the lower court in a flagrant manner or that the finding of facts was based on a violation of law.[6] Apart from such (rare) corrections of the facts, the Supreme Court only addresses questions of law.

The dispute before the Supreme Court and the legal grounds relevant to deciding the case are primarily defined by the parties. The Supreme Court applies the law *ex officio*,[7] but only within the grounds of the appeal brought forward by the parties involved.

III. ORGANISATION OF THE COURT

The organisation and procedure of the Supreme Court are governed by statutory law,[8] namely the *Bundesgerichtsgesetz* or BGG. The Supreme Court consists of

---

2 Unless otherwise provided by law, any person against whom civil proceedings have been raised has the right to have their case decided by a court within the jurisdiction in which they reside.

3 Unless the law provides otherwise, court hearings and the delivery of judgments shall be in public.'

4 The Federal courts are the *Schweizerisches Bundesgericht/Tribunal fédéral suisse* (Swiss Federal Supreme Court, here referred to as Swiss Supreme Court or Supreme Court), the *Schweizerisches Bundesverwaltungsgericht* (Swiss Federal Administrative Court), the *Schweizerisches Bundesstrafgericht* (Swiss Federal Criminal Court) and the *Schweizerisches Bundespatentgericht* (Swiss Federal Patent Court). There are, however, specific laws regarding the organisation of each of the Federal courts: *Bundesgesetz vom 17. Juni 2005 über das Bundesgericht* (*Bundesgerichtsgesetz* or BGG; SR 173.110), *Bundesgesetz vom 17. Juni 2005 über das Bundesverwaltungsgericht* (*Verwaltungsgerichtsgesetz* or VGG; SR 173.32), *Bundesgesetz vom 20. März 2009 über das Bundespatentgericht* (*Patentgerichtsgesetz* or PatGG; SR 173.41), and *Bundesgesetz vom 19. März 2010 über die Organisation der Strafbehörden des Bundes* (*Strafbehördenorganisationsgesetz* or StBOG; 173.71).

5 Lack of space prevents this contribution describing and discussing all of the different solutions adopted in respect of different courts The focus here lies on the Swiss Supreme Court. However, some specific cantonal solutions which may be of interest from an international perspective will also be mentioned in passing.

6 Article 105 BGG.

7 Article 106 BGG.

8 Article 188 (2) of the Swiss Federal Constitution (BV).

seven Chambers, two dealing with public law, two dealing with civil (private) law, two dealing with social security law and one dealing with criminal law. In addition to 38 ordinary judges serving full-time the Supreme Court has 19 deputy judges. These deputy federal judges serve in a part-time capacity. Their primary occupations are professors, practicing lawyers or cantonal judges. In general, the deputy judges serve as replacements for judges who have recused themselves from a case or have taken sick leave, or when the workload of the Supreme Court becomes overly heavy. In the proceedings in respect of which they sit, the deputy judges have the same rights and obligations as ordinary judges.[9]

IV. CASELOAD[10]

In 2019, the Supreme Court had to deal with 7,884 new cases in total.[11] It has no means of controlling its caseload. A project to change the law with the intention of permitting the Supreme Court to focus more on relevant cases by excluding certain cases of lesser importance from appeal to the Court was discussed in 2018/2019 in the two Chambers of Parliament, but the necessary majority could not be found.[12]

V. WORKING PROCEDURES

Incoming appeals are distributed among the Chambers according to the legal subject involved. Then the President of the competent Chamber,[13] assisted by his staff of court clerks and office personnel, undertakes the preliminary work concerning a given case, such as organising the exchange of written arguments between the parties, taking decisions as regards requests for an advance of costs, etc. The President is also competent in respect of decisions of (manifest)

9 With the exception of the procedure according to Article 25 BGG, (*cf* under heading VIII. below, 'Consistency of Case Law'), where all – and only – the ordinary judges of the Chambers concerned have the right to participate.

10 See *Geschäftsbericht 2019 des Bundesgerichts* (available under https://www.bger.ch/files/live/sites/bger/files/pdf/Publikationen/GB/BGer/de/GB19_DE_BGer.pdf, last accessed 2 April 2020).

11 It is worth noting that about 40% of the cases disposed of in 2019 were based on a refusal to consider the case on its merits (*Nichteintreten*): *cf Geschäftsbericht 2019*, ibid 19, figure 3.1.2.

12 See https://www.parlament.ch/de/ratsbetrieb/suche-curia-vista/geschaeft?AffairId=20180051#/AffairSummary (last accessed 2 April 2020).

13 The President of the Chamber is elected for two years by the full Supreme Court on a proposal from the Chamber. He (or she) can be re-elected twice.

inadmissibility. Once the preliminary phase is over, the President assigns a case to an individual judge ('Reporting Judge'). With regard to such an assignment, a main criterion is the language of the case,[14] with a second criterion possibly being the special judicial knowledge of a judge or of the law clerks in a particular judge's team. It seems obvious that this margin could in theory give the President of the Chamber the possibility of influencing the direction of the outcome of a case by selecting the Reporting Judge according to his (likely) tenor. In practice, however, this problem does not arise since the other judges of the Chamber would notice if such behaviour occurred on a regular basis and would intervene.

The Reporting Judge is responsible for the drafting of a judgment. He does so himself or has it done by a law clerk. The law clerks are the judicial staff of the judges.[15] Currently the Court has 132 clerks. Previously, their primary task was to draft the written judgments after the decisions had been taken in court. Given the increasing caseload of the Supreme Court, the law clerks are now also tasked with drafting the Reporting Judges' decisions in many cases. They work under the responsibility of the Reporting Judge, and it is up to the Reporting Judge to define the allowance he gives to his law clerks.[16] It is the Reporting Judge's decision whether and when to put a draft into circulation, and it is his proposition that is up for the discussion within the panel. In all cases, however, the law clerks have a consultative vote. If they do not agree with the opinion of the Reporting Judge, they can add their remarks to the files to be circulated.[17] The law clerks also are involved, in an advisory capacity, in the preparatory stages of proceedings and during deliberations.

Another task of the court clerks is to draft the final text of rulings based on the remarks made by the members of the Chamber (either in circulation or during oral debate) once the decision is taken. They sign the judgment, together with the President of the Chamber.

The drafting is based on the case file, especially the judgment in question, the appeal and the other party' s reply. Neither the parties nor experts nor third parties are heard. The draft judgment is circulated among the judges.

For reasons of impartiality, the composition of the panel, apart from the President and the Reporting Judge, is determined by a computer program within parameters set by the President. These parameters relate, inter alia, to the

---

14 Each judge uses his native language, ie French, German, or Italian, in written statements as well as in oral debates. The judges must have at least a passive understanding of the other two languages.

15 A former judge of the Supreme Court used to refer to the law clerks to foreign visitors as 'junior judges'.

16 In general, the free space given to a law clerk to elaborate a draft depends on the knowledge and experience of the law clerk and the complexity of the case.

17 See Article 24 BGG as well as Articles 38 et seq BGerR. It goes without saying that this might cause tensions between a judge and his law clerk, depending on how even-tempered the judge is in his reaction to objections: *cf* S Risi, 'Die beratende Stimme der Gerichtsschreibenden' [2017] *Justice – Justiz – Giustizia*, issue 3.

question of whether there should be a mixed gender panel and/or a specialist in the particular field of law on the panel. The President can override the composition of the computer-generated panel, but there must be good reasons to do so, and these must be documented.

A panel normally consists of three judges. In cases involving questions of principle or at the request of one of the judges on the panel, a larger panel of five judges can be created.[18]

VI. DECISION-MAKING PROCESS

Cases are usually decided by circulation alone. Given the caseload of the Court,[19] this course of action is indispensable. Nevertheless, it also has its downsides: The Reporting Judge has great responsibility and a large leeway. Very often, his colleagues on the panel do not have enough time to study all the documents in detail themselves, and they thus rely on the work of the Reporting Judge and maybe his law clerk.[20] This reliance can even reach a point (particularly when the case concerns a legal field in which the participating judges are not experienced) where the contribution of the participating judges is limited to a mere 'plausibility check' of the proposed judgment.[21]

If a judge does not agree with the draft – entirely or in part – he may either submit written comments or directly ask for a (public oral) deliberation. Usually, the former is preferred, and the President will then decide whether to let the draft with the annotations circulate a second time or whether an oral deliberation would be more useful. If there is a possibility of finding a common solution in discussion, the panels usually have internal meetings.[22]

---

18 Article 20 BGG. In contrast to the US system with its '*en banc* procedure', neither the parties nor the other two or three – not yet involved – judges of the Chamber can request a panel of five judges.

19 See under heading IV above ('Caseload').

20 The potential influence this way of proceeding generates for the Reporting Judge will be obvious. There could, for instance, be a considerable 'framing effect', meaning that it may be decisive which information is presented in what way in the draft judgment (*cf* in this context the remarks in n 36 below concerning the discussion of the role of the individual judge).

21 It should be noted that this might lead to a substantive preponderance for experienced and/or established judges in their function as Reporting Judges (this might for example occur by effect of an authority bias).

22 The law provides for only two forms of deliberation: either in a public oral debate or by way of circulating the dossier (Article 58 BGG). In the view of the Court, internal oral debates are admissible for editorial discussions of the judgment (ie discussions concerning differences in the motivation, but not in the outcome of a case: see S Heimgartner and H Wiprächtiger in *Basler Kommentar zum Bundesgerichtsgesetz*, 2nd edn (Basel, Helbing & Lichtenhahn, 2011) Art 59, paras [32] et seq. In practice, internal discussions are used on a regular basis to search for a common solution after divergences have emerged during the circulation.

The panel may debate a case orally not only following an order of the President, but also at the request of a panel judge. A case must be debated orally if unanimity within the panel is not found during circulation.[23] In the case of an oral debate, the panel deliberation and the voting must take place in public.[24]

In 2014, a motion in the Swiss Parliament requested that the public deliberations should be broadcast live, but this motion was dismissed.[25] A broad majority of the Court was happy with this decision, mostly for two reasons: One is connected with the Swiss system of rather short terms of tenure – six years in the case of the Supreme Court judges – and the need of being re-elected. There was a fear that live broadcasting could be misused to create profiles of the judges' ('political') attitudes and to use such profiles to refuse re-election for mere political reasons. Another fear concerned the quality of the deliberation. It was said that live broadcasting might increase the tendency of judges not really to enter substantive discussing with each other during the public deliberation, instead exchanging pre-elaborated statements.

It might be observed that the above-mentioned point addresses a weakness of the public deliberation process which already exists today: The usual understanding of a 'deliberation' would be that the participants try to find a solution by the means of a constructive dialogue. Their aim should be to improve the outcome of cases by discussing pros and cons of different approaches and to find additional answers in the process. Yet a public deliberation has a different primary purpose: it makes the finding of the judgment and the diverging opinions of the judges transparent to the public. Of course, this goal could also be reached if the public deliberation were held in the form of a constructive dialogue. But practical reality shows that most judges are a lot less inclined to enter open-ended discussions in public than they are to conduct them behind closed doors. This should not come as a surprise: it is quite a widespread attitude to think that by discussing open-endedly, one might give the impression of being insecure or still in search of a result; so it is common for panellists to prefer giving the impression that they have already reached a conclusion and have sound and convincing reasons for the solution they are proposing. It seems obvious that such a starting point is not ideal for a deliberation in the sense of a panel finding the best solution by means of constructive dialogue.

---

23 Article 58 BGG. However, the fact that there was a public deliberation does not necessarily mean that the panel was not unanimous in its conclusions: The President of the Chamber or one of the judges of the panel might well consider it useful to discuss the case in public to demonstrate publicly the possible way of reasoning even, when there is no substantive difference amongst the judges regarding the outcome.

24 Article 59 BGG.

25 See https://www.parlament.ch/de/ratsbetrieb/suche-curia-vista/geschaeft?AffairId=20133660 (last accessed 17 February 2020).

In 2015, another motion of the Swiss Parliament requested that, following a public deliberation, it should be possible to publish dissenting opinions.[26] Under the law currently in force, however, neither dissenting nor concurring opinions are published, nor are details of the voting process published.[27] Some literature suggests that deliberating and presenting the different opinions in public already includes the possibility of publishing dissenting and concurring opinions.[28] This view argues from the position of the outside observer. By doing so, however, the stages of deliberation on the one hand and of decision-making on the other are mixed up. If there is a vote on the bench to conclude on a joint decision, this means that the minority opinion is eliminated. Opinions which were rejected over the course of the deliberation can no longer be part of the judgment of the bench.[29] Therefore, under a civilian/continental approach, some concrete legal basis is essential if separate opinions are to be allowed.[30]

Public deliberations are regulated in detail in some points, and insufficiently or not at all in other points: On the one hand, there are stipulations on seating arrangements and speaking order.[31] On the other hand, there is no provision at all concerning the question of how to proceed in a situation where there are several conflicting motions.[32]

---

26 The motion was accepted on 11 March 2015 and 18 June 2015, respectively (https://www.parlament.ch/de/ratsbetrieb/suche-curia-vista/geschaeft?AffairId=20143667, last accessed 2 April 2020), but the proposal was finally rejected by Parliament (https://www.parlament.ch/de/ratsbetrieb/suche-curia-vista/geschaeft?AffairId=20180051, last accessed 2 April 2020). It has to be mentioned, that the effect of such an amendment would have had only a minor effect, bearing in mind that it would have introduced separate, dissenting opinions only for those cases which were deliberated in public (about 1% of all cases of the Swiss Supreme Court). Within the Supreme Court, supporters of a system change – from the system of public deliberation to a system with the possibility of separate opinions – are still a minority; yet voices suggesting that such a change could increase the overall quality of the deliberation process are on the rise.

27 It is clear, though, that a decision was unanimous if there was no public deliberation – the presence of a public deliberation would be noted in the decision. (As regards the connection between 'unanimity' and public deliberation, see comment in n 23 above.)

28 P Egli, 'Dissenting Opinions: Abweichende Richtermeinungen im Schweizer Recht', in F Lorandi and D Staehelin (eds), *Innovatives Recht: Festschrift für Ivo Schwander* (Zürich/St Gallen, Dike, 2011) 849.

29 See W Ernst, 'Abstimmungen in Richterkollegien' [2012] *Justice – Justiz – Giustizia*, issue 4, para [15].

30 *Cf* also M Baldegger, 'Der wiederkehrende Ruf nach „dissenting opinions" am Bundesgericht: Wünschbarkeit, Auswirkungen und Ausgestaltung richterlicher Sondervoten in der Schweiz' (2017) 118 *Schweizerisches Zentralblatt für Staats- und Verwaltungsrecht* (ZBl) 131. Note that there are several cantonal laws establishing the possibility of dissenting opinions. They vary significantly in the details (see the outline by Baldegger). It is especially worth mentioning the regulations regarding Zurich, which provide for the possibility not only of the judges, but also the law clerk in a given case (who – it will be recalled – in fact has only consultative vote), inserting his/her dissenting opinion into the files.

31 Article 44 BGerR.

32 On this subject, see heading VII below ('Voting').

Regarding the order of statements, the relevant regulation stipulates that the Reporting Judge presents the draft and his motion first, then the judge with a counter-motion gets the floor. After that, the baton is passed to the other judges counter-clockwise (starting from the Reporting Judge),[33] and the President speaks last.[34] Afterwards, the law clerk – who has a consulting vote – may take the floor. In general, there is a second round in the same order,[35] and in rare cases there can be a third round or a free exchange of arguments. The fact that there rarely is such a 'third round' before the final vote, and even less frequently a free discussion among the judges, shows the disadvantage of the public deliberation system: The very formalised procedure hinders a free exchange of opinions with the objective of finding a potentially better solution by constructive discourse.

Apart from these basic rules, there are neither regulations on the deliberations nor generally shared principles concerning the role of the individual judge within a panel of judges. Therefore, there are judges fostering the idea that their task is to find the best solution by themselves and to fight for this solution within the panel, whereas others have the image of the individual judge as part of a team, whose task is to discover the best solution together. It is obvious that these kinds of divergent self-conceptions do not facilitate collaboration.[36]

VII. VOTING

A very specific topic within the public deliberation process concerns voting. To begin with, one can state that the awareness for the complexity of voting problems is quite weak at the Swiss Supreme Court. The law only stipulates that abstention from voting is not allowed[37] and decisions are taken by a majority.[38] This principle is applicable not only to the adjudication itself, but also for the

33 This detail is not expressly stipulated, but is mere custom.
34 Unless the President himself is the Reporting Judge or the one presenting the counter-motion.
35 Whereupon, in general, the law clerk will not take the floor a second time.
36 The role and tasks of the individual judge, and especially his obligation towards the other members of the panel, seem obvious only at first sight. The challenge is in the details: For example, is a judge obliged to inform a colleague if he is noticing that this colleague is following his opinion, but based on the misunderstanding of some relevant point? It may be helpful to establish a sort of meta-discussion on the role and task of the individual judge within a panel at the Court and to achieve a shared understanding in doing so. For an example of such an understanding, see U Kranenpohl, *Hinter dem Schleier des Beratungsgeheimnisses: Der Willensbildungs- und Entscheidungsprozess des Bundesverfassungsgerichts* (Wiesbaden, VS Verlag für Sozialwissenschaften, 2010). Kranenpohl describes the shared view of the role of the Reporting Judge at the German *Bundesverfassungsgericht* as follows: it is broadly understood that the Reporting Judge has to present all the legal aspects, the ones in favour of his solution, but also the ones which are against it.
37 Article 21(3) BGG.
38 Article 21(1) BGG.

reasoning of a decision. The commentaries to the statute governing the operation of the Swiss Supreme Court first stipulated rather laconically that if there is a dispute about how to vote, this dispute should be resolved by a vote.[39] Newer editions of the commentaries propose voting in a similar way to Parliament, ie carrying out contingent voting.[40] It is only just very recently that the conference of the Presidents of the Chambers gave one of the members the mandate to prepare a short report on case examples regarding voting. The discussion came up because problems with voting began to accumulate in one of the Chambers.[41]

Over the course of the last few years, the Second Public Law Chamber had several public deliberations where voting procedures were discussed. There was no disagreement on the fact that voting had to be done in a sequential procedure. Neither was there a disagreement that voting on procedural questions has to come first, for example, whether or not a case is admissible. In some cases, it was clear that there must be a logical order in voting. For example, first the vote on whether or not a certain income would in principle be tax-exempted based on a specific statutory provision, before there could be a vote on whether in the specific case at hand the provision should not be applied due to tax evasion concerns.

Yet there were intensive discussions regarding situations where more than two proposals had been put forward. At first, a quite simplistic approach was adopted: if one had more than two opinions to vote on, then there was the proposal to have an eliminating vote, as used in the Federal Assembly.[42] After a while, the panels of the Chamber realised that this approach might lead to 'wrong' results if the different proposals are all on the same logical level. One example concerned a tax case, where the discussion was about whether an income ought to be taxed as ordinary revenue,[43] as a lump sum payment,[44] or as capital payment from a

---

39 See M Féraud in *Basler Kommentar zum Bundesgerichtsgesetz*, 2nd edn (Basel, Helbing & Lichtenhahn, 2011) Art 21, para [2].

40 *Cf* n 42 below. See also H Seiler in H Seiler and others (eds), *Bundesgerichtsgesetz*, 2nd edn (Bern, Stämpfli, 2015) Art 21, para [5]; Ys Donzallaz, *Loi sur le Tribunal fédéral*: commentaire (Bern, Stämpfli, 2008) Art 21, para [292]; L Kneubühler in *Basler Kommentar zum Bundesgerichtsgesetz*, 3rd edn (Basel, Helbing & Lichtenhahn, 2018) Art 21, para [2a].

41 It may well be that in the other Chambers there were no less difficult starting points in voting constellations, but that there was a lack of sensitivity for the problem and its consequences.

42 Article 97(1) and (2) of the Federal Act on the Federal Assembly (Parliament Act or ParlA; SR 171.10) of 13 December 2002 provide:

'(1) If more than two proposals have been made on the same subject matter, then an eliminating vote must be held until a vote can be held on which of the two proposals is to be accepted.

(2) The order of voting on the proposals must be structured in such a way that a vote is held first on- the proposals that differ the least from each other in content, working through the proposals until those that differ the most are reached.'

43 According to Article 36 of the Swiss Federal Direct Tax Law (DBG; SR 642.11).

44 According to Article 37 DBG.

pension institution.[45] The panel realised that an eliminating vote might produce different outcomes depending on the preferences of the individual judges.[46] The concrete case was nevertheless solved in the usual way – by an eliminating vote – but this had no influence on the outcome at the time because the preferences of the judges were allocated in a way that produced identical results irrespective of the voting order.

It is worth emphasising that the Second Public Law Chamber of the Supreme Court has indeed noticed the problem, but that it has not yet found a consistent solution by which to resolve it. Therefore, there were in fact cases where the outcome depended on the order in which the eliminating vote took place. Maybe the clarification initiated by the conference of the Chamber Presidents of the Supreme Court will give a stimulus for developing adequate solutions in future. And maybe more input for these questions should come from scholars.[47]

A related problem concerns the understanding of the role and the behaviour regarding voting: Is it legitimate to vote with a view to the desired outcome? Or does a judge have to decide each and every vote separately, to the best knowledge of the law? And would he then subsequently have to vote in the consecutive voting process based on the anterior decision taken by the majority?

To date, there has been no explicit discussion of these questions at the Swiss Supreme Court, and it seems that the views diverge. Some judges think that every separately presented question has to be answered separately and that consecutive voting has to observe the principle of 'stante concluso'; others find it hardly acceptable that such a procedure might produce an outcome which is in fact supported by a minority of the panel. This unsolved situation provokes unpleasant disputes, as it is not clear who plays according to which rules. The following example shows how the voting process may have taken place.

The Court had to decide whether a taxpayer could deduct a loss carry-forward. One proposal (a) was that he could do so in an unlimited way; the optional proposal (b) was that he could at least deduct the loss carry-forward insofar as he had no clearable income in the previous years; and the counterproposal (c) was that he could not deduct it at all.

During the discussion, it became clear that two judges were in favour of the main proposal (a) and would also support the optional proposal (b); that two judges were in favour of the counterproposal (c) opposed to the main proposal (a) and totally opposed to the optional proposal (b); and that the fifth judge preferred the optional proposal (b) and – in case there were to be no majority for this – would prefer the counterproposal (c) over the main proposal (a).

---

45 According to Article 38 DBG.

46 See the discussion of the case in T Stadelmann, 'Abstimmungsverfahren des Spruchkörpers' [2012] *Justice – Justiz – Giustizia*, issue 1.

47 The conference in Oxford could become a most welcome starting point.

Table 1. Priorities of individual judges

	Priority 1	Priority 2	Priority 3
Judge A:	(a)	(b)	
Judge B:	(a)	(b)	
Judge C:	(c)	¬ (a)	¬¬ (b)
Judge D:	(c)	¬ (a)	¬¬ (b)
Judge E:	(b)	(c)	(a)

Source: Compiled by the author.
Note: ¬ = 'Not'. ¬ ¬ = 'Absolutely not'.

Solutions (a), (b) and (c) are on the same level, and the panel could have chosen a method for voting on multiple-same-level candidates like the so-called Condorcet or Borda method, or even an 'election-like' method, having the effect that those who are 'falling out of the race' with their first vote get the decisive vote in the next round (with their second choice), whereas the preferences of the others are of no importance.

If the panel had chosen one of these procedures, the outcome would have been as follows:

Table 2. Condorcet method

	(a)	(b)	(c)	
(a)	–	4	2	**6**
(b)	1	–	3	4
(c)	3	2	–	5

Source: Compiled by the author.

Table 3. Borda method

	Judge A	Judge B	Judge C	Judge D	Judge E	
(a)	3	3	2	2	1	**11**
(b)	2	2	1	1	3	9
(c)	1	1	3	3	2	10

Source: Compiled by the author.

Table 4. Election-like method

	(a)	(b)	(c)
1st round	2	1	2
2nd round	2	–	**3**

Source: Compiled by the author.

The panel chose another method and decided first to vote on the main proposal (a) and then to juxtapose either (a) – if it got a majority in the first vote – or (b) – if (a) were not to get a majority – with (c).

The first vote for or against the main proposal (a) then surprisingly gave a result of 4:1 for (a) – surprisingly because judges C and D had made it very clear that they were opposed to the main proposal (a) –, with only the fifth judge voting against (a). Eventually the counterproposal (c) got 3 votes against 2 votes for the main proposal (a).

One can observe that the outcome was apparently the same as with the Election-like method, but the chosen procedure – which was arguably not appropriate (but based on the assumption that (a) and (b) were just sub-proposals, (a.1) and (a.2), so to speak, and that therefore not all 3 proposals were on the same level) – should have led to another result: if each judge were to have voted according to his opinion on the concrete question as it was expressed during the deliberation, the outcome would have been (b).[48]

VIII. CONSISTENCY OF CASE LAW

Even though each Chamber has its distinct competences, a question of law can actually involve several Chambers. If a Chamber has to decide a question that affects other Chambers, it must request the consent of the other Chambers concerned, provided that this would appear to be expedient for the development of the law or for the uniformity of legal practice.[49] If a Chamber wishes to decide a question that involves dissenting from a previous decision of one or more of the other Chambers, it can do so only if the Chamber(s) concerned consent.[50]

This procedure and its application by the Court has some flaws: First of all, the decision on whether to initiate the procedure lies in the discretionary power of the relevant Chamber. So, if a panel knowingly dissents from previous decisions of other Chambers without consulting the other Chambers concerned, there is no remedy against this. Equally there is no remedy if a Chamber decides on a question that affects other Chambers as well, without liaising with those other Chambers. Moreover, it is not clear who exactly is targeted when the law stipulates that 'the Chamber' has to request the consent of other Chambers. Normally the judicial panel in a case consists of five judges. One of these five judges might be a deputy judge. This raises the question of the role of this deputy judge in the decision of initiating the procedure of exchange of opinions: Does he have a vote in this decision, given the fact that he will not have a vote in

48 Stadelmann (n 46), paras [21] et seq.
49 Article 23(2) BGG.
50 Article 23(1) BGG.

the decision of the unified Chambers on the matter?[51] Or does the fifth – and potentially the sixth in a Chamber with six judges – have a vote on the question if the procedure of exchange of opinions has to be initiated, despite the fact that in the case itself he is not involved and hence does not have a vote? Such questions remain yet to be resolved.

51 See Article 23(3) BGG.

CHAPTER 10

DECISION-MAKING IN APPELLATE COURTS

An Austrian Experience

Georg KODEK*

I. INTRODUCTION

In this chapter, I am going to share with you a few observations on decision-making in Austrian courts. Before I do so, I should describe my own role and the nature of my involvement in the Austrian justice system. I can be described as a 'professional hybrid' because I am both a sitting judge and a law professor. Over the past 24 years, I have been sitting on many panels and tribunals of various sorts. While most of this work was as a judge of intermediate appellate courts, I have now been a member of the Austrian Supreme Court for some eleven years. Consequently, I will be talking mostly about the Austrian Supreme Court and, more specifically, about appellate decisions in civil cases. Criminal cases are different for a number of reasons, and the same holds true for intermediate appellate courts, where the smaller number of judges in a panel

* Professor Georg Kodek is a judge of the Austrian Supreme Court. In addition, he is Professor of Civil and Commercial Law at WU, the Vienna University of Business and Economics. The chapter is based on the written version of a paper delivered on 21 July 2017. The style of the oral presentation has been retained in large measure, with a few citations added.

(normally three) and the workload often tends to reduce the time spent for deliberation and discussion.

Obviously, I am bound to observe the limits imposed by my professional duties of confidence. Therefore, regrettably I will not be able to disclose the actual course of deliberations in any specific case. Instead, I will confine myself to more general observations. All I am going to say is, in some form or another, available from public sources. While there is no equivalent to Kranenpohl's monumental study of the German Constitutional Court,[1] in recent years some empirical work in this field has been done in Austria as well. I will rely heavily on papers published in a 2012 volume on access to the Austrian Supreme Court,[2] which includes an article by myself on the working method of our Court,[3] and on a book by sociologist Veronika Haberler which originated as a master's thesis I supervised and is based on interviews with some of the judges.[4]

II. INSTITUTIONAL FRAMEWORK

1. THE AUSTRIAN COURT SYSTEM

Continental European court systems have been described as 'bureaucratised' by common law observers, and there is some truth to that (and I realise that the term 'bureaucratised' has a somewhat negative connotation). Certainly Austria, like most civil law countries, has a career judge system. This means that judges are typically appointed at an early age, after only a few years of training spent with various courts and other authorities such as public prosecutors. Typically, a judge will start his or her career at a district court (*Bezirksgericht*), a court of limited jurisdiction, and may later be promoted to the regional court (*Landesgericht*), a court of full original and appellate jurisdiction, and eventually, to one of Austria's four Courts of Appeal (*Oberlandesgericht*) or to the Austrian Supreme Court (*Oberster Gerichtshof*). While occasionally cases on the trial court level are decided by a panel of judges, this is extremely rare in civil cases. Thus, deliberations among several judges involved typically only occur on the appellate level. There, most cases are decided by panels of three professional judges (with some minor matters such as appeals against orders determining the

1 U Kranenpohl, *Hinter dem Schleier des Beratungsgeheimnisses: Der Willensbildungs- und Entscheidungsprozess des Bundesverfassungsgerichts* (Wiesbaden, VS Verlag für Sozialwissenschaften, 2010).

2 GE Kodek (ed), *Zugang zum OGH: Vorträge des Symposiums „Zugang zum OGH in Zivil- und Strafsachen"* (Wien, Manz, 2012).

3 GE Kodek, 'Funktion und Arbeitsweise des OGH – die Binnensicht', ibid 99.

4 V Haberler, *Die höchstgerichtliche Entscheidung: Eine empirische Studie zur Entscheidungsfindung in Zivilrechtssachen am OGH* (Wien, Wiener Advocatur Bureau, 2014).

costs of court-appointed experts being decided by a single judge). In commercial cases the panel is composed of two professional judges and a layperson, an experienced businessman.

2. THE AUSTRIAN SUPREME COURT

One striking feature of the Austrian Supreme Court is its size. Obviously I do not mean the physical size of its building (although that, too, is quite impressive), but the number of judges serving there. In the past years, the Court has had between 58 and 60 judges. Ironically, this is the same number as 150 years ago when the Court's jurisdiction included all territories of the Austrian Hungarian monarchy except Hungary.

To give you some idea of the case load, let me provide some figures: The Court disposes of 2,500 to 3,000 civil cases per year (though, fortunately, some of them are dismissed summarily by way of a decision which contains no motivation or only a very short motivation).[5] As a matter of simple arithmetic, this means that each of the ten panels hearing civil cases will have assigned to it 250 to 300 cases per year. In civil matters, cases are typically decided on the basis of written pleadings, with an oral hearing being an absolute exception.[6] Perhaps more importantly, there is virtually no interaction between the Court and the parties. The Court generally does not disclose its concerns and invites the lawyers to address them. Rather, the Court ordinarily confines itself to reading the briefs submitted by the lawyers and deciding the case on that basis. In a recent case, we invited the appellee to address certain issues 'in particular' in his reply to the appeal, but this was about as far as the Court would go in written proceedings.

III. COMPOSITION AND ORGANISATION OF PANELS

Depending on the nature of the case, the court sits in panels of three, five, seven or eleven judges. Most cases are disposed of by a panel of five judges.

---

5 Statistical information on the work of the Court is published in the Court's annual activity reports (*Tätigkeitsberichte*), available online via http://www.ogh.gv.at/medien/taetigkeitsberichte/ (last accessed 20 February 2020). For a history of the rules governing access to the Supreme Court, see K-H Danzl, 'Die Anrufbarkeit des OGH in streitigen Zivilrechtssachen – von Franz Klein bis zur Gegenwart: Analyse – Rückblick – Ausblick' in B König (ed), *Historiarum ignari semper sunt pueri: Festschrift Rainer Sprung zum 65. Geburtstag* (Wien, Manz, 2001) 39.

6 While intermediate courts of appeals hold oral hearings slightly more often (until a recent reform, hearings were mandatory), these tend to be very short. Thus, even second instance proceedings are in large measure written proceedings. In criminal cases, there is an oral hearing in about half of all cases.

Thus, the Court is organised into several panels of five judges each. Typically, each panel will have judges who also serve on other panels to function as 'liaison' among the various panels. Each of these panels has its own special area of expertise. There are ten panels hearing civil cases (with some judges sitting in more than one panel) and five panels hearing criminal cases. Specialty fields include corporate law (the type of work I do), insurance law, negligence law, labour and social law, etc. The composition of the panels remains fairly constant. Thus, in my eleven years on the Court, one judge has served with me for all eleven years and two others for nine and ten years respectively. The structure of the panels is organised hierarchically, with the Presiding Judge being appointed to this post by the government. Among the other members of the panel, too, seniority plays an important role, not merely for things such as size and location of offices (which is regarded as a matter of prestige) or allocation of parking lots (of which we have only a few),[7] but also for the order in which the judges speak or vote during deliberations. Thus, the oldest member of the panel is the 'first deputy' of the Presiding Judge and takes part in all decisions (even if the case is decided by only three judges). One judge will act as the *rapporteur* and will typically prepare a draft of the decision which is then discussed with the other judges.

Occasionally cases are decided by a so-called 'enlarged panel' (*verstärkter Senat*). This procedure is used if a panel wants to depart from well-established case law or if there is a discrepancy in the Court's case law. On average, this occurs once every two or three years in civil cases (and slightly more often in criminal cases). In these cases, the regular number of five judges is augmented by six additional judges, chosen according to seniority. This tends to make the enlarged panel a somewhat conservative body. I once wanted to use this procedure to depart from the recent decisions of three other panels and failed miserably. In my opinion, the case was clearly wrongly decided. Writing extrajudicially, I later suggested that the Supreme Court 'placed continuity above consistency of reasoning'.[8]

---

7 Due to the length of time I have served on the Court, I am lucky in both respects, having a big office on the *beletage* of the Court as well as a parking space in the yard.

8 See GE Kodek and P Leupold in A Wiebe and GE Kodek (eds), *UWG:Gesetz gegen den unlauteren Wettbewerb*, 2nd edn (Wien, Manz, 2016), §14 para [186]. I should point out that I was not a member of the enlarged panel deciding the case. The case concerned a very technical problem, namely whether an action asking for an injunction against unfair terms and conditions was available where defendant hat agreed to the claimant's request out of court to stop the use of the unfair terms, but expressly reserved the right to leave other terms unchanged which were lawful. Incomprehensibly (although, maybe not unsurprisingly in light of the previous decisions) the Court held that a defendant was not entitled to make such a reservation and could only flatly agree to or deny claimant's request.

IV. THE 'WORKFLOW' WITHIN THE COURT

When a new case comes in, it is assigned to one judge as *rapporteur*.[9] Cases are distributed among all judges in a way which ensures that all have the same workload. The assignment of cases takes into account whether the case falls into the special field of expertise of a panel. If there are not enough such cases, so-called 'general civil law cases' are used to 'fill up' the panel's docket. Thus, if we run out of corporate cases, I may get assigned a divorce case or a normal sales contract.

The judges' work is assisted by the Research and Documentation Service which operates under the old-fashioned name of *Evidenzbüro* (a term incomprehensible even to native speakers of German and a term which, coincidentally, was formerly also used for the army intelligence service in the Austrian-Hungarian monarchy). Since the name of this institution is determined by statute, efforts to use a more modern term have not been successful so far.[10] The Research and Documentation Service is made up by young judges appointed to other courts (some of whom sit part-time in their court and spend the remaining time in the Supreme Court), law clerks (judgeship candidates in training) and university assistants seconded by their university under various cooperation agreements. They will draw up a report which typically contains a summary of the curial history of the case and of the arguments presented by the parties. Also, they will append copies of all authorities cited by the courts below and by the lawyers.[11] Often the report will also contain a discussion of the merits of the case.

The next stage will typically be a draft decision prepared by the *rapporteur*. We take great pride in writing our decisions ourselves, although I have to admit that, depending on the individual judge's working habits, an astute observer might occasionally be able to spot similarities between the draft decision and the report of the Research and Documentation Service. The draft is then sent to the Presiding Judge. Sometimes the *rapporteur* may not draft a decision, but will want to discuss the case first. This is likely to be done in cases which are expected to be highly controversial. Also, if a *rapporteur* is voted down, he need not (but, of course, may) write the decision. In this case the judge whose view is adopted by the majority has to write the decision.

---

9 The German term is *Berichterstatter*. Colloquially, he may also be referred to as *Referent* (especially by the Presiding Judge). In my view, this term is not a fortunate one in this context since in German *Referent* may also denote a subordinate official.

10 I suggested renaming this institution *Wissenschaftlicher Dienst* (Scientific Advisory Service).

11 Austrian courts generally rely quite heavily on academic writing in addition to precedents (which, in civil law countries, are not technically binding, but, of course, constitute very important persuasive authority).

The next phase is a bilateral dialogue between the Presiding Judge and the *rapporteur*. The way in which this dialogue is used varies greatly depending on the personalities involved. In my opinion, this dialogue should be limited to questions of form or to determining whether or not certain additional arguments should be addressed in the draft. Every disagreement as to the outcome of the case should be reserved for determination by the full panel.

However, particularly in the courts of appeals, the Presiding Judge may assume a very strong role. Bear in mind that he or she is appointed to that post on the ground (typically) of being the most senior judge on the panel and often, through his or her assessment of the other judges, will have a potentially important influence on their future careers. Until recently, it was extremely rare for the other two judges to vote down the Presiding Judge, although I personally feel that this possibility can sometimes be beneficial to the quality of the outcome. I recall that during my time on the Vienna Court of Appeals, we once voted down the Presiding Judge. According to an anecdote (which, however, is of course entirely apocryphal) I said that 'according to a rough estimate, it's two to one'. Certainly, at that time it was highly unusual for a Presiding Judge to be outvoted by the other members of the panel. This was – and probably still is – all the more true in commercial cases which are decided by two professional judges and a layperson, since the laypersons tends to take the side of the Presiding Judge (whom the layperson tends to regard more reliable on the grounds of the Presiding Judge's greater age and expertise) rather than that of the *rapporteur*.

The case is then set for deliberation by the Presiding Judge. This deliberation normally takes place during one of the regular meetings of the members of the panel, although obviously in urgent matters *ad hoc* meetings or decisions by way of circulation are possible. (Intermediate appellate courts nowadays often do not deliberate, but decide by way of circulation, a practice which I personally do not approve of but for routine cases.)

It should be pointed out that, ordinarily, the file is only available to the *rapporteur* and to the Presiding Judge, but of course the other judges could also obtain it if they wanted.[12] Thus, the case is generally decided on the basis of the draft decision and of the presentation of the case by the *rapporteur*. This led one German Supreme Court judge, the famous criminal lawyer Professor Sarstedt, to comment that 'even assuming that the *rapporteur* and the Presiding Judge know the file, those who do not know it are still in the majority'. Even in former times, however, files were circulated in more difficult cases. Nowadays drafts are also exchanged by way of email beforehand, thus giving all judges an opportunity to read the draft before the deliberations.

---

12 Most intermediate appellate courts and the Supreme Court in criminal cases follow a different practice, routinely making the entire file available to all members of the panel.

The identity of the *rapporteur* is not made public.[13] Nor are there dissenting or concurring opinions. Thus, the general public will never know whether a decision was unanimous or the result of, eg, a three-to-two split. (What the general public could know, however, is that in at least 27 cases the decision was not unanimous since in these cases our computerised data base (*Rechtsinformationssystem – RIS*) mentioned that there is a dissent (*Kontravotum*) on file,[14] a result of the index cards for internal use of the Court being made public from the 1990s onwards without proper redaction.)

After deliberations the decision is proof-read and redacted by clerks or assistants, but no changes in substance are made. Even minor changes (other than simple typos or mis-citations) require the approval of a judge.

V. THE ACTUAL DELIBERATION PROCESS

The panel meets about once or twice a month for deliberations. Even though the meeting takes place *in camera* with no parties or lawyers present, it is still quite a formal event with judges dressing up for the occasion, thus recognising the importance of the event (although I note that in the past couple of years this practice sometimes is not as well observed as it used to be in the past). Typically, the judges will also have lunch together. Depending on the panel, the deliberations may well last into late evenings, sometimes running on as late as 9.30 pm. The reason for this strong focus on a few deliberation days is that some judges do not live in Vienna and work from offices throughout the country; they only come to Vienna for meetings or hearings.

On deliberation days I typically have breakfast with another judge of my panel.[15] On this account, a former Presiding Judge (now retired) was afraid that we might discuss our cases beforehand, thus coordinating the way we would

---

13 Some lower courts divulge the name of the *rapporteur* by always mentioning the name of the *rapporteur* (typically without an express reference to his function, but sometimes with the addition of the letters 'BE' for *Berichterstatter* (*rapporteur*) second right after the Presiding Judge in the list of judges taking part in the decision given in the judgment. This practice, however, is by no means universal. The Supreme Court always lists the judges in order of seniority.

14 *Cf* http://www.ris.bka.gv.at/Ergebnis.wxe?WxeFunctionToken=a6d76a3f-929d-4099-93c8-e3a61e7ebca5&Abfrage=Justiz&Gericht=&Rechtssatznummer=&Rechtssatz=&Fundstelle=&AenderungenSeit=Undefined&SucheNachRechtssatz=True&SucheNachText=False&GZ=&VonDatum=&BisDatum=06.12.2017&Norm=&ImRisSeit=Undefined&ResultPageSize=100&Suchworte=Kontravotum (last accessed 20 February 2020). See, by way of example, the syllabus of the decision 5 Ob 94/61, referring to an unpublished dissenting opinion of the Presiding Judge.

15 Readers may remember that legal realism is sometimes ridiculed as looking into what the judge had for breakfast. See A Kozinski, 'What I Ate for Breakfast and Other Mysteries of Judicial Decision Making' (1993) 26 *Loyola of Los Angeles Law Review* 993, available online via http://digitalcommons.lmu.edu/llr/vol26/iss4/5 (last accessed 20 February 2020).

vote during deliberations. I can assure you that these concerns were unfounded for the simple reason that we do not know our files well enough. But seriously: Of course, in difficult cases there are often informal discussions before the actual deliberations, over lunch (or breakfast), in the hallway, etc. The motives for these discussions can be quite diverse; they range from genuine interest in other judges' views on a case to a search for 'allies' for a certain view or position. Clearly, the latter is only acceptable if it is done honestly and involves a full presentation of all issues involved. I should add that such a search for 'allies' is also highly unreliable. I recall an occasion when I had (I thought) assembled six votes in an eleven-judge panel and yet the panel decided differently than I expected.

The deliberations always start with a report from the *rapporteur* who presents a draft or, occasionally, several alternatives. The case is then discussed among the judges. While traditionally judges spoke in order of seniority, nowadays the style of discussion is quite informal. One reason for this, in addition to the judges' professionality, is that all have reached the summit of their career and nothing could be gained by trying simply to boost one's profile during the course of discussions. Also, ordinarily, rhetoric skills or an academic record do not play an important role (but – even today – seniority might).

Clearly, the style of the discussion depends on the personalities involved. Typically (but – I regret to say – maybe not universally) it is highly professional, courteous and collegial. However, there are rumours about colleagues who vigorously defend their 'holy decisions', regarding criticism as a sacrilege. On the other hand, I recall a case where I stepped as a substitute onto another panel where I managed to talk the majority (but, sadly, not the *rapporteur*) out of the approach laid down in the draft of the *rapporteur*. This shows that, generally, the judges are quite open-minded and are prepared to depart from their previous views if confronted with good counter-arguments.

Deciding a case may take everything from five minutes to several days, although the latter is clearly an exception. There was an enlarged panel in a criminal case which took one day for preliminary discussions and two days of full discussions with the judgment being announced in open court on a separate day. This, of course, is not typical. Since 15 to 30 cases are disposed of on a normal day of deliberations, routine cases which are dismissed summarily may take a few minutes and others receive 10 to 20 minutes of discussion. However, in more difficult cases this may well be different. I recall a case (it was about a question of inheritance law) which was discussed on two separate days. On the second day a new aspect came up. The Presiding Judge adjourned for an hour or so and asked us to think it over. We then reconvened, continued the discussion, and ultimately came up with a unanimous decision.

While there are rules on voting in our Judicature Act (*Jurisdiktionsnorm*), it may come as a surprise to the reader that these rules are rarely applied. According to section 10 of the Judicature Act, the *rapporteur* is to vote first, then (if applicable) the lay member of the panel, then the most senior judge and the other judges in descending order of seniority, with the Presiding Judge always voting last. According to section 14 of that statute, minutes of the voting have to be kept, but these are not available to the parties (but may be inspected by a higher court in appellate proceedings). In fact, so rarely are these provisions used that occasionally we had to look them up when they were in fact applied.

Under the statute, voting should take place on grounds and preliminary questions, rather than on the overall outcome. Whether this rule is sound may well be debated. Clearly, it can lead to strange results. I recall a case, many years ago, about whether something (I forgot what) could be entered into the company register. The courts below had refused the application. All of us felt that the courts had decided correctly. However, when we discussed the reasons for refusing the application, it turned out that each of us had a different argument in mind. It was not possible to find a majority for any one ground for refusal. Under the statute, the result would have been that the application (which all of us felt was unfounded) would have been granted. I do not recall how that case was resolved eventually, but it clearly illustrates how the statutory rule works.

In 80 to 90 percent of all cases, the draft prepared by the *rapporteur* is approved, sometimes with amendments or reductions. Some parts may be regarded as going too far, or as being unnecessary for the determination of the case, and thus it may be prudent to err on the side of caution. Thus, often a compromise is reached and parts of the decision certain members of the panel consider offensive are 'diluted' or 'watered-down'. Clearly, there is tendency to search for a compromise, and even if a member of the panel is not fully convinced, a formal vote is quite rare. But there are exceptions. In a recent case (which I cannot describe in detail for reasons of confidentiality) pending before an enlarged panel of eleven judges, authorities in Austria and Germany were divided on the issue with about half the sources supporting one view and the other half the opposite view. More importantly, the issue had been decided differently by two panels of the Supreme Court a few years earlier, when the second panel which considered the question a few weeks after the first one did not know of the prior decision. The case was decided by an extremely narrow margin, by six to five. Although this is a matter of pure speculation, it is said that the outcome would have been different if one judge had not been sick (and replaced by a substitute) or if one more judge had been unable to sit (and would have been replaced by the next substitute).

There is also a tendency (but by no means a universal one)[16] to avoid *dicta* not necessary for the disposition of the case. Sometimes the actual problem

---

16 A former Chief Judge strongly disapproved of *dicta* in court decisions. Yet her panel wrote what was certainly the most extensive *dictum* in recent history. While the appeal was clearly inadmissible (as a result of some technical provisions designed to limit appeals on questions of jurisdiction), the decision, in a long *dictum*, stated that the joinder of several claims in one complaint was permissible, thus paving the way for what is called the Austrian

may be circumvented (an easy task under our technical rules of procedure), and sometimes it may turn out that the case is not suited for addressing a certain problem, thus resulting in a dismissal of a case that had already been accepted for decision.

VI. CONCLUSION

The way of decision-making in Austrian appellate courts is clearly designed to promote standardisation. It also secures a certain minimum quality (with an emphasis on 'minimum'). It also leads to a highly assimilated style of decisions, with all traces of individuality being carefully eliminated.[17] This is perhaps not only a result of the decision-making process, but reflects the culture of country in general. Thus, children are already trained in elementary school to avoid using the word 'I'. This tendency is also evident in German-language academic writings, but particularly clearly in court decisions. Observations like Lord Denning's 'It was blue-bell time in Kent'[18] are totally unthinkable in Austria.

While the system has some merit, it comes at a cost. Some observers have claimed that this way of decision-making leads to mediocrity.[19] Certainly, the system encourages a result which is acceptable to the majority (or even to all members of the panel) and thus encourages compromises.[20] Arguably it also leads to reluctance to adopt new views and theories.

I would love to tell you more specifics and share with you further insights I have gained in my some 26 years (24 years of which I spent with appellate work) in the Austrian court system. Yet unfortunately my duties of confidentiality prevent me from doing so. I hope that I could nonetheless share with you some insights on how our Austrian Supreme Court operates 'behind the scenes'.

---

version of class action. On this case, see GE Kodek, 'Funktion und Arbeitsweise des OGH' (n 3) 116. On group litigation in Austria in general, see GE Kodek, 'Collective Redress in Austria' in DR Hensler, C Hodges et al (eds), *The Globalization of Class Actions, Annals of the American Academy of Political and Social Sciences*, vol 622 (Thousand Oaks/California, SAGE Publication, 2009) 86, and GE Kodek, 'Class Actions – Some Reflections from a European Perspective' in E Lein, D Fairgrieve et al (eds), *Collective Redress in Europe – Why and How?* (London, BIICL, 2015) 117.

17 Lawyers sometimes engage in educated guesswork, based on a linguistic analysis, as to who was the author of a certain decision. For the reasons described in the text, these efforts are not very successful (and, given the Court's refusal to divulge the name of the *rapporteur*, can never be proven or disproved).

18 The opening words of his judgment in *Hinz v Berry* [1970] 2 QB 40 (CA) 42.

19 W Ernst, *Rechtserkenntnis durch Richtermehrheiten: "group choice" in europäischen Justiztraditionen* (Tübingen, Mohr Siebeck, 2016) 319.

20 Which is why during our discussions following my presentation in Oxford an English participant (somewhat disapprovingly) described our decisions as being 'like those of a committee'.

PART IV

COLLEGIATE COURTS IN A NON-EUROPEAN CIVIL LAW JURISDICTION: THE CASE OF JAPAN

CHAPTER 11

COLLECTIVE JUDGING BY COLLEGIATE COURTS IN JAPAN

Akira OJIMA* and Naoki ONISHI**

* Judge Akira Ojima MA (Tokyo), LLM (Cornell) is Chief Judicial Research Official at the Supreme Court of Japan and a former Presiding Judge of the Tokyo High Court. He is responsible for sections II–IV of this chapter, which is based on a joint presentation given at the 'Collective Judging' conference. Its text is rendered here with some stylistic adaptations and supplementary information provided in light of the question-and-answer session following the presentation.

** Judge Naoki Onishi MA (Keio), LLM (Cantab), MJur (Oxon) is a Presiding Judge of the Otsu District Court (Head of the Criminal Division) and a former judge of the Tokyo High Court. He is responsible for sections V–VI of this chapter.

I. INTRODUCTION

In this chapter, we will begin by briefly explaining the Japanese judicial system in order to provide a background for the discussion. We will then explain the decision-making process followed by the courts in Japan: first, in the Supreme Court, and second, in High Courts and District Courts.

II. JUDICIAL SYSTEM IN JAPAN[1]

1. OVERALL STRUCTURE AND THE COMPETENCE OF DIFFERENT COURTS

Let us first give you an outline of the judicial system in Japan. As shown in figure 1, it is a three-instance system. The first instance is District Court and Family Court. There are 50 District Courts and 50 Family Courts. They decide issues of both facts and law. The next instance is the High Court level. There are eight High Courts. They handle appeals from District Courts and Family Courts, and also decide issues of both facts and law. The final body of appeal is the Supreme Court. It is located in Tokyo and it handles appeals from High Courts, and it usually decides on issues of law only.

---

[1] Further details may be found in the following books: Supreme Court of Japan, *Court System of Japan* (2018, available under www.courts.go.jp/english/vcms_lf/2018_Court_System_of_Japan.pdf, last accessed 24 February 2020); The General Secretariat of the Supreme Court of Japan, *Justice in Japan* (Tokyo, Supreme Court of Japan, 2016); CJ Milhaupt, JM Ramseyer and MD West, *The Japanese Legal System: Cases, Codes, and Commentary*, 2nd edn (New York, Foundation Press, 2012).

Figure 1. Judicial system in Japan

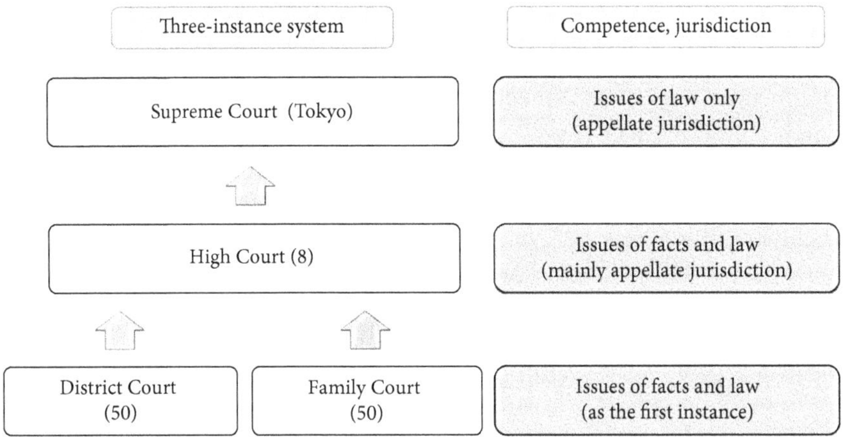

Source: Produced by the authors.

2. JUDICIAL BODIES WITHIN EACH INSTANCE

Let me move on to the next part, concerning the kinds of judicial bodies and the cases they handle (see figure 2).

Figure 2. Judicial bodies within each instance

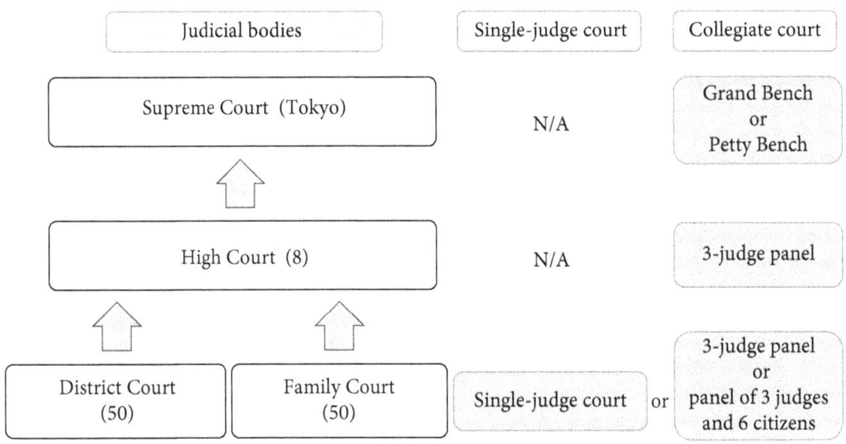

Source: Produced by the authors.

At District Court level, most cases are handled by single judges, with all remaining cases being handled by a three-judge panel.

As regards civil cases, a single-judge court in theory has the power to handle any case whatsoever. However, in practice, complex cases involving important legal or factual questions are generally referred to three-judge panels. Some examples are administrative law cases, medical malpractice cases, patent cases, and cases involving judicial constitutionality review.

As regards criminal cases, while most are similarly handled by single-judge courts, the law requires that cases concerning certain major offences are to be handled by a collegiate court.

There are two kinds of collegiate courts, one being a three-judge panel, the other being a panel of three professional judges and six citizens selected at random from registered voters. The latter court deals with cases in which there is a possibility of severe punishment, for instance the death penalty or life imprisonment. We will explain this unique court later on in our contribution.[2]

Figure 3. Judicial bodies at District Courts

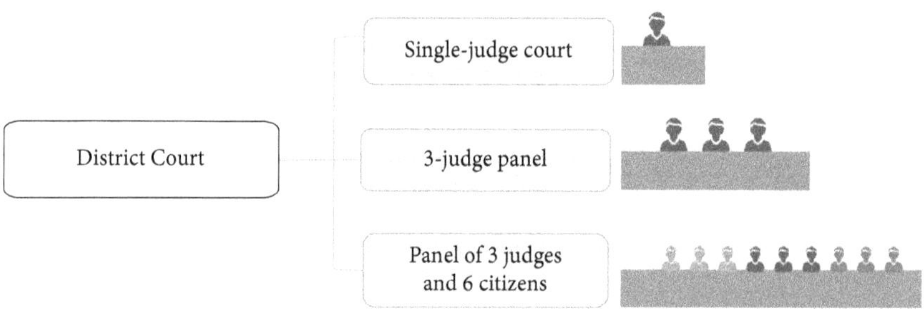

Source: Produced by the authors.

At High Court level, all cases are handled by a collegiate court, mostly a three-judge panel, with a few exceptions where a five-judge panel handles cases. Such cases include patent and other intellectual property litigation as well as the review of decisions by the Fair Trade Commission.

Figure 4. Judicial bodies at High Courts

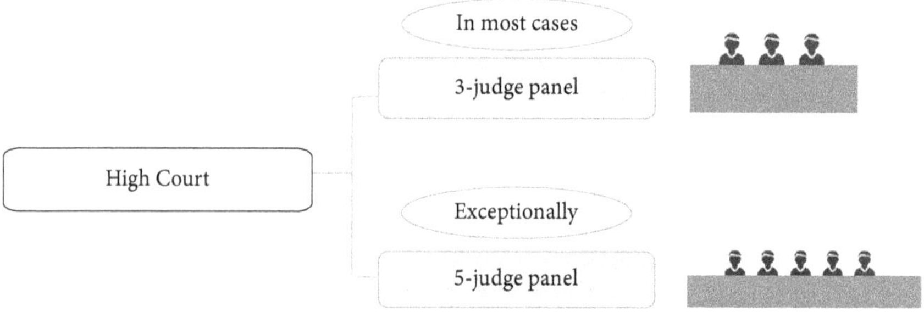

Source: Produced by the authors.

2 See under heading IV.2 below (at p 216).

At the Supreme Court, all cases are dealt with by collegiate courts, either a Grand Bench consisting of all the 15 Justices or a Petty Bench composed of five Justices.

Figure 5. Judicial bodies at the Supreme Court

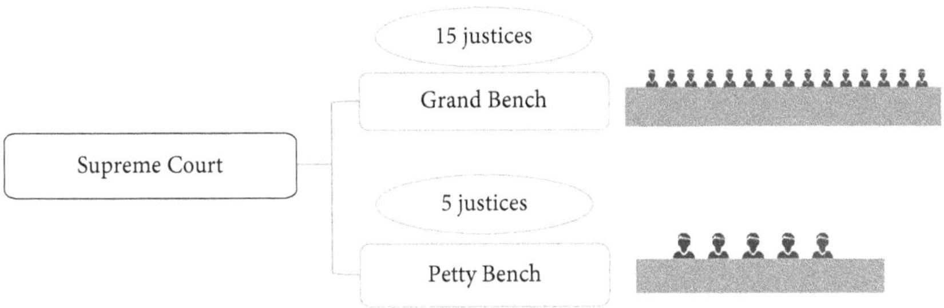

Source: Produced by the authors.

3. COLLECTIVE JUDGING AND EXPRESSIONS OF OPINION BY INDIVIDUAL JUDGES

Let us now move on to how Japanese courts prepare and render their judgments, and how individual judges can express their opinions. Courts should always prepare a written judgment in advance and then read out the document in the courtroom which is open to the public. It is the Presiding Judge who delivers the judgment. In civil cases, only the conclusion is usually read out, but occasionally a summary of the reasoning is also explained in the courtroom. Afterwards, an authentic copy of the judgment is served to both parties. In criminal cases, it is necessary for Presiding Judge to read out both the conclusion and the reasoning.

4. CONTENT OF JUDGMENTS AND EXPRESSIONS OF OPINION BY INDIVIDUAL JUDGES

The next question is *what* is written in the judgment. This differs depending on the court concerned.

a) District Court and High Court

In District Courts and High Courts, only a unitary set of conclusions and the reasoning reached by majority is contained in the judgment. This is because the Procedural Code mandates judges to provide not only the conclusion, but also to indicate their reasoning in the written judgment. 'Reasoning' here means a unitary reasoning of the whole court, adopted by its majority.

Even where there is a dissenting opinion during the process of deliberation, neither the content of the dissenting opinion nor the simple fact that there was a dissenting opinion is written down. As a result, together with the rule that deliberation shall be secret,[3] no one, except the judges themselves, knows whether the judgment was unanimous or a majority decision. This is on account of Japan operating a 'continental/civilian' system as defined by Professor Ernst.[4]

Figure 6. Content of judgment (District Court and High Court)

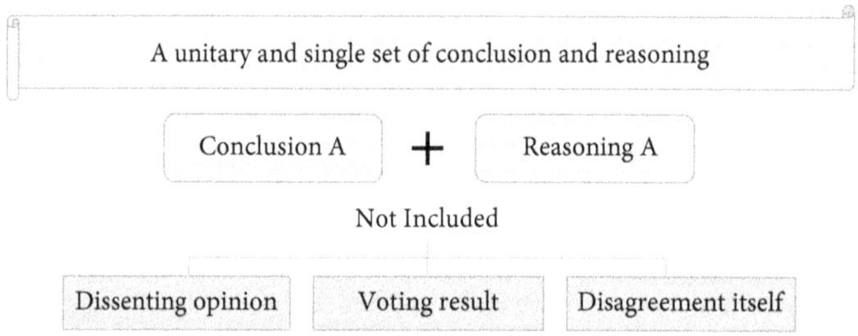

Source: Produced by the authors.

b) The Supreme Court

As for the Japanese Supreme Court, a unitary set of conclusions and reasoning reached by the majority is contained in the judgment, just as is the case in lower courts. The Supreme Court, however, is unique in the sense that individual opinions, either concurring or dissenting, are indicated together with the names of the Justices who wrote them. It can therefore be said that the Anglo-American system is introduced in part.

Figure 7. Content of judgment (Supreme Court)

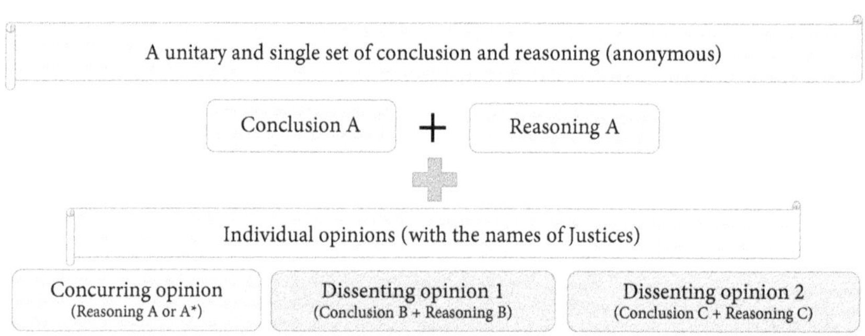

Source: Produced by the authors.

---

3 See immediately below, under section III.1 of the present chapter.

4 See W Ernst's contribution in chapter 1 of the present collection (at pp 4 et seq).

III. LEGAL PROVISIONS AND PRACTICES GOVERNING COLLECTIVE JUDGING

1. PROVISIONS AND PRACTICES CONCERNING DELIBERATION

Let us now move on to the next part, namely the legal provisions and practices regarding collective judging within Japanese collegiate courts.

The exact procedure of deliberation is widely entrusted to the discretion of each individual collegiate court, except for the following statutory provisions which set out the basic rules. As prescribed by the 'Court Law', they are as follows:

- Deliberations of decisions in a panel shall not be disclosed.[5]
- Deliberations shall be initiated and regulated by the Presiding Judge. Strict secrecy must be observed with respect to the deliberation proceedings, the opinions of each judge and the number of opinions constituting the majority and the minority.[6]
- Judges must express their opinions in deliberations.[7]
- Decisions shall be rendered by a majority of opinions.[8]

2. LEGAL PROVISIONS GOVERNING JUDGMENT BY COLLEGIATE COURTS

Let us now look at the legal provisions governing judgments which reflect the result of deliberations. The Procedural Law provides judgments in both civil and criminal cases must indicate not only the court's conclusion, but also its reasoning in a given case.[9] As already indicated, 'reasoning' here means the operative reasoning by which the conclusion was reached, in other words, a unitary reasoning of the whole collegiate court, adopted by its majority.

While the same rule also applies to the Supreme Court, in addition to the majority conclusion and the reasoning supporting it, individual opinions – whether concurring or dissenting – are also included in an appendix to the Supreme Court's judgment.

---

5 Article 75(1) of the Court Law.
6 Article 75(2) of the Court Law.
7 Article 76 of the Court Law.
8 Article 77(1) of the Court Law.
9 Article 253(1) of the Civil Procedure Law; Article 44 of the Criminal Procedure Law.

IV. COLLECTIVE JUDGING IN THE JAPANESE SUPREME COURT

1. DECISION-MAKING IN THE SUPREME COURT

Next, we will consider the decision-making process of the Supreme Court. The Supreme Court is composed of 15 Justices. The Chief Justice is appointed by the Emperor, and 14 Associated Justices are appointed by the Cabinet. They are selected from lower court judges, public prosecutors, private attorneys, legal scholars, or government officials. The mandatory retirement age is 70 years.

The Supreme Court has one Grand Bench consisting of 15 Justices and three Petty Benches each of which consists of five Justices. The Grand Bench hears only a few cases, usually less than five cases, per year, while the remainder of the cases (several thousand cases) are handled by Petty Benches. The grounds of appeal to the Supreme Court are limited to constitutional issues and important issues of law.

The Supreme Court has a special supporting body which lower courts do not have. This is the 'Judicial Research Office' consisting of 39 lower court judges as judicial research officials (see figure 8). These research officials are responsible for assisting the 15 Supreme Court Justices. The Research Office is divided into three divisions: civil, administrative, and criminal. Judicial research officials differ from law clerks in the United States. They serve the Supreme Court as a whole, not individual Justices. Judicial research officials are chosen among experienced judges, who usually have more than 15 years' worth of experience as judges, and they are assigned to the post to examine cases. They serve the Research Office for about four years on average.

Figure 8. Justices and the Judicial Research Office

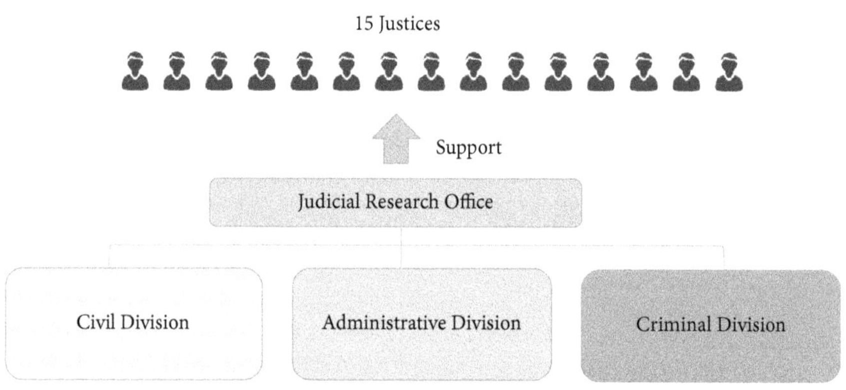

Source: Produced by the authors.

Given that one of us (Akira Ojima) has a long record of serving the Research Office,[10] it may be appropriate for us to explain the decision-making process of the Japanese Supreme Court through this lens. It is further buttressed by experience in presiding over a three-judge panel at the Tokyo High Court, and the Tokyo District Court, and – more than 25 years ago – acting as a law clerk for a judge of the United States District Court for the District of Columbia (Ojima). This allows us to contribute a genuine comparative perspective to the discussion of collective judging.

Going back to the decision-making process of the Supreme Court (see figure 9), every case brought to the Court is allocated to one of the three Petty Benches. One judicial research official is assigned to examine the case, and he or she prepares a written report on it. After the report is submitted to the Bench, the Justices consider the case. Approximately 98% of petitions are dismissed through summary approval, without discussion in the conference room. The remainder, approximately 2%, are accepted as cases requiring discussion in the conference room.

Following the conference, some cases proceed to the oral argument stage in the courtroom. Only few cases are referred to the Grand Bench. The Grand Bench hears only two types of claim. One concerns constitutional cases, the other cases in which the Court overrules a precedent of the Supreme Court. For the Grand Bench, the judicial research officials responsible for the case again submit a report in advance of the conference, this time a very detailed one.

Figure 9. Decision-making process of the Supreme Court

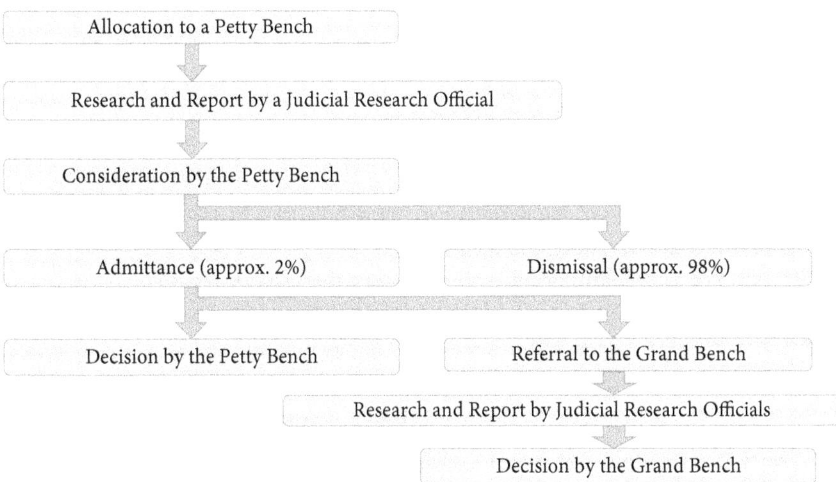

Source: Produced by the authors.

[10] Judge Ojima, who is responsible for this part of the present chapter, twice in the past served the Research Office as a research official, for nine years in total, and he has been the Chief Judicial Research Official since January 2018.

Since the new Japanese Supreme Court was created after the World War II, its decision-making system was crafted under the strong influence of the Anglo-American judicial system. This is why only Supreme Court Justices can express their individual opinions in the judgment. Although the court opinion (the majority opinion) is anonymous, each Justice can also put on record his or her own opinion.

2. CONFERENCE OF THE SUPREME COURT

Each Petty Bench holds a conference twice a week. At the conference, the Presiding Justice, whose identity varies from case to case, first states his or her opinion, and then Associate Justices should state their opinions. The judicial research official responsible for the case is allowed to attend the conference. After the discussion, when majority opinion is formed, it will be an anonymous opinion of the court. The judicial research official then prepares a draft judgment based on the results of the conference. This draft is carefully examined at the next conference. After the opinion of the court is completed, Justices may themselves write concurring or dissenting individual opinions.

3. THE ROLE OF THE JUDICIAL RESEARCH OFFICE

As stated above, the Judicial Research Office is a unique body which exists only in the Supreme Court. The main task of judicial research officials is to prepare case reports before the conference and drafting court opinions after the conference. Case reports usually include an outline of the case, the pleadings of both parties, a summary of appellate courts' opinions, and an analysis of the legal issues involved. When analysing cases, judicial research officials comprehensively review all the relevant legal issues, such as importance of constitutional and other legal issues in question, precedents of the Supreme Court and any lower courts, the legislative history, scholars' commentary, the background of social situations, or practices in foreign countries.

Since the number of Justices of the Supreme Court is limited to 15 and since, under Japanese procedural law, we do not have an *amicus curiae* or so-called amicus briefs, it may sometimes be difficult to collect information for the Court, especially in lawsuits between private citizens. It is therefore necessary to have an organised research body like the Judicial Research Office.

As previously mentioned, in civil cases 98% of petitions do not reach the face-to-face conference of Justices; it is simply declared that 'the petition is not accepted'. This is because most petitions do no more than blame or criticise the fact-finding of High Courts. Concerning such cases, judicial research officials write brief reports recommending simple denial of the petition. If and where all five Justices of the Petty Bench agree with the report, then the case is finished without a face-to face conference.

Concerning cases where different and competing legal opinions exist, judicial research officials may state their recommendation that a particular opinion is appropriate, based on the nature of the case, legal conformity with precedent, or reasonableness of result. In some cases, they present two or more options of opinions which can reasonably be adopted.

Judicial research officials only provide the materials or information needed by the Justices as the basis for their discussion. In the course of discussion, however, judicial research officials may provide comments on the opinions given by the Justices. Such comments could be, for instance, that a certain opinion provided by a Justice possibly contradicts former Supreme Court precedent, or that it is not based on the legally binding facts the High Court has found. The final decision is always made by Justices as a matter of course.

4. VOTING AND OPINIONS

Since the Supreme Court is mandated to decide only the specific constitutional and legal issues raised by petitioners, the vote of each Justice is cast to the specific issue at hand. Let us present a couple of examples of the recent cases of the Grand Bench.

They are taken from judgments of 16 December 2015. One concerns the requirement for a married couple to use the same surname (family name).[11] In this case, the claimants sought a damages award against the defendant (the Japanese government) on the basis that a provision of the Civil Code obliging a husband and a wife to select one of their surnames as a new family name upon getting married was unconstitutional. As regards the conclusion of whether or not the claimants could be awarded damages, the votes were split 14:1 for the defendant. The complaint was therefore dismissed. However, as regards the issue of whether or not the Civil Code was constitutional, the votes were split 10:5 in favour of the defendant. It meant that four Justices declared the Code unconstitutional, yet the claimants could not seek damages for that reason.

Another case concerned marriage restrictions for women after divorce.[12] In this case, the claimant sought a damages award against the defendant (the Japanese government) on the ground that the Civil Code was unconstitutional in restricting the right of divorced women to marry again. The Court's unanimous opinion pronounced the relevant provision of the Code to be unconstitutional; however, with respect to the conclusion of whether or not the claimants could

11 Minshu vol 69, no 8, p 2586.
12 Minshu vol 69, no 8, p 2427.

be awarded damages, the votes were split 14:1 in favour of the defendant. The complaint was therefore dismissed. Since it was dismissed under the construction of the relevant Government Compensation Act, the unanimous decision on the unconstitutionality of the Civil Code did not directly dictate the outcome of the case at hand. However, the decision was respected as a precedent of the Supreme Court, and a national Diet amended the Civil Code soon afterwards. Thus the precedential value of a case remains even where a finding does not form part of the *ratio decidendi*. In the marriage restriction case, the Supreme Court itself had actually put its decision into the formal case reporter.

V. COLLECTIVE JUDGING IN DISTRICT COURTS AND HIGH COURTS

Now that we have provided a picture of the decision-making process in the Supreme Court, we would like to illustrate how deliberations are conducted in the lower courts. Our focus will be on collective judging in the District Courts.

As already mentioned, there are two types of collegiate court at the District Court level, namely a three-judge panel and a panel of three judges and six citizens, called *saiban-in*. Both of these will be explained in turn.

1. DELIBERATION BY THREE-JUDGE PANEL

Generally speaking, all the judges constituting a collegiate court belong to the same division and work in the same room. This environment enables them to carry out deliberation in a more flexible and less formal way than would otherwise be the case. While deliberation may be held at a certain time scheduled in advance specifically for the meeting, it is not uncommon to start talking and exchanging views on pending cases spontaneously and thus gradually to form an opinion as a collegiate court.

It may also be worth mentioning the educational aspect of deliberation for younger judges. In Japan, judges are appointed from those who graduated from a law school, passed the bar examination and have completed one year of legal training. As a result, it is possible to become a judge as early as in one's mid-20s, without ever having practiced as a lawyer. The first few years after one's appointment as a judge are therefore in the character of on-the-job training; and deliberation is occasionally used of as an opportunity for such training, especially in District Courts.

Let us give you an example of the procedure – from deliberation to the rendering of judgment – in District Courts. Since the deliberation process may in practice differ widely from one collegiate court to another, and also depending on the cases at hand, the example presented here is what we would consider typical (see figure 10).

It is common practice for the most junior judge, ie the judge appointed most recently, to play the role of *rapporteur* in District Courts.

Generally, the *rapporteur* prepares a memorandum first. It may take the form of a draft judgment, or, in a complex case, it could well take the form of an issue paper which may include, for instance, factual and legal points to be determined, the *rapporteur*'s opinions on these points, and his/her conclusion(s).

The Presiding Judge starts and facilitates the judges' conference. It usually starts with a presentation by the *rapporteur* based on the memorandum, and then the judges exchange views on the case. If the case is a simple one, both the conclusion and the reasoning will be discussed at the same time – as a package. On the other hand, if the case is complex with several legal or factual questions to be determined, it appears to be common practice to take a step-by-step approach. In other words, the conference arranges the questions into a logical order and decide each question one-by-one, in order eventually to reach a unitary conclusion with a unitary reasoning.

While all the judges have an obligation to express their opinions, opportunities to do so are not limited to a single one. They can intervene as many times as they wish, and they are free to change their mind after listening to other judges speak. Frank and free exchange of opinions is regarded as being of utmost importance in order to arrive at the best possible decision. The length of the deliberation is not limited and, if necessary, the judges' conference may be held more than once.

Although there is no rule determining the speaking order, in many cases, the *rapporteur* speaks first, followed by the other associate judge, and finally the Presiding Judge will speak. This practice is based on customary wisdom fostered through long practice; it enables junior judges to express more candid opinions and thus to enrich the quality of deliberation.

In cases where disagreement remains even after thorough deliberation, a vote will be taken so as to reach a unitary decision of the collegiate court. Each and every judge has an equal vote. While much depends on the case at hand, the usual procedure is for the conference to vote step-by-step, just as in the deliberation process mentioned above, rather than immediately taking a vote on the final outcome Voting will then normally follow the logical order of reasoning by which the final conclusion is reached.

Even if a judge's opinion was rejected by the majority in a previous round of voting, he or she is not allowed to abstain in subsequent rounds. He or she is instead required to participate in the following vote on the basis of majority opinion in the previous questions.

Having said that, it is our experience that the free and frank exchange of views, and sufficient time for that process, will often enable the collegiate court to resolve disagreements between judges and thus to reach a unanimous decision, even without formal votes.

Once the collegiate court reaches its decision, the conclusion and the supporting reasoning are written down in a document in accordance with the result of the deliberation. Dissenting opinions are not included in this document. Generally speaking, the *rapporteur* prepares the first draft, circulates it to the other associate judge and then to the Presiding Judge for their comments; the draft is thus finalised. The Presiding Judge renders judgment by reading out the entirety or summary of it in the open court.[13]

Figure 10. Process to reach collective judgment by three-judge panel (an example)

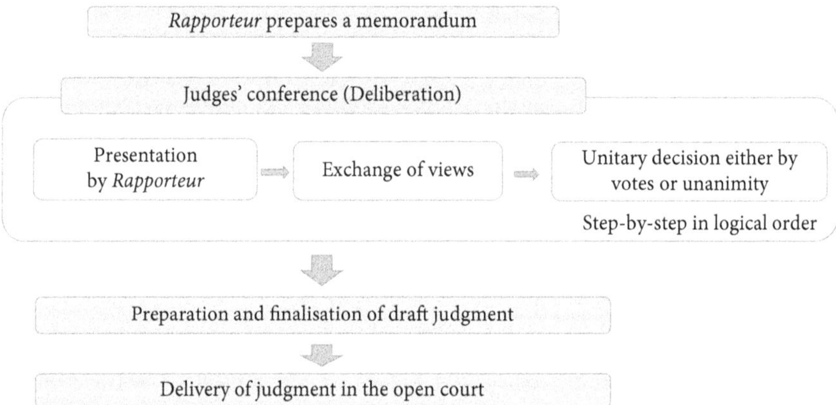

Source: Produced by the authors

2. DELIBERATION BY A PANEL OF THREE JUDGES AND SIX CITIZENS

Let us move on to the deliberation by a 'mixed collegiate court' composed of three judges and six citizens. Before going into details, it may be useful briefly to explain the Japanese version of a jury system, which is known as the *saiban-in* system.

The *saiban-in* system is similar to the jury system in the United Kingdom, in the sense that ordinary citizens participate in the criminal justice process. However, our system is also unique, in the sense that the collegiate court – composed of professional judges and ordinary citizens called *saiban-in* – decide

13 While it is common to read out the entirety of the judgment in criminal cases, the common practice in civil and administrative cases is to read out a brief summary of the judgment, in most cases, the conclusion(s) only in the open court. In the latter cases, however, the written judgment shall be served on both parties immediately after the delivery of the judgment in the court room.

not merely whether or not the accused is guilty, but also the sentence in case of a guilty verdict.[14] Unlike in the jury system, professional judges and citizens deliberate together as a team in the *saiban-in* system.

The *Saiban-in* Law provides that a collegiate court composed of three professional judges and six citizens selected at random from the electoral register should handle criminal cases involving the most serious offences – those for which the death penalty or life imprisonment are provided as possible penalties.[15]

The system was first introduced in May 2009. Since then a little over 1,000 cases have been handled by such collegiate courts annually.

3. DELIBERATION IN *SAIBAN-IN* CASES

Let us now turn to the deliberation in *saiban-in* cases (see figure 11). In principle, the same basic rules for deliberation as in other cases also apply to *saiban-in* cases: secrecy, the duty to express opinions, and majority rule. However, a number of new procedural devices were introduced in order to achieve substantial collaboration between professional judges and *saiban-in*.

---

14 The constituting judge explains the basic principles of sentencing; the team including *saiban-in* discuss mainly the relevant facts concerning the crime as such, then refer to the database of sentences imposed in previous cases for the same type of crime, and finally decide the sentence by taking a vote after thorough deliberation.
The basic principles of sentencing here means the principles which can be inferred from the Criminal Law of Japan – that the sentence should primarily be based on the evaluation of the criminal act, as opposed to that of the accused as a person, and that considerations concerning general and specific prevention, such as the environment and motivation for rehabilitation, or compensation, can also be considered, but only as subsidiary and secondary elements.
As to the database mentioned above, the sentences and the main circumstances relevant to the sentencing have been compiled since 2008, a little before the start of the *saiban-in* system. The database can be consulted according to types of crime, and the data set can be limited by certain conditions, such as the result, modus operandi, or motivation of the crime committed. By doing so, a range of sentences imposed in previous cases appears as a kind of distribution map – for instance, four years' imprisonment to ten years' imprisonment, with seven years' imprisonment being the most common sentence. Judges and *saiban-in* place the case at hand into the distribution map, considering all the circumstances of the crime being tried. For example, a *saiban-in* might think that a particular case is relatively serious compared with the same type of crime in respect of one or the other circumstance, and so eight to nine years' imprisonment might be the appropriate sentence to impose.
After exchanging views on these matters, the team discuss other subsidiary circumstances, and then each member of the panel decides the sentence as a concrete figure. At this point, a vote will be taken, and thus the sentence handed down by the panel is decided. The result of the deliberation on sentencing (not merely the sentence as such, but also the reasons for its imposition) will be written down in the judgment and read out in the open court.

15 Article 2 of the *Saiban-in* Law.

First of all, a pre-trial arrangement procedure is mandatory for all *saiban-in* cases.[16] Judges, prosecutors and defence attorneys in charge of the case get together before starting the hearing with a view to sorting out the main point(s) of issue, the best evidence to be examined and to lay a timetable for the hearing and deliberation. The point(s) of issue, identified in the pre-trial arrangement procedure, will then become the focal point of the hearing and deliberation. The main task of *saiban-in* is thus to determine the point(s) of issue.

At the deliberation, professional judges explain the role and competence of *saiban-in*, and provide them with the legal knowledge necessary for carrying out their functions.

Not only professional judges, but also *saiban-in* are under an obligation to express their opinion. In order for *saiban-in* to express their opinion freely, professional judges provide them with legal knowledge, and clearly indicate the issue(s) and topic(s) on which they are expected to express their opinion.[17] Professional judges also make utmost efforts to foster an atmosphere in which *saiban-in* can freely express their opinion, for instance by visualising the process of deliberation using a white board, or by providing sufficient time for everybody to reflect by themselves before starting a winder discussion, and so on.

The voting procedure is basically the same as that in 'judges only' deliberation. All the members of the collegiate court, either professional judges or *saiban-in*, have an equal vote, and decisions are taken by a simple majority, with a slight modification to the effect that the collegiate court cannot decide against the defendant unless the simple majority in question includes the opinions of both professional judge(s) and *saiban-in*.[18] This rule applies to all the *saiban-in* cases, including cases where the death penalty may be imposed if the accused is found guilty. Generally speaking, votes are taken step-by-step, normally following the logical order determined in the pre-trial arrangement procedure. In our experience, it is common to reach a unanimous decision, especially concerning the question of whether or not the accused is to be found guilty.

---

16 Article 49 of the *Saiban-in* Law.

17 Article 66 of the *Saiban-in* Law.

18 Article 67(1) of the *Saiban-in* Law provides that the decision with participation of *saiban-in* at the deliberation under para 1 of the preceding Article shall be rendered by a majority of opinions of the number of persons constituting the panel, which must include the opinions of both professional judge(s) and *saiban-in*, notwithstanding the provisions of Article 77 of the Court Law. This slightly modified simple majority rule reflects not only the purpose of the *Saiban-in* Law, ie a joint decision by a mixed panel sharing the responsibility and burden between professional judges and *saiban-in*, but also the spirit of the Japanese Constitution, which guarantees the right to fair trial. According to the provision, even if all the six *saiban-in* agree upon conclusion A (which is more disadvantageous for the accused than conclusion B, which all three professional judges support), it shall not be the decision of the panel, since the majority does not include any professional judge. Needless to say, arithmetically, the three professional judges alone cannot form a majority. In short, at least one judge and four *saiban-in* together are needed in order to constitute the majority prescribed in the provision.

Once the collegiate court reaches its decision, the conclusion and the court's reasoning are written down in a document by professional judges, reflecting the outcome of the deliberation. Dissenting opinions, or the result of the votes, are not included in this document.

The Presiding Judge renders judgment by reading out the document. All other panel members – ie the associate judges as well as the *saiban-in* – are present in the courtroom while the judgment is delivered.

Figure 11. Process to reach collective judgment in *Saiban-in* cases (an example)

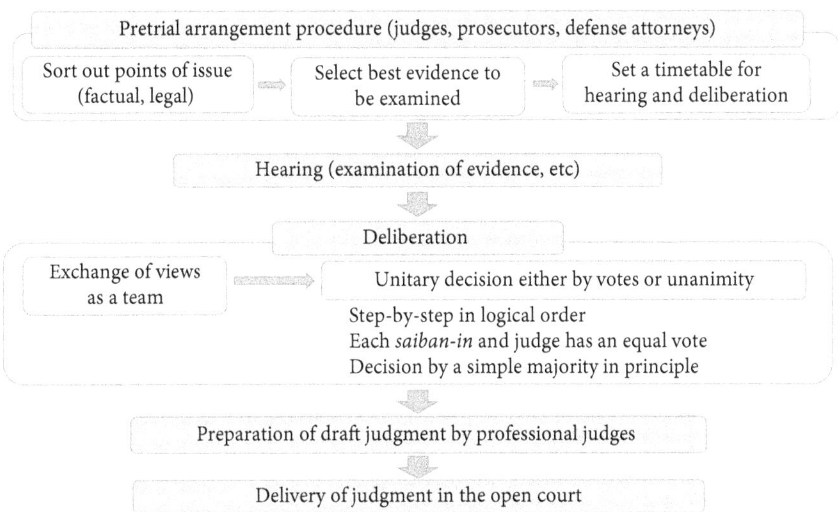

Source: Produced by the authors

Over ten years have passed since the *saiban-in* system started. Our impression is that it has by-and-large operated properly and smoothly, partly thanks to the efforts of those involved in the preparation and operation of the system. However, we cannot overemphasise the sincerity and feeling of responsibility demonstrated by most *saiban-in*, which is no doubt essential to the system. In addition, it is worth stressing that the decision by the collegiate court with *saiban-in* can often be particularly persuasive and profound, reflecting various point of view and being tested from multiple perspectives.

VI. IMPROVEMENT AND REINFORCEMENT OF THE FUNCTION OF COLLECTIVE JUDGING IN JAPAN

As Japanese society transform from a 'pre-regulation' society to a 'post-remedy' society, the role of the judiciary is becoming increasingly important. There are cases where the judgment in an individual case may have significant ramifications far beyond it. We have been facing the important task of improving and reinforcing the function of collective judging. In other words, the question is how the Japanese judiciary can constantly provide appropriate, high-quality decisions.

While it is not a task which can be achieved in a day, it will be possible for us to produce great results by improving daily practice, which is widely entrusted to each judge and each collegiate court individually.

To conclude, Japanese collegiate courts are engaged in ongoing improvements to their collective judging procedures, and they may well find that valuable lessons can be learnt from other collegiate courts around the world. In our chapter, we have focused on two main topics, namely decision-making in the Japanese Supreme Court, and the deliberation process involving *saiban-in*. Being neither Anglo-American nor Continental in origin, both of these are unique to Japan, and we are delighted to have been able to present them to a wider audience.

Figure 12. Improvement and reinforcement of the function of collective judging (image)

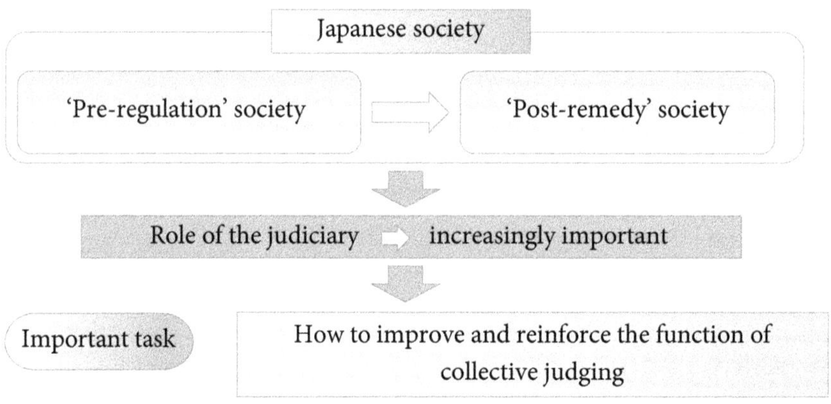

Source: Produced by the authors

PART V

SUPRANATIONAL AND INTERNATIONAL COLLEGIATE COURTS

CHAPTER 12

THE FINE-MECHANICS OF JUDICIAL DECISION-MAKING AT THE EUROPEAN COURT OF HUMAN RIGHTS

Angelika NUSSBERGER*

* Professor Dr Dres hc Angelika Nussberger was Judge at the European Court of Human Rights elected on behalf of Germany (between January 2011 and December 2019) and its Vice-President (between February 2017 and December 2019). This chapter expresses the author's personal opinion and does not bind the Court in any way.

I. COURTS AS BLACK BOXES?

Judges are bound by their oath. At the European Court of Human Rights (ECtHR) every judge, before being allowed to form part of a decision-making body, has solemnly to declare 'to keep secret all deliberations'.[1] As a natural consequence of this collective promise of silence, the Court seems to be transformed into a black box. Facts and judicial arguments are put in on one side, judgments come out on the other side. What happens in between remains in the realm of mystery.

But: transparency is an important value in a system based on the rule of law. To a certain extent, it might even be considered a precondition for the acceptance of judgments in the 'outside world'. Judgments without adequate reasoning are considered to be incompatible with basic requirements of fair trial – a standard well entrenched in the jurisprudence of the European Court of Human Rights itself.[2] Nevertheless, the reasoning is communicated to the outside world as a whole, not as work in progress. The mechanics of putting the arguments together, of moulding them into a specific form, smoothening them if necessary, is not visible from outside.

In reality, however, the black box is not as 'black' as it might appear to be. Neither is it really non-transparent. Many signs show that the decision-making process can be cumbersome and that it is all but easy to make 17 European

---

1 Rule 3 of the Rules of Court.

2 See eg *H v Belgium*, app 8950/80, 30 November 1987, para 53; *Suominen v Finland*, app 37801/97, 1 July 2003, para 36.

judges in Grand Chamber cases or seven European judges in Chamber cases speak with one voice. Very often they do not find a compromise acceptable to all, but write dissenting and concurring opinions and explain their personal convictions. Furthermore, whenever judges ask questions in public hearings, this might betray their preoccupations and reflections, even if the questions are worded in a neutral manner.

The decision-making process at the ECtHR is worthy of consideration in many respects, not least as it is an international court with judges coming from 47 different (European) jurisdictions, having a variety of professional, social and personal backgrounds and working together only for a limited period of time. At the same time, their judgments have to be acceptable in 47 different jurisdictions. So they are not only bound to speak with a common legal language, but this common legal language also has to be understood everywhere in Europe. Therefore, in a first step, the structural peculiarities of the Court's various decision-making bodies have to be explained (section II). The second question to be asked is how the judges – despite their dissimilarities – manage to come to unequivocal conclusions about 'what the law is' (section III). In this context, it is necessary to analyse the voting procedures in some detail (section IV). These results have to be summarised and evaluated in their specificity (section V).

II. FACTORS DETERMINING DECISION-MAKING

The ECtHR is different from all other national and international courts. Its decision-making process cannot be understood unless some basic features of the Court's composition and functioning are explained.

1. DIVERSITY OF JUDGES

a) Cultural and Educational Background

Context matters for judges' work. Judges are not abstract creatures, but formed by the environment in which they have been living for many years, even if they are all integrated into the international community of Strasbourg as soon as they start their job. The very fact that the 47 judges of the Court come from 47 different countries[3] suggests cultural diversity. At the outset, they can be

3 In the present-day composition of the Court, the judge elected on behalf of Liechtenstein is a Swiss national. Some other judges have double nationality or have a multicultural background in their family. In the original version of the European Convention on Human Rights (ECHR) of 1950, it was forbidden for two judges to be nationals of the same State (Article 38); however, this provision has been abolished.

grouped into judges educated in a continental legal system,[4] judges educated in the common law system,[5] and judges influenced by the specific traits of what used to be called 'socialist law', at least if they were educated before the breakdown of the respective legal systems in Central and Eastern Europe.[6] It is true that in an open, modern world such differences become more and more blurred due to, among other things, international study programmes and students mobility. But this also depends on the generation. For the older generation, studying abroad was not possible either because of closed borders or because of a lack of options, while such hindrances no longer exist for the younger generation. Furthermore, not all judges were in their 'former life' professional judges. According to the requirements set out in the Convention, they 'must either possess the qualifications required for appointment to high judicial office or be jurisconsults of recognised competence'.[7] In practice the largest groups among the judges are on the one hand former judges, some of whom have been presidents of their respective supreme or constitutional courts,[8] and on the other hand former law professors. A non-negligible number of judges are also former practising lawyers,[9] who have sometimes even brought important cases to the Court themselves,[10] or government agents.[11]

While it might be assumed that all judges are equal in their work at the Court, a closer look betrays important differences here as well. It is true that it does not matter whether a judge comes from a small or a big Member State, a common law or a civil law jurisdiction, a so called 'old' or 'new' democracy. Nor is it relevant what he or she was in a 'former life'. The position within the Court is only determined by seniority. However, judges coming from or educated in French- or English-speaking countries do have certain

---

4 This is the vast majority of Member States of the Council of Europe.

5 The United Kingdom and the Republic of Ireland; Malta and Cyprus have mixed systems using the common law.

6 On these differences, which also concern what is meant by 'judging', see P Glenn, *Legal Traditions of the World*, 4th edn (Oxford, Oxford University Press, 2010). The relevance of the 'origin' of the judges is visible from the rules about the composition of the Sections of the Court (Rule 25(2)) and the Grand Chamber (Rule 24(2)(e) of the Rules of Court).

7 See Article 21(1) ECHR.

8 For instance, Egidius Kuris, who was former President of the Constitutional Court of Lithuania, or Pauliine Koskelo, who was former President of the Supreme Court of Finland.

9 For instance, the former President of the Court Dean Spielmann, who was a lawyer in Luxembourg, and the former Vice-President of the Court Josep Casadevall, who was a lawyer in Andorra.

10 For instance, the British judge as of 12 September 2016, Tim Eicke, who appeared before the Court as representative of the applicant in the case *Christine Goodwin v United Kingdom*, app 28957/95, 11 July 2002, and as representative of the Government in the case *N v United Kingdom*, app 26565/05, 27 May 2008; or the Bulgarian judge as of 13 April 2015, Yonko Grozev, who was representative for the applicants in the case *Hasan and Chaush v Bulgaria*, app 30985/96, 26 October 2000.

11 For instance, the former President of the Court, Nicolas Bratza.

advantages (and perhaps also responsibilities). Interpreting the law is a hermeneutic and linguistic task; language matters. It also matters in setting out the reasons for a judgment. Unavoidably, in questions concerning precise and correct wording, native speakers will be given the last word in deciding on linguistic subtleties. Such incongruences do not exist in national courts, where all are trained in the same language, unless they work in more than one language as, for instance, in Switzerland.

b) Different Status of Judges in Different Procedures

Equality among judges is also undermined by the status of the so-called 'National Judge', ie the judge elected on behalf of the Member State against whom a complaint is directed. The National Judge is *ex officio* a member in all Chamber and Grand Chamber formations deciding on cases against the High Contracting Party concerned.[12] This means that there is always one judge with a 'special knowledge' both of the respective national legal system and of the potential consequences a judgment might have in the country concerned. This is a non-negligible factor in the decision-making process. Judges coming from so-called 'high-count countries' with the highest number of applications brought to the Court (at present Turkey, Romania, Ukraine and Russia) are much more often 'National Judges' than others.

If a case is referred to the Grand Chamber, the National Judge is, as a rule, bound to sit twice in the same case.[13] He or she is thus called upon either to confirm or to reject the position taken on the first level,[14] whereas for all the other judges sitting in a Grand Chamber case referred under Article 43 of the Convention, the subject matter is a completely new one.

12 See Article 26(4) ECHR and Rule 24(2)(b); different regulations are applied for committees and single judge cases. National Judges are not allowed to examine applications against their own State (Article 26(3) ECHR). For committee cases this is an optional rule (Article 28(3) ECHR).

13 See Article 26(5) 2nd sentence ECHR and Rule 24(2)(d) of the Rules of Court. In as far as this regulation also allows Presidents of Section to sit twice in a case, it is not applied in practice.

14 See the famous concurring opinions of Nicolas Bratza in the case of *Al-Khawaja and Tahery v United Kingdom* (GC), app 26766/05 22228/06, 15 December 2011, where he justifies his change of position: 'Having re-examined the two cases in the light of these principles, I agree with the majority that, contrary to my original view in the Chamber, Article 6(1) ECHR was not violated in the Al-Khawaja case but that there was a violation of that Article in the Tahery case' (para 4 of his concurring opinion); in a similar vein, see also the concurring opinion of Paul Lemmens in the case of *Paposhvili v Belgium* (GC), app 41738/10, 13 December 2016; in the case of *Paradiso and Campanelli v Italy* (GC), app 25358/12, 24 January 2017, the Grand Chamber's finding of a non-violation was the one supported by the National Judge Guido Raimondi in the Chamber. In his concurring opinion, he explains his position in view of the changed line of argument: 'If I find it necessary to express myself through a separate opinion, it is purely because I wish to note that the Grand Chamber's decision to analyse this case in the light of protection of the applicants' private life, rather than in the light of their family life, is, in my view, particularly appropriate.'

2. DIVERSITY OF PROCEDURES

a) *Four Courts in One*

It is always 'the Court' which decides a case. But behind this notion lies a number of very different decision-making 'formations'. For understanding the fine-mechanics of judicial majoritarianism, it makes a difference whether seven judges sitting as a 'Chamber' decide a case which is just one out of many on the weekly agenda of their 'Section', or whether seventeen judges in the 'Grand Chamber' decide in a complex procedure including a hearing and two deliberations. Chamber cases are, as a rule, adopted 'in one go', whereas the elaboration of a Grand Chamber judgment may easily last for more than a year even after the hearing.

The choice of the formation or composition is related to the matter decided. Basically, the Grand Chamber decides on serious questions affecting the interpretation (or application) of the Convention, be it on the basis of a relinquishment (Article 30 of the Convention) or a referral (Article 43 of the Convention). The competence of the regular Chambers might thus be seen as defined *ex negativo* – in all cases not touching upon 'serious' questions of interpretation. This would, however, be misleading, particularly since the criterion of 'seriousness' is very vague. As a matter of fact, the Chambers decide in all legally intricate non-repetitive questions, and only the most difficult and serious questions are sent to the Grand Chamber. Many Chamber judgments can without any doubt be regarded as 'landmarks' in the Court's jurisprudence.[15]

But the distribution of cases cannot be seen solely in light of the relationship between Chamber and Grand Chamber. On the contrary, only a small selection of cases is dealt with by those two formations. The vast majority of cases are decided by Committees and Single Judges. These are meant to be the right *fora* for uncontroversial, repetitive and manifestly unfounded or inadmissible cases.[16] Decision-making in those bodies is completely different. Obviously, there is no majoritarian element involved in single judges' decisions. Committees of three judges always have to reach a unanimous decision, otherwise the case is

---

15 See, for instance, *Oleksandr Volkov v Ukraine*, app 21722/11, 9 January 2013, on the requirements of fair trial in dismissing a judge; *M v Germany*, app 19359/04, 17 December 2009, on retrospective security detention; *Tagayeva and others v Russia*, app 26562/07, 14755/08, 49339/08, 49380/08, 51313/08, 21294/11 and 37096/11, 13 April 2017, on the requirements for police operations to free hostages.

16 The new competences of Committees and Single Judges were introduced by Protocol No 14 to the Convention, opened for signature in 2004 and entered into force in 2010. As explained in the Preamble, it responded to the 'urgent need to amend certain provisions of the Convention in order to maintain and improve the efficiency of the control system for the long term, mainly in the light of the continuing increase in the workload of the European Court of Human Rights and the Committee of Ministers of the Council of Europe'.

automatically referred to a Chamber. A simple vote decides; a procedure for finding compromise is dispensable.

Decision-making in Chambers and in the Grand Chamber is thus nothing but the famous tip of the iceberg. The bulk of the work, far more than 95%, is done by Single Judges and Committees without any deliberations. It might not even be an exaggeration to talk of a 'decision-making factory' in this context.[17] It is only the Chamber and the Grand Chamber who do 'classical' judicial work.

b) *Elements of a Lottery*

i) Composition of the Chamber

Comparing the number of judges deciding on specific cases (seven) and the number of judges forming a so-called 'Section' (nine or ten), it is clear that the Sections decide cases in different compositions. While some details, such as the inclusion of the President of Section and of the National Judge[18] are clearly regulated in the Convention and the Rules of Court,[19] other questions are left within the discretion of the President. Thus, according to Rule 26(1)(b) of the Rules of the Court, 'the other members of the Chamber shall be designated by the President of the Section in rotation from among the members of the relevant Section.' The President may follow different models in this respect. According to one model, compositions are fixed in advance for a longer period of time. Another model allows deciding on the composition on a case-by-case basis by drawing lots. The principle of a 'subjective right to the lawful judge' (known in German as the '*gesetzlicher Richter*')[20] is not an explicit Convention requirement

---

17 The Court's strike-out decision in the case of *Burmych and others v Ukraine*, app 46852/13, 47786/13, 54125/13, 56605/13 and 3653/14, 12 October 2017, documents a specific facet of this problem. After the failure of a pilot judgment against Ukraine, complaints about non-execution of final court judgments kept being brought to the Court. The Court summed up that it had already dealt with 14,430 such cases while 12,143 more were pending (para 153). It then commented: 'The Court observes that it runs the risk of operating as part of the Ukrainian legal enforcement system and substituting itself for the Ukrainian authorities in directing "appropriate and sufficient redress for the non-enforcement or delayed enforcement of domestic decisions", as required under the fifth operative provision of the Ivanov judgment. That task is not compatible with the subsidiary role which the Court is supposed to play in relation to the High Contracting Parties under Article 1 (obligation to respect human rights) and Article 19 of the Convention, and runs directly counter to the logic of the pilot-judgment procedure developed by the Court.'

18 On the so-called 'National Judge', see the text accompanying n 12 above.

19 See Article 26 ECHR and Rule 26(1)(a) of the Rules of Court.

20 On the details of this constitutional tradition, see the references to the Belgian, Slovenian and Italian Constitutions in the opinion of the Venice Commission, *Report on the Independence of the Judicial System. Part I: The Independence of Judges*, adopted by the Venice Commission at its 82nd Plenary Session on 12-13 March 2010, CDL-AD(2010)004, para 39.

for the composition of the Chambers. Neither is there a consensus in Europe that the predetermination of the individual judges forming part of a judicial decision-making body on the basis of abstract criteria would be a *conditio sine qua non* for a fair trial.[21]

ii) Composition of the Grand Chamber

The composition of the Grand Chamber is an even more controversial issue. Based on the Convention, the President of the Court, the two Vice-Presidents and the three Section Presidents as well as the National Judge are *ex officio* members of the Grand Chamber. All the other judges are drawn by lot. In order to guarantee a regionally diverse composition, the lots are drawn on the basis of preformed regional groups of judges.[22] That means that while the Chambers have a relatively stable composition and can build up a specific 'culture of discussion', the same is not true for the Grand Chamber.

iii) Substitute Judges

Judges of the Section not included in the deciding formation are 'Substitute Judges'. Their role is clear insofar as they have to step in as soon as a judge of the composition drops out. But quite a lot of questions remain unresolved. Thus it is not clearly regulated whether the Substitute Judges are allowed to intervene in the deliberations. Whether or not they do so is a factor hidden to the outside world, as only the names of the judges included in the composition are listed. On the other hand, if they are excluded from the deliberations, but have to replace a colleague later on, they have to take part in the final vote without having been included in the substantive discussion.

The same problem besets the position of the Substitute Judges in the Grand Chamber, all the more so as the first and second deliberations have a different focus (discussed further below).[23]

---

21 According to the Venice Commission (ibid para 79), however, such a regulation would be recommendable: 'It is not enough if only the court (or the judicial branch) competent for a certain case is determined in advance. That the order in which the individual judge (or panel of judges) within a court is determined in advance, meaning that it is based on general objective principles, is essential. It is desirable to indicate clearly where the ultimate responsibility for proper case allocation is being placed.'

22 See the respective regulation in Rule 24(2)(e) of the Rules of Court: 'The judges and substitute judges who are to complete the Grand Chamber in each case referred to it shall be designated from among the remaining judges by a drawing of lots by the President of the Court in the presence of the Registrar. The modalities for the drawing of lots shall be laid down by the Plenary Court, having due regard to the need for a geographically balanced composition reflecting the different legal systems among the Contracting Parties.'

23 See section III.3 below, text in the paragraphs preceding n 42.

Thus Substitute Judges can be considered as undefined elements in the decision-making process. Nevertheless, for pragmatic reasons they are important as they help to avoid time-consuming repetitions of parts of the procedure. This is the price to be paid for not allowing a change in the quorum of seven judges for Chamber judgments and seventeen judges for Grand Chamber judgments. The advantage is that – due to the uneven numbers of judges – a majority will always be clearly established.[24]

III. COMPLEXITY OF DECISION-MAKING

There are two distinct models for decision-making in courts.[25] Either the decision-making power lies uniformly with the conference of judges, who have to arrive at one common finding conveyed as 'the Court's decision'. Or the decision-making is based on individual judges' conclusions. Their different approaches are then not melted into one whole, but remain visible in the judgment. While the first model creates the fiction of several judges deciding with one voice, the second model presents judgments as an agglomeration of different opinions. What is put to the forefront in the '*per curiam* model' is the result, what is central in the '*seriatim* model' is the process of decision-making.

It is the first model that has been chosen for the judgments and decisions of the European Court of Human Rights. The underlying assumption is that the judgments represent the unanimous opinion of the judges. It is the exception to the rule which is explicitly expressed in the Convention:

> 'If a judgment does not represent, in whole or in part, the unanimous opinion of the judges, any judge shall be entitled to deliver a separate opinion.'[26]

Allowing for dissenting and concurring opinions means, however, that the fiction of judges speaking with one voice can be undermined and – in practice – is often undermined. The exception can even turn into the rule.[27] Nevertheless, the Court's majority judgments are binding; only the line of argument

---

24 The rules concerning a tie in the voting procedure (Rule 23(1) 2nd sentence of the Rules of Court) are therefore not of practical relevance in this regard.

25 G Lübbe-Wolff, 'Cultures of Deliberations in Constitutional Courts' in P Maraniello (ed), *Justicia Constitucional* (Buenos Aires, Contexto Libreria Editorial, 2016), 37, 42; W Ernst, 'Abstimmen über Rechtserkenntnis' (2012) *Juristenzeitung* 637.

26 Article 45(2) ECHR.

27 This is shown by the statistics on the voting results in the Grand Chamber. Many important judgments are adopted on the basis of a tight majority, for recent examples see *Moreira Ferreira v Portugal No. 2* (GC), app 19867/12, 11 July 2017, *Béláné Nagy v Hungary* (GC), app 53080/13, 13 December 2016, both adopted by nine to eight votes. Grand Chamber judgments are in fact rarely unanimous.

supported by the majority forms part of the Court's case law. Arriving at a conclusive majoritarian approach can be difficult. It is remarkable that neither the Convention nor the Rules of Court contain detailed regulations. The only relevant rule is Rule 22(3) of the Rules of Court which reads as follows:

> 'Before a vote is taken on any matter in the Court, the President may request the judges to state their opinions on it.'

It therefore does not come as a surprise that this is an issue of intense debate within the Court.

1. DIFFERENT STEPS IN THE DECISION-MAKING PROCESS

In order to understand how the Court fulfils its task of producing convincingly reasoned Committee, Chamber and Grand Chamber judgments, it is necessary to see the decision-making process in its entirety.

a) *Acceptance of Incoming Complaints*

Incoming complaints have to comply with the formal requirements set out in Rule 47 of the Rules of Court. While the Court's practice was quite permissive until 2015, due to the enormous influx of cases and the backlog in the Court's work, the approach has significantly changed since then.[28] The date of introduction of the application for the purpose of Article 35(1) of the Convention is now the date on which an application form satisfying all the formal requirements is sent to the Court. Before 2015 it was sufficient for meeting the deadline of six months to bring the complaint to the Court in whatever form; it could even be the famous scribbling on a slip of toilet paper sent out of prison.

The idea behind Rule 47 in its present form is that the information set out in the application form has to be 'sufficient to enable the Court to determine the nature and scope of the application without recourse to any other document'.[29] It is true that, due to the Court's mission of effectively protecting human rights, exceptions to this harsh rule are necessary.[30] Nevertheless, statistics show that roughly 15% of the incoming complaints are rejected on the basis of Rule 47 without being seen by a judge.[31]

---

28 See the new Rule 47 of the Rules of the Court, as amended by the Court on 5 October 2015.

29 Rule 47(2)(a) of the Rules of Court.

30 See Rule 47(6)(b) of the Rules of Court: 'Where it finds it justified, the Court may nevertheless decide that a different date shall be considered to be the date of introduction.'

31 See eg the data for the year 2016: while 80,568 complaints were registered, 11,734 were rejected on the basis of Rule 47 of the Rules of the Court.

According to the Court, the new Rule 47 has achieved its aim as it facilitates the efficient sifting of incoming applications. It is therefore seen as a contribution 'to the Court's success in diminishing the overall backlog of cases and dealing with cases more speedily.'[32] Comparing the rather generous time limit of six months (between the last final decision on the national level and the introduction of the complaint) to more restrictive regulations of other courts,[33] it can be argued that access to the Court is – even after the reform of 2015 – not restricted in a way that would endanger its mission. The new Protocol No 15 to the Convention, which has not yet entered into force, however, will reduce the period to four months.[34]

b) *Filtering*

A decisive step in the decision-making procedure is the filtering of those complaints which fulfil all formal requirements and have thus passed the first hurdle. Filtering lies mainly in the hands of the registry, but is supervised by the judges at a later stage. The relevant Rule 49(1) of the Rules of Court reads as follows:

> 'Where the material submitted by the applicant is on its own sufficient to disclose that the application is inadmissible or should be struck out of the list, the application shall be considered by a single-judge formation unless there is some special reason to the contrary.'

It is thus at this early stage that it is decided whether the complaint is worth being sent to a Committee or Chamber. Otherwise it can immediately be dismissed by a Single Judge. While, before the reform introduced by Protocol No 14,[35] inadmissible complaints would pile up, nowadays the Court deals with them based on the principle 'one in – one out'. Any complaint identified as being non-meritorious should not remain on the Court's dockets for more than a few months.

Single Judge decisions do not form part of the following analysis, as there are no fine-mechanics of judicial majoritarianism to be observed. When a Single Judge decides, the relevant decision is based on preparatory work done by the Registry, in which the so-called Non-Judicial *Rapporteurs*, ie experienced lawyers appointed by the President, play a crucial role.[36] The Single Judge has four options. He or she can accept the Non-Judicial *Rapporteur's* proposal, ask

---

32 See Report on Rule 47 of the Rules of the Court, available online via the Court's home page under http://www.echr.coe.int/pages/home.aspx?p=basictexts/rules&c (last accessed 29 February 2020).

33 Compare, for instance, the one-month time limit for individual complaints before the Federal Constitutional Court of Germany in §93(1) 1st sentence BVerfGG.

34 See Article 4 of Protocol No 15 to the Convention.

35 On which see n 16 and the accompanying text.

36 See Article 24(2) ECHR and Rule 27A(4) of the Rules of Court.

for more information and adjourn the case, refer the case to a Committee of three judges or to a Chamber.[37] The latter decision is not binding for the then appointed *Rapporteur* who is free to prepare a draft for a Committee instead of bringing the case immediately to the Chamber. Between 2010 (when Protocol No 14 entered into force) and 2017, the Single Judge decisions were not reasoned.[38] Since 2017, summary reasons have been provided.[39]

Human rights lawyers have criticised the Single Judge procedure harshly. It is true that it does not comply with all the requirements of fair trial set out in Article 6 of the Convention. But the procedure before the Court is not an ordinary judicial remedy; it should be reserved for well-founded complaints about human rights violations. A Court of 47 judges competent to decide on complaints coming from 820 million people living in 47 Member States must, at least to a certain extent, be able to concentrate on well-founded complaints. The summary reasoning provided as of 2017 is meant to be a compromise between the complainants' wish to get reasoned decisions even in the case of inadmissibility and the community's wish of seeing the Court deal quickly and thoroughly with well-founded applications.

Not all inadmissible complaints are decided by the Single Judge. It is also possible to bring them to a Committee or to the Chamber and to decide *de plano*. Even questions of inadmissibility can be intricate. They can have important consequences, especially when explaining which national remedies are deemed to be effective and have to be exhausted before bringing a case to the Court. This is a very controversial issue in complaints concerning measures taken by the authorities, for instance in a number of cases about dismissals and pretrial detention brought to the Court after the attempted coup d'Etat in Turkey.[40]

c) *Communication*

Communication of an application to the Government signals that it is not obviously inadmissible or without merits, but may, on the contrary, be well-founded. Therefore the respondent Contracting Party has to be given the opportunity to comment on all relevant questions of admissibility and merits, comments which are then forwarded to the applicant.[41] At this moment in the

37 See Rule 52A of the Rules of Court, inserted by the Court on 13 November 2016.

38 The only information contained in the letter sent to the applicant read as follows: 'In the light of all the material in its possession and in so far as the matters complained of are within its competence, the Court found that the admissibility criteria set out in Articles 34 and 35 of the Convention have not been met.'

39 See the Court's Press Release of 1 June 2017, ECHR 180 (2017) 'Launch of new system for single judge decisions with more detailed reasoning'.

40 See, eg, *Mercan v Turkey*, app 56511/16, 8 November 2016; *Zihni v Turkey*, app 59061/16, 29 November 2016.

41 See Rule 54(2) of the Rules of Court.

procedure, the application becomes known to the public. The communication report is put on the Court's website. This enables third party interventions and a public debate on pending cases.

With the communication report the complaint is 'put on the rails'. The questions asked by the Court show which human rights problems are identified. At the same time, the President can – acting as a Single Judge – declare parts of the application inadmissible. This shows that the decision-making process by the collegiate body does not necessarily embrace all the aspects of a case. Some parts may be cut off already, some parts are already channelled in a certain direction. Corrections on the basis of re-communications are possible, but, for the sake of efficiency, are meant to be avoided.

It is not only the President of Section, but also the *Rapporteur*, who is involved in this part of the procedure. According to the Rules of Court, the President designates the Judge *Rapporteur*, 'who shall examine the application' (Rule 49(2) of the Rules of Court). No further specification is given on the criteria by reference to which the Judge *Rapporteur* should be chosen. The same is true for Grand Chamber cases (Rule 50 of the Rules of Court). The name of the *Rapporteur* is not publicly known in order to protect those working on especially 'hot' cases.

It is important to see that the *Rapporteur* is not left alone working on a case, but is assisted by the Registry. While judges come to the Court and leave it after the end of their mandate of nine years, the Registry, at least in as far as it is composed of long-term employees, represents the institutional memory of the Court. Even if the Registry lawyers stay in the background, they fulfil crucial functions, supporting the Judge *Rapporteur* in preparing – together with him or her – the communication report as well as the draft judgments, always strictly in line with the existing case-law and based on the simple rule of 'how it is always done'. While the Judge *Rapporteur* is free to change and modify the text according to individual preferences, the basis of the text is drafted in what might be called 'Registry style'. The cooperation between Registry lawyer and Judge *Rapporteur* starts, as a rule, with the decision on communication. If a communication is not deemed to be necessary, a *de plano* inadmissibility decision can be prepared for the Chamber.

If President and Judge *Rapporteur* disagree on the communication, the Chamber decides.

All these preparatory steps show that the analysis of the collective decision-making process at the ECtHR cannot focus exclusively on the oral deliberations among the judges, but must also take into account the context in which the deliberations are embedded. Deliberations and voting are the two last decisive steps, but form part of a much more complex procedure. The preparatory work facilitates the decision-making process, but also reduces the scope of the judges' choices.

2. PREPARATION OF THE JUDGES' CONFERENCE

Deliberations on the level of the Chamber and on the level of the Grand Chamber are different. Chamber deliberations are based on a draft with one or several alternatives; it can be adopted within one Section meeting. The deliberations are relatively free and flexible; the final vote is taken immediately after the deliberations. By contrast, Grand Chamber deliberations are stretched out over several meetings, two meetings of the full composition and one or more meetings of the drafting committee. Deliberations among the 17 judges have to be relatively structured and rigid in order to allow all judges to take the floor while keeping the discussion within reasonable time limits. The first deliberations take place immediately after the hearing and take up all legal questions raised by the case, while the second deliberations are focussed on the concrete wording of the draft. It is only at the very end of the whole procedure – which can last for over a year – that the vote becomes binding.

These differences are also mirrored in the preparatory steps taken. The Rules of Court do not contain detailed regulations on the questions raised in this context.[42]

a) Preparation of Written Material for the Judges

i) Procedure before the Chamber

An important distinguishing feature between the preparation of deliberations in courts on the national constitutional level and on the international level is the accessibility of the contents of the original court files. Cases brought before the ECtHR have, as a rule, been discussed during two, three or even four instances of court proceedings at the national level. The relevant court decisions have to be included in the application to the Court.[43] Due to language barriers, however, they are often not directly accessible to the judges of the Court with the exception of the National Judge; there are 42 different languages spoken in the Member States of the Council of Europe. The material provided in the original language is read and analysed by the Registry and forms the basis for the summary of the facts of the case, which has to be approved by the parties and is taken up in the judgment. Yet summaries are only summaries. The quality of

42 The Rules of Court do not systematically distinguish between proceedings before the Chamber and the Grand Chamber. Most regulations apply to 'the Court' in whatever formation; according to Rule 71(1) of the Rules of Court, provisions governing proceedings before the Chambers 'shall apply, *mutatis mutandis*, to proceedings before the Grand Chamber.'

43 See Rule 47(2) of the Rules of Court.

the parties' observations before the Court – including annexes with translations of the relevant national court judgments – is therefore of crucial importance in order to bring all relevant arguments to the judges' attention.[44]

The *Rapporteur* is responsible for collecting all the relevant material for deciding a case. If deemed necessary, he or she can ask for translations of specific judgments of national courts, be it the text as a whole or parts thereof. As a rule, such excerpts are then also quoted in the Court's judgments. The documentation can vary in length, but will, as a rule, also include dissenting opinions and judgments of courts on different levels if they are based on different arguments or come to different solutions.

It is true that working in languages different from the languages of the original court procedure is quite a challenge. Summaries, excerpts and translations are always only 'second best'. But this is the price to be paid for allowing an international court to decide on national human rights cases. Safeguards such as the adversary procedure before the Court and the integration of the National Judge into the Chamber's formation are important for making sure that the national legal system is well understood. In analysing the mechanisms of decision-making, the restricted accessibility of the original case material for all judges but the National Judge[45] is a factor that should not be forgotten.

ii) Procedure before the Grand Chamber

The material provided for Grand Chamber deliberations is, as a rule, much more comprehensive. It is the *Rapporteur* who decides what to include, depending on the topic to be discussed. The material may comprise comparative law reports, international law reports, specific statements of facts in addition to the observations of the parties, and summaries of relevant case-law as well as other material. Third parties ask for the right to intervene much more often than in procedures before the Chamber and thus provide additional analytical elements.

b) Oral Hearing

According to Rule 59(3) of the Rules of Court, the Court has full discretion in deciding whether or not to hold a hearing:

> 'The Chamber may decide, either at the request of a party or of its own motion, to hold a hearing on the merits if it considers that the discharge of its functions of the Convention so requires.'

44 See the detailed regulation on the use of languages in Rule 34 of the Rules of Court.
45 In cases where the material is in English or French, these problems obviously do not arise.

In almost all the cases brought before the Grand Chamber, a public hearing is organised. An exception may be made in especially 'technical' cases.[46] In proceedings before the Chamber, by way of contrast, hearings are the exception rather than the rule. They are deemed to be useful in highly sensitive or controversial cases. Examples in recent years are *Tymoshenko v Ukraine*, a case concerning the pretrial detention for the allegedly contemptuous behaviour of the former Prime Minister of Ukraine before the trial court,[47] *Oleksandr Volkov v Ukraine*, a case concerning the dismissal of a judge of the Supreme Court of Ukraine,[48] and *Al Nashiri v Poland*, a case about secret rendition.[49]

Public hearings are very structured and do not allow for much interaction. The representatives of the parties are allocated a certain amount of time for their pleadings, without being interrupted by the judges. Judges ask questions in one block after the pleadings and before the break. After the break, the parties have an opportunity for rebuttal and answering the judges' questions. Where answers are unsatisfactory, the judges can repeat or explain their questions. This was introduced only very recently in order to enhance a real dialogue instead of a series of monologues.

Nevertheless, the function of the public hearing cannot be described as enabling a lively debate on the subject – as it seems to be in other courts. It is rather the opening of a door for outsiders, allowing them to witness the discussions before the Court. Hearings are important for showing the Court in action and for conveying information about its work; they thus contribute to the Court's mission, not least in making human rights victims' voices heard. This is all the more true as the public hearings are webcasts.

c) *Channelling of the Deliberations*

As mentioned above, the debate in the Chamber is generally based on a draft proposing one concrete solution or – if deemed helpful – alternatives. If only one solution is proposed, colleagues either have to accept it, perhaps with modifications to the text, or may reject it. A draft which does not proffer an alternative solution will thus channel the deliberations in a certain way, while the debate is *per se* more open where alternative solutions are provided from the outset.

---

46 See, eg, *Burmych and others v Ukraine* (GC), app 46852/13, 47786/13, 54125/13, 56605/13, 3653/14, 12 October 2017: division of responsibility between the Court and the Committee of Ministers following failure to execute a pilot judgment; *Sabri Güneş v Turkey* (GC), app 27396/06, 26 June 2012: determining expiry date of six-month time limit; *Nagmetov v Russia* (GC), app 35589/08, 30 March 2017: award of non-pecuniary damage in the absence of a properly submitted claim.

47 *Tymoshenko v Ukraine*, app 49872/11, 30 April 2013.

48 *Oleksandr Volkov v Ukraine*, app 21722/11, 9 January 2013.

49 *Al Nashiri v Poland*, app 28761/11, 24 July 2014.

In clear-cut cases, alternatives are not necessary. However, in the light of work efficiency, there is a tendency to bring clear-cut cases, even those concerning important human rights questions, to the Committee, and to reserve the Chamber for truly controversial cases.

The *Rapporteur's* note prepared for the Grand Chamber is not a draft judgment, but outlines the relevant facts and the case-law together with a detailed legal analysis.

d) *Further Preparatory Steps*

i) Procedure before the Chamber

Efficiency is an important factor in the work of a Court faced with about 60,000 pending cases. The better the deliberations are prepared, the easier it is to arrive quickly at a well-founded solution to a case.

This is the reason why the Jurisconsult's department, a specific division of qualified lawyers, has been created within the Court's Registry.[50] Every week, they read all the judgments on the agenda of the five Sections of the Court and send critical comments to all judges. The comments may concern the omission of references to relevant case-law, potential contradictions between the solution proposed and existing case-law, information on cases not yet decided, but pending before other sections, and even information on international hard or soft law that might additionally be included in the draft. The Jurisconsult's analysis is a very important tool for the preparation of the judgments and for securing the consistency of the Court's jurisprudence. The recommendations are, however, not binding on the judges, who are free to take them on board or to ignore them.

Comments on draft judgments on the agenda may already be shared before the meeting. This helps the *Rapporteur* in his or her preparation of the case and facilitates the debate. Yet there is a general consensus that such comments should not replace the deliberations. In any case, in as far as such comments are sent to all colleagues, they are much preferable to 'corridor chats'. All judges forming part of the decision-making body should dispose of the same information when deliberations start.

It can thus be argued that the preparatory stage is decisive. Deliberations in the judges' conference are shaped by the work done beforehand. What may be called a 'tentative testing of arguments' takes place at this stage already. The preparation of Section meetings is not regulated in detail. It is thus more

---

50 See Rule 18B of the Rules of Court: 'For the purposes of ensuring the quality and consistency of its case-law, the Court shall be assisted by a Jurisconsult. He or she shall be a member of the Registry. The Jurisconsult shall provide opinions and information, in particular to the judicial formations and the members of the Court.'

a question of style, depending on personal preferences and well-established practice in the five Sections of the Court.

ii) Procedure before the Grand Chamber

As the procedure before the Grand Chamber always comprises several steps – from the hearing, to the first deliberations, to the drafting Committee, and finally to the second deliberations – there is no need of an additional preparatory phase, as in the procedure before the Chamber.

3. ORGANISATION OF THE JUDGES' CONFERENCE

a) Order of the Judges' Addresses

i) Procedure before the Chamber

As in many courts, there are unwritten rules about the order of the judges' addresses, although, according to the Rules of Court, it is the President who has the final say concerning the structuring of the deliberations.[51] Generally, all judges are free to take the floor whenever they want to, with the exception of the Judge *Rapporteur*, National Judge and President, who are allocated specific time slots for their interventions.

There is no obligation to speak. In 'easy cases', there is even a gentleman's agreement not to take the floor if there is nothing important to add.

Deliberations among seven judges based on a draft judgment are comparatively easy to organise. The discussion can go back and forth and be very lively. At the end, the Judge *Rapporteur* has to make a proposal, either to take the final vote on the case or to adjourn it and come back to the Chamber with a revised draft.

ii) Procedure before the Grand Chamber

Deliberations at Grand Chamber level are more difficult to organise. Due to time constraints, the discussion has to be more rigid and structured. But, although certain rules about speaking order and interventions have been formed on the basis of long-standing practice, nothing is carved in stone. The President can always opt for a different approach to follow.

In organising Grand Chamber deliberations, the Court is confronted with a dilemma. It is well-known that the more participants there are, the less intense the debate. Decision-making in bodies with between five and eight members may

---

51 See Rule 22(3) of the Rules of Court, quoted above, at the top of p 236.

be regarded as ideal – a model followed by many courts worldwide. However, for the authority of the Grand Chamber of the ECtHR, it is important to include a substantial part of the 47 judges representing the different legal systems and geographical regions of Europe. A composition of 17 judges has thus to be seen as a compromise. Deciding in the plenary would be virtually impossible; deciding by an even smaller number of judges would no longer be considered as representative and would undermine the Grand Chamber's authority.

Reform debates concerning the work in the Grand Chamber are on-going. The *status quo* is not considered as wholly satisfactory, although it does allow for a debate to which every judge can contribute.

Grand Chamber deliberations take place immediately after the hearing and end, as a rule, with a provisional vote after all interventions on the evening of the first day of deliberations have been heard.

b) *Role of President and the Judge* Rapporteur

i) Chamber Cases

The role of the Judge *Rapporteur* is decisive in the preparatory phase, but also during the deliberations. He or she has been working on the case for a long time, has been in an intense dialogue with the lawyer(s) preparing the case, has knowledge of the whole file, is thus the drafter of the judgment and has the right to make proposals on which all the judges involved vote.

The President steers the deliberations and decides which questions are put to a vote.

The deliberations end with a final vote on the draft. Basically, when the Judge *Rapporteur* has prepared a draft proposing only one solution, there are two scenarios: Either he or she 'wins' the case and convinces the colleagues to vote for the proposed solution; it is then adopted, often with minor textual changes. Or the case is 'lost' and the Judge *Rapporteur* remains in the minority. In the latter scenario, it is a somewhat schizophrenic exercise for the Judge *Rapporteur* to write a new draft judgment against his or her own conviction and arguments. Even though it should not be problem for a professional lawyer to argue a case from different angles, it might be better for an *ad hoc* drafting committee or another judge to take over at this point. A dose of pragmatism and flexibility as well as teamwork for the 'common good' can be helpful in such a situation, even if the assignment of the Judge *Rapporteur* is not changed. Where there are two alternatives proposed from the outset, such problems do not arise.

ii) Grand Chamber Cases

For Grand Chamber cases, the *Rapporteur's* analysis provides a panoply of solutions. Thus potential tensions between the *Rapporteur's* opinion and the majority's finding are felt less deeply, all the more so as the final draft of the judgment is elaborated not by the *Rapporteur* alone, but by a drafting committee assisted by the Registry.

In the Grand Chamber – in contrast to the Chamber – the end of the deliberations is not marked by a final vote, but by a provisional vote only. Where there are abstentions or the vote is very tight, the final outcome might not yet be clear before the drafting process has to start, particularly as judges are free to change their opinion up to the final vote during the second deliberations. In such a scenario, the President will ask for the preparation of two alternative drafts and will appoint a 'mixed drafting committee' composed of representatives of both the supposed majority and the supposed minority opinion.

4. DISSENTING OPINIONS

The centrepiece of the decision-making process both in Chamber and in Grand Chamber is the deliberation on the case, where judges lay open their opinions about the case in all details. Those who find themselves in the minority are allowed to express their divergent views, be it on the relevant line of argument, be it on the result. It is doubtful whether writing dissenting and concurring opinions is a 'right' protected by freedom of expression, or whether it forms part of the institutional set-up of an independent and impartial judicial authority. In any event, there is an explicit guarantee under the Convention, at least so far as judgments on the merits rather than admissibility decisions are concerned (Article 45(2) of the Convention). There is no common approach about how to proceed when the Court takes the decision on admissibility together with the judgment on the merits.

The practice of writing separate opinions goes back to the early days of the Convention system, to the year 1958. Interestingly, the very first dissenting opinion concerned the decision of the Commission in an interstate case between Greece and the United Kingdom about measures used for quelling an insurgence in Cyprus, at that time still a British colony.[52] The Commission had refrained from deciding on a breach of the Convention in a situation where the legislative act allegedly violating the Convention had been repealed before the decision was taken. There was good reason for a dissent – the legislative act had allowed flogging as collective punishment. The abolition of the law could not alter the fact that the physical integrity of the victims had been infringed. This view was clearly expressed by the minority.[53]

---

52 *Greece v United Kingdom (I)*, app 176/56, 26 September 1958.

53 See the dissenting vote of four of the eleven members of the Commission (Eustatkiades, Süsterhenn, Petren and Janssen-Pevtschin): '... the Commission in determining whether or not the Convention has been violated, has no authority to disregard measures which have been, but are no longer, applied' (para 97).

Since then innumerable separate opinions have been written. Still, some controversies on the use of this instrument persist.

First, it is not clear whether there is an obligation to signal a dissent in accordance with the vote. Some deem it to be a tacit rule, others do not accept it and refrain from expressing any opinion. While in most cases, it will be clear who has voted for and who has voted against which part of the operative part when reading the separate opinions, in some cases there may be an incongruity in the vote.[54] The divergence of views on this point can be explained by different conceptions of the role of a judge. While some stress that the individual judge forms part of the collective decision-making body and should, for the sake of neutrality and impartiality, not be individually identifiable with a certain opinion, others emphasise the value of transparency and the right to know who has decided in which way. It is clear that this also reflects an element of legal culture, where judges' opinions might well be influenced by their home jurisdictions.[55]

Another controversy concerns the style of the dissent. While it is clear that a judge writes a dissent because he or she does not agree with the majority's judgment and thus has something to criticise, the limits of criticism are not always clear, especially if the reputation of the Court as a whole is called into question. A famous example is the dissent in the very controversial case of *Lambert v France* about the 'right to die'. The majority did not find a violation of the Convention in the decision to discontinue nutrition and hydration (with the consequence that the patient in a state of total dependency would no longer be kept artificially alive). The dissenting judges did not agree with this finding and concluded their opinion with the following statement:

> 'In 2010, to mark its fiftieth anniversary, the Court accepted the title of The Conscience of Europe ... We regret that the Court has, with this judgment, forfeited the above-mentioned title.'[56]

Despite these open questions, it is generally acknowledged that dissenting opinions have a very important function in the decision-making process. They serve as a valve. If a compromise solution is possible, it is fine. But, if it is not – and often the different positions are so firmly entrenched that it is impossible to bridge the gaps – then it is not necessary to search for a futile compromise and to soften and change what would otherwise be a consistent and clear approach.

---

54 See, for instance, *Paradiso and Campanelli v Italy* (GC), app 25358/12, 24 January 2017. It was found by eleven to six votes that there was no violation of Article 8 of the Convention. Nevertheless, only five judges appended a joint dissenting opinion to the judgment.

55 On the cultural background, see T Bingham, *The Rule of Law* (London, Penguin Books, 2010) 44. For a historical perspective, see Ernst (n 25) 638 ff.

56 *Lambert v France*, app 46043/14, 5 June 2015, dissenting opinion of judges Hajiyev, Šikuta, Tsotsoria, De Gaetano and Griţco (para 11).

At the same time, it cannot be denied that judgments based on tight votes – adopted with nine votes against eight, or ten votes against seven – do not convey a very strong message, particularly when the arguments of the minority are spelled out very convincingly. Nevertheless, what counts is the majority's view, unless the Court's approach is explicitly changed at a later time.

All in all, the separate opinions may well move the ECtHR's model from the '*per curiam* model', where decision-making is based on the decision of the conference of judges, to the '*seriatim* model', where the individual judges' conclusions are bundled together.[57] To a certain extent, it combines the positive elements of both models: clarity on the one hand, and transparency and openness of the decision-making process on the other hand.[58]

IV. VOTING PROCEDURES

1. MOMENT OF VOTING

In the Chamber, the final vote is taken at the end of the deliberations after scrutinising the text. When more than one alternative is proposed, a provisional vote may be necessary.

In the Grand Chamber, the first deliberations end with a provisional vote. The final vote is taken at the end of the second deliberations. Here again, when alternatives are proposed, a provisional vote may be necessary at the beginning of the second deliberations, in order to know which alternative needs to be worked on.

2. VOTING RESULTS

Voting is based on simple majority. As the number of judges is always uneven, the result is always clear. Abstention in the final vote is not allowed.[59]

Although these rules seem to be very clear, one critical remark may be allowed. Cases referred to the Chamber by the panel are decided twice – once by the Chamber, once by the Grand Chamber. What is decisive is the final vote in the Grand Chamber. However, it is possible that this final result is supported only by a narrow majority, eg 9:8. By contrast, when the vote in the

57 See in section III above, n 25 and the text accompanying and following it.

58 See Bingham (n 55) 45, who praises the advantages of 'multiple judgments and the freedom to dissent' thus: 'this practice fosters beneficial development of the law and avoids unsatisfactory compromises which result in a final judgment commanding the wholehearted support of no one.' According to him, this is true only under the condition that, first, judgments are clear and, second, judicial activism does not go beyond certain limits.

59 See Rule 23(2) 2nd sentence of the Rules of Court.

Chamber was clear, eg 7:0, the result can be somewhat paradoxical. Out of a total of 24 (viz 17 + 7) judges, nine will have voted for one and a total of fifteen for the other result. The final result will be the one supported by a total of nine judges only. This is open to criticism, as the votes of all judges are equal; it is a mere coincidence whether a judge sits in a case at the Chamber level or at the Grand Chamber level.

A qualified majority is never required. It is true that a qualified majority could be an additional argument in conflicts between the Convention law and national constitutional law in order to enhance the authority of the Court's judgments. However, such a change in the Convention mechanism would considerably weaken the whole execution system based on Article 46 of the Convention:

> 'The High Contracting Parties undertake to abide by the final judgment of the Court in any case to which they are parties.'

As far as execution is concerned, all final judgments have to be executed without allowing for any counter-arguments based on national – even national constitutional – law. Any change to this established rule would be difficult to reconcile with the basic principle of international law enshrined in Article 27 of the Vienna Convention on the Law of the Treaties, according to which a 'party may not invoke the provisions of its internal law as justification for its failure to perform a treaty'. Furthermore, a constitutional proviso would allow the national legislator to predetermine the procedure before the Court by integrating a specific provision into the national constitution rather than at the level of a 'normal' legislative act. The current rule should thus not be altered – a final judgment of the Court is a final judgment, be it adopted unanimously, by a qualified majority, or by a narrow vote.

While the judges' voting is, as a rule, clear and well-understood, there is one particularity that seems to give rise to misunderstandings. A case can be declared 'inadmissible' either because the admissibility criteria are not fulfilled (exhaustion of domestic remedies, six-months' time limit, etc) or because it is 'manifestly ill-founded'. This verdict means that the complaint is clearly without merits. Yet, opinions can be divided on this finding as well. Thus, a case may be declared inadmissible as 'manifestly ill-founded' by 4:3 votes. At first sight, this seems to be paradoxical – can there really be a split vote on something that is qualified as 'manifest'?

3. INTEGRAL OR SEQUENTIAL VOTING

The judges at the ECtHR have to vote separately on admissibility and on the merits; here again a separate vote is taken on each point of the operative part.

However, the vote as such is integral and concerns the end result: 'admissible' versus 'inadmissible', 'violation' versus 'non-violation'.[60] Sometimes, other alternatives are offered, eg 'not necessary to analyse'.[61] There is no option to vote on a violation 'because of …'. A judge who disagrees (only) with the arguments underlying the solution preferred by the majority has to vote with 'yes', but is then free to write a concurring opinion.

If no agreement is found on the wording of a specific passage of the text of the judgment, additional voting may be necessary. It is controversial whether dissenters should be allowed to take part in these 'auxiliary votes', which concern details of the majority's draft. On the one hand, it is clear that they dissociate themselves from the judgment as a whole. Thus it may be argued that they should not be allowed to water down or influence the majority's draft, not even the 'general principles'. On the other hand, it is the responsibility of all judges to elaborate 'general principles'; dissenters might disagree only with the application of the general principles to the specific case, but not with the general principles themselves, or vice versa.[62] Here, clear rules might be helpful.

Furthermore, it is unclear how judges who consider a complaint inadmissible should vote when the majority holds the complaint admissible. Sequential voting would mean deciding on the merits irrespective of the decision on the inadmissibility of the complaint – and thus being free to make a 'detached' assessment of the merits. Integral voting, on the other hand, would mean drawing the consequence of inadmissibility – thus finding no violation. An illustrative example of this difficulty is the Chamber judgment in the case of *Al-Dulimi v Switzerland*. One judge argued that the case was inadmissible, but was outvoted by the other judges by 4:3. Based on sequential voting, he then held that the complaint was well-founded.[63] The end result was not

60 On the different types of voting, see W Ernst, *Le vote en assemblée* (Génève, Schulthess Médias Juridiques, 2016) 95.

61 This is often used in cases concerning potential discrimination. If a violation of the main provision is found, an analysis of a violation of Article 14 ECHR is considered 'not necessary'.

62 On the controversy about general principles, see eg the dissenting opinion of Judge Ranzoni and the concurring opinion of Judge O'Leary in the case of *JK and others v Sweden*, app 59166/12, 23 August 2016. Both judges outline explicitly why they do not agree with parts of the general principles concerning risk assessment in asylum cases. See on this issue also the dissenting opinion of Judges Jäderblom, Gritco, Dedov, Kjølbro, Kucsko-Stadlmayer and Poláčková.

63 See the dissenting opinion of Judge Sajó in the case of *Al-Dulimi and Montana Management inc v Switzerland*, app 5809/08, 26 November 2013: 'I do not share the view of the majority with regard to the admissibility of this case. I believe that under Articles 25, 48, and 103 of the United Nations (UN) Charter, the obligations set forth in Security Council Resolution 1483 are binding and prevail over any other international agreement. Moreover, the provisions of the Resolution provide little room for interpretation or flexibility with regard to State implementation measures. Consequently, I believe this case should have been declared inadmissible ratione personae. As the case has proceeded, however, to a judgment on the merits, I join the majority regarding the finding of a violation with respect to Article 6 of the Convention.'

wholly satisfactory as there was a merely fictitious majority for finding a violation in the case.[64]

Nor is it clear whether 'once dissenter' means 'always dissenter', even in follow-up cases. There is no rule on voting *stante concluso*;[65] it seems that judges decide individually. A famous example is the case of the prisoners' voting rights. One of the judges who had been strongly opposed to the majority's finding in the case of *Hirst v United Kingdom*[66] accepted the majority's approach as part of the case-law in the follow-up case of *Frodl v Austria*, another judge did not.[67]

These examples show that voting rules, even if they seem to be clear, leave many important questions unanswered.

4. CHOOSING BETWEEN MORE THAN TWO SOLUTIONS

The decision on non-pecuniary damage[68] is not only a 'yes-or-no' decision. If an award in respect of non-pecuniary damage is deemed necessary to compensate for a human rights violation, the amount has to be defined as well. It is well known that the Court uses tables indicating maximum and minimum amounts, but they are not binding. The judges' discretion may lead to a sort of negotiation. The President will ask for a vote on the Judge *Rapporteur's* proposal, which is not necessarily the arithmetic average of the amounts proposed.

V. SUMMARY

The European Court of Human Rights decides in different formations. Different rules apply to Single Judge, Committee, Chamber, and Grand

---

64 The case was subsequently sent to the Grand Chamber: *Al-Dulimi and Montana Management inc v Switzerland* (GC), app 5809/08, 21 June 2016. The finding of a violation was upheld, but based on a different reasoning.

65 Voting '*stante concluso*' in the narrow sense is related to the individual steps within one and the same procedure only: see Ernst (n 25) 647.

66 *Hirst v United Kingdom No. 2* (GC), app 74025/01, 6 October 2005, on prisoners' voting rights; dissenting opinion of judges Wildhaber, Costa, Lorenzen, Kovler, Jebens.

67 See *Frodl v Austria*, app 20201/04, 8 April 2010, a case which concerned the same topic (prisoners' voting rights), but in relation to another State (not the UK, but Austria). Here Judge Jebens voted with the majority finding a violation, while judge Kovler upheld his dissent with the following words: 'I voted against finding a violation of Article 3 of Protocol No. 1 to the Convention in the present case for the reasons expressed in the joint dissenting opinion of Judges Wildhaber, Costa, Lorenzen, Kovler and Jebens in the case of *Hirst v. the United Kingdom* (no. 2) [GC], no. 74025/01, ECHR 2005-IX).'

68 According to Article 41 of the Convention, the Court can grant 'just satisfaction'. This comprises pecuniary and non-pecuniary damages. Details are regulated in the Practice Directive issued by the President of the Court in accordance with Rule 32 of Court on 28 March 2007.

Chamber formations. While the fine-mechanics of judicial majoritarianism are inexistent on the first and rather simple on the second level, the procedure both at the Chamber and the Grand Chamber level is sophisticated and complex, providing for different solutions in respect of a number of important factors, such as the number of judges involved, the preparatory phase, the structure of the deliberations, and the timing of the final vote. Allowing concurring and dissenting opinions to be attached to Chamber and Grand Chamber judgments serves as a valve and enhances the clarity and transparency of the judgments; it also moves the Court's decision-making from the '*per curiam* model' used in the continental legal tradition, at least to some extent, towards the '*seriatim* model' developed in Common Law. Although the Convention and the Rules of Court contain detailed regulations on the Court's working methods, many issues, especially as far as the deliberations and the voting are concerned, remain open. The gaps are often filled in a pragmatic and flexible way.

CHAPTER 13

COLLECTIVE JUDGING IN THE COURT OF JUSTICE OF THE EUROPEAN UNION

Thomas VON DANWITZ*

As in all legal systems, collective decision-making in the Court of Justice of the European Union (CJEU) has to meet the principal requirements of the rule of law to structure the judicial process in a way that ensures fair and rational decision-making and leads to decisions which do not merely produce a legal finding, but provide a *ratio decidendi* allowing for acceptance by the legal community and the public in general. As I shall underline, these requirements might be of particular importance in the legal order of the European Union (EU), due to its supranational nature. But let me approach the subject step by step.

---

* Professor Dr Dr hc Thomas von Danwitz is judge of the Court of Justice of the European Union. He is also Professor of Public Law and European Union Law at the University of Cologne (on leave).

I. THE NATURE OF THE LEGAL ORDER OF THE EUROPEAN UNION

Judicial decision-making in the European Union is indeed profoundly linked to its supranational character and its specific mission to create common rules – which, by their very purpose, are to be given a uniform meaning across the Union – in a wide variety of areas. Needless to say that such a legal order entails rather specific requirements in terms of equivalence, effectiveness and non-discrimination and favours legal evolutions which are easy to incorporate into the national law of the Member States or at least a significant number of them.

The reason for the very existence of the European Union and its legal order is, first and foremost, the historic choice to abandon centuries of power play between nations, characterised by domination and political pressure, in which at best a balance of powers could be attained. But that kind of order in international relations mostly ended up, in essence, in a permanent threat to peace, prosperity and well-being of European citizens. In stark contrast to this historic tradition, the European Integration brought about the rule of law between its Member States – appreciated particularly by smaller Member States – and a legal protection of Union citizens against acts both of the institutions of the Union and of Member States when implementing European Union law. The rule of law in the European Union has given the Court of Justice, in addition to its function as supreme authority in interpreting Union law, a set of powers fully comparable to a constitutional court, allowing notably for judicial review and annulment of secondary legislation found to be in breach of primary law of the Union and, in particular, of fundamental rights. These enjoy an increasing importance in the European legal order since the entry into force of the Charter of Fundamental Rights in 2009. In my experience, some of the reluctance to follow the Court's jurisprudence is simply due to the fact that the concept of a constitutional jurisdiction on the European level has not been fully embraced.

From the perspective of Europe's historic heritage, securing the rule of law is intrinsically linked to the integration of Europe, the law being at the same time the principal tool of integration which the Union has at its disposal and the most fundamental guarantee for peace, prosperity and well-being all across Europe.

A lot has been written about European integration through law,[1] its historical and conceptual foundations, its advantages and the practical limits

---

1 M Cappelletti and P Golay, 'The Judicial Branch in the Federal and Transnational Union: Its Impact on Integration' in M Cappelletti, M Secombe and J Weiler (eds), *Integration Through Law*, vol 1, book 2 (Berlin/New York, de Gruyter, 1986) 261; D Kommers and D Waelbroeck, 'Legal Integration and the Free Movements of Goods: The American and European

of its application. Let me just briefly touch upon some aspects concerning the judicial side of law-making in the course of European integration. According to the Treaties, the Court of Justice of the European Union is not entrusted with an institutional mandate to promote European integration or to make choices on European policy alternatives or priorities. As a general rule, the Court has to proceed wisely in its decision-making in order to find balanced solutions which do not neglect the limits of what national law or the national judiciary is capable of absorbing. But it is undoubtedly correct that Union law, and its primary law in particular, is generally characterised by a considerable openness to divergent solutions, thus giving quite some leeway to the Court's interpretation. And for our national counterparts, it is sometimes surprising to see that EU law confers, at times, much greater latitude to judicial interpretation than would exist in national legislation governing the same area. Furthermore, it goes without saying that the Court's case law has to live up to the values of the Union as they are enshrined in Article 2 Treaty on European Union (TUE) and, in particular, in the Charter of Fundamental Rights. As the political situation in some Member States and candidate countries illustrates, the Court would miss out on its function as supreme guardian of the historic achievement of the rule of law in Europe, more precisely of what Walter Hallstein termed the 'community of law' (*Rechtsgemeinschaft*) if it refused to reflect those values in its case law. But the latitude which – due to these circumstances – the Court certainly enjoys when interpreting Union law, should not be confused with making political choices.

II. OPERATING CONDITIONS OF THE CJEU

In essence, three factors can be identified explaining the specificities of the case law of the Court of Justice of the European Union: The normative characteristics of EU legislation, the particularities of the preliminary ruling procedure and the values of European Union.

Experience' in M Cappelletti, M Secombe and J Weiler (eds), *Integration Through Law* vol 1, book 3 (Berlin/New York, de Gruyter, 1986) 165; U Haltern, 'Integration Through Law' in A Wiener and T Diez (eds), *European Integration Theory* (Oxford, Oxford University Press, 2004) 177; R Streinz, 'European Integration Through Constitutional Law' in HJ Blanke and S Mangiameli (eds), *Governing Europe Under a Constitution* (Berlin/Heidelberg, Springer, 2006) 1; D Augenstein, *'Integration Through Law' Revisited: The Making of the European Polity* (London, Ashgate, 2012); C Joerges, 'Integration Through Law and the Crisis of Law in Europe's Emergency' in D Chalmers, M Jachtenfuchs and C Joerges (eds), *The End of the Eurocrats' Dream* (Cambridge, Cambridge University Press, 2016) 299.

1. CHARACTERISTICS OF EU LEGISLATION

A first specificity of the Court's case law is down to the characteristics of EU legislation. It is a well known fact that EU law in general is characterised by a lack of precision, maybe even a certain ambiguity. This is not only true for provisions of the Treaties, but can be observed in particular as regards secondary legislation. The principal reason for this specificity is to be found in the complexity of the legislative process, which tries to take into account as many of the diverging positions as possible. The textual openness of EU legislation is quite often due to the difficulties in finding an acceptable compromise amongst the various actors in the legislative process. This is regularly reflected in a great number of recitals, outnumbering by far the operative provisions of a legislative act and seeking, as it sometimes seems, to dilute the essence of the legislative content.[2] In addition, the terms used in EU legal provisions, even when they are defined in the legislative act, can rarely be said to use a legally coded language conveying to the judge an implicit understanding of how the provision ought to be applied. In a significant number of cases, this legislative practice comes close to an implicit delegation of decisional powers to the Court to resolve the imprecision of a legislative product.

The multi-linguistic nature of EU law contributes significantly to this specificity. Since all official language versions of EU legislation have, according to our constant case law, the same value for interpretation, differences between these language versions do not allow placing too much weight on the mere text of a provision. In particular, in EU law, it cannot easily be said that the textual meaning of a provision will put limits to its possible interpretations. It occurs quite frequently that the particular language version on which a party relies is indeed favourable to the advocated interpretation, but that a comparison with other language versions shows that there is little certainty in that respect.[3] In that kind of situation, which could certainly be avoided by a more rigorous control of the different language versions, the Court has to base its interpretation of EU legislation on other methods than the mere textual meaning of a provision.[4]

---

2 See, for example, Directive 2014/24/EU of the European Parliament and of the Council of 26 February 2014 on public procurement and repealing Directive 2004/18/EC (OJ 2014 L 94, p 65); Directive 2016/343/EU of the European Parliament and of the Council of 9 March 2016 on the strengthening of certain aspects of the presumption of innocence and of the right to be present at the trial in criminal proceedings (OJ 2016 L 65, p 1).

3 See, for example, judgment of 26 April 2017, *Popescu*, C-632/15, EU:C:2017:303, paras 32 to 34.

4 See, for example, judgment of 4 September 2014, *Vnuk*, C-162/13, EU:C:2014:2146; judgments of 15 October 2015, *Axa Belgium*, C-494/14, EU:C:2015:692, paras 30 to 32; of 28 July 2016, *Edilizia Mastrodonato*, C-147/15, EU:C:2016:606, paras 28 and 29; of 28 July 2016, *JZ*, C-294/16 PPU, EU:C:2016:610, paras 38 and 39; of 17 May 2017, *ERGO Poisťovňa*, C-48/16, EU:C:2017:377, paras 37 and 38.

Unfortunately, there are an important number of divergences between different language versions. This explains the rather frequent recourse to systematic and teleological interpretation in the case law of the Court, though the textual interpretation remains statistically the interpretation tool that the Court uses most often.[5] Besides those difficulties, the textual argument sometimes simply does not allow a satisfactory answer to the question raised. As an example, let me refer you to a pending case in which the Court has to decide whether Bridge is to be considered a 'sport' under the mandatory exoneration of VAT provided for in the VAT Directive.[6]

In this context, it is important to note that, in situations governed by secondary EU legislation, the Court has, as a general rule, always been rather cautious to derive solutions from primary law contrary to what seemed to be the traceable policy choices of the legislator. This is particularly true for questions concerning the validity of EU legislation which might have interpreted fundamental freedoms rather restrictively and for which a certain degree of judicial self-restraint can be observed. As a recent example, let me refer you to the *Dano* and *Alimanovic* cases on access of migrant union citizens to social benefits of host Member States.[7] It is as true that, depending on national traditions, the Court's jurisprudence is sometimes considered to be less cautious in other areas, in particular in those involving the respect of fundamental rights. In *Digital Rights Ireland*, the Court addressed the question of the intensity of its judicial review of the requirements of the principle of proportionality in general terms. Referring to the *Marper* judgment of the European Court of Human Rights (ECtHR), the Court of Justice stated that, where interferences with fundamental rights are at issue, the extent of the EU legislature's discretion may prove to be limited, depending on a number of factors, including, in particular, the area concerned, the nature of the right at issue guaranteed by the Charter, the nature and seriousness of the interference, and the object pursued by the interference. Reference to such criteria can also be found in the jurisprudence of constitutional or Supreme Courts of Member States.[8] In view of the importance of the protection of personal data and the extent and seriousness of the interference, the Court concluded that its review of the Data Retention Directive should be strict.[9]

5 See M Dederichs, 'Die Methodik des Gerichtshofes der Europäischen Gemeinschaften', (2004) 39 *Europarecht* 345, 349 ff.

6 *The English Bridge Union*, C-90/16, 26 October 2017.

7 Judgments of 11 November 2014, *Dano*, C-333/13, EU:C:2014:2358, and of 15 September 2015, *Alimanovic*, C-67/14, EU:C:2015:597.

8 See, for example, the decisions of the German Federal Constitutional Court of 1 March 1979, ref 1 BvR 532, 533/77, BVerfGE 50, 290; and of 14 July 1986, ref 2 BvE 2/84, BVerfGE 73, 40.

9 Judgment of 8 April 2014, *Digital Rights Ireland and Others*, C-293/12 and C-594/12, EU:C:2014:238, paras 47 and 48.

In sum, the Court is very well aware that the legitimacy of a purposive interpretation, relying on vaguely phrased recitals, can easily – but unfairly – be criticised as representing judicial policy choices based on opportunism rather than what is classically understood as an application of the law. But it should be understood that this difficulty is due to the normative quality of EU legislation and not to the will of a self-empowering institution. In particular, the Court would certainly welcome any improvement of the quality of EU legislative drafting and, as a matter of principle, is definitively not looking for occasions to embark on any autonomous constructive or even creative development of the law to promote a certain view of European integration. The simple reality is that the Court has to give an answer to a question as it has been posed by a national judge on the basis of EU legislation as it is and may not escape its responsibility.

2. PROCEDURAL INTERACTION BETWEEN THE CJEU AND NATIONAL COURTS

A proper understanding of the nature of judicial decision-making by the CJEU has, as a second important consideration, to take into account the procedural interaction between the Court of Justice of the European Union and national courts. It is, to a large extent, the preliminary ruling procedure which organises the process of judicial implementation of European law, building – in its turn – upon the national legal orders. According to the functioning of this process, the preliminary ruling procedure interacts quite strongly with national law.

In the absence of specific legislation of the Union, and as long as the objectives of Union law and the requirements of its uniform application are not impeded, the task of ensuring a proper application of the substantive law of the European Union is left to the procedural law of the Member States. In this regard, national legal orders enjoy what has been termed 'procedural autonomy', which is – of course – not unlimited. This joint application of EU substantive and national procedural law to one single situation explains quite self-evidently the basis on, and the perspective from, which national courts address their questions on interpretation and on validity of Union law to the Court of Justice. Quite often, a certain legal concept deeply rooted in a national law tradition,[10] or the way in which a Directive has been implemented,[11] or the specific difficulties of a particular mechanism of national law,[12] explain why the Court is confronted

10 See, for instance, judgment of 5 April 2016, *PFE*, C-689/13, EU:C:2016:199.

11 See, for instance, judgment of 10 November 2016, *Private Equity Insurance Group*, C-156/15, EU:C:2016:851.

12 See, for instance, judgment of 22 June 2010, *Melki and Abdeli*, C-188/10 and C-189/10, EU:C:2010:363.

with a certain set of questions which may not arise in legal systems of other Member States. In bringing such questions to the attention of the CJEU, the referred question places its mark on the European legal order which might otherwise have been shaped differently.

From the perspective of the CJEU, we pay much attention to the fact that the preliminary ruling procedure under Article 267 of the Treaty on the Functioning of the European Union (TFEU) organises a dialogue between judges, not a decentralised instrument of access by private parties to the Court. But the impact of Member States' governments and the Commission's legal service on the proceedings before the Court, which has no equivalent in national procedures, should not be neglected. The main difficulty for the CJEU is finding out what precisely is the legal question raised by the referring court, in particular since it may only arise on an understanding of European law that is not fully expressed or might result from a concept of national law which the Court is not fully aware of. Giving a useful answer in such circumstances is not an easy task. The awareness of the need to ensure an open dialogue between judges is, unfortunately, not always shared by all our national colleagues, thereby calling into question the procedural framework within which we operate, such as the presumption of pertinence of a posed question, which itself reflects this relationship of trust between judges. The same is true for the duty of national courts to establish the facts of a case before referring it to the CJEU and to explain the referred question adequately. Despite all best efforts, undertaken by means of enquiry demands and by questioning the parties in the course of the pleadings, the Court is sometimes confronted with a delicate choice, particularly when preliminary rulings originate from Supreme Courts. In such circumstances, the Court either has to give preference to a diplomatic approach, which implies giving judgment on rather unsatisfactory foundations concerning the facts and the pertinence of a question according to national law, or to declare a request inadmissible although it might in essence raise an important point in law. In the past, the Court has opted for the diplomatic approach, which might explain why some of its judgments are not characterised by the same precision as those of national Supreme Courts. These have, of course no hesitation to declare applications inadmissible. Even recent efforts undertaken by the Court to limit the increasing caseload have not really been fruitful, so that the traditional practice might have to be reconsidered in due course.

3. THE NATURE OF THE EUROPEAN LEGAL ORDER

The nature of the European legal order entails a third essential consideration which must be taken into account in analysing the decision-making of the Court of Justice of the European Union. It relates to the particular and often challenging responsibility of the Court in questions involving fundamental values of the Union as embodied in Article 2 TEU and, notably, elaborated in the Charter of Fundamental Rights. Despite their most prominent position in the supreme law of the land, it has become evident that those values sometimes go beyond national traditions and, more often, are not supported by the same understanding amongst all Member States, governments and private individuals. In recent years, it could be observed that political parties and even governments were expressly advocating 'political projects' (to put it diplomatically) which are in essence quite squarely incompatible with those values, be it in matters of non-discrimination or, in particular, in terms of the rule of law.

From this perspective, the specific task of the Court could be understood as having to take the fundamental values of the Union into consideration in order to judge on the validity or the interpretation of EU legislation or on national legislation coming in the ambit of EU law. Of course, the Court may, at times, be inclined to take constitutional traditions and national practices into account,[13] but, in principle, the relevant standards may only be derived from Union law, be it from constitutional traditions common to the Member states. In a Union of Member States with considerable differences regarding their respective human rights culture and the ways in which the rule of law is respected, the Court might, at times, even be driven to adopt solutions which are inspired by merely a minority of legal traditions or even only by a single one. Given the great practical importance of the values of the European Union, the Court is, in the first place, not looking for an intermediate solution, nor for one which might, as a matter of principle, be the least conflicting with national traditions, but rather gives preference to what it considers to be the most convincing answer with regard to the values of the Union. In matters which are sometimes too delicate for national jurisdictions to embark upon, it is for the Court of Justice of the European Union to take the lead. Just take the *Kadi*-jurisprudence as a prominent example for this challenge, which was certainly innovative at the time, but has been widely accepted afterwards.[14]

III. DECISION-MAKING IN THE COURT OF JUSTICE

These rather substantive considerations on the specific nature of the European Union's legal order, its challenges and the role of the Court are, it seems to

---

13 See Article 52(4) and (6) of the Charter of Fundamental Rights.

14 Judgments of 3 September 2008, *Kadi and Al Barakaat International Foundation v Council and Commission*, C-402/05 P and C-415/05 P, EU:C:2008:461; of 18 July 2013, *Commission and Others v Kadi*, C-584/10 P, C-593/10 P and C-595/10 P, EU:C:2013:518; of 28 November 2013, *Council v Fulmen and Mahmoudian*, C-280/12 P, EU:C:2013:775; of 28 November 2013, *Council v Manufacturing Support & Procurement Kala Naft*, C-348/12 P, EU:C:2013:776; of 5 March 2015, *Europäisch-Iranische Handelsbank v Council*, C-585/13 P, EU:C:2015:145; of

me, indispensable to allow for a sound understanding of the decision-making of the Court, since the written rules and non-written practices of the Court's deliberations are designed to meet precisely those challenges.

1. A PRELIMINARY REMARK

The following description of the decision-making process in the Court of Justice follows the normal course of dealing with a case. But before setting out, let me emphasise that the deliberation process in the CJEU lies exclusively in the hands of the judges, assisted by the Advocate Generals. All questions, be they procedural or substantive, are decided by members of the Court. In the preparation of deliberations, judges are generally assisted by members of their cabinets, in particular in drafting written notes for deliberations; but the oral deliberations take place in the working language of the Court solely amongst judges, and without the presence of any interpreters, referendaires or other persons. A judgment and any modification of it has to be decided in oral deliberation. Only in rare cases, concerning in practice decisions by Chambers of three judges, is it allowable for a written deliberation to take place, if and to the extent that the nature of the question and the state of discussion do not require an oral exchange of arguments.

2. THE ROLE OF THE REPORTING JUDGE

As soon as possible after the introduction of a case, the President of the Court designates the Reporting Judge according to Article 15 of the CJEU's Rules of Procedure, mainly on grounds of the seniority of judges and the connection between cases, while respecting the basic rule that a judge may not report on a matter emanating from or involving his or her home country. The importance attributed to a case and its preparation depend largely on the Reporting Judge, acting in accordance with the Advocate General to whom the case is assigned.

The Reporting Judge of a case enjoys a particular status due to his precise knowledge of the technicalities of the subject-matter and the most intensive

21 April 2016, *Council v Bank Saderat Iran*, C-200/13 P, EU:C:2016:284; see also the judgments of the European Court of Human Rights in *Nada v Switzerland* (GC), app 10593/08, 12 September 2012, ECLI:CE:ECHR:2012:0912JUD001059308, and *Al-Dulimi and Montana Management Inc v Switzerland* (GC), app 5809/08, 21 June 2016, ECLI:CE:ECHR:2016:062 1JUD000580908; moreover, the decision of the Swiss Federal Court of 14 November 2007, *Youssef Nada v State Secretariat for Economic Affairs and Federal Department of Economic Affairs*, Administrative appeal judgment, Case No 1A 45/2007 BGE 133 II 450.

study of the applicable case law. The Reporting Judge submits a preliminary report to the General Assembly of the Court, which contains a first assessment of the case and procedural proposals regarding, in particular, the panel of judges (15, 5 or 3 judges) and the necessity of an oral hearing and of an opinion by the Advocate General. Once this preliminary report has been approved by the General Assembly, it serves as the basis for the opinion of the Advocate General. The role of the Reporting Judge furthermore remains crucial for the deliberation of a case. In case of divergent views between the Advocate General and the Reporting Judge, the latter will, as a general rule, ask for an 'orientation debate' amongst the judges of the panel, but the Reporting Judge can also submit a first draft in his own responsibility, an option which might be preferable in complex cases. But any judge of the formation can ask for an orientation debate. On the basis of the results of that discussion, the Reporting Judge will prepare the draft that serves as the basis for deliberations. It goes without saying that the way in which a proposition is drafted contributes significantly to the decision-making of the Court.

3. THE PROCESS OF DELIBERATIONS

The deliberative process takes place in two phases, a written and an oral one. After the draft of the Reporting Judge has been circulated, the other members of the formation will submit written observations, including alternative propositions for the draft which the Reporting Judge may take into account or reserve for the oral deliberation on the final draft. Such observations may sometimes amount to a real alternative draft and are, apart from their confidential treatment, quite often fully equivalent to a dissenting or concurring opinion.

Even after an orientation debate, it is sometimes necessary to have more than one oral deliberation, if orientations change or differences over the reasoning are difficult to overcome. But most importantly, the written and the oral deliberation is always a profoundly discursive process requiring an openness of mind and a willingness to better understand the value of another proposition and, eventually join in. In the Court's practice, deliberations are certainly not a matter of counting heads, but neither are they limited to exchanging views which have been definitively fixed beforehand. For the functioning of the CJEU, it is essential that judges are ready to adapt their views in response to the arguments of others. This is why we rarely vote on legal questions, and why we have not developed finely structured rules on how to do this. We do not even practice a precisely determined speaking order, but it is for the Reporting Judge to introduce the deliberation, after which the President of the formation may make a suggestion on how to structure the debate; but on the substance he or she intervenes only at the end of it.

After an initial discussion of horizontal questions of a judgment, and if the orientation of the proposition of the Reporting Judge is confirmed, the panel will continue with a page by page review of the draft, a process during which significant modifications may still be added. The orientation debate may therefore be concluded provisionally and remain subject to acceptable modifications. Despite often being of crucial importance to finding common ground or acceptance for the proposed draft amongst the members of the panel, such modifications do not necessarily add to the logical precision or coherence of a judgment, and they may even dilute the principal reasoning.

4. THE ROLE OF THE PRESIDENT OF THE COURT

Concerning the role of the President of panel, it is worth noting that the President of the Court (who has to chair the deliberations of the full Court and the Grand Chamber) as well as the Vice-President and each of the Presidents of the Chambers of five judges are elected by an assembly of all judges in secret ballot. The President and Vice-President are the only born members of the Grand Chamber whose principal task is to ensure the coherence of the jurisprudence. In a comparable manner, the Presidents of the Chambers of five judges have to ensure that the jurisprudence of the respective Chamber does not contradict the case law of the Grand Chamber. In the course of a deliberation, it might turn out that a case is more difficult than expected, thus touching upon the prerogatives of the Grand Chamber, or that a Chamber's preferences might run counter to the jurisprudence of the Grand Chamber or of another Chamber of five judges. In such circumstances, which occur rather regularly, but in a very limited number of cases, the case is transferred to the Grand Chamber, which implies a(n) (re) opening of the oral procedure.

In view of this internal structure, it follows naturally that the President enjoys an important role in the decision-making of the Court. The way in which he directs the deliberations of the Grand Chamber is doubtlessly of great significance to the decision-making of the institution. Some judges of the Court, according to their national traditions, even tend to attribute a particular weight to the opinion expressed by the President, namely in questions of particularly great political and institutional importance. In sum, the President of the CJEU enjoys a natural authority and is therefore certainly more than a *primus inter pares*. But, of course, any President is aware that he or she has to exercise this function wisely. And since all judges and, in particular, the Reporting Judge are quite vigilant of a discursive deliberation, the President's arguments have to be as convincing substantively as those of any other judge.

5. DEBATE ABOUT DISSENTING AND CONCURRING OPINIONS

In academic debate, a lot of attention is paid to the question of whether the CJEU should allow for dissenting and concurring opinions. Amongst members of the Court, several discussions have been organised in recent years to reflect on the advantages and disadvantages of such an instrument. Even though dissenting or concurring opinions do not form part of the continental tradition of collective decision-making, it should be noted that constitutional courts of major European Member States in particular have reported positive experiences with such more recently introduced instruments. It seems to me that this is why this question has received so much attention. There can be little doubt that dissenting and concurring opinions can greatly contribute to enhancing the transparency and, in particular, the rationality of judicial decision-making. But they may also lead to a more individualised and personalised perception of the role of judges. This could bear the danger that judges wish – for whatever reason – to express a particular view on a case or, even more delicately, wish to respond to an undefined need to state a certain point of view in a given matter, which can be problematic, for instance in a situation of reappointment.[15]

After fruitful discussions inside the Court, a majority of members came to the conclusion that dissenting and concurring opinions would profoundly alter the nature and inherent logic of decision-making in the CJEU. It was feared by some members that dissenting and concurring opinions might not contribute to the ultimate objective of our deliberations, which is to ensure a large consensus inside the Court and full acceptance amongst the Member States. But much more decisive than the fear of a potentially negative impact on the quality of our judgments are the consequences of dissenting and concurring opinions for the acceptance of the Court's judgments in the Member States. As far as concurring opinions are concerned, they would certainly make it more difficult properly to understand the prevailing interpretation of Union law which – especially in a preliminary ruling – is crucial for the correct application of Union law by national courts following a judgment of the CJEU. And above all, as regards dissenting opinions, can we be sure that, particularly in politically controversial cases, an outspoken dissent by the judge coming from a particular Member State would not seriously affect the acceptance of the majority judgment in precisely that Member State? As long as it seems that such a dissent could or would be a relevant, if not important, factor for ensuring acceptance of the Court's jurisprudence, it might be wise not to play with fire.

---

15 In this context, it should be recalled that the term of office at the CJEU lasts only six years, but reappointment is possible without limitation.

Of course, each generation of judges of the Court bears the responsibility to evaluate all questions relating to its decision-making. But the long-standing continuity in the practice of the Court is a remarkable feat which should not be neglected. It simply indicates that judges of different generations have, in general, been satisfied with the rules and practices governing the decision-making procedure inside the CJEU, ensuring an intense discourse for adopting truly European solutions.

CHAPTER 14

THE ANATOMY OF THE DELIBERATION PROCESS AT INTERNATIONAL CRIMINAL TRIBUNALS

Theodor Meron* and Christos Ravanides**

* Theodor Meron CMG is former President and Presiding Judge of the Appeals Chambers for the International Criminal Tribunal for the former Yugoslavia and for the International Criminal Tribunal for Rwanda, and of the International Residual Mechanism for Criminal Tribunals; Judge of the Mechanism; Visiting Professor at the University of Oxford and Honorary Fellow of Trinity College, Oxford. The views expressed in this chapter are personal to the authors and do not reflect the views of the MICT, the ICTY or the United Nations.

** Christos Ravanides is Legal Officer at the Office of Legal Affairs of the United Nations and former deputy *chef de cabinet* to Judge Theodor Meron, then-President of the ICTY. The views expressed in this chapter are personal to the authors and do not reflect the views of the MICT, the ICTY or the United Nations.

I. INTRODUCTION

It is an honour to contribute to this unique forum, which brings together distinguished members of domestic and international judiciaries with the goal of discussing matters that remain largely mystical to the public (each judiciary's very constituents), confined as they are within the hallowed corridors of justice. Although the internal workings of some domestic courts, such as the US Supreme Court, are frequently the subject of public fascination and scrutiny,[1] little is known about the decision-making process at international courts.

The goal of this brief chapter is to lift, to the extent possible, this veil of secrecy covering the deliberations at the *ad hoc* international criminal tribunals – namely, the International Criminal Tribunal for the former Yugoslavia (ICTY), which closed its doors at the end of 2017, and the (now also defunct) International Tribunal for Rwanda (ICTR). The focus of this chapter will, more specifically, be the Appeals Chambers shared by the ICTY and the ICTR for about 20 years. The ICTR having ceased operations in 2015 and the ICTY in 2017, the demystification of the deliberation process at the last instance body of these remarkable institutions can only be meant as a tribute to their enormous contributions to the development of international criminal law. Inevitably, any discussion about the *ad hoc* tribunals must also extend to the innovations introduced by the ICTY's and ICTR's successor institution, the Mechanism for International Criminal Tribunals (MICT).

It goes without saying that the actual content of judges' discussions and their votes on particular issues in specific cases fall beyond the scope of this chapter. These aspects of the deliberation process are squarely covered by time-honoured principles of secrecy and confidentiality that must be respected at all times and at all costs if judges, both domestic and international, are to deliberate impartially and fulfil their duties uninfluenced by external factors.[2]

What the secrecy of deliberations does not protect, however, is the decision-making process itself, ie the distinct procedural steps judges follow to resolve

---

1 See, inter alia, J Toobin, *The Nine: Inside the Secret World of the Supreme Court* (New York, Anchor Books, 2007); E Lazarus, *Closed Chambers: The First Eyewitness Account of the Epic Struggles Inside the Supreme Court* (New York, Penguin Books, 1998); B Woodward and S Armstrong, *The Brethren: Inside the Supreme Court* (New York, Simon & Schuster, 1979).

2 As mentioned at the 105th Annual Meeting of the American Society of International Law, 'secrecy in judicial deliberations plays a crucial role in ensuring the independence and impartiality of the bench … [and] also lends greater authority to the ultimate decision that the judges pronounce': see T Meron, *The Making of International Criminal Justice – The View from the Bench (Selected Speeches)* (Oxford, Oxford University Press, 2011) 284. For a slightly different perspective, see R Posner, *How Judges Think* (Cambridge/Massachusetts, Harvard University Press, 2008) 3, referring to the secrecy of deliberations as 'an example of professional mystification'.

the controversies before them. Judges at international criminal tribunals have formulated, over the years, specific working methods and procedures to determine the liability of the indicted individuals for the crimes charged. Our intention in this chapter is to shed some light on these internal processes and, more in tune with the theme of this agora, at times explore their provenance.

This discussion will enable a closer inspection of the holy of holies of the international judicial tabernacle.[3] Even though the jurisprudence and the adjudicatory practices of international criminal tribunals have been the subject of extensive investigation from a comparative – civil law *versus* common law – perspective,[4] the judicial deliberation process remains shrouded in mystery.

In dispelling this mystery, this chapter will often draw comparisons to the deliberative practices of domestic courts of second and last instance emblematic of either the civil or the common law tradition, such as the *Cour de Cassation* or the *Conseil d'État* in France, the *Bundesgerichtshof* and the *Bundesverfassungsgericht* in Germany, the UK and the US Supreme Courts. Even though not all of these courts deal exclusively (or at all) with criminal cases, the length and breadth of the judgments of international criminal tribunals makes a comparison of internal working practices both possible and useful. For a more elaborate description of the basic features of the decision-making models followed by civil law and common law courts, from which the international tribunals have drawn inspiration, deference must be paid to the relevant analyses by other participants here and elsewhere.[5] Suffice it to mention here, in summary fashion, that in continental courts of second and last instance, judges deliberate and all but decide the cases assigned to them *before* the oral hearing, by appointing a *juge rapporteur* or 'Reporting Judge' who prepares a thorough draft decision that reflects as broad a consensus among the members of the bench as feasible. Appellate and supreme courts in common law systems, on the other hand, deliberate in earnest *after* oral arguments, which play a very central role in every common law judicial proceeding.

---

3 In my remarks at the Annual Meeting of the American Society of International Law in 2011, I described, summarily, some aspects of the decision-making process within the ICTY Appeals Chamber, without, however, providing a step-by-step overview of our deliberations and without examining the origins of those internal procedures: Meron (n 2) 283–84.

4 See, inter alia, M Fairlie, 'The Marriage of Common Law and Continental Law at the ICTY and its Progeny, Due Process Deficit' (2004) 4 *International Criminal Law Review* 243; CJM Safferling, *Towards an International Criminal Procedure* (Oxford, Oxford University Press, 2003); PM Wald, 'The International Criminal Tribunal for the former Yugoslavia Comes of Age: Some Observations on Day-to-Day Dilemmas of an International Court' (2001) 5 *Washington University Journal of Law and Policy* 87; PL Robinson, 'Ensuring Fair and Expeditious Trials at the International Criminal Tribunals for the former Yugoslavia' (2000) 11 *European Journal of International Law* 569.

5 See, eg, M Cohen, 'Ex Ante Versus Ex Post Deliberations: Two Models of Judicial Deliberations in Courts of Last Resort' (2014) 62 *American Journal of Comparative Law* 401, 413–30.

II. DELIBERATIONS AT THE ICTY/ICTR

Unsurprisingly, the working methods of international criminal courts have been an amalgam of both civil law and common law practices. Since international criminal tribunals have been composed of judges hailing from different legal systems,[6] their model of deliberations could not but reflect the diversity of the judicial body.

We will start by describing how the ICTY/ICTR Appeals Chamber deliberated on and decided appeals from judgments, because this was the core of the judicial 'business' at the *ad hoc* tribunals. All references to the ICTY, the oldest and longest operating *ad hoc* criminal tribunal (1993–2017), should also be construed as applying equally to the ICTR, which officially closed its doors in December 2015.

1. APPEALS FROM JUDGMENTS

At the ICTY, an appeal from a judgment lay as of right for both the Prosecution and the Defence – a feature borrowed from the continental criminal justice system. Once an appeal was filed, the ICTY President – and Presiding Judge of the ICTY and the ICTR Appeals Chamber – would appoint a five-member panel to decide the appeal. If the President sat on the panel, he or she would also preside over the appeal *ex officio*; otherwise, the judges of the panel would elect the Presiding Judge in the case.[7] The office of the Presiding Judge was critical, because, as explained below, he or she essentially combined the functions of both the *juge rapporteur* in civil law appellate courts and the judge designated in common law courts to write the court's opinion. Customarily, the Presiding Judge would also be the 'pre-appeal' judge, who decided, *solo*, motions relating to the briefing of the case – such as extensions of time and word limits – and other house-keeping matters; more complex pre-appeal matters, however, would be submitted to the consideration of the whole panel.[8]

Two clarifications are necessary at this juncture. First, cases handled by international criminal courts were immensely more complex than any criminal case brought before domestic courts. Cases decided by the ICTY and the ICTR implicated high-ranking individuals accused of egregious mass crimes

---

6 See, in this respect, Meron (n 2) 103, 281–83, describing the process of selection of judges at the *ad hoc* Tribunals and the diversity of their professional backgrounds.

7 ICTY Manual on Developed Practices (The Hague, UNICRI, 2009) ('ICTY Manual') para [26].

8 Ibid para [28].

covering extended periods of time. International trials, therefore, involved the presentation of voluminous evidence – dozens, sometimes hundreds of witnesses and thousands of documents, video-recordings, and even pieces of physical evidence – and unexceptionally culminated in the issuance of very lengthy judgments. The Appeals Chamber was thus required to review and analyse not only sizeable trial judgments but also the lengthy briefs of the parties' on appeal, as well as the original evidence, to the extent required by the submissions.

Precisely because of this complexity of international criminal cases, judges at the *ad hoc* tribunals (as well as other international criminal courts) relied on the assistance of legal staff significantly more than domestic courts rely on clerks. Consistent with the common law tradition, each judge at the Appeals Chambers was assisted by a legal officer specifically assigned to that judge; in addition, numerous lawyers were employed 'in Chambers' as a whole, who would offer their assistance in the resolution of specific cases on a 'floating' basis. The Chambers' legal staff actively participated in the decision-making process, by reviewing evidence, analysing the parties' submissions on every matter, and preparing first drafts of the memoranda, orders, decisions on motions, and judgments to be issued. The ultimate decision-making power rested, of course, with the judges who would consider and edit these drafts, resorting to the evidence and the other materials on the record as necessary, and finalise them again with the assistance of legal staff.[9]

The complexity of the proceedings and the critical role of legal staff have been two important features of the adjudication model at international criminal tribunals in general, not only the *ad hoc* tribunals, which allow a better understanding of the decision-making process at those adjudicatory bodies, including the International Criminal Court.

a) *Before the Hearing*

The most important phase of the appeal process involved the drafting of a document that in ICTY/ICTR parlour was called the 'preparatory document' (or, colloquially, 'prepdoc'). This was historically the primary material used by the judges of the panel to *prepare* for the appeal hearing – hence, the document's name. The 'prepdoc' would summarise the findings of the trial chamber, the appellant's challenges against these findings and the appellees' responses, much like the 'bench memorandum' in a common law appellate court. The 'prepdoc', however, would also analyse the parties' submissions, discuss how these arguments could or should be disposed of, and propose very concrete

9 See also Meron (n 2) 283.

conclusions on each specific legal question. If an issue could be resolved in more than one way, the 'prepdoc' would offer alternative analyses.[10] The 'prepdoc', in that sense, resembled much the draft judgment prepared by the *juge rapporteur* in the continental deliberative model. Indeed, the 'prepdoc' would even adopt the format of a draft 'judgment' of the Appeals Chamber.

It must be stressed, nevertheless, that the 'prepdoc' was *not* a draft judgment: detailed though it was, it lacked the requisite judicial input to constitute a draft judgment. Indeed, the 'prepdoc' was not drafted by a judge but by a team of legal officers headed by an experienced senior lawyer. The drafting of the 'prepdoc' would take place under the general direction and oversight of the Presiding Judge of the case and his or her legal advisers – including the Tribunal's *chef de cabinet*, if the Presiding Judge was the President – who would review the legal analysis proposed by the drafting team on each issue of the appeal. In this role, the Presiding Judge would engage in extensive exchanges with the drafting team, but would not usually reach out to other judges to seek their views on specific issues, unlike the *juge rapporteur*. However, consistent with the civil law adjudication model, the 'prepdoc' was not supposed to merely reflect the personal views of the Presiding Judge but present the bench with the entire spectrum of possible solutions to the issues involved so that the judges would not have to conduct significant additional research on their own.

Importantly, in the early years of the Tribunal, the only document prepared in advance of the appeal hearing was a typical common-law bench memorandum, summarising the parties' positions. Yet, as the caseload of the Appeals Chamber grew and the complexity of the cases and the volume of the parties' submissions on appeal increased, the need for efficiency and speed required that judges familiarise themselves in-depth with each case before the hearing. This gave rise to calls for a more detailed pre-hearing document that would delve into the merits of the appeal. The 'prepdoc', in other words, emerged as a more advanced version of the 'bench memorandum' in common law courts but something less than the draft judgment drafted by the *juge rapporteur*. Consistent with this shift towards a more civil law-oriented deliberative model, the drafting teams made a conscious effort to foresee and address in the 'prepdoc' all the issues arising from the parties' submissions and propose every analysis possible, often not entirely in agreement with the views of the Presiding Judge. The tacit goal was to present the bench with a document that would face as little opposition as possible. The extent to which a 'prepdoc' would gain praise by judges, in fact, became the unofficial yardstick of the quality of the work done before the hearing.

Notably, while the drafting team would work on the 'prepdoc' under the supervision of the Presiding Judge, the other judges of the panel were free to

---

10 ICTY Manual (n 7) paras [38]–[39].

read the trial judgment, review the parties' submissions, and conduct their own research in preparation for the hearing, but were generally not required to do so. As a rule, they also abstained from interfering with the 'prepdoc' drafting. Consistent with the continental adjudication model, the principal responsibility at the pre-hearing stage fell upon the Presiding Judge; the other judges' input was minimal. For this reason, the composition of the panel could change at any point before the circulation of the 'prepdoc' to the bench: the ICTY President could replace one or more judges sitting on a case, in exercise of his coordinating powers under the Tribunal's Statute and Rules, after assessing the need for more effective management of the caseload and typically, with the agreement of both the replacing judge and the replaced judge. Once the 'prepdoc' was circulated, the composition of the panel would become definite.

The 'prepdoc' would be circulated, per internal custom, at least a month before the scheduled hearing.[11] In more complicated cases, the 'prepdoc' would be distributed several months in advance, to allow judges sufficient time to review it carefully. Upon receipt of the 'prepdoc', the judges would embark earnestly upon the preparation for the hearing. Much like in common law courts, each judge would study the 'prepdoc' and prepare mostly individually, in the privacy of his or her Chambers, with the assistance of his or her assigned legal officer. Also like in common law courts, judges were not bound in any way by the analysis in the 'prepdoc'. Judges were free to perform their own research and communicate their views to their colleagues and the drafting team, even before the hearing. When the time for hearing came, the judges would sit on the bench with at least partially formed views as to what the main issues on appeal were and how these issues should be framed, analysed and disposed of.

b) The Hearing

The distribution of the 'prepdoc' set the stage for the oral hearing, which, consistent with the common law adjudication model, was not perfunctory and largely ceremonial, as in civil law appellate courts. Questions by judges during the hearing were, most of the time, a genuine attempt to seek clarifications from the parties on legal and factual issues that remained unanswered in their briefs. The parties' responses thus elucidated their positions and may have convinced the panel to see a critical question through the parties' own preferred prism. A masterful presentation could sway the panel in the party's favour.

It was not unusual for the Appeals Chamber, in the order scheduling the hearing, to draw the parties' attention to specific issues and invite the parties to

11 Ibid para [39].

discuss these issues explicitly during their presentations.[12] This was a genuine novelty of the Tribunal's own devise. In the case against *General Tolimir*, for example, the Appeals Chamber invited the parties to discuss explicitly during the hearing, inter alia, whether certain incidents constituted genocide and whether the defendant could be found guilty of charged crimes under modes of liability other than physical commission (eg aiding and abetting).[13] Such highly specific questions would offer a glimpse into the panel's thinking about the case (despite the usual disclaimers included in the scheduling order). In any event, confining the scope of the appeal hearing to particular issues was often inevitable given the limited time at the parties' disposal and the magnitude of the cases heard by the Appeals Chamber.

Because of its important function, the appeal hearing for a single case could have lasted several days, depending on the size of the case and the number of accused. The last appeal hearing by the ICTR Appeals Chamber, for example, in the so-called *Butare* case, involved seven consolidated appeals and lasted seven full business days;[14] the hearings in the *Popovic et al* case at the ICTY, which involved the physical perpetrators of the Srebrenica genocide, and the *Prlic et al* case, the last appeal heard by the ICTY, lasted several days too as they involved multiple defendants and appeals.[15] At the end of the hearing, it became customary to allow the defendant(s) to make a brief personal address to the Chamber.

c) *After the Hearing*

The deliberations would enter their main stage after the hearing, consistent with the Anglo-American deliberative model. Shortly after the hearing, the Presiding Judge would circulate to the other members of the panel the agenda for the post-hearing conference. The agenda took the form of a detailed questionnaire on all the issues that the judges were required to explicitly decide by vote, which ensured that no issue remained unresolved.

In addition to this critical agenda-setting power, the Presiding Judge would also open and preside over the post-hearing conference. He or she would go

---

12 Ibid para [41]. See, eg, *Prosecutor v Naser Oric*, Case No IT-03-68-A, *Addendum* to Order Scheduling Appeal Hearing, 10 March 2008.

13 *Prosecutor v Zdravko Tolimir*, Case No IT-05-88/2-A, *Addendum* to the Scheduling Order for Appeal Hearing, 31 October 2014, 1–2. See also *Prosecutor v Pauline Nyiramasuhuko et al*, Case No ICTR-98-42-A, Order for the Preparation of the Appeals Hearing, 25 March 2015.

14 *Prosecutor v Pauline Nyiramasuhuko et al*, Case No ICTR-98-42-A, Order Setting the Timetable for the Appeals Hearing, 19 March 2015.

15 See *Prosecutor v Prlic et al*, Case No IT-04-74-A, Scheduling Order for Appeal Hearing, 15 December 2016, and Order for the Preparation of the Appeal Hearing, 1 March 2017; *Prosecutor v Vujadin Popovic et al*, Case No IT-05-88-A, Order for the Agenda of the Appeal Hearing, 7 November 2013.

through the items in the pre-circulated agenda and request the members of the panel to vote on each of the issues on appeal. The Presiding Judge would express his or her views and cast an often-decisive vote at the end of each voting round, so as not to influence the other judges. The only issue on which judges would not deliberate at this stage was sentencing – this was the subject of a separate round of deliberations that would take place once the appeal judgment was all but finalised.

Much like the Anglo-American deliberative model, the post-hearing conference at the Appeals Chamber was intended more as a preliminary voting session than a forum for detailed discussions on the merits of the case. Given the size of each appeal and the myriad of issues that had to be decided, the panel could not afford to engage in extensive debates about the substance of the appeal. The primary objective of this conference was to canvass the judges' stance on the analysis proposed in the 'prepdoc', so that guidance could be provided to the drafting team for the preparation of the first draft judgment. This was the reason why, as in some continental courts, the leader of the drafting team, as well as each judge's legal officer, would attend the conference in order to note each judge's positions and initial votes and prepare a draft judgment in accordance with these votes.

Yet judges were free – much more so than in civil law courts – to deviate from or even reject the analysis of a given issue in the 'prepdoc'. In practice, such deviations were not infrequent and could involve central portions of the 'prepdoc'. In any case, like in the Anglo-American tradition, the votes cast at the conference were not definite; judges reserved the right to revisit their earlier positions and change their votes once they would receive the first draft of the appeal judgment.

On the other hand, an important difference from the common law model is that the preparation of the draft appeal judgment at the ICTY would not be assigned to a single judge but the drafting team, which acted pursuant to the judges' views as expressed at the post-hearing conference. The Presiding Judge would continue to supervise the drafting process, as before the hearing, even when he or she would not be in agreement with the majority as to the resolution of a specific issue or even the entire appeal. Unlike in common law courts, the Presiding Judge did not aspire to prepare a draft reflecting primarily his or her own views, but a draft echoing the views of the majority, which would thus be likely to be approved without extensive modifications.

The deliberations would enter their most intense phase when the first draft judgment would be delivered to the bench. Judges would be given ample time – a minimum of four weeks – to review the draft and circulate their comments. During this time, judges would consult the staff within their Chambers – ie their assigned legal officers or interns – but they would also be free to reach out to their colleagues and exchange views. Such interactions among judges would not be unusual, especially in controversial cases in which only a tentative majority emerged at the post-hearing deliberations. Informal discussions in search for compromise solutions are a natural part of the decision-making process at all courts, domestic and international. In civil law courts, such informal exchanges occur mostly before the hearing, while in Anglo-American courts, as well as the ICTY, the time for such exchanges is after the hearing. Yet it must be noted that not all international judges – and not only at the *ad hoc* tribunals – are equally comfortable with such 'behind-the-scenes' communications.

Judges would communicate their views by means of confidential memoranda containing their position on the draft judgment along with substantive comments and editorial suggestions, which the drafting team would then review, in consultation with the Presiding Judge, and decide whether to incorporate in the draft. If a proposal gained the support of the majority of the panel, it had to be implemented. Otherwise, the drafting team had to weigh carefully whether the draft could be revised in accordance with a judge's request without undermining its overall reasoning. This delicate task required a certain degree of drafting acrobatics to satisfy the requests of as many judges as possible while keeping intact the existing majority.

A refined draft judgment would then be re-circulated to the members of the panel, who would, again, review and comment upon it. The same process would be repeated until a solid majority emerged. Each new draft judgment inched closer to the final resolution of the appeal. Even though there was no limit in the number of revised drafts that could be circulated before the finalisation of a judgment, it was unlikely that no majority would emerge after the circulation of the first or second draft judgment. In more controversial cases, contentions among the judges over major issues could persist even after several drafting rounds, and a second round or even a third round of in-person deliberations could have been needed, but these instances were exceptional.

d) Sentencing Deliberations

Once judges cast their final votes on each issue on appeal and the judgment was finalised, the drafting team would prepare the disposition of the case, ie a list of the Appeals Chamber's conclusions on each count of appeal. On the basis of that list, the judges would confer a second time in person, without any legal officers present, to deliberate exclusively on the length of the sentence to be imposed, provided that the defendant was not to be acquitted *in toto*. In general, judges had absolute discretion as to the length of the sentence. Typically, an expansion of the scope of criminal liability on appeal (for instance, the entry of fresh convictions or a conviction for commission of a crime in lieu of a conviction for aiding and abetting) was likely to result in an increased sentence. Reversals of convictions could lead to a shorter sentence, but this would necessarily depend on the gravity of the surviving convictions. Notably, all the members of the panel would attend the sentencing deliberations, even judges who had voted in favour of acquitting the defendants. All judges' views about sentencing issues were to be heard before a consensus was reached on the appropriate sentence. The verdict on the sentence would be announced confidentially to the leader of the drafting team who would insert it in the final version of the appeal judgment. At that point, the judgment was ready for signature and delivery.

e) Separate/Dissenting Opinions

Before the judgment was delivered, separate opinions, dissenting from or concurring with the majority opinion (albeit on a different basis), would also have to be finalised. The weight of such individual opinions depended on the strength of the majority opinion. In cases decided by a weak majority (3 out of 5 votes), concurring opinions may have shed more light on the majority reasoning, while dissenting opinions may have been relied upon by the parties in subsequent cases seeking to attack the earlier holding. In some cases, a majority opinion would be rendered even more fragile as a result of multiple concurrences that diluted the majority opinion's strength and undermined legal certainty on specific issues. The saga on 'specific direction' (a controversial element of aiding and abetting liability according to ICTY/ICTR caselaw) and especially the appeal judgments in the *Perisic* and *Sainovic et al* cases are the most recent examples of such borderline cases.[16] However, there was never an ICTY or ICTR appeal judgment that was not decided by a clear majority.

Normally, drafts of concurring and dissenting opinions would be circulated well in advance of the scheduled delivery of the judgment so as to afford the majority the opportunity to reconsider their position. In this regard, deliberations at the ICTY Appeals Chamber did not differ much from deliberations at common law courts. Judges could use their dissenting or concurring opinions to persuade their colleagues to adhere to their views. In the past, well-crafted concurrences or dissents succeeded in attracting the support of the majority in favour of a different outcome in later decisions.

f) Finalisation and Delivery of the Judgment

Once all these stages of deliberations were completed, the judgment was ready to be issued on the scheduled date. Judgments were issued in the name of the Appeals Chamber as a whole and – importantly for the legitimacy of the

---

16 Compare *Prosecutor v Momčilo Perisic*, Case No IT-04-81-A, Judgment, 28 February 2013, paras [25]–[40] (discussing specific direction as a component of aiding and abetting liability) and separate and dissenting opinions attached thereto, with *Prosecutor v Nikola Sainovic et al*, Case No IT-05-87-A, Judgment, 23 January 2014, paras [1617]–[1651] (concluding that specific direction is not an element of the *actus reus* of aiding and abetting liability) and dissenting opinions attached thereto.

verdict – were signed by all the judges, including dissenters, as a certification of the integrity of the deliberation process and indirectly, an acknowledgment of the historical importance of the ICTY/ICTR judgments.

2. INTERLOCUTORY APPEALS, PRE-APPEAL DECISIONS, AND PETITIONS FOR REVIEW

In addition to appeals from final judgments, there were three other categories of matters handled by the ICTY/ICTR Appeals Chamber outside the normal decision-making process outlined above.

First, pre-appeal motions: pending an appeal, judges assigned to it had to also decide, in the first instance, numerous pre-appeal motions on matters as diverse as the provisional release of the defendants, the admission of newly discovered evidence, or the variation of protective measures granted to trial witnesses.

A second source of appeal work consisted in interlocutory appeals, ie appeals from non-final rulings of the trial chambers on a wide variety of issues, such as the violation of the prosecution's obligation to disclose exculpatory evidence to the defence, the judicial notice of factual propositions adjudicated in earlier cases, the *prima facie* sufficiency of the evidence to support a conviction, or challenges to the fairness of the proceedings. Under the Rules of the *ad hoc* tribunals, appeals as of right would only lie from certain categories of such trial rulings.[17] Appeals from all other interlocutory decisions had to be certified to the Appeals Chamber by the trial chamber that issued the decision. Certification was theoretically granted only in limited instances,[18] but trial chambers tended to certify appeals quite generously, so as to benefit from the Appeals Chamber's guidance before the issuance of the trial judgment.

---

17 Immediately appealable were decisions on (i) the provisional release of the accused individuals, (ii) motions challenging jurisdiction, (iii) the referral of indictments to domestic courts and (iv) motions by the parties for orders to States for the production of documents, as well as from (v) directions to the Prosecution to proceed on only specific counts in the indictment. See ICTY Rules 65, 72(B)(i), 11*bis*, 54*bis*(C), and 73*bis*(E), respectively.

18 Certification would be granted only when the trial ruling would involve an issue that would significantly affect the fair and expeditious conduct or the outcome of the trial and thus warrant the immediate intervention of the Appeals Chamber so as to materially advance the proceedings. See ICTY Rules 72(B)(ii) and 73(B). Earlier versions of this Rule provided that the permission to file an interlocutory appeal was to be sought and granted by a three-judge bench of the Appeals Chamber, not the trial chamber that issued the impugned decision. This practice was eventually abandoned, however, because it put a considerable strain on the Appeals Chamber's docket and resources, as appeal judges had to decide a constant stream of requests for leave to file an interlocutory appeal, in addition to the merits of the limited number of appeals that met the filing threshold.

Another part of the Appeals Chamber's workload was the post-appeal review of final judgments.[19] A party could petition the Appeals Chamber to revisit an earlier final judgment, if new facts of decisive importance for the outcome of the case were discovered after the completion of all proceedings.[20] Although the review of a final judgment was not a second appeal, parties would not hesitate to take advantage of this last resort opportunity to re-litigate issues decided on appeal. In 2013, the exclusive competence over such petition for review of either ICTR or ICTY judgments was transferred to the ICTY and ICTR's successor organisation, the Mechanism for International Tribunals (MICT), which has since handled an increasing number of such petitions.

All of this additional workload had the potential of interfering with and delaying pending appeal proceedings, the Appeals Chamber's main work. For this reason, these three categories of matters (pre-appeal motions, interlocutory appeals and review petitions) would be handled in a more expedited fashion. No oral hearings would take place on such matters – the judges would deliberate and issue their decision on the basis of the written submissions alone. ICTY Rule 116*bis* explicitly precluded hearings on interlocutory appeals, whether as of right or certified, while hearings on pre-appeal motions were to be held only upon the request from the parties and if the Appeals Chamber would affirm the need for a hearing, which was rarely the case. Hearings on review requests would only be held if the majority of the judges on the bench determined that the new fact, if proved, could have been 'decisive' as to the outcome of the case, ie after the judges would reach the preliminary determination that the request to reopen the judgment was warranted.[21]

Except where a hearing on a review was held, no 'prepdoc' would be drafted on these matters. Instead, once the parties' briefs were filed, the Presiding Judge would prepare, with the assistance of legal officers, a draft decision and circulate it to the bench. Judges would not deliberate in person, but communicate their views via written memoranda. Revised versions of the draft decision would then be prepared and commented upon, and concurring and dissenting opinions could be circulated, until a solid majority supported the decision, which was finalised and filed.

This simplified procedure bears more resemblance to the continental adjudication model, which relies more on written submissions and written

---

19 Final would be either judgments rendered by the Appeals Chamber in the second degree, or trial judgments not challenged on appeal, which became final upon the expiration of the deadline for the filing of an appeal.

20 See ICTY Rule 119. This standard would be applied strictly by the Appeals Chamber, which only granted it once, agreeing to overturn its own judgment in the *Mrkšić and Šljivančanin* case. Petitions for review would have to be filed before a trial chamber as well, in which case the decision on review would be subject to further appeal pursuant to ICTY Rule 121. This part of the chapter focuses on how the Appeals Chamber would decide review requests.

21 See ICTY Rule 120.

exchanges among the Judges. Yet similar streamlined procedures have been adopted by common law courts, too, vis-à-vis certain categories of matters, such as appeals relating to sentencing or asylum matters, which raise relatively less complex legal issues. The aim is to expedite the disposition of the matter, without undermining the integrity or fairness of the deliberation process.

III. CHALLENGES FOR THE MICT

This chapter would not be complete without a reference to the MICT, the organisation that has succeeded the ICTY and the ICTR. Created in 2010, the MICT introduced a novel model of international adjudication. The main feature of this new model is its lean and efficient structure – the only full-time judge of the MICT is the President, appointed by the UN Secretary General after consultations with the president of the Security Council and the other MICT judges.[22] All other judges of the MICT are only working on MICT matters, as assigned by the MICT President, on a part-time basis and (mostly) without being physically present at the seats of the MICT at The Hague in The Netherlands or Arusha, Tanzania, unless their presence is deemed necessary for the conduct of trial or appeal hearings or in-person deliberations. Judges' remuneration is also determined on a *per diem* salary basis, depending on working days.

As a result of such and other innovations,[23] deliberations at the MICT are mostly conducted remotely, often via electronic mail by judges located thousands of miles apart. This mode of deliberating from distance poses challenges not only about the secure nature of judges' communications (and thus the secrecy of deliberations) but also about the quality of the deliberative process, which is widely considered to benefit from in-person exchanges among the judges.[24]

Nonetheless, the MICT's decision-making process has not been as revolutionary as it might have seemed at first. For one, the absence of in-person meetings is not catholic – the first appeal judgment issued by the MICT Appeals

22 See Articles 8, 10, and 11 of the Statute of the International Residual Mechanism for International Criminal Tribunals, UN Security Council Resolution 1966, UN Doc S/RES/1966, 22 December 2010, Annex I.

23 See, inter alia, GL McIntyre, 'The International Residual Mechanism and the. Legacy of the International Criminal Tribunals for the Former Yugoslavia and Rwanda' (2011) 3 *Goettingen Journal of International Law* 923; S Maurice and J Soufi, 'Structure, Functions and Initial Achievements of the Mechanism for International Criminal Tribunals (MICT)' (2015) 15 *International Criminal Law Review* 544.

24 As Cohen notes, there is no consensus as to 'the effects of computer-mediated deliberations' as opposed to face-to-face deliberations: Cohen (n 5) 448–49 (and references cited therein).

Chamber in the *Ngirabatware* case[25] was decided pursuant to the regular decision-making process followed by the ICTY, because the judges sitting on that appeal were double-hatting as judges of the ICTY and were thus physically present at the MICT premises in The Hague. The two subsequent appellate cases adjudicated by the MICT, namely the *Karadžić* and *Šešelj* appeals,[26] were assigned to judges located in several different countries around the world. These judges were deciding pre-appeal matters from a distance, in the same way in which pre-appeal matters were decided by the *ad hoc* tribunals' Appeals Chamber, ie based on a draft decision prepared in advance by a drafting team under the supervision of the Presiding Judge, without oral hearings or in-person meetings. In the meantime, a drafting team in The Hague was working on the 'prepdoc' in those two appeals, under the guidance of the Presiding Judge, who is *ex officio* the MICT President and also based in The Hague. A hearing in both appeals took place in The Hague, with all panel members participating in person, and the post-hearing deliberation process followed the decision-making procedure described above, with judges from other countries relocating to The Hague for the hearing and also for the post-hearing deliberations. The same process has also been followed in the pending appellate proceeding in the *Ratko Mladić* case. In other words, despite institutional innovations, the decision-making process at the MICT so far does not deviate considerably from the deliberative model of its predecessor tribunals. It remains to be seen, however, how the MICT will address the challenges created by the judges' physical distance from the MICT headquarters.

IV. DELIBERATIONS AT OTHER INTERNATIONAL CRIMINAL TRIBUNALS

Unsurprisingly, the same decision-making model described above has largely been followed by other international and hybrid criminal tribunals that came to being after the creation of the ICTY and the ICTR – such as the Special Court for Sierra Leone (SCSL), the Extraordinary Chambers in the Courts of Cambodia (ECCC), the Special Tribunal for Lebanon (STL), and the ICC, the first permanent court for international crimes in history. As the ICTY was the first international criminal court created since the end of World War II, it has become a source of inspiration for the internal regulations and the basic parameters of adjudication at the ICTR and other subsequent institutions. A detailed presentation of the

---

25 See *Prosecutor v Augustin Ngirabatware*, Case No 12-29-A, Judgment, 18 December 2014.

26 See *Prosecutor v Vojislav Šešelj*, Case No 16-99-A, Judgment, 11 April 2018; *Prosecutor v Radovan Karadžić*, Case No 13-55-A, Judgment, 20 March 2019.

decision-making processes at all these international and semi-international courts would exceed the scope of this chapter. It is worth mentioning, perhaps, that, as far as the ICC is concerned, the only notable difference is that oral hearings are to be held on requests for revision of a conviction or sentence – the equivalent to petitions for review under the ICTY Rules.[27]

V. CONCLUDING REMARKS

The goal of this brief chapter of the internal workings of the *ad hoc* tribunals has been to promote transparency, which 'is essential to building public confidence in the fair administration of justice', which, in turn, is essential to fostering 'a broad understanding of and support for the Tribunals' work'.[28] As must by now be clear, the decision-making process at these tribunals, as well as other international criminal judicial institutions – in spite of the prevalence of the common law/adversarial model of criminal adjudication at international criminal courts – has been a combination of ingredients from both the civil and the common law tradition, with special importance for civil law impact in the field of evidence. The sheer volume of the cases tried by these tribunals has required judges and legal officers to work tirelessly at all stages of the deliberation process. Appellate judges, thus, deliberate in-depth both before the hearing, as in civil law courts, and after the hearing, consistent with the common law tradition, so as to issue the fairest judgment possible. Whether that goal is actually achieved, it is not up to judges to determine. History and time will tell.

27 See ICC Rule 161.
28 See Meron (n 2) 278.

CHAPTER 15

COLLECTIVE JUDGING IN THE CATHOLIC CHURCH

Markus GRAULICH*

To consider collective judging in the Catholic Church presupposes a knowledge of the fact that the Church has her own tribunals, which are separate and independent of the ordinary civil courts and tribunals run by the state. These tribunals are normally situated in dioceses around the world, that is, on the local level; but they are also to be found on the level of the universal Church as tribunals of the Holy See. Regarding collective judging, both types of tribunals are regulated by the same principles, but there are also specific rules when it comes to the tribunals of the Holy See. The rules binding all tribunals within the Church are found in the general law that governs the universal Church, but the tribunals at the local level will be considered first in this chapter.

I. THE TRIBUNALS OF THE CHURCH AT THE LOCAL LEVEL

In talking about collective judging within the Church, we have to keep in mind, first of all, that in the Catholic Church, the Bishop is *the* judge. From the very beginning, people came to him to present their cases or to seek his

* Msgr Dr Markus Graulich is Undersecretary of the Pontifical Council for Legislative Texts and a former Prelate Auditor of the Tribunal of the Roman Rota (*Tribunal Rotæ Romanæ*) at the Vatican.

judgment in a controversy, be it ecclesial or civil. The history of law, therefore, shows how great an influence the workings of Church tribunals had on the evolution of general civil tribunals.

A good example of the way in which Bishops exercised their juridical duty is provided by the canon law collection of Regino of Pürm, *Libri duo de synodalibus causis et disciplinis ecclesiasticis*, a handbook for the Bishop during his visitation of the diocese, first published at the end of the 9th century.[1]

Apart from this general role, which is also emphasised in the Code of Canon Law,[2] the canonical tradition suggests that the Bishop should not act as a judge in person but set up a tribunal to handle controversies.[3] With the Code of Canon Law of 1917, we have an organisation of these collegial tribunals for the whole Church, which is repeated in the revised Code of Canon Law (1983).

It is the Code of Canon Law that determines the working of tribunals in the Church and contains the law binding the whole Church all over the world. Some aspects of this law are illustrated in the Instruction[4] *Dignitas Connubii* of 2004 in order to facilitate the work of tribunals, especially in marriage cases, which are mostly treated within the tribunals of the Church.

1. THE COLLEGIATE TRIBUNALS

These determinations of the law allow us to know how collective judging works in tribunals of the Church all over the world. We find the relevant indications in the seventh Book of the Code of Canon Law containing the provisions about processes in the Church. The first part of the provisions regarding collective judging is to be found in the general norms for the process

---

1 W Hartmann (ed and trans) *Das Sendhandbuch des Regino von Prüm*, Freiherr vom Stein-Gedächtnisausgabe, vol 42 (Darmstadt, Wissenschaftliche Buchgesellschaft, 2004).

2 *Cf* Canon 1419:

> 'In each diocese and for all cases not expressly excepted by law, the judge of first instance is the diocesan bishop, who can exercise judicial power personally or through others according to the following canons.'

3 *Cf* Canon 1420 §1–2:

> 'Each diocesan bishop is bound to appoint a judicial vicar, or offcialis, with ordinary power to judge, distinct from the vicar general unless the small size of the diocese or the small number of cases suggests otherwise.
>
> The judicial vicar constitutes one tribunal with the bishop but cannot judge cases which the bishop reserves to himself.'

4 *Cf* Canon 34:

> 'Instructions clarify the prescripts of laws and elaborate on and determine the methods to be observed in fulfilling them. They are given for the use of those whose duty it is to see that laws are executed and oblige them in the execution of the laws. Those who possess executive power legitimately issue such instructions within the limits of their competence.'

regarding tribunals in general; the second part is to be found in the chapter regarding the pronouncement of the judge.

First of all, a general rule states: 'In any trial, a single judge can employ two assessors who consult with him; they are to be clerics or lay persons of upright life.'[5] Yet these assessors are not judges, so that we cannot really describe this as a form of collective judging. What this rule provides is a kind of collaboration when it comes to a judicial decision.

Nevertheless, some cases cannot be treated by a single judge:

> 'With every contrary custom reprobated, the following cases are reserved to a collegiate tribunal of three judges:
>
> 1/contentious cases: a) concerning the bond of sacred ordination; b) concerning the bond of marriage …;
>
> 2/penal cases: a) concerning delicts which can entail the penalty of dismissal from the clerical state; b) concerning the imposition or declaration of an excommunication.'[6]

While the collegiate tribunal is normally composed of three judges, 'the bishop can entrust more difficult cases or those of greater importance to the judgment of three or five judges.'[7]

The Judicial Vicar, who presides over the tribunal, plays an important role when it comes to the assignation of the single cases: 'Unless the bishop establishes otherwise in individual cases, the judicial vicar is to assign the judges in order by turn to adjudicate individual cases.'[8]

Given the fact that there are not always a sufficient number of canon lawyers available, the Bishop can also make an exception from the general rule: 'If it happens that a collegiate tribunal cannot be established in the first instance of a trial, the conference of bishops can permit the bishop, for as long as the impossibility continues, to entrust cases to a single clerical judge who is to employ an assessor and auditor where possible.'[9] This auditor hears the parties and their testimonies; the assessor's role is to assist the judge. Nevertheless, we cannot talk about collective judging in these cases.

Once the penal or *turnus* of judges is determined, 'the judicial vicar is not to substitute judges once they have been assigned except for a most grave cause expressed in a decree.'[10] This rule promotes legal certainty, for the parties have the right to know who will be handling and deciding their case.

---

5 Canon 1424.
6 Canon 1425 §1.
7 Canon 1425 §2.
8 Canon 1425 §3.
9 Canon 1425 §4.
10 Canon 1425 §5.

'A collegiate tribunal must proceed collegially and render its sentences by majority vote.'[11] Taking a decision collegially means that all the judges involved in the case must be present and involved in the decision.

Within a collegiate tribunal there are several roles. First of all, there is the President of the tribunal: 'The judicial vicar or an adjutant judicial vicar must preside over a collegiate tribunal insofar as possible.'[12] He has the task of 'designat[ing] one of the judges of the college as the *ponens* or *relator* who is to report about the case at the meeting of the judges and put the sentence into writing. For a just cause the president can substitute another in place of the original *relator*.'[13] During the proceedings, the *ponens* has several special tasks to fulfil and can do this without the other judges, who have to be informed about the procedural steps taken by the *ponens*.

2. COLLECTIVE DECISION-MAKING

'In a collegiate tribunal the president of the college is to establish the date and time when the judges are to convene for deliberation; unless a special reason suggests otherwise, the meeting is to be held at the tribunal office.'[14] Prior to this meeting, every judge has to study the case and form an opinion about the controversy. The law of the Church urges the judges to give their judgment with moral certitude.[15] This means, studying the findings of the process, each judge has to reach a conclusion without a positive doubt, weighing the proofs according to his conscience.

'On the date assigned for the meeting, the individual judges are to submit their written conclusions on the merit of the case with the reasons in law and in fact which led them to their conclusions; these conclusions are to be added to the acts of the case and must be kept secret.'[16] These written conclusions are to be used for the writing of the sentence, that is, the definite judgment.

As the decision takes place in a court room of the Church, the session begins with a prayer. 'After the invocation of the Divine Name, the individual judges are to present their conclusions in order of precedence, always beginning, however, with the *ponens* or *relator* of the case. A discussion then follows under the leadership of the tribunal president, especially to determine what must be established in the dispositive part of the sentence.'[17] This norm appeals once

11 Canon 1426 §1.
12 Canon 1426 §2.
13 Canon 1429.
14 Canon 1609 §1.
15 *Cf* Canon 1608 §1.
16 Canon 1609 §2.
17 Canon 1609 §3.

again to the individual responsibility of the judges. Every judge has the right to emphasise certain aspects.

'In the discussion each judge is permitted to withdraw from his or her original conclusion. The judge who is unwilling to assent to the decision of the others, however, can demand that his or her conclusions be transmitted to the higher tribunal if an appeal is made.'[18] The judges themselves cannot appeal the sentence, but they can ask that their minority vote be included into the files.

Normally, a collegiate tribunal reaches a decision, but 'if the judges are unwilling or unable to arrive at a sentence during the first discussion, the decision can be deferred to a new meeting, but not for more than a week, unless the instruction of the case must be completed according to the norm of can. 1600.'[19] This possibility allows every judge to reach a decision with moral certainty.

When it comes to the writing of the sentence, the norm for the single judge is that 'he will write the sentence himself.'[20] But 'in a collegiate tribunal, it is for the *ponens* or *relator* to write the sentence, selecting the reasons from those the individual judges brought forth during the discussion, unless a majority of the judges have already determined the reasons to be presented. The sentence must then be submitted for the approval of the individual judges.'[21] This rule ensures that all opinions and all aspects are included in the sentence.

The judges in the Church work within a certain time frame: 'The sentence must be issued no more than a month from the day on which the case was decided unless in a collegiate tribunal the judges set a longer period for a grave reason.'[22]

As far as the content of the sentence is concerned, the Code of Canon Law provides:

> 'The sentence must:
>
> 1/decide the controversy deliberated before the tribunal with an appropriate response given to the individual doubts;
>
> 2/determine what obligations have arisen for the parties from the trial and how they must be fulfilled;
>
> 3/set forth the reasons or motives in law and in fact on which the dispositive part of the sentence is based;
>
> 4/determine the expenses of the litigation.'[23]

18 Canon 1609 §4.
19 Canon 1609 §5.
20 Canon 1610 §1.
21 Canon 1610 §2.
22 Canon 1610 §3.
23 Canon 1611.

Whereas in the Church a sentence is not given in the name of an authority, canon law establishes that 'after the invocation of the Divine Name, the sentence must express in order the judge or the tribunal, the petitioner, the respondent, and the procurator, with their names and domiciles correctly designated, and the promoter of justice and defender of the bond if they took part in the trial.'[24]

Other elements of the sentence are listed subsequently: 'Next, it must briefly relate the facts together with the conclusions of the parties and the formula of the doubts. The dispositive part of the sentence follows the above, preceded by the reasons on which it is based. It is to conclude with the indication of the date and the place where it was rendered, with the signature of the judge or, if it is a collegiate tribunal, of all the judges, and the notary.'[25]

In the end, 'the sentence is to be published as soon as possible, with an indication of the means by which it can be challenged. It has no force before publication even if the dispositive part was made known to the parties with the permission of the judge.'[26]

II. THE TRIBUNALS OF THE CHURCH AT THE UNIVERSAL LEVEL

The procedure hitherto discussed is that for the local courts. Regrettably, there are fewer and fewer canon lawyers in the Church, so that in the future it could be difficult to set up collegiate tribunals. As mentioned at the beginning of this chapter, the tendency is normally to have a single judge; but this brings with it a number of disadvantages, for the tribunals of the Church frequently deal with extremely delicate questions concerning the marriage of two people, their intention and their readiness to get married. While it may be easy to evaluate proofs concerning an alleged simulation in the marriage consent, it is less easy to assess the capacity someone has to marry. Here, the counsel of other judges be often be quite helpful.

At the level of the universal Church, collective judging works more or less in the same way as on the local level. In the Roman Rota, the judges form several fixed tribunals (*turnus*) to which cases are assigned as they come in. The only exception is where the case requires a special panel (for instance because of its language).

In the Rota, too, every judge has to present his opinion in writing (it goes without saying that the written opinion has to be delivered in Latin).[27]

24 Canon 1612 §1.
25 Canon 1612 §2–4.
26 Canon 1614.
27 *Cf* Article 89 of the Norms of the Roman Rota.

These written opinions are to be kept in the archive of the Dean of the Roman Rota and they are burnt after ten years.[28] The discussion of a given case begins with the opinion of the *ponens* and follows the order of precedence.[29] Just as in the local courts, a judge is permitted to resile from his opinion and change his *votum* if arguments brought forward during the discussion make him change his mind.[30] There is also the possibility to defer the decision if the judges do not reach a unanimous verdict.[31] If after a second discussion – which has to take place within a week after the first session – a peaceful agreement cannot be reached, the *ponens* has to present the case to the Dean who may enlarge the panel.[32] This does not happen often, however.

After the decision, the *ponens* has two months to write the sentence,[33] taking into consideration the opinions of the judges expressed during the discussion.[34] As in other tribunals, the sentences of the Rota are published to the parties. Every judge can select three decisions in which he acted as *ponens* to be published in the annual volume of the tribunal. They are anonymised and may serve judges in lower tribunals as an example of jurisprudence, since the jurisprudence of the Roman Rota is a model for the correct application of the law, or at least should be.

In the Appeal Court of the Signatura Apostolica, which treats only administrative cases, there are several levels of decisions: the first is the decision of the Secretary on whether or not to reject an appeal *in limine*, that is from the start. The second level is a decision of the Prefect on whether or not an appeal can be admitted for judicial discussion. This decision is taken by the Prefect in a congress. This means that the members of the congress are not acting as judges, but as councillors to the Prefect.

The final judgement is found in the meeting of the college of judges (normally five of them) by majority vote. The case is assigned to a *ponens* who makes a report and suggests the solution. Only few sentences of the Signatura are published.

III. CONCLUSION

Regarding collective judging in the Church, we are basically counting votes, ensuring that all opinions are considered. In an organisation like a tribunal of

28 *Cf* Article 89 §3 of the Norms of the Roman Rota.
29 *Cf* Article 90 of the Norms of the Roman Rota.
30 *Cf* Article 91 of the Norms of the Roman Rota.
31 *Cf* Article 93 of the Norms of the Roman Rota.
32 *Cf* Article 94 of the Norms of the Roman Rota.
33 *Cf* Article 96 §1 of the Norms of the Roman Rota.
34 *Cf* Article 96 §3 of the Norms of the Roman Rota.

the Church, unanimity is always a goal, but not always reached. Given the fact that a judge should decide with moral certainty, this involves the conscience of the judges – something which cannot be forced. At most, a judge can be invited not to oppose the decision of the majority.

As stated at the beginning of this chapter, the judicial culture worldwide has learnt a great deal from the way the Church has handled cases in history. Nowadays, of course, the Church may also learn from the various different legal traditions which have become established around the world.

PART VI

VOICES FROM THE AUDIENCE AND CLOSING REMARKS

CHAPTER 16

DECISION-MAKING BY THE BOARDS OF APPEAL OF THE EUROPEAN PATENT OFFICE

Kevin GARNETT*

I. INTRODUCTION

The 1973 European Patent Convention (EPC) established a system for the grant of 'European' patents, such patents extending in scope throughout the territories of its Contracting States (or those of them which the applicant has designated). Upon grant, a European patent takes effect as a bundle of national patents, each being enforceable by national law in the state for which it was designated.[1] The system of law established by the EPC is both independent of national legal systems and autonomous. Its institutions and proceedings are not connected

* Kevin Garnett QC, London, was formerly a Member of the Boards of Appeal and of the Enlarged Board of Appeal at the European Patent Office, Munich.

1 Thus a European patent is to be treated in the state for which it is granted as having 'the effect of and be subject to the same conditions as a national patent granted by that state.' (Article 2(2) EPC).

with those of the European Union, and the Contracting States include states that are not members of the EU. There are presently 38 such states.[2]

Although, as with any patent granting authority, the system may have some failings, in general terms the EPC has been an outstanding success, measured not just by the large number of Contracting States. Thus in 2019 there were over 181,000 applications for a European patent,[3] and nearly 138,000 were granted.[4]

The European Patent Office (EPO) is the organisation charged with carrying out the aims of the EPC.[5] It is subject to the overall control of an Administrative Council, composed of representatives from the Contracting States.[6] The day-to-day running of the EPO is the responsibility of its President, who is in turn answerable to the Administrative Council.[7]

The EPO has two core functions, carried out by two separate administrative departments or 'Divisions':[8] first, the granting of European patents by the 'Examining Division'; second, following a request filed by an 'opponent', the revocation or amendment by the 'Opposition Division' of European patents in cases where it is established that the granted patent does not in fact comply with the EPC.[9] There is no restriction on the national identity of those who may apply for a patent or file an opposition.[10] Questions of infringement of a European patent are not dealt with by the EPO, but by national courts.[11]

---

2 Alphabetically: Albania, Austria, Belgium, Bulgaria, Croatia, Cyprus, Czech Republic, Denmark, Estonia, Finland, France, Germany, Greece, Hungary, Iceland, Italy, Latvia, Liechtenstein, Lithuania, Luxembourg, Malta, Netherlands, Norway, Poland, Portugal, Republic of Macedonia, Romania, San Marino, Serbia, Slovakia, Slovenia, Spain, Sweden, Switzerland, Turkey, United Kingdom. Accession is open to 'European States': Article 166(1)(b) EPC.

3 This, and some of the following statistics are taken from: https://www.epo.org/about-us/annual-reports-statistics/statistics/2019.html (last accessed 23 May 2020).

4 However, this latter figure does not indicate a 'success' rate for applications since the 138,000 granted patents were based on applications filed in earlier years.

5 The EPO is one of the larger public service organisations in Europe, employing some 7,000 staff of 35 different nationalities.

6 Article 26(1) EPC.

7 Article 10(1) EPC.

8 Articles 15, 18 and 19 EPC. There is also a Search Division, which is responsible for drawing up European search reports: Article 17 EPC.

9 Of granted patents, about 3% are subsequently challenged in opposition proceedings, leading to revocation in about 30% of cases.

10 In 2019, about 45% of all European patent applications came from the EPC Contracting States, followed by the US, Japan, China and South Korea.

11 This is because a European patent takes effect as a bundle of national patents. Such a national patent is also subject to revocation/nullity proceedings in the relevant national court. The Unified Patent Court (established by the UPC Agreement, EU Document 16351/12) is intended to enable European patent disputes to be tried in one court rather than, as often happens at present, in parallel proceedings brought in separate European states. It has yet to come into force.

The fundamental principles for the grant and revocation/amendment of European patents are laid down in the EPC itself; more detailed, regulatory provisions are provided by Implementing Regulations. Proceedings take place in one of three official languages, English, French or German. The language of the first filing dictates the language of the proceedings, ie the language in which the EPO maintains the official register and issues communications and decisions to the parties. Any party may, however, use any one of the three official languages when communicating with the EPO or making submissions during an oral hearing.

II. THE BOARDS OF APPEAL

The Boards of Appeal (the 'Boards'), established within the European Patent Office by the EPC,[12] are the single judicial appeal body with power to review first instance decisions of the departments of the EPO. This may be done at the request of an applicant who is aggrieved by a decision not to grant a patent on the terms requested, or at the request of a proprietor or an opponent who is dissatisfied with a decision made in opposition proceedings. There is no appeal from a decision of a Board of Appeal,[13] whether to the Court of Justice of the European Union, the European Court of Human Rights or elsewhere.[14] Neither can the Boards refer any question of law to the European Court of Justice (or elsewhere): the legal systems are not connected. Accordingly, if an application for a European patent is refused or if a European patent is revoked by a Board, there is no further legal remedy, whether at national level or elsewhere.

The structure and functioning of the Boards are laid down by the EPC[15] and the Implementing Regulations,[16] and further regulated by Rules of Procedure.[17] An underlying principle is that the Boards are independent of the Office in their decisions and are bound only by the European Patent Convention.[18] The Boards are headed by the President of the Boards of Appeal,

---

12 Article 15 EPC.

13 But see later as to the jurisdiction of the Enlarged Board of Appeal, in section IV below.

14 The fact that, almost uniquely amongst modern legal systems, there is only one level of appeal, particularly on questions of law, has been controversial.

15 Article 21 EPC.

16 Article 23(4) EPC; Rules 12–13 of the EPC Implementing Regulations.

17 As laid down by the 'Boards of Appeal Committee', established by the Administrative Council: Rule 12c of the EPC Implementing Regulations.

18 'In their decisions the members of the Boards shall not be bound by any instructions and shall comply only with the provisions of this Convention': Article 23(3) EPC.

who carries out administrative and managerial duties delegated to him by the President of the Office.[19]

The Boards currently have about 170 members, comprised of both technically qualified and legally qualified members, reflecting the different skills required to deal with patent appeal cases. The overwhelming number of appeals are concerned with so-called technical issues, ie with core patent issues such as the novelty or inventiveness of the claimed invention.[20] The present discussion is limited to these kinds of appeals, which can serve to illustrate the decision-making characteristics of the Boards generally. In 2018 over 3,000 technical appeals were filed.

In order to be able to deal with these cases, the Boards are divided into different technical fields, namely chemistry, mechanics, electricity and physics, and further subdivided to deal with particular specialisms (eg polymer chemistry). Typically, each particular 'Board' will be made up of a chairman, four to five technically qualified members and three to four legally qualified members (who will also work with other technical Boards). The chairman will usually have been appointed after having served for a number of years as a technically qualified member of a Board in the same general technical field and so gained relevant experience.[21] Currently there are 28 technical boards of appeal.

When an appeal is filed it is allocated to a particular Board, depending on the technical field in question. The Chairman of this Board then appoints a panel of three (also called a 'Board') to deal with the case, consisting of two technically qualified members and one legally qualified member chosen from the Board members. The Chairman will usually be one of the three members. The Chairman also allocates one of the members of the Board to act as *rapporteur*, usually the other technical member.[22] The *rapporteur* system is central to the work of the Boards, as will be explained. The method of choosing the *rapporteur* is not fixed. In some Boards this is done purely by rotation. In others, the Chairman will make the choice depending on existing expertise in the technical field

---

19 Rule 12a(2) of the EPC Implementing Regulations. But in exercising such functions and powers, he is responsible solely to the Administrative Council and is subject to its hierarchical and disciplinary authority. These provisions were part of the changes to the organisational structure of the Boards of Appeal introduced in 2017 intended to deal with criticisms that the Boards of Appeal were not sufficiently independent from the administration of the EPO, including its President. See, eg, https://www.epo.org/law-practice/case-law-appeals/about-the-boards-of-appeal.html (last accessed 23 May 2020). As to the judicial function of the President of the Boards of Appeal, see under 'Enlarged Board of Appeal' (text following n 40 below).

20 Even though cases or the issues are often conveniently described as either 'technical' or 'legal', they are of course all based on the law.

21 Although a legally qualified member may also be chairman of a Board.

22 Article 5 of the Rules of Procedure of the Boards of Appeal ('RPBA').

in question, ability to work in the language of the proceedings[23] and existing workload.

After preliminary checks for any obvious defects in the appeal, the file will then take its place in the *rapporteur's* queue of work. Subsequent filings, eg by a respondent, are added to the file as and when they arrive.

III. DECISION-MAKING BY THE BOARDS OF APPEAL

1. PRELIMINARY STEPS

Substantive work on the file, and the beginning of the collective decision-making process, starts when the *rapporteur* first looks at the file in detail.[24] This work involves a thorough examination of the issues and the evidence with a view to preparation of an internal written assessment of the case (in a '*votum*') and a written communication to the party or parties drawing attention to matters that seem to be of particular significance for the decision to be taken. This may also include the Board's preliminary assessment of the case. The type of work carried out may vary according to whether the case is an appeal by a dissatisfied applicant (an '*ex parte*' case) or an appeal in opposition proceedings. In an *ex parte* case the *rapporteur* may *ex officio* carry out some research of his own (for example, into published materials) if there seem to be deficiencies in what is on file, or speak to the appellant's representative by phone to deal with a particular problem; the Board's role here may be relatively pro-active. In opposition cases, however, the *rapporteur* will generally restrict himself to the submissions of the parties and the evidence filed by them. The process is not necessarily done in isolation. A *rapporteur* works in physical proximity to his Chairman and colleagues, and will often discuss particular points informally in cases of difficulty or uncertainty.

The *votum* and draft communication will be circulated by email for consideration and approval to the other two, usually first to the Chairman. Given the Chairman's experience and authority, his view will often carry considerable weight, but the process is one of discussion and eventual agreement. Where there is no agreement on a particular issue, it can be left open until later. The process is not fixed in stone, and the legally qualified member may be involved at an early stage if difficult legal issues arise.

23 Although all members are required and expected to work in all three of the official languages.
24 Given the backlog of appeals, and the *rapporteur's* workload, this may not take place until a year or more after the appeal is filed.

In proceedings before the EPO, including those before the Boards, parties have a right to be heard in oral proceedings, and parties usually ask for such a hearing, if only as a precautionary measure. Of course, if in an *ex parte* case the Board agrees that the appeal can be allowed on the terms requested by the appellant, the appeal can be disposed of without an oral hearing. Otherwise, the next step will be to fix a date for the hearing, and to issue a summons. This will usually be about six months' ahead. This delay is partly a matter of scheduling and partly to give the parties time to digest the Board's communication and to file any observations or alterations to their case to take into account the Board's preliminary views.

From the Board's point of view, the next step will take place a week or so before the hearing, when the *rapporteur* will examine the file once again, particularly in the light of any new filings from the parties. Usually, a further *votum* will be prepared (or updated) and circulated by the *rapporteur*, setting out the issues which are now on the table and also the *rapporteur's* views. Except in very straightforward cases, a meeting of the three members of the Board will then take place on the day before the hearing, at which the issues are discussed in detail. Before this meeting the other two members will have read into the case and prepared themselves for the hearing. The discussion is not limited to the content of the *votum*, but may include anything which the other two see as being relevant. It may include an explanation from the *rapporteur* of particularly complicated technical issues which the other two, particularly the legal member, may need help in understanding. This discussion will typically last one hour, but there is no fixed rule.

2. THE ORAL HEARING

Oral proceedings are usually fixed for one day, and will continue (sometimes even into the night!) until a result is achieved. The course of the proceedings is heavily influenced by two factors which are peculiar to patent cases. The first is the fact that it is common for there to be a number of different objections to what the applicant or patentee is seeking, based on the various different requirements for patentability. Any single objection may be fatal. Second, it is generally acceptable that an applicant or patentee may file a number of hierarchical fall-back positions (in the form of different sets of claims defining the extent of patent protection sought), claiming ever narrower protection. As a result of these factors, the debate is usually taken in stages, with the various points at issue being taken one by one. After each point has been debated, the Board will usually interrupt the proceedings, deliberate in private and then announce its conclusion. The result may be either that the set of claims currently on the table survives for the next round of argument or that it is knocked out, to be replaced by a lower-ranking set of claims which the applicant or proprietor believes will get round the objection. This process does not result in a number of separate, formal 'decisions', but rather a series of non-binding announcements indicating the Board's conclusion on a particular point, which then enable the debate to move forward.[25] A decision comes only at the end of the hearing, when the appeal is either dismissed or allowed, in whole or part.

The debate with the parties is relatively informal, and while the Chairman does have some (rather ill-defined) powers to control the proceedings, it is common for each point to be argued back and forth until the parties consider that there is nothing more which can be said on it. The parties' representatives will often be asked questions by members of the Board to clarify particular points, either during or at the end of their submissions.

When it comes to breaking off the hearing for the Board to reach a conclusion on a particular point, the Board discusses the point in private and in confidence.[26] Where the point is a technical one, the *rapporteur* will usually give his view first.[27] Although the Rules of Procedure provide that the Chairman should speak last,[28] this rule is 'more honour'd in the breach than the observance.'[29] The discussion is informal, going backwards and forwards until, hopefully, a consensus is reached. Even where the point is purely technical, the legally qualified member will often take a full part, asking for explanations and expressing his own view on the issue. As regards the dynamics of the decision making-process, as already noted, clearly the Chairman's views, by virtue of his seniority and experience, will usually have great weight. On the other hand, the *rapporteur* will often have most to contribute, usually having studied the technical background and the documents in greater depth. The Rules of Procedure do not allow for a dissenting judgment, and the same is true for the series of intermediate conclusions. Where no consensus can be reached, the majority view will prevail.[30] Where the two technically qualified members cannot agree, it follows that the legally qualified member must decide between them, even if the issue is highly technical. For this reason alone, the legally qualified member needs properly to understand the issues.

At the end of the proceedings, it will have become clear which, if any, of the ranking sets of claims of the applicant or proprietor has survived the battle,

---

25 But a Board would not later go back on such a conclusion, at least not without making it clear in the oral proceedings that it had changed its mind.

26 Article 19(1) RPBA.

27 But where the point is purely legal one, eg a procedural point, the legally qualified member may be asked by the Chairman to speak first.

28 Article 19(2) RPBA.

29 See W Shakespeare's *Hamlet*, Act I, scene 4.

30 The RPBA provide that voting should essentially take place in the same order as the expressing of views, but again this rule is not usually strictly observed.

and the Chairman will announce the decision of the Board accordingly. This decision is final and cannot be re-opened by the Board.[31] A Board can, in a difficult case, 'reserve' its decision, to be communicated later in writing, together with its reasons, but this is very unusual.

3. DRAFTING THE REASONS FOR THE DECISION

There then follows the process of drafting the reasons for the decision. Written reasons for Board decisions are generally detailed and follow a set pattern, first setting out the background facts and then the reasons for the decision. They are often long and highly technical, and may in addition contain detailed citations from existing case law of the Boards. The first draft is prepared by the *rapporteur*[32] and then circulated to the others, usually first to the Chairman. There then follows an iterative process of amendment until the three members are satisfied with the decision and it can be signed. It is then transmitted to the parties.

As already noted, no dissenting judgment is possible under the Rules, and any dissents will normally have been dealt with at the oral proceedings. When it comes to producing the reasons for the decision, it is rare that any further dissent arises that cannot be ironed out by a compromise formulation. It might be thought that since the various points in the case have been discussed amongst the Board members in detail during the oral hearing, and the reasons for any conclusion usually noted informally by one or more of the Board members, it would be a simple and quick process to produce a written statement of the reasons. The truth is otherwise, and it can often take some time.[33] This can be explained partly by the workload of the *rapporteur* and the other members of the Board, but also by the fact that while it may be relatively easy to reach a definite yes/no conclusion on a particular point in a face-to-face deliberation, it can be much more difficult to formulate the precise reasons for this decision *ex post facto*.[34] This is no doubt one reason why the Boards often take considerable time during oral proceedings to reach their conclusions. But the Boards must be unusual as a judicial body in announcing their decision at the end of oral

31 T 843/91 (OJ EPO 1994, 818).

32 Article 5(5) RPBA.

33 As a rule, the written reasons must be sent out within three months of the oral proceedings; if the Board is unable to meet this timetable, it must tell the parties when the reasons are to be sent out: Article 15(9)(a) RPBA.

34 In the author's personal experience, this way of proceeding can be a dangerous one, since it is often only by the disciplined process of writing that the various logical steps in the decision-making process are properly worked through.

proceedings (which cannot later be re-opened) before detailed written reasons have been produced and circulated amongst its members for agreement.[35]

Decisions of the Boards are frequently cited in national courts as giving guidance on particular patent law issues. All are published (in the language of the proceedings)[36] and are available to the public on the EPO website.[37]

IV. THE ENLARGED BOARD OF APPEAL

For completeness the functions of one other organ of the Boards of Appeal need to be mentioned, namely the Enlarged Board of Appeal (the 'EBA'). The EBA is not a superior court to the ordinary Boards but rather, as its name suggests, an enlarged version. It has two main functions. First, to answer questions which in a particular case have been referred to it by a Board, where the Board considers that a ruling is required to ensure uniform application of the law (eg because there are conflicting earlier decisions of the Boards) or where a point of law of fundamental importance has arisen.[38] In addition, the President of the Office, independently of any existing proceedings before the Boards, may refer a point of law to the EBA for its opinion where two Boards have given different decisions on that question.[39] The Enlarged Board of Appeal deals with two to three such referrals per year. The decisions and opinions of the EBA are generally of considerable importance to the patent community and treated with respect by national courts.

The EBA in these cases consists of five legally and two technically qualified members,[40] taken from a standing panel of EBA members drawn from existing members of the Boards of Appeal, chosen in the light of their experience. The Chairman for the case will usually be the President of the Boards of Appeal. In cases where the question has implications extending, for example, beyond procedural issues under the EPC, at least one and sometimes two of the legally qualified members will be an external judge appointed from a court of one of the Contracting States.

The process of decision-making by the EBA follows very closely that of the ordinary Boards of Appeal, with the appointment of a *rapporteur*, preparation of

---

35 Even under the English system where, in a (straightforward) case, a decision is given orally at the end of a hearing, the judge or judges will first orally give a 'judgment', summarising the facts and explaining the reasons for the decision, which is then formally announced.

36 See the text in the paragraph at the top of p 295 above.

37 Via https://www.epo.org/law-practice/case-law-appeals/advanced-search.html (last accessed 23 May 2020).

38 Article 112(1)(a) EPC. The proceedings before the technical Board are suspended pending the outcome of the reference.

39 Article 112(1)(b) EPC.

40 Article 22(2) EPC.

a *votum* and a communication to the parties, discussion of the case amongst its members before the hearing, the hearing itself and the preparation of the written reasons for the decision or opinion. However, the EBA differs from the ordinary Boards in that a dissenting opinion is permitted, although only if a majority of the members of the Board agrees.[41] The identity of the dissenter or dissenters, or their number, may not be disclosed.[42]

The second main jurisdiction of the EBA relates to deciding on so-called petitions for review. A party who considers that (inter alia) a fundamental procedural defect occurred during proceedings before a Board, may file a petition asking the EBA to set the decision aside.[43] These petitions are first screened by a three-person panel of the EBA to weed out hopeless cases, those petitions which survive then being heard by a five-person panel of the EBA. The decision-making process follows the procedure already outlined for other EBA cases, except that no external judges are involved and no dissenting judgment is possible. Currently, less than ten such review cases are filed per year.

V. SUMMARY

It can be seen that the decision-making process of the Boards of Appeal of the European Patent Office shows something of a hybrid character. Partly it follows what might be thought of as a typical continental European 'civilian' approach, with considerable internal work being done by the Board on the papers, coupled with a *rapporteur* system. But it also has elements of the Anglo-Saxon 'common law' tradition, where the role of oral proceedings at which there is an extended debate, with participation by the judges, is important.

---

41 Article 18(2) of the Rules of Procedure of the Enlarged Board of Appeal.

42 Ibid.

43 Article 112a EPC. This article sets out the full list of grounds on which such a petition may be filed.

CHAPTER 17

COLLEGIALITY AND COLLECTIVITY IN COMMON LAW COURTS

James LEE*

I. INTRODUCTION

This chapter examines the question of collegiality in relation to judgment-writing in two common law apex courts: the United Kingdom Supreme Court (UKSC) and the High Court of Australia (HCA). During 2017, when the conference that gave rise to this collection took place, both courts went through periods of transition after the retirements of Lord Neuberger PSC and French CJ with new leadership and new appointments: Lady Hale as President of the UKSC and Susan Kiefel AC as Chief Justice of Australia, respectively. Lady Hale has since retired and been succeeded by Lord Reed,

* James Lee is Reader in English Law and Vice Dean for Education at The Dickson Poon School of Law, King's College London, and an Associate Academic Fellow of the Honourable Society of the Inner Temple. I thank the editors and publishers for the opportunity to update the chapter with statistics to the end of 2019. I am grateful to Gabrielle Appleby, Brice Dickson, Wolfgang Ernst, Birke Häcker, Simon Lee, and Alan Paterson for helpful discussions of the issues here, and to Andrew Lynch for valuable comments on a draft. None of these people should be taken to join in my judgements here, however: all views, and any errors, are my own.

who has reiterated the Court's preference for 'single judgments or at least a single majority judgment … where possible'.[1] The aim of this chapter is to draw upon statistics for each court, in order to provide context for reflections on the practice in respect of collective judging, and to complement other chapters in this collection.

In order to keep within the necessary confines, the chapter relies upon a study of the statistics for each court from 2017 to 2019:[2] these statistics reveal a significant level of continuity and settled practice in the case of each court. I also draw upon the extra-curial comments of leading Justices of each court.

I argue that judicial individuality is not incompatible with collegiality on a multi-member appellate court.[3] In so doing, I respectfully suggest some reservations about the approach taken by the HCA. I suggest that there may be lessons to be learnt for the HCA from the process of gradual reform over the first decade of the UKSC. The divergences in practice between the UKSC and HCA[4] demonstrate that there is no common 'common law' approach to judgment-writing in apex courts, which has implications for the dynamics of decision-making.

II. THE COURTS AND THEIR ERAS

The UK Supreme Court was inaugurated in 2009,[5] having been provided for by the Constitutional Reform Act 2005 (UK), Part 3. Prior to that, the final

---

1 Lord Reed, 'The Supreme Court Ten Years On', The Bentham Association Lecture 2019, available online via https://www.supremecourt.uk/docs/speech-190306.pdf (last accessed 30 April 2020) 9.

2 The UK Supreme Court sits in legal years from October to July (albeit there are occasionally judgments issued in August and September). There is therefore some potential discrepancy in comparing the calendar year statistics, but it is justified in that all bar five of the Michaelmas (autumn) Term 2017 decisions of the Court where heard during Lord Neuberger's Presidency. The 2017 calendar year figures therefore represent the end of Lord Neuberger's Presidency and the remaining years were under the Presidency of Lady Hale, who retired at the end of Michaelmas Term 2019 in January 2020. For an analysis of Lord Neuberger's legacy on the court, see A Paterson, 'Presidency and the Supreme Court: Lord Neuberger's Legacy', available online via https://www.ucl.ac.uk/judicial-institute/sites/judicial-institute/files/presidency_and_the_supreme_court_lecture_-_final.pdf (last accessed 30 April 2020).

3 J Lee, 'The Judicial Individuality of Lord Sumption' (2017) 40 *University of New South Wales Law Journal* 862–96.

4 See the leading annual studies of the High Court of Australia's decisions for 2017 and 2018: A Lynch and G Williams, 'The High Court on Constitutional Law: The 2017 Statistics' (2018) 41 *University of New South Wales Law Journal* 1134 and A Lynch and G Williams, 'The High Court on Constitutional Law: The 2018 Statistics' (2019) 42 *University of New South Wales Law Journal* 1443. The methodology employed by Lynch and Williams differs slightly from mine here, but the trends identified are common.

5 Constitutional Reform Act 2005 (UK), section 23(1): 'There is to be a Supreme Court of the United Kingdom'.

court of appeal in the United Kingdom has been the Appellate Committee of the House of Lords. Its status as a committee of the Upper Chamber of Parliament meant that formally, each judgment was a 'speech', and the general practice therefore was that each sitting Law Lord gave a separate judgment, and speeches were always delivered in order of seniority, even if the most senior Lord was simply concurring in a formulaic way with a colleague's speech.[6]

Upon the move to the Supreme Court, the Justices took the opportunity to introduce some changes to practice. The first judgment, a procedural application decided by three Justices, was delivered by Lord Hope DPSC, but his Lordship used 'We' throughout.[7] The second case, *Re Sigma Finance*,[8] saw the first substantive decision, with the lead judgment given by Lord Mance, who was in terms of seniority the second most junior Justice on the panel. The judgment is listed as being given by 'Lord Mance (with whom Lords Hope, Scott and Collins concur)';[9] there is a short concurrence on a point of interpretation from Lord Collins (with whom Lords Hope and Mance agreed). Lord Walker issued a short dissent, and his judgment was identified as a dissenting judgment.[10] This was the first case in which the top UK court had delivered its judgments in such a fashion: identifying a lead judgment, then concurring speeches and listing dissents at the end. The third decision of the Court reverted to *seriatim* opinions in the House of Lords style.[11] But the general practice[12] has been to take advantage of the flexibility provided by the creation of the new Court: doing so makes judgments easier to follow.[13]

---

6 In the style of, eg, 'I have had the advantage of reading the speech of my noble and learned friend, Lord Diplock. I agree with it and have nothing further to add'.

7 *R (on the application of E) v Governing Body of JFS* [2009] UKSC 1, [2009] 1 WLR 2353.

8 *Re Sigma Finance* [2009] UKSC 2, [2010] 1 All ER 571.

9 Ibid [1].

10 Ibid, noting at [41] that 'in respectful dissent from the majority of this Court I prefer the view taken by the judge and the majority of the Court of Appeal. Since no issue of principle is involved it would be quite inappropriate to give any lengthy explanation of my reasons. I will limit myself to three fairly general points.'

11 *R (on the application of L) v Commissioner of Police of the Metropolis* [2009] UKSC 3, [2010] 1 AC 410. Lord Hope delivered the main judgment, Lord Saville issued a formulaic concurrence. Lord Brown issued a short concurring opinion, noting at [62] that he had 'had the advantage of reading in draft the opinions of Lord Hope and Lord Neuberger. I agree with both of them and there is really very little that it might be helpful to add.' Lord Neuberger's longer concurring opinion concluded by noting that he would dismiss the appeal '[for] these reasons, which are little more than an echo of those more fully expressed by Lord Hope, with whose judgment I agree.'

12 Indeed, so much so that the court has only exceptionally reverted to its prior practice: as in *In the matter of an application by the Northern Ireland Human Rights Commission for Judicial Review (Northern Ireland); Reference by the Court of Appeal in Northern Ireland pursuant to Paragraph 33 of Schedule 10 to the Northern Ireland Act 1998 (Abortion) (Northern Ireland)* [2018] UKSC 27, [2019] 1 All ER 173.

13 There are a limited number of examples of a judgment being listed as 'Lady/Lord X delivered the judgment of the Court', as opposed to 'Lady X (with whom the others agree)'.

This approach continued under Lord Neuberger, who became President in 2012. Writing shortly after his appointment, his Lordship strongly supported restraint with respect to judgment-writing:

> 'Basically, concurring judgments should only be written where they really add (or, I suppose, subtract) something to (or from) the leading judgment. On the whole, there is much to be said for giving a concurring judgment only where the topic really would benefit from judicial dialogue.'[14]

Writing in 2013, after the first four years of the Court, Professor Paterson noted that there was 'now a prevailing view amongst the Justices that concurrences should be curbed unless they are going to add something to the lead judgment',[15] and as President, Lord Neuberger did take the view that single judgments were desirable where possible.[16] In a 2017 restitution case, his Lordship wryly noted 'the ability of ingenious lawyers to identify possible differences between concurring judgments'.[17] Earlier scholarship has shown that the percentage of single judgments[18] was significantly higher during his time as President of the Supreme Court when compared to his immediate predecessors.[19] We shall see in section IV below that this trend continued in his Lordship's final year and throughout Lady Hale's tenure.

The early predictions for Kiefel CJ's tenure in the High Court were that it would be one of continuity: as Justice Bell observed, 'there is no reason to think that there will be a departure from the collegial decision-making

---

This occurred twice in 2019: in *Cape Intermediate Holdings Ltd v Dring (Asbestos Victims Support Groups Forum UK)* [2019] UKSC 38, [2019] 3 WLR 429 (Lady Hale) and *R (on the application of Miller) v The Prime Minister* [2019] UKSC 41, [2020] AC 373 (Lady Hale and Lord Reed).

14 Lord Neuberger, 'No Judgment – No Justice', speech delivered on 20 November 2012, available online via https://www.supremecourt.uk/docs/speech-121120.pdf (last accessed 29 February 2020) para 29. See also Paterson (n 2) 18–19 and 35.

15 A Paterson, *Final Judgment* (Oxford, Hart Publishing, 2013) 108.

16 Although, with respect, it was not quite accurate of Kiefel CJ to state in 'The Individual Judge' (2014) 88 *Australian Law Journal* 554, 560, that Lord Neuberger was a 'proponent of *joint* judgments' (my emphasis) – that is equating the HCA and UKSC practices which, as this chapter seeks to show, have certain clear differences.

17 *Lowick Rose LLP v Swynson Ltd & Anor* [2017] UKSC 32, [2018] AC 313 at [121]. See similarly, Lord Reed, 'The Supreme Court Ten Years On' (n 1) 9.

18 Note that, as made clear below, 'single judgment' means a single judgment of the Court determining the case, regardless of how many authors, not a judgment by a single judge.

19 Paterson, *Final Judgment* (n 15) 102 and 143. See also J Lee, 'The United Kingdom Supreme Court: A Study in Judicial Reform' in E Guinchard and M-P Granger (eds) *The New EU Judiciary – An Analysis of Current Judicial Reforms* (Alphen aan den Rijn, Kluwer, 2017) 77, 91–95. For more recent work, see R Cahill-O'Callaghan, *Values in the Supreme Court: Decisions, Division and Diversity* (Oxford, Hart Publishing, 2020); R Hunter and E Rackley, 'Judicial leadership on the UK Supreme Court' (2018) 38 *Legal Studies* 191; and the political science analysis of the judicial behaviour on the UKSC, see C Hanretty, *A Court of Specialists: Judicial Behavior on the UK Supreme Court* (Oxford, Oxford University Press), 2020.

which characterised the French Court under the stewardship of Kiefel CJ',[20] and Lynch and Williams wrote that it was 'reasonable to anticipate a smooth transition'.[21] The statistics for the first three years set out below seem to vindicate these initial views. During Kiefel CJ's tenure, the HCA has had a period of stability, as the next mandatory retirement is not until that of Nettle J, in December 2020. By contrast, in the same period between Justice Edelman's appointment in January 2017 and Nettle J's mandatory retirement, the UKSC will have appointed ten new Justices out of twelve,[22] and changed President twice. Reviewing the past three years therefore offers an opportunity to reflect upon the development of practices with respect to delivery of judgments. In the remainder of this chapter, we shall see reasons offered for the differing practices, and then consider the extent to which the statistics support those reasons.

III. JUDGMENTS AND JUDGEMENT

The delivery of multiple judgments has been the subject of extra-curial consideration by Justices of both the UKSC and the HCA.[23] The contemporary discussion of the issues of collective (or otherwise) judging in Australia has been influenced by the role of particularly individualistic Justices who were prone to issuing their own separate judgments: as Professor Lynch has observed, 'Kirby J and Heydon J appeared to embrace their outlier status, speaking candidly and persuasively about the value of judicial individualism and the

---

20 Justice Bell AC, 'Examining The Judge', speech at the launch of volume 40 of the *University of New South Wales Law Journal* on 29 May 2017, available online via http://www.hcourt.gov.au/assets/publications/speeches/current-justices/bellj/bellj29May2017.pdf.pdf (last accessed 29 February 2020) 2. See also A Lynch, 'Susan Kiefel era signals continuity, not change', *The Australian*, 20 January 2017.

21 Lynch and Williams, 'The 2017 Statistics' (n 4) 1135.

22 Three Justices were appointed in October 2017: Lady Black, Lord Lloyd Jones and Lord Briggs (at the same time as Lady Hale was elevated to the Court's Presidency); succeeding the late Lord Toulson (who retired in September 2016), Lord Clarke and Lord Neuberger PSC. In 2018, three appointments were announced (to replace Lords Mance DPSC, Lord Hughes and Lord Sumption): Lady Arden and Lord Kitchin became Justices in October 2018 and Lord Sales was sworn in in January 2019. Three new appointments are taking place in 2020, as three further Justices reach their mandatory retirement age in the first half 2020: Lady Hale PSC, Lord Carnwath and Lord Wilson. Lord Hamblen (January 2020) and Lord Leggatt (April 2020) have already been appointed, with Professor Andrew Burrows to join the Court in June 2020. As this chapter was at proof stage, the Court has announced that Lord Kerr, the last member of the Court to have served on the Judicial Committee of the House of Lords, is to retire in September 2020.

23 In addition to the speeches discussed below, see, eg, Sir Anthony Mason, 'Reflections on the High Court: Its judges and judgments' (2013) 37 *Australian Bar Review* 102. For a recent New Zealand perspective broadly sympathetic to the Australian practice, see Justice Susan Glazebrook, 'Academics and the Supreme Court' (2017) 48 *Victoria University Wellington Law Review* 237.

importance of dissent'.[24] For example, Lynch and Williams have shown that during his time on the French Court, Heydon J participated in a single judgment in only 22.99% of cases, separately concurring in 48.13% and dissenting in 28.88%.[25] Heydon J's defence[26] of his practice in giving individual judgments, which he framed as a necessary feature of individual judicial independence, led to 'an unprecedented public "debate" between serving Justices who addressed the collaborative-individualist tensions on a multi-member court'.[27]

Kiefel CJ has been particularly vocal in her support for joint judgments, in speeches while a puisne Justice[28] and as Chief Justice,[29] deprecating 'unnecessary [additional] judgments'.[30] Her Honour has noted on several occasions that Lord Neuberger expressed similar views, particularly with respect to the disapproval of 'vanity' judgments[31] which add nothing to what has already been

---

24 A Lynch, 'Introduction – What Makes a Dissent "Great"?' in A Lynch (ed), *Great Australian Dissents* (Cambridge, Cambridge University Press, 2016) 1, 7–8. See also the specific chapters by G Appleby and H Roberts, 'He Who Would Not Be Muzzled: Justice Heydon's Last Dissent in *Monis v The Queen* (2013)', ibid 335, and AJ Brown, 'When Liberty Divides: Judicial Cleavages and their Consequences in *Al-Kateb v Godwin* (2004)', ibid 311, 320 et seq (on Kirby J); and further A Lynch, 'Keep Your Distance: Independence, Individualism and Decision-Making on Multi-Member Courts' in R Ananian-Welsh and J Crowe (eds), *Judicial Independence in Australia – Contemporary Challenges, Future Directions* (Alexandria/NSW, The Federation Press, 2016) 156.

25 A Lynch and G Williams, 'The High Court on Constitutional Law: The 2016 and French Court Statistics' (2017) 40 *University of New South Wales Law Journal* 1468, 1482.

26 See both JD Heydon, 'Varieties of Legal Method in the Late 20th Century' (2012) 34 *Sydney Law Review* 219 and idem, 'Threats to Judicial Independence: The Enemy Within' (2013) 129 *Law Quarterly Review* 205.

27 H Hobbs, A Lynch and G Williams, 'The High Court under Chief Justice Robert French' (2017) 91 *Australian Law Journal* 53, 56. See generally Lord Neuberger, 'Twenty Years a Judge: Reflections and Refractions' (Neill Lecture 2017, Oxford Law Faculty, 10 February 2017) paras 31 and 34.

28 The Hon Justice Susan Kiefel AC, 'Reasons for Judgment: Objects and Observations', Sir Harry Gibbs Law Dinner, Emanuel College, University of Queensland, 18 May 2012, available online via https://www.hcourt.gov.au/assets/publications/speeches/current-justices/kiefelj/kiefelj-2012-05-18.pdf (last accessed 6 May 2020); eadem, 'On Being a Judge', Public Lecture, Chinese University of Hong Kong, 15 January 2013, available online via https://www.hcourt.gov.au/assets/publications/speeches/current-justices/kiefelj/kiefelj-2013-01-15.pdf (last accessed 6 May 2020); eadem, 'The Individual Judge' (n 16).

29 The Hon S Kiefel AC, 'Judicial Methods in the 21st Century', Supreme Court Oration, Brisbane, 16 March 2017, available online via http://www.hcourt.gov.au/assets/publications/speeches/current-justices/kiefelj/KiefelCJ16Mar2017.pdf (last accessed 29 February 2020). See the analysis of this speech in Lynch and Williams, 'The 2017 Statistics' (n 4) 1147–55.

30 Ibid 4. See also S Kiefel's contribution in chapter 4 of the present collection (pp 53–55).

31 Kiefel, 'Judicial Methods in the 21st Century' (n 29) 8–9, citing Lord Neuberger, 'Sausages and the Judicial Process: The Limits of Transparency', Annual Conference of the Supreme Court of New South Wales, Sydney, 1 August 2014, available online via https://www.supremecourt.uk/docs/speech-140801.pdf (last accessed 6 May 2020) para 32.

written by a colleague: such a judgment, says Kiefel CJ, is 'not the voice of the Court, it is the sound of self'.[32]

The HCA practice of 'joining in' judgments means that the authorship of such an opinion is never disclosed. What does it mean to 'join a judgment'? A remarkable feature to English eyes is that it is openly acknowledged that '[t]ruly joint judgments, where two or more judges contribute to a single draft, are rare':[33]

> 'Whilst it is not unusual for suggestions, sometimes substantial in content, to be made to the author of the first draft, it is not often the case that two or more justices will work together to produce a judgment.'[34]

'Joining in' is therefore not the same as joint authorship. Yet is it necessarily apparent to the general reader of a joint judgment that the judges listed as joining in it have not all directly contributed to it?

The justifications offered for the approach in the High Court of Australia include the authority of the judgment being enhanced by the weight of several Justices, it being practically difficult for Justices to work together on a judgment,[35] and that disclosing the author would lead to Justices writing separately more often.[36] However, the evolution in the practice of the UK Supreme Court demonstrates that it is possible to attribute authorship without leading to a proliferation in judgments. The HCA approach has caused some unease about a lack of transparency:[37] whether for litigants, the legal professions, the academy or the wider public,[38] and has led to interesting work using computational linguistics to attempt to attribute authorship of HCA joint judgments.[39]

---

32 Kiefel, 'Judicial Methods in the 21st Century' (n 29) 9, although five years earlier her Honour had suggested that Lord Neuberger's description of extraneous judgments as a form of vanity 'may be a little harsh': Kiefel, 'Reasons for Judgment: Objects and Observations' (n 28) 4: one may speculate that the subsequent experiences of the HCA have hardened her Honour's view.

33 Kiefel, 'Reasons for Judgment: Objects and Observations' (n 28) 4.

34 Kiefel, 'Judicial Methods in the 21st Century' (n 29) 6. See also the interview with French CJ, ABC Radio National, 'Retiring Chief Justice Robert French', The Law Report, 13 December 2016 (Chief Justice Robert French), available via http://www.abc.net.au/radionational/programs/lawreport/retiring-chief-justicerobert-french/8105828#transcript (last accessed 29 February 2020) cited in Lynch and Williams, 'The High Court on Constitutional Law' (n 25) 1469.

35 Kiefel, 'On Being a Judge' (n 28) 9. Lord Reed has, by contrast, emphasised how technology enables collaboration: Lord Reed, 'The Supreme Court Ten Years On' (n 1) 10.

36 Kiefel, 'Judicial Methods in the 21st Century' (n 29) 7.

37 See, eg, J Gans, 'Catch-22 in the Court of Disputed Returns: *Re Culleton (No 2)*', Opinions On High, 8 February 2017, available via http://blogs.unimelb.edu.au/opinionsonhigh/2017/02/08/gans-culleton/ (last accessed 29 February 2020).

38 A Partovi, R Smyth, I Zukerman and J Valente, 'Addressing "Loss of Identity" in the Joint Judgment: Searching For "The Individual Judge" in the Joint Judgments of the Mason Court' (2017) 40 *University of New South Wales Law Journal* 670.

39 Ibid.

Although Bell J has suggested that she is unconvinced by such approaches,[40] French CJ, since retiring, has noted that this work

> 'might encourage movement towards express attribution of authorship in judgments, particularly if the technique of computational linguistics creates a non-trivial probability of identifying the wrong person.'[41]

In the UKSC, if there is a joint judgment, the inference is that it is the work of the relevant Justices who join in it, and Justices have been quite transparent about the process. For example, Lord Reed has viewed joint judgments as

> 'a good solution where more than one Justice would like to write and their views of the case are broadly aligned, particularly where the case raises a number of issues which the Justices can divide between them.'[42]

Occasionally, a joint judgment will be done to make a statement: in 2016–17, the Court was the focus of media, political and public attention[43] when it had to decide whether legislative authorisation was required for the UK Government was entitled to issue a notification under article 50 of the Treaty of Lisbon of the UK's intention to leave the European Union. The Court sat *en banc* for the first time,[44] with eleven Justices hearing *R (on the application of Miller) v Secretary of State for Exiting the European Union*.[45] The Court divided 8:3. The majority judgment is a joint judgment of all eight Justices,[46] with the Court

40 Bell, 'Examining The Judge' (n 20).

41 Hon Robert French, 'Foreword' (2017) 40 *University of New South Wales Law Journal* 665, 666.

42 Lord Reed, 'The Supreme Court Ten Years On' (n 1) 10.

43 The case saw 'the Supreme Court [find] its way into public consciousness to an unprecedented degree': Mark Ormerod, Introduction to *The Supreme Court Annual Report and Accounts*, 2016–17 (HC 31) 7. See also The Hon S Kiefel AC, 'Some Reflections, Following the Brexit Decision, on Secession, on the Roles of Australian and English Courts with Respect to the Validity of Executive and Legislative Action and on Responses to Controversial Decisions of this Kind', Anglo Australian Lawyers Association, London, 12 July 2017, available online via http://www.hcourt.gov.au/assets/publications/speeches/current-justices/kiefelj/kiefelcj12jul2017.pdf (last accessed 29 February 2020).

44 For the reasons why, see Lord Neuberger, 'Twenty Years a Judge' (n 27) para 31, Lady Hale, 'Judges, Power and Accountability: Constitutional Implications of Judicial Selection', Constitutional Law Summer School, Belfast, 11 August 2017, available online via https://www.supremecourt.uk/docs/speech-170811.pdf (last accessed 29 February 2020) and Paterson, 'Presidency and the Supreme Court' (n 2) 17–18.

45 *R (on the application of Miller) v Secretary of State for Exiting the European Union* [2017] UKSC 5, [2018] AC 61.

46 Lord Neuberger of Abbotsbury PSC, Baroness Hale of Richmond DPSC, Lord Mance, Lord Kerr of Tonaghmore, Lord Clarke of Stone-Cum-Ebony, Lord Wilson, Lord Sumption, Lord Hodge JJSC.

presenting as united a front as possible.[47] The more general practice of joint judgments would mean the reduced ability of the Court to make a particular statement as a show of unity, as in the *Miller* decision.[48] 'Attribution matters'.[49]

A further concern for Kiefel CJ is that a practice of each decision featuring several opinions risks leading to delay in the delivery of judgments.[50] There is no doubt some risk of duplication of work, too, but the examples alluded to by Kiefel CJ are equally evidence of difficult working relationships. But, as I would argue is shown by other chapters in this collection,[51] there are other norms or rules which can better deal with the problem of recalcitrant authors than an expectation in respect of joint judgments.

IV. STATISTICS

The statistics which follow represent a study of the decisions of the UKSC reported on www.bailii.org and of the High Court of Australia reported on www.austlii.org for 2017 to 2019. In 2017, the UKSC decided 82 cases, in 2018 a total of 67 cases,[52] and in 2019 a total of 60 cases. while the HCA decided 56 cases in 2017, 63 in 2018, and 50 in 2009. Since the focus here is on judgments of multi-member apex courts, some HCA decisions have been discounted in the analysis below: the High Court retains an original jurisdiction on some matters, and some decisions were interim applications heard by a single Justice.[53] Therefore, the figures for the HCA consider only the decisions which were heard by at least three Justices:[54] 50, 59 and 43 for each respective year.

---

47 In the subsequent case of *R (on the application of Miller) v Prime Minister* [2019] UKSC 41, concerning the 2019 proroguing of Parliament, Lady Hale and Lord Reed (the Court's President and Deputy President) gave the judgment of the unanimous panel of eleven Justices (although this was not *en banc*, since there were now twelve serving Justices: Lord Briggs was the only Justice not to sit).

48 Although there are instances in the HCA, particularly in recent cases concerning the potential disqualification of members of Parliament: see Lynch and Williams, 'The 2018 Statistics' (n 4) 1456.

49 Partovi, Smyth, Zukerman and Valente (n 38) 672.

50 Kiefel, 'The Individual Judge' (n 16) 556–57; eadem, 'Judicial Methods in the 21st Century' (n 29) 1.

51 See, eg, the contribution by HT Edwards in chapter 5 (pp 85 et seq), but *cf* the arguments in favour of joint judgments presented by G Lübbe-Wolff in chapter 8.

52 Not counting the reasons for not granting permission to appeal in the exceptional case of *R (on the application of Conway) v Secretary of State for Justice* [2018] UKSC B1.

53 There were six such decisions in 2017, four in 2018 and seven in 2019. For a similar approach in this respect, see eg Lynch and Williams, 'The High Court on Constitutional Law' (n 25) 1470.

54 The HCA decisions were generally heard by at least five Justices (sometimes six or seven), with the exception of appeals from the Supreme Court of Nauru, when only three Justices heard the appeals. In all bar one of those cases, the Court gave a joint judgment from all

1. COURTS COMPARED

The following two tables divide the respective Courts' decisions into three categories – those where there was a single judgment (whether from a single Justice or a joint judgment of all Justices); then cases where the Court was unanimous as to the outcome but where there was at least one additional concurring opinion;[55] and those in which there was at least one dissent.[56] In this chapter, I use 'univocal' to refer to cases where the Court spoke with one voice, and 'unanimous' to refer to cases where the Court was agreed as to the outcome, but where there may have been more than one judgment offering a different view.[57] I have classified dissents as instances of a judge disagreeing with one of the orders of the court: it is of course – as discussed further below – possible for a Justice to disagree vehemently with the majority's reasoning but to still concur for different reasons in the disposal of the appeal.

Table 1. 2017–2019 High Court of Australia Decisions

	2017 Percentage (Number in brackets)	**2018 Percentage (Number in brackets)**	**2019 Percentage (Number in brackets)**	**Overall (2017 to 2019)**
Single Judgment	34% (17 cases)	47.46% (28 cases)	13.95% (6 cases)	33.55% (55 cases)
Unanimous with at least one separate concurrence	38% (19 cases)	40.68% (24 cases)	48.84% (21 cases)	42.10% (64 cases)
Cases with Dissents	17.07% (14 cases)	11.86% (7 cases)	37.21% (16 cases)	24.34% (37 cases)
Total	50	59	43	100% (152 cases)

Source: Compiled by the author

In the High Court, there is a significant variation in the figures. The level of dissent ranged from 11.86% to 37.21% (albeit that in 2019 there were fewer cases), while the level of single judgments also varied widely, with a swing from nearly half in 2018 to only 13.95% in 2019.

three Justices: the exception was *CRI028 v The Republic of Nauru* [2018] HCA 24, in which Bell J issued a separate concurring opinion alongside the joint judgment of Gordon and Edelman JJ.

55 For reasons explained below, I have included the 'welcome case' (see the text between n 69 and n 71) of *Kendirjian v Lepore* [2017] HCA 13 in this category.

56 This approach therefore includes partial dissents, such as the judgment of Edelman J in *Lordianto v Commissioner of the Australian Federal Police; Kalimuthu v Commissioner of the Australian Federal Police* [2019] HCA 39. On the meaning of 'dissent' for present purposes, see the text following n 57 below.

57 I have discussed this further elsewhere: J Lee, 'A Defence of Concurring Speeches' [2009] *Public Law* 305, 309. I thus take a different approach on this point of terminology from Lynch and Williams, 'The High Court on Constitutional Law' (n 25).

Table 2. **2017–2019 UK Supreme Court Decisions**

	2017 Percentage (Number in brackets)	**2018 Percentage (Number in brackets)**	**2019 Percentage (Number in brackets)**	**Overall (2017 to 2019)**
Single Judgment	67.07% (55 cases)	65.67% (44 cases)	75% (45 cases)	68.89% (144 cases)
Unanimous with at least one separate concurrence	15.85% (13 cases)	14.9% (10 cases)	8.33% (5 cases)	13.40% (28 cases)
Cases with Dissents	17.07% (14 cases)	19.4% (13 cases)	16.67% (10 cases)	17.7% (37 cases)
Total	82	67	60	100% (209 cases)

Source: Compiled by the author

It is clear that in the UKSC there is a high percentage of single judgments, ranging from 65% to 75%. The overall level of unanimity was very consistent, with the dissents between 16.67% and 19.4%. The overall 2017–2019 averages of 68.89% single judgments and 17.7% dissents for the UKSC are remarkably consistent with 2016, the last full year of Lord Neuberger's Presidency when 68% of cases were resolved by a single judgment and 18% of cases saw a dissent.[58]

Figure 1. 2017–2019 HCA and UKSC decision statistics compared

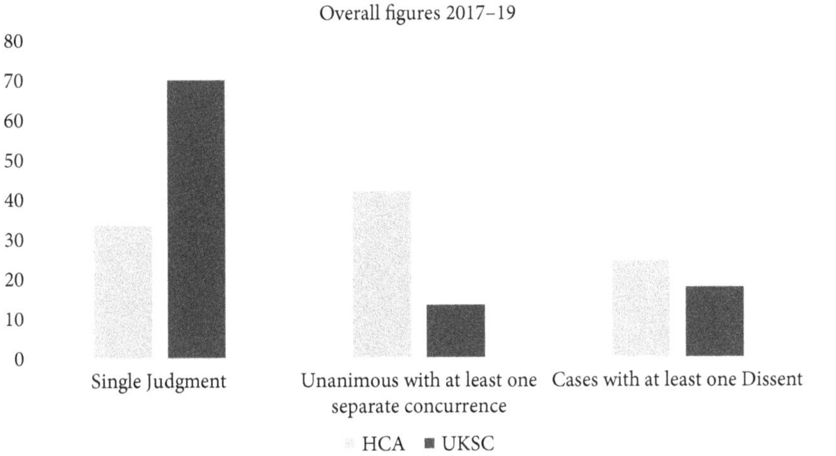

Source: Produced by the author

There are numerous caveats here: the many different judicial personalities on the courts, the changes in personnel on the UKSC during the three-year period,

58 B Dickson, 'Supreme Justice' (2017) 167 *New Law Journal*, issue 7736, p 20.

and the categorisations are necessarily somewhat impressionistic. But the raw figures are clear in showing that the UKSC practice leads to more cases being decided by a single judgment than the HCA's practice of 'joining in' judgments. As Paterson has noted, the rise in UKSC single judgments 'can only be achieved by the Justices working together (rather than as individuals)'.[59] The statistics show that over the three years, the courts were unanimous in a similar percentage of cases: 75.6% in the HCA and 82.3% in the UKSC. But we can see that the proportion of cases decided by a single judgment is radically different between the two courts: just over 36% for the HCA and just under 70% for the UKSC. If therefore, as we saw earlier, an aim of the Australian practice of joint judgments is to discourage the issuing of further separate concurring opinions, then it seems this is an approach with limited success. One potential reason is that it may be more palatable for a judge to agree with a colleague's disposal of an appeal in their colleague's name than if the judge also has to put his or her name to it. And indeed, some Justices may not be comfortable with joint attribution for what is not joint work. The difference may seem cosmetic, but may be significant.

2. HIGH COURT OF AUSTRALIA STATISTICS BY JUSTICE

Coper, writing in 2001, described the HCA as having been 'marked by rugged individualism, though with bursts of collective effort from time to time'.[60] With the retirements of Kirby and Heydon JJ, there is no pattern of a 'Great Dissenter'. But there is nevertheless a notable variation amongst the HCA Justices in terms of their willingness to join in judgments. Analysing the decisions of each Justice, the results are as follows (generally taking 'lead judgment' as the first listed in the report or that which commands the support of a plurality of Justices):[61]

59 Paterson, *Final Judgment* (n 15) 144.

60 M Coper, 'Joint Judgments and Separate Judgments' in in M Coper, T Blackshield and G Williams (eds), *The Oxford Companion to the High Court of Australia* (Oxford, Oxford University Press, 2001) 367.

61 In *Frugtniet v Australian Securities and Investments Commission* [2019] HCA 16, the first judgment is a joint judgment of Kiefel CJ, Keane and Nettle JJ, while the second judgment is a joint judgment of the remaining four Justices. The judgment of the four Justices has been counted as the lead judgment for these purposes. Similarly, there were two three-Justice judgments in the unanimous decision in *Carter Holt Harvey Woodproducts Australia Pty Ltd v The Commonwealth* [2019] HCA 20: although Kiefel CJ, Keane and Edelman JJ's judgment comes first, the joint judgment of Bell, Gageler and Nettle JJ is counted as the lead judgment because the seventh Justice, Justice Gordon, expressly agreed with their reasons in her separate concurrence (at [106]).

Table 3. 2017–2019 Joined Judgment Delivery in the High Court of Australia by Justice

Justice	Kiefel CJ	Bell	Gageler	Keane	Nettle	Gordon	Edelman
Number of cases	134	115	124	121	129	114	114
Joined in Lead Joint Judgment	120	105	61	107	84	77	64
Percentage of 'Joining In' the Lead Judgment	89.6%	91.3%	49.1%	88.4%	65.1%	67.5%	56.1%

Source: Compiled by the author

This data shows that the seven Justices of the High Court of Australia can broadly be arranged into three groups. The two most senior Justices, Kiefel CJ and Bell J, are the most willing to join a joint judgment: as we shall see below, their Honours have expressed strong extra-curial support for the practice with respect to joint judgments. Keane J leans in the same direction, joining in over 88% of judgments. In the middle group are Nettle and Gordon JJ who joined in the joint judgment around two thirds of the time. The clear outliers on this analysis are Gageler and Edelman. Edelman J joined in the joint judgment in 56% of cases overall, but in 2019, joined in the joint lead judgment in fewer than half of the decisions on which his Honour sat. Overall Gageler J joined in the judgments in fewer than half of the cases in which his Honour sat. Justice Gageler has also spoken extra-curially on the subject of judgment-writing,[62] noting the importance of clarity but also emphasising the individual responsibility of each judge to reach their own view. Writing judgments as an individual on a multi-member appellate court can contribute to 'maximis[ing] the probability that the court as an institution will give the best of possible judgments'.[63] Both Gageler and Edelman JJ are willing to articulate their reasons for issuing concurring judgments in the given case, which include the importance of the issues engaged,[64] expressly wanting to explain their own reasons,[65] or to issue a qualification on the reasoning in the joint judgment.[66] In *Tony Strickland v Commonwealth Director of Public Prosecutions*,[67] Edelman J noted that he agreed with the reasons of the joint judgment and the judgment of Keane J,

> 'However, in light of (i) the importance of the power to stay proceedings as an abuse of process, and (ii) the divergence of views about its scope and application, this is an

62 S Gageler, 'Why Write Judgments?' (2014) 36 *Sydney Law Review* 189.

63 Ibid 203.

64 See, eg, *Clubb v Edwards; Preston v Avery* [2019] HCA 11, [134] (Gageler J); *UBS AG v Tyne* [2018] HCA 45 (Gageler J).

65 *Brisbane City Council v Amos* [2019] HCA 27, [44] (Gageler J).

66 *Northern Territory v Mr A Griffiths (deceased) and Lorraine Jones on behalf of the Ngaliwurru and Nungali Peoples* [2019] HCA 7, [240]–[241] (Gageler J) and [254] (Edelman J).

67 *Tony Strickland (a pseudonym) v Commonwealth Director of Public Prosecutions* [2018] HCA 53.

instance where the expression of separate reasons may help the common law to "work itself pure"'.[68]

For completeness, we may note that there are also other joint judgments which do not appear to serve as the lead judgment for the Court (whether as concurrences or dissents) and so we can add those to the previous figures:

Table 4. 2017–2019 Any Joined Judgment Delivery in the High Court of Australia by Justice

Justice	Kiefel CJ	Bell	Gageler	Keane	Nettle	Gordon	Edelman
Total of Joining any Joint Judgment	128	105	69	114	98	90	71
Percentage of Joint Judgments Overall	95.5%	91.3%	55.6%	94.2%	75.9%	78.9%	62.3%

Source: Compiled by the author

Kiefel CJ's commitment to her conception of collegiate judgment-giving is shown by the fact that in the relevant period, her Honour gave only six solo judgments (two per year). One of those six was dictated by tradition: *Kendirjian v Lepore*.[69] This case saw the first judgment of Edelman J, who was sworn in as a Justice of the High Court of Australia on the same day as Kiefel CJ became Chief Justice. High Court tradition dictates[70] that, where a Justice gives their first lead judgment for the Court, the other Justices offer *seriatim* concurrences: this is known as a 'welcome' case.[71] Kiefel CJ's judgment (and that of Bell, Gageler and Keane JJ) was simply 'I agree with Edelman J',[72] while Nettle J concurred but expressed some reservations.[73] It is worth noting that the first judgment of Kiefel J (as she then was) saw the tradition observed by five of the other Justices, with Kirby J offering his own additional comments on the point in issue.[74] These welcome cases are a neat tradition, but if it is not problematic for Justices to indicate their specific agreement individually with their colleague's maiden opinion, rather than being joined in that opinion, why could that not also be the case with subsequent opinions?

68 Ibid [255], quoting *Omychund v Barker* (1744) 1 Atk 21, 33; 26 ER 15, 23.

69 *Kendirjian v Lepore* [2017] HCA 13.

70 The tradition is of somewhat unclear heritage, but appears to go back at least as far as the first judgment delivered by McHugh J in 1989: *Jones v Hyde* [1989] HCA 20, (1989) 85 ALR 23.

71 Lynch and Williams, 'The High Court on Constitutional Law' (n 25) 1473, see further K McLoughlin, '"A Particular Disappointment?" Judging Women and the High Court of Australia' (2015) 23 *Feminist Legal Studies* 273.

72 *Kendirjian v Lepore* (n 69) [1].

73 Ibid [5]–[9].

74 *Queensland Premier Mines Pty Ltd v French* [2007] HCA 53. See further McLoughlin (n 71).

Finally, we may note that the institutional preferences with respect to judgments even extend to the press summaries produced by each court. The HCA press summaries speak only of the Court deciding – there is no account of what individual Justices said, even where there are differences amongst the Court as to the reasons.[75] Indeed, the press summary for *Hughes v The Queen*,[76] which was the only 2017 decision to see a 4:3 split, notes that the decision was by a majority, but does not refer to any of the individual Justices or explain the reasons of the dissentients. By contrast, the UKSC press summaries do speak to what individual judges have decided, and also generally identify the lead judgment and any dissents.

V. COLLEGIALITY AND COLLECTIVITY

A noticeable feature of the positions of Kiefel CJ and Bell J is their equation of collegiality with the *willingness* to join in judgments. Bell J, for example, has stated that she does not see 'why we should encourage judges to be other than collegial in their decision-making'.[77] But arguments for the attribution of authorship or the potential value of concurring opinions are not antithetical to collegiality – they simply rest on a different conception of what it means to be collegial. For Kiefel CJ, a determination to issue individual judgments is incompatible with collegial decision-making: 'What is the vice in seeking to persuade colleagues, one's equals, to one's point of view?'[78] Instead, a judge can learn 'the virtue of judicial restraint and the need to quell that sense of self on occasions when institutional responsibility requires it.'[79] Her Honour concluded that 'collegiality is not compromise'.[80]

Although it is understandable that previous experiences have led to a hardening of positions, this argument succeeds only in presenting a false opposition. For the choice is not between joint judgments and multiplicity of unnecessary or wilfully individualistic opinions: a sole-authored, single judgment can be published with the indication of the other Justices' agreement. The figures above suggest that that general practice is more likely to lead to a univocal decision of the court than joint judgments.

---

75 See, eg, the press summary for *Rizeq v Western Australia* [2017] HCA 23, one of the two decisions in which Kiefel J issued a separate solo judgment, and in which Edelman J expressed some doubts as to the scope of the decision. The press summary notes only that the decision was unanimous: http://www.hcourt.gov.au/assets/publications/judgment-summaries/2017/hca-23-2017-06-21.pdf (last accessed 29 February 2020).

76 *Hughes v The Queen* [2017] HCA 20.

77 Bell, 'Examining The Judge' (n 20) 4.

78 Kiefel, 'The Individual Judge' (n 16) 557.

79 Ibid 558.

80 Ibid 560.

In previous work, I have supported the practice of each Law Lord or Justice being able to issue a separate concurring opinion,[81] and I continue to adhere to that view. Concurrences can appropriately be used to delimit the extent of agreement[82] or to 'sound a note of … caution'.[83] But although concurring opinions can add value, it does not follow that judges should always avail themselves of the opportunity to issue a separate concurrence:[84] 'in some cases, it will be an unhelpful repetition or a source of unnecessary ambiguity (particularly if it fails to deal at all with some of the issues)'.[85] I thus wish to be clear that my position is not to support the intransigence of Justice Heydon's approach in his latter years on the HCA. Indeed, for his part, Justice Heydon's objections based on individual independence apply equally to single judgments commanding agreement, whether they are joint or composite judgments.[86] But support for concurring opinions in appropriate circumstances 'is not to justify grandstanding or self-indulgence'.[87]

The views of Lady Hale, the recently retired UKSC President, evolved over time. In a case towards the end of the House of Lords era, her Ladyship said that 'there would be much to be said for our adopting the practice of other supreme courts in having a single majority opinion to which all have contributed and all can subscribe without further qualification or explanation'.[88] But Lady Hale has also recognised the value in bringing a diverse perspective through concurring opinions. Such an opportunity for a judge is reduced by the practice of joint judgments:[89] a feature which potentially raises questions about

---

81 Lee, 'A Defence of Concurring Speeches' (n 57); idem, 'The United Kingdom Supreme Court: A Study in Judicial Reform' (n 19). Professor Ernst has offered wider comparative perspectives in W Ernst, *Rechtserkenntnis durch Richtermehrheiten: "group choice" in europäischen Rechtstraditionen* (Tübingen, Mohr Siebeck, 2016) (reviewed in English by J Bell, (2017) 76 *Cambridge Law Journal* 433). See also M Andenas and D Fairgrieve, 'Simply a Matter of Style? Comparing Judicial Decisions' (2014) 25 *European Business Law Review* 361.

82 See, eg, *Four Seasons Holdings Incorporated v Brownlie* [2017] UKSC 80, [2018] 1 WLR 192, per Lord Clarke at [68]. *Michalak v General Medical Council* [2017] UKSC 71, [2017] 1 WLR 4193, per Lord Mance at [37], agreeing with Lord Kerr but making some additional observations. See also P Daly, 'The Signal and the Noise in Administrative Law' (2017) 68 *University of New Brunswick Law Journal* 68, 78: 'Concurring and dissenting reasons tend to concentrate attention on particular points of dispute that might otherwise be obfuscated by a bland set of majority reasons.'

83 *Four Seasons Holdings Incorporated v Brownlie* (n 82), per Lady Hale at [35].

84 Lee, 'A Defence of Concurring Speeches' (n 57) 315. I am reminded of the line from Jeff Goldblum's Dr Ian Malcolm in *Jurassic Park* (1993): 'your scientists were so preoccupied with whether or not they could, they didn't stop to think if they should'.

85 Coper (n 60).

86 Heydon, 'Threats to Judicial Independence' (n 26) 212.

87 Baroness Hale, 'Judgment Writing in the Supreme Court', First Anniversary Seminar, 30 September 2010, available online via https://www.supremecourt.uk/docs/speech_100930.pdf (last accessed 29 February 2020) 5.

88 *OBG Ltd v Allan, Douglas v Hello! Ltd (No.3), Mainstream Properties Ltd v Young* [2007] UKHL 21, [2008] 1 AC 1, [303].

89 Hale, 'Judgment Writing in the Supreme Court' (n 87).

the ability of judges from diverse backgrounds to contribute meaningfully.[90] This does not just apply where a judge seeks to offer such a view in a concurring speech. For example, Lady Hale's first lead judgment as President of the Supreme Court, began as follows:

> '"We lead women's lives: we have no choice". Thus has the Chief Justice of Canada, the Rt Hon Beverley McLachlin, summed up the basic truth that women and men do indeed lead different lives. How much of this is down to unquestionable biological differences, how much to social conditioning, and how much to other people's views of what it means to be a woman or a man, is all debateable and the accepted wisdom is perpetually changing. But what does not change is the importance, even the centrality, of gender in any individual's sense of self.'[91]

The other four Justices are listed as agreeing with Lady Hale. But the power and symbolism of the first female President of the Court opening a judgment in such a way would be lost if the other Justices had 'joined' in such a judgment.[92] On a related point, Justices of the UK Supreme Court may in concurring opinions offer *obiter* comments on the position in other parts of the United Kingdom, based on their relevant experience.[93]

A successful collegiate and collegial multi-member apex court requires the distinctive individual contributions of the relevant judges: as Lord Mance (now retired) has remarked, the discipline of judging depends upon specific controls found in the judicial method.[94] 'Judiciaries usually also develop

---

90 Lee 'A Defence of Concurring Speeches' (n 57) 330–31. See also Dame Mary Arden, 'Are Shorter Judgments Achievable?', and eadem, 'A Matter of Style' in her book *Common Law and Modern Society: Keeping Pace with Change* (Oxford, Oxford University Press, 2015), at 241 and 247 respectively. Justice Bell has suggested that she is somewhat sceptical about the need for diversity to feed explicitly into decision-making of top courts: Bell, 'Examining the Judge' (n 20).

91 McLachlin CJ retired as Chief Justice of Canada in December 2017. Compare part of the opening paragraph to one of Lady Hale's final judgments in *Whittington Hospital NHS Trust v XX* [2020] UKSC 14, [2020] 2 WLR 972, [1]: 'For some women, the ability to bear and to rear children is a vital part of their identity. What then should be the measure of damages for a woman who has been wrongfully deprived of the ability to bear children herself?'

92 See further on this general theme (rather than this case in particular) McLoughlin (n 71) and eadem, '"Collegiality Is Not Compromise": Farewell Justice Crennan, The Consensus Woman' (2016) 42 *Australian Feminist Law Journal* 241; E Rackley, *Women, Judging and Judiciary: From Difference to Diversity* (Abingdon, Routledge, 2013); and Lady Justice Hale, 'Judging Women & Women Judging' (2002) *Counsel*, August issue, 10.

93 Most commonly in relation to differences between Scots Law and the law of England and Wales: see, eg, Lady Hale in *Gow v Grant* [2012] UKSC 29, 2012 SLT 829, [44]: 'I add a few words because there are lessons to be learned from this case in England and Wales'; and Lord Hodge in *Marley v Rawlings* [2014] UKSC 51, [2015] AC 157, [87] et seq: 'I agree and confine myself to some observations on how Scots law might have dealt with the problem if it were the governing law.'

94 Lord Mance, 'The Role of Judges in a Representative Democracy', Lecture given during the Judicial Committee of the Privy Council's Fourth Sitting in The Bahamas, 24 February 2017,

an internal collegiality. This aids cohesive jurisprudence, but should never degenerate into cliqueness or arrogance.'[95] Echoing the approach of Justice Gageler earlier,[96] Lord Reed has noted the necessary balance between teamwork and individuality: 'the value of the team depends on everybody using their own individual intelligence and their own experience and so forth and bringing all that to the party, but our working method is very collaborative.'[97]

VI. CONCLUSIONS

In one of the High Court's 2017 decisions, *Perara-Cathcart v The Queen*,[98] Gageler J observed:

> 'The institutional responsibility of a court is to produce an order that resolves the justiciable controversy before it. That is the court's "unique and essential function". In the performance of that function by a multi-member court, each member of the court has an individual duty to give effect to his or her own true view of the law and of the application of the law to the facts of the case.'[99]

This chapter has addressed the individual and institutional responsibilities borne by judges on leading apex courts. I have argued that contrasting conceptions of collegiality amongst judges bear upon the respective courts' decision-making processes. Using recent statistics, the approaches in the High Court of Australia and the United Kingdom Supreme Court have revealed some common concerns, but different approaches to resolving them. My argument has been that some of the main reasons given for the prevailing practice of 'joining in' in the High Court of Australia do not justify its current operation – as opposed to speaking to a general desirability for judges to understand the collective enterprise of judging on a multi-member appellate court. Some diversity of opinion is to be expected amongst top judges dealing with the most complex, intensely controversial issues.[100]

---

available online via https://www.supremecourt.uk/docs/speech-170224.pdf (last accessed 29 February 2020) para 22.

95 Ibid para 42.

96 See Gageler (n 62).

97 In an interview with Paterson, *Final Judgement* (n 15) 141.

98 *Perara-Cathcart v The Queen* [2017] HCA 9.

99 Ibid [73]. See also Gordon J at [137]: 'A disagreement in reasoning should not and cannot render a court unable to make an order. A single judge does not need support from other members of the court to reach a conclusion that an appeal should be allowed or dismissed.'

100 Lee, 'A Defence of Concurring Speeches' (n 57) 327. See also Coper (n 60).

The legacy of prior divisions over irreconcilable conceptions of independence and collegiality understandably continues to reverberate in the High Court. No doubt, free-wheeling individualism is not to be encouraged, but a drive for joint judgments is not the only way of dealing with the problem. The incremental changes which the UKSC has made since its inauguration demonstrate that there are other ways to accommodate such reservations while enhancing clarity and transparency, which can in turn serve to improve our understanding of the working of top courts.

CHAPTER 18

SHOULD JUDGES TELL US WHAT THEY THINK?

Richard HYLAND*

This delightful conference provided a rare opportunity to learn more about how judges think. In the courses I teach in an American law school, my students and I try to understand how judges reach their decisions. We follow the logic of the court's argument and then reconstruct the argument for the losing side – which often seems to us at least as persuasive as the argument that convinced the court. By the end of the term, after we have discussed several dozen appellate opinions, the students conclude that a cogent legal argument can usually be made for each side. It is clear to us that judicial decision-making involves more than simply choosing a good legal argument over a bad one. When we try to decide one of the cases ourselves, whichever way we come out, we sometimes find that the arguments that convince us are not mentioned in the opinions. A judge sometimes reveals a significant fact or argument – borrowing a term from poker, we call it the *tell* – a fact, factor, or argument that finds its way into the opinion even though it is not relevant to the elements of the cause of action. We can never be certain about the role the factor played in the decision, and we often wish we could ask the judge. This conference promised the kind of opportunity I have long been seeking.

The conference focused on the complicated questions that arise when judges decide cases collectively. As the distinguished judges reflected on that process, it seemed to me they would first have to discuss how they reach their individual decisions. And since they are of course aware of the difficulty of the task, it also seemed they would want to discuss among themselves how they decide between competing legal arguments when both are good enough to anchor the decision in the law.

---

* Professor Richard Hyland is Distinguished Professor of Law at the Rutgers Law School, Camden, New Jersey.

My hopes, however, were somewhat disappointed. The judges avoided discussing both how they reach their conclusions and why it seems best to suggest that the correct result is always clear. At the same time, several judges described elements of the process that suggest that deciding cases involves more than simply applying the law to the facts. Though many judges expressed views about whether dissents and concurrences should be published, none acknowledged the theoretical problem that arises from the fact that judges differ in their legal evaluation of the cases. If judges who read the same briefs and examine the same record disagree about how the law is to be applied, and if they occasionally feel so strongly about the matter that they would like to make their disagreement public, then it must be true that, at least in many cases, a good legal argument can be made for each side. Several judges also mentioned that they are occasionally swayed by the advocates at oral argument. The critical role of oral argument suggests that the ability of the advocates makes a difference, and that a case might have come out differently if the parties had hired different lawyers or if a different panel of judges had heard the case. If the theoretical difficulty had been recognised, the discussion might have shifted to a consideration of how judges proceed when they have to decide not against a bad legal argument but against a good one. Especially with regard to those cases that reach the higher courts, it probably is not generally the case that one of the positions is clearly right and the other clearly wrong. The relevant factors can frequently be balanced in different ways. In such situations, how do judges know which position to choose? None of the judges addressed this question.

Several judges mentioned that their courts prohibit the publication of concurring and dissenting opinions. In the discussion period, I asked whether it is wise to repress the fact that different judges approach the case differently and come to different results. One judge responded that the conflict is not repressed. The weaker argument is presented and refuted in the published opinion. The answer is not entirely satisfying. If dissents were allowed, the argument for the losing side would receive a more thorough appreciation than it obtains in the majority opinion. What is actually suppressed is not the existence of an opposing argument but rather the difficulty of decision. I continue to wonder, more so after attending the conference, whether it is wise to continue to imply that there is one right answer to every case.

Other judges suggested that the court system would lose legitimacy if it became known that the decision is not the only one possible. In the common law, at least in America, the heritage of legal realism teaches that, on any given day, pretty much any case might come out differently depending on the ability of the advocates and the proclivities of the judges. And yet even we do not publicise this fact. If the views of my first-year students are representative, Americans generally consider the judicial decision to be the only legally permissible resolution of the dispute.

So, the question remains: Is it helpful for the courts to conceal the difficulties they encounter in the process of reaching a decision? Would we be better off if these difficulties were more widely appreciated? After all, we all confront difficult personal decisions, and it should surprise no one to learn that judicial decisions are no less difficult than the decisions we face in daily life.

Would public respect for the courts diminish if judges did not portray the decision as the only possible result? Meir Dan-Cohen suggested that society may benefit when the public is ignorant about certain aspects of the legal process.[1] And yet the contrary may also be true. If we were to become aware of the factors that persuade the judges, that knowledge might change the way we act – and the way lawyers advise their clients.

It is important not to overestimate the extent to which individuals structure their conduct to satisfy the applicable legal norms. Many know little of the law that governs their lives. Nonetheless, I think we all would benefit if the opinions offered a more transparent discussion of the power of competing legal arguments, why it is difficult to choose between them, and the considerations, to the extent the judges are aware of them, that lead judges to decide as they do. Those considerations, since they actually decide the cases, are the real law that governs our society. The more we know of it, the better off we are. Moreover, the factors that guide the decisions are honourable; they serve to achieve justice and to assure that the decisions are fair and equitable. If the public were to become aware of this, I believe it would increase rather than decrease the law's legitimacy. If it became known that fairness, however difficult to articulate in the abstract, proves to be an important aspect of case adjudication, it might convince individuals that they will fare better before the courts if they act equitably in their dealings with others.

I am not proposing that judges offer gratuitous statements of preference, such as the one that found its way into an opinion by Jerome Frank about the parol evidence rule: 'Candor compels the admission that, were we enthusiastic devotees of that rule, we might so construe the record as to bring this case within the rule's scope …'[2] But I think it makes sense for the judges to admit the power of the argument for the losing side and to mention the factors that turned the scales. Courts in contemporary society are, among other things, educators. Providing insight about how decisions are made would serve to instruct both the legal profession and the general public about the considerations that should guide our conduct.

---

1 See M Dan-Cohen, 'Decision Rules and Conduct Rules: On Acoustic Separation in Criminal Law' (1984) 97 *Harvard Law Review* 625.

2 *Zell v American Seating Co*, 138 F.2d 641, 644 (2d Cir 1943) (Frank J), rev'd, 322 US 709, 64 SCt 1053, 88 LEd 1552 (1944).

I understand that this approach to opinion-writing might be a bridge too far in those jurisdictions that do not publish dissents or concurrences and that believe that the role of the judge is limited to applying the law to the facts. Nonetheless, this conference, in the background, created the theoretical foundation for a different view of how courts might proceed.

CHAPTER 19

BEYOND ANECDOTE AND SYNECDOCHE

Matthew Dyson*

A retiring domestic bursar of an Oxbridge College was recently interviewed about his working life, first at Her Majesty's Foreign and Commonwealth Office and then in charge of 500-year-old buildings and slightly younger academics. In the interview, he suggested that there were cultural differences between academics and civil servants. Academics, he implied, were self-serving, seeking personal fame through being recognised for an idea or a discovery; civil servants worked collectively and without a belief that their own contribution should be recognised. While this implication is open to serious challenge, it is perhaps best not taken at face value, but understood within the special cultural practices of a retiring British diplomat. Until recently, an ambassador leaving his or her post was permitted to send a 'valedictory despatch', a frank but confidential communiqué, a parting shot, sent without fear of repercussions, covering local customs, manners and morals or even the state of their drains.[1] These missives can be particularly revealing about how diplomats, famed for their discretion,

* Dr Matthew Dyson is Associate Professor in the Faculty of Law, University of Oxford and Tutorial Fellow of Corpus Christi College, Oxford. With particular thanks to Wolfgang Ernst, Birke Häcker, James Lee, Catarina Sjölin Knight, and Elizabeth Fisher.

1 The practice ended in 2006; see a collection of previously unpublished despatches in M Parris and A Bryson (eds), *Parting Shots: Undiplomatic Diplomats – he ambassadors' letters you were never meant to see* (Penguin, London, 2011).

actually felt about their lives in post. That said, the frankness of the despatch should not be taken to convey truth in their contents.

The provocative report about glory-hunting academics and self-effacing civil servants might also prompt us into thinking more about what judges are doing when they collectively make decisions. Often our only insights into the judicial process are from similarly personal stories. That is quite understandable, and such glimpses can be both informative and amusing. There is also some more recent work adding layers of statistical analysis. This chapter suggests that to get whatever mileage we can out of such anecdotal comparisons and generalisations, we need to push past their face value and, in particular, put them in their proper context. This even applies to some of the language that comes most easily to hand for discussing judicial decision-making. For example, 'collegiality' may be a false friend, meant to express an attitude, but each use might imply different accompanying actions, from avoiding dissent where possible to expecting reproach if a peer's draft judgment is not read within a matter of weeks. Unpacking some of this accompanying baggage might let us make the right comparisons, whether within a legal system, or across systems and actors.[2] Such comparisons and resulting understanding is vital to unlocking the core of judicial decision-making: when, and why, it is better to come to a decision as an individual or as a group? The chapter pushes in that direction by examining three key aspects of collective judicial decision-making: (I) the nature of the decision; (II) who decides it; (III) and how it is decided as a group.[3]

I. NATURE OF DECISION-MAKING

Collective judicial decision-making is shaped by the *nature of the decisions* to be made. Judges make many decisions in their work, but the classic example is a decision in respect of litigation. Relevant decisions include procedural questions, from case management to correct documentation, evidential questions, questions of principle, and questions of substantive law. We might start by thinking of each decision's *size*, *importance* and *urgency*. Decisions are easier when judges agree on those three things. To take a homely example, it

---

2 See generally, R Sacco, 'Legal Formants: A Dynamic Approach to Comparative Law' (1991) 39 *American Journal Comparative Law* 1 (instalment I) and 293 (instalment II), esp 397–401.

3 On English judicial process generally, see A Paterson, *Final Judgment: The Last Law Lords and the Supreme Court* (Oxford, Hart Publishing, 2013); P Darbyshire, *Sitting in Judgment: The Working Lives of Judges* (Oxford, Hart Publishing, 2011); M Zander, *The Law-Making Process*, 7th edn (Oxford, Hart Publishing, 2015) esp ch 7; and M Dyson, 'Judicial Decision-Making in England Today' in J Basedow, H Fleischer and R Zimmermann (eds), *Legislators, Judges, and Professors* (Tübingen, Mohr Siebeck, 2016), 97. For a wider ranging piece which also refers to English material, see JD Heydon, 'Threats to Judicial Independence: The Enemy Within' (2013) 129 *Law Quarterly Review* 205.

is hard to believe that groups of judges are necessarily better than non-judges at deciding what restaurant to eat at or what newspapers the court should buy. Such matters are mundane but contentious, in part because their size, importance and urgency might well vary amongst those taking part. Whatever the character of the decision, a primary step is getting to the key issues: 'triaging' to allocate the right resources to each decision. Two examples would be deciding on whether to grant leave to appeal to your court and how many judges should hear a particular appeal. On the one hand, it would not be surprising to find more *important* cases typically having large panels, while on the other hand, *large* and *urgent* cases depend more on their facts and the available resources. It would also not be surprising to find that larger, important and novel cases create a greater risk that not all of what a given judge thinks of as key to a decision fits into one agreed judgment, leading to pressure for a concurring or dissenting judgment.[4]

In addition to size, importance and urgency, each judicial decision fits into a wider picture which includes *purpose* and *scale*.[5] Let us take as an example a decision on an appeal. In addition to resolving the dispute, the importance of assessing, or correcting, lower courts on the law also varies from legal system to legal system. For example, while the most common translation of what the French *Cour de cassation*, the highest civil and criminal court, does is dealing with an 'appeal', that choice of English terminology is potentially misleading. The idea of *cassation* connotes a purpose more about a correction of the application of law, rather than an engagement with a particular dispute. The French *appel* is used for the appeal to the *Cour d'appel*, but from there a *pourvoi en cassation* or *recours en cassation*, not an *appel* is brought to the *Cour de cassation*. The only possible outcomes are to 'quash' the decision or not to quash. If quashed, the *Cour de cassation* cannot substitute its own decision, it can only remit the dispute back to a lower court to decide again. Form follows function, and cassation judgments are short, technical, famously so, and claim simply to be correcting errors of application of the law rather than creating new law.[6] Yet merely such a process of quashing does not tell the whole story. The key fact is that the cassation process is available *as of right* in many

4 Where such further judgments are possible; the alternative approach leads to more difficult negotiations and perhaps a 'fudged' text. Even some legal systems which have dissents do not have them in certain areas of law. One example is in England and Wales, where the Court of Appeal Criminal Division must have a single judgment unless a senior judge decides to the contrary (section 59 of the Senior Courts Act 1981), but this prohibition does not apply formally to other criminal appeals.

5 It might also be argued that *novelty* and *effect* are further factors, and legal systems acknowledge and accept judicial law-making to varying degrees; but both are set aside here for reasons of space.

6 Specifically on the French *Cour de cassation*, see the contribution by D Hascher in chapter 6 of the present collection.

countries, a statement about the role of the higher courts in keeping a permanent check on lower judges' interpretation of the law. In France, this check was previously in the form of a report to Parliament, an approach in place since its revolutionary origins in 1790.[7] Since cassation is available essentially as of right,[8] the task of the *Cour de cassation* is massive, hearing thousands of cases every year. That burden of cases also promotes a narrower response in court judgments. It might even promote a less personalised response from judges. If the decision to quash or not to quash a lower court's judgment must express the law itself, not a personal view of it, and that decision has to be taken hundreds of times by any one chamber of the court each year, it is less likely to appear as a composition of individual voices. Judges working under that kind of case load must have significant abilities as good bureaucrats as well as judges.[9]

II. WHO IS MAKING THE DECISION

Collective judicial decision-making also depends on *who* is performing this task, in particular the number and background of judges. For instance, an appeal could be thought even more important than a decision at trial, as the appeal might imply a challenge to a trial judge's decision. Such appeals therefore merit more judges on the panel. Even within appeals, each stage of appeal often involves more judges due to the added importance of full and careful scrutiny of the appeal. Multi-handed decision-making also seems to be more common in certain substantive areas of law, and one example is criminal law. In a case of theft in England, facts might be found and law applied by a panel of three lay magistrates, by a judge with a jury of 12 or even, sometimes, by a single legally trained 'district judge (magistrates' court)'.[10] But while lay magistrates and a single district judge decide both the law and the facts, in a jury trial the judge decides the law and the jury decide facts. The same is true in the Japanese *saiban-in seido*, where three professional judges and six lay jurors decide questions

7 The review of a decision of a *Parlement*, a court of appeal prior to the Revolution was carried out by a similar body and that tradition was deliberately continued by the revolutionaries.

8 Subject only to procedural limits, such as time limits to submit, and limits on the seriousness of the grounds, which lead to a streamlined non-admission procedure.

9 Case load is of course a problem for many legal systems. The English and Welsh senior judiciary are struggling to fill their ranks, particularly at the level of the High Court, in part because of case load issues (as well, perhaps, as pay and conditions). Nonetheless, there is a very different expectation of how cases should be handled when, for example, tens of cases come each year rather than hundreds.

10 Theft under section 1(1) of the Theft Act 1968 is triable either way, either in the Magistrates court or on indictment in the Crown Court (with stronger procedural safeguards, a jury and a greater sentencing range).

of fact by a qualified majority (a majority which must include at least one judge).[11] There appears to be a general rule of thumb that the lower the legal expertise of the decision-makers, the more of them are needed, even to decide matters of fact rather than law.[12]

In respect of judicial background, one of the key questions is perhaps incapable of resolution: how do you make the best judge? In many legal systems, being a judge is a career that law students can apply for like any other, sitting as judges before they have reached thirty years of age. By contrast, in the common law tradition, senior judges are drawn almost exclusively from proven advocates. In England and Wales, this also means the youngest high court judge is rarely much under fifty years of age, and a judge retires at 70 years old (if appointed after 1995; if before, s/he must retire by 75).[13] These former top advocates unsurprisingly tend to continue to value advocacy, especially oral advocacy. It might even be that forms of advocacy and legal practices are perpetuated by their practitioners being elevated to the bench and looking for them from there. More generally, it might mean that the judge values the independence and personal reputation that mark the English advocate, which itself might carry over into how judicial decisions are made. But it is hard to believe that judges are unable to see merit in new techniques at the bar or bench. The advantages in new technologies for presenting cases must be just such an example. How long before judges find advocacy in massed bundles of hardcopy to be unhelpful, rather than digital courtrooms, even though it was what everyone cut their teeth on? It is also important to recall that many English lawyers did not do law degrees, but some other subject and then did a one-year legal qualification before legal practice.[14] There is thus a much wider base of expertise at the bar and on the bench than a joint formative experience in law faculties. There is instead a focus on facts and argument as something of a unifying approach if nothing else is. That approach is also one infinitely adaptable, rather than bound to a particular

---

11 On the Japanese system, see the contribution by A Ojima and N Onishi in chapter 11 of the present collection (esp at p 222) This system might be particularly suited to a legal setting where potentially young judges deal with conviction rates of almost 100%, and confession rates are not much lower, while on the other hand violent and particularly firearms offences are rare. Consider also the lay *jurat* in Jersey and Guernsey, on the history of which see CEA Bedwell, 'IV – The office of the Jurat in the Royal Courts of Jersey and Guernsey' (1908) 34 *Law Magazine and Review: A Quarterly Review of Jurisprudence* (5th series) 159.

12 This logic is inverted for an appeal, where it is very common to have at least three professional judges.

13 Judicial Pensions and Retirement Act 1993, section 26.

14 It was only from the 1970s that a law degree (whether a three-year undergraduate degree or a one-year conversion after another degree) was required for legal practice; even then, it was to be followed by a vocational training period (typically of a year) before traineeship as a lawyer: see generally, A Boon and J Webb, 'Legal Education and Training in England and Wales: Back to the Future?' (2008) 58 *Journal of Legal Education* 79, 87. The point was to learn on the job, and law was not, until relatively recently, regarded by many in practice and beyond, as an academic discipline.

structure or form. Finally, senior judges are also often relatively few in number, which is certainly the case in England and Wales: the High Court having around 110, the Court of Appeal having 38 and the Supreme Court having 12, with the four heads of court divisions in addition. This makes for a very small group of repeat players, where a judge has argued before, or sat with, most of the judges he is likely to sit with on any given case. That said, there are many thousand more circuit judges, tribunal judges and even tribunal members (who are typically lay people), and collective decision-making is particularly prevalent in tribunals. What little research has been done on judicial decision-making has tended to focus on senior judges, for reasons of scale, access and legal significance.[15]

III. HOW DECISIONS ARE MADE

Collective judicial decision-making finally depends on *how decisions are made*, and three aspects are particularly important here: mechanisms for engagement, techniques for persuasion, and expressions of decision-making.

1. MECHANISMS FOR ENGAGEMENT

First, there are different *mechanisms for engagement* between colleagues. Obvious examples of this are the conferences or discussions before, during and after a hearing.[16] Other examples are about how, especially how soon, draft judgments must be responded to, and the possible sanctions in case of delay.[17] Formal mechanisms like these can be incredibly effective in promoting group decision-making. However, as is clear from many legal transplants, a mechanism rarely works in precisely the same way when it is transplanted from one judiciary to another.[18] One obvious problem is different judicial cultures. A system for open debate, where judges are of different seniorities, might need careful integration

---

15 See n 3 above, esp Paterson, but *cf* Darbyshire.

16 Even during an oral hearing, one judge might shoot a question to an advocate, but intending the point to rebound to a colleague on the bench. This was neatly described by one participant at the workshop as akin to a game of squash (where a player hits a ball against a wall and the rebound is what the opposing player must respond to).

17 In US Courts of Appeals, for example, different mechanisms are employed to encourage panel members to respond to a draft in a timely manner: see the contribution by HT Edwards in chapter 5 of the present collection (at pp 85–86, 100).

18 See generally D Nelken, 'Legal Transplants and Beyond: of disciplines and metaphors' in A Harding and E Örücü (eds), *Comparative Law in the 21st Century* (London, Kluwer, 2002) 19; A Watson, *Legal Transplants* (Edinburgh, Scottish Academic Press, 1974). *Cf* W Ewald 'Comparative Jurisprudence (II): The Logic of Legal Transplants' (1995) 43 *American Journal of Comparative Law* 489; P Legrand, 'What "Legal Transplants"?' in J Feest and D Nelken (eds), *Adapting Legal Cultures* (Oxford, Hart Publishing, 2001), and most importantly Sacco (n 2).

into cultures where hierarchies are common and individuality is frowned upon.[19] But informal effects can persist whatever the system. To take just one example, personal interactions have always been important, perhaps particularly so in the world before discussion and debate took place so frequently by email. The office of Lord Brown of Eaton-under-Heywood in the House of Lords was perfectly positioned next to the kitchen and the secretaries: when other Law Lords went to get tea or coffee, social interactions and chance (or deliberate) discussions could take place. This might explain why Lord Brown was commonly in a majority decision.[20]

2. TECHNIQUES OF PERSUASION

Second, there are *techniques of persuasion*. Are judges as a group, rather than judges alone, persuaded more effectively by certain ways of formulating arguments? Certainly many would suggest that persuading a smaller group is usually easier than persuading a larger group. Three seems to be thought the ideal number for a court hearing a first appeal from a trial. But it is very hard to say any more than that. Some judges might be persuaded more easily by argument on paper from counsel,[21] or by their colleagues, than others; some judges might have more stamina to read the papers in fine detail before a case than others, and thus might have already formed more of a view of the case before discussion. Judges themselves talk of colleagues 'thinking again', or 'weighing the arguments again' and being 'persuaded', but opening up that process to scrutiny is as hard, if not harder, than understanding why anyone is persuaded of anything. Alan Paterson's work on the Supreme Court is the benchmark for scholarship in this area, but his decades of work have only unlocked some aspects of how the UK Supreme Court works. In large part this is because such painstaking academic work necessarily has a lag, typically of at least half a year and often significantly more.[22] One aspect of techniques of persuasion is how the judge views his or her role as part of a court. There is much in Lord Neuberger's remark that:

> '[English] appellate courts consist of a number of judges who happen to be sitting on the same bench, whereas courts such as the CJEU consist of a single bench which happens to comprise more than one judge.'[23]

---

19 An example would be the Japanese proverb, 'The head of the nail that sticks up is pounded down', suggesting that standing out leads to criticism.

20 Paterson (n 3) 157–58; see there also the table on p 153 and generally at 167–69.

21 In England and Wales, the outline of counsel's argument, or 'skeleton argument' became more common in the 1980s and is now standard: Zander (n 3) 388–92.

22 Paterson (n 3).

23 Lord Neuberger, 'Tweaking the Curial Veil', The Blackstone Lecture 2014, delivered on 15 November 2014, (available online via www.supremecourt.uk/docs/speech-141115.pdf, last accessed 29 February 2020), para 9.

Lord Neuberger was speaking as President of the Supreme Court, that Court having begun the UK court of final appeal in 2009, taking over from the Appellate Committee of the House of Lords. Since then the Court has handed down significantly more single majority opinions, as opposed to individual ones,[24] and had also engaged in more discussion before and after the hearing. Perhaps its identity as a formally independent body has helped develop a self-identity as a court, rather than as a number of judges who happen to sit on the same bench.

There are also significant differences in how a court perceives itself: in Germany it is simply stated that there are five Supreme Courts (as well as the Federal Constitutional Court), all different but parallel,[25] while in France it is stressed that there is only one *Cour de cassation*, even though it has hundreds of members and tens of Chambers.[26] By contrast, the individual judge is seen as having a greater role, whatever court he is on, within the common law tradition. A large part of this individual influence lies in how much colleagues are persuaded, and part of that is in how much each judge seeks to persuade others. As Lord Wilberforce wrote about Lord Diplock (each of whom became, during his period in office, Senior Law Lord in the House of Lords):

> 'You cannot really estimate a judge's influence without knowing from behind the scenes what influence he had on his colleagues … Lord Diplock possessed the quality of persuading his colleagues to the extreme. It almost got to the stage of a mesmeric quality. He had this sort of intellectual superiority, coupled with enormous hard work. He had always done his homework far better than anyone else, which enabled him to persuade his colleagues to follow his point of view. He would work on persuading people to his point of view during the conduct of the case, in the lunch intervals, in the corridors, in their rooms … Lord Diplock was a very persuasive man.'[27]

---

24 Paterson (n 3) 105–06. They were, in part at least, responding to pressure from the Court of Appeal that five substantive speeches put too much work on lower courts: ibid 104, and see particularly *Doherty v Birmingham CC* [2006] EWCA Civ 1739, [2007] LGR 165, [62] (per Carnwath LJ). Baroness Hale also points out that the freedom from Parliamentary procedure has aided the Justices of the new Supreme Court, such as being able to print the speeches in any order, thus putting a more junior judge who does the 'donkey-work' first: B Hale, 'Judgment Writing in the Supreme Court', speech delivered on 30 September 2010, available online via https://www.supremecourt.uk/docs/speech_100930.pdf (last accessed 29 February 2020).

25 On the German Federal Supreme Court and the German Federal Constitutional Court, see – respectively – the contributions to the present collection by J Schmidt-Räntsch (chapter 7) and G Lübbe-Wolff (chapter 8).

26 See https://www.courdecassation.fr/about_the_court_9256.html (last accessed 29 February 2020).

27 According to G Sturgess and P Chubbs, *Judging the World* (Sydney, Butterworth, 1988) 275.

3. EXPRESSIONS OF DECISION-MAKING

Third, there are the *expressions of decision-making*, most commonly the judgment. The judgment speaks to the litigants, to other judges and, of course, to advocates. A judgment might even contain 'rumblings from Olympus', implications from the court to other lawyers on what might be interesting or valuable for future cases.[28] But are the judgments statements of law, or stories of how a problem has come to be resolved? A Spanish *Tribunal Supremo* decision is typically quite business-like in its expression of the underlying legal questions and their resolution on the facts. In England, personalised, and often narrative judgments, are still the norm. Even when in agreement, there was for many decades a tradition that each judge would speak, if only to say 'I agree'. The test of a decision was not simply whether there was one judgment, but whether there was any dissent as opposed to concurrence.[29] Dissent in the UK Supreme Court is statistically somewhat rare, and it has been suggested that the careful debates between judges before, during, and after the oral hearing promote the resolution of disagreement.[30] Nonetheless, in the UK, but even more so in other common law jurisdictions, there have been significant movements towards composite or single judgments. This process seems to represent a cultural shift towards viewing single judgments as an expression of clarity of understanding, rather than individual attempts to constructing the problem as the best way to find the best possible approach. In a sense, 'individual paths to truth' and 'collective clarity' are either ends of a spectrum, and many courts seem to be moving along it, towards fewer judgments.

Yet this brings greater focus to the process of judgment writing as a mechanism of persuasion in itself. Judges hope to persuade the litigants. They also hope to persuade the wider legal community, even though the paradigm of judicial authority makes persuasion formally unnecessary. But more than that, judges might hope to persuade their peers through a draft. That draft might even be deliberately different to what is intended ultimately to be handed down. The Justices of the UK Supreme Court are open to seeing hyperbole and insult of each other's ideas in drafts on the condition that it is removed before the judgment becomes public, thus to have the fun of reading the insult amongst

---

28 P Devlin, *The Judge* (Oxford, Oxford University Press, 1979) 11.

29 For an informative look at concurring judgments in Canada at the start of Chief Justice Beverley McLaughlin's term, see P McCormick, 'The Choral Court: Separate Concurrence and the McLachlin Court, 2000–2004' (2005) 37 *Ottawa Law Review* 1; on England, see J Lee, 'A Defence of Concurring Speeches' [2009] *Public Law* 305 as well as J Lee's contribution in chapter 17 of the present collection (esp at pp 304 et seq, 318 et seq).

30 Lord Kerr of Tonaghmore, 'Dissenting Judgments – Self Indulgence or Self Sacrifice?', The Birkenhead Lecture, 8 October 2012, (available online via https://www.supremecourt.uk/docs/speech-121008.pdf, last accessed 29 February 2020), esp 17–19.

colleagues, not the sting of having it read outside the court.[31] A persuasive draft will be one that accounts not only for the law, but how that law has been argued by other judges and lawyers. In the High Court of Australia, it appears that this weaving in of arguments is accompanied by a depersonalised drafting style, the better to attract others who could see it as their own words. This is because in the last twenty years or so, the High Court has adopted moved away from one judge simply agreeing with another, to 'joined in' judgments, where one writes a draft and others add their names seamlessly, so there is no external record of who has added what to it.[32] Such a process seems also to happen in the Court of Appeal of England and Wales, and at times in the UK Supreme Court (but it is rare and not always discernible).[33]

The Australian example also reminds us of the important link between how judges justify their decisions and what the judges are actually doing. Many academics and judges in Australia have debated the possible loss of transparency and accountability in judgments,[34] and some stinging judicial rebukes have resulted.[35] Both sides have valid points. One of the more amusing aspects is a group of academics together write a paper which criticises judges for writing together.[36] Such combined judgments obviously mean fewer judgments. A notable trend towards fewer judgments has also been evident in the Supreme

31 Lord Neuberger, 'UK Supreme Court Decisions on Private and Commercial Law: The role of public policy and public interest', Centre for Commercial Law Studies Conference 2015, speech delivered on 4 December 2015 (available online via www.supremecourt.uk/docs/speech-151204.pdf, last accessed 29 February 2020), para [26].

32 An account of collective judging from an Australian perspective is given by Chief Justice S Kiefel in chapter 4 of the present collection. See also the analysis by J Lee in chapter 17 (esp at pp 307 et seq, 312 et seq).

33 See Lee, 'A Defence of Concurring Speeches' (n 29); idem, 'The United Kingdom Supreme Court: A Study in Judicial Reform' in E Guinchard and M-P Granger (eds) *The new EU Judiciary – An analysis of current judicial reforms* (Alphen aan den Rijn, Kluwer, 2017) 77, 91, §4.05.

34 See, eg, E Campbell, 'Reasons For Judgment: Some Consumer Perspectives' (2003) 77 *Australian Law Journal* 62; Heydon (n 3); Sir A Mason, 'Reflections on the High Court: Its Judges and Judgments' (2013) 37 *Australian Bar Review* 102, available online via http://www.austlii.edu.au/au/journals/SCULawRw/2013/1.pdf (last accessed 29 February 2020); P Heerey, 'The Judicial Herd: Seduced by Suave Glittering Phrases?' (2013) 87 *Australian Law Journal* 460; the particularly novel Justice S Gageler, 'Why Write Judgments?' (2014) 36 *Sydney Law Review* 189, available online via http://www.hcourt.gov.au/assets/publications/speeches/current-justices/gagelerj/2014%2036%20sydney%20law%20review%20189.pdf (last accessed 29 February 2020); Justice S Kiefel, 'The Individual Judge' (2014) 88 *Australian Law Journal* 554, available online via https://www.actlawsociety.asn.au/documents/item/944%3E (last accessed 29 February 2020); and, most recently, the volume of the *UNSW Law Journal* on the topic: (2017) 40 *University of New South Wales Law Journal*, issue 2, *The Individual Judge*.

35 Most recently, see Bell J: http://blogs.unimelb.edu.au/opinionsonhigh/2017/06/21/news-bell-j-on-the-individual-judge/ (last accessed 29 February 2020).

36 The contexts are of course, somewhat different, but the reasons of principle remain the same. For a recent example, see A Partovi, R Smyth, I Zukerman and J Valente, 'Addressing "Loss of Identity" in the Joint Judgment: Searching For the "Individual Judge" In the Joint Judgments of the Mason Court' (2017) 40 *UNSW Law Journal* 670.

Court of Canada.[37] It has been suggested that unanimity is only rarely an explicit aim, but when it is, the result is actually to reduce the depth and breadth of consensus in the legal or policy outcomes in the written reasons.[38] Peter McCormick has written in detail about this trend, tracing its beginnings to the 1960s, decades after the same process in the USA, and decades before the Australia 'joined in' trend. McCormick suggests that it was the institution of regular judicial conferences after hearings which changed the judgment writing paradigm. But he adds that moving to fewer judgments was not a neutral process. A *seriatim* court, where each judge gives a judgment, he thought:

> 'is well-suited to applying long-standing legal principles to immediate disputes: if several judges pursue independent enquiries and reach the same outcome supported by similar reasons, this demonstrates that previously established neutral principles direct a particular outcome. In redundancy lies reassurance; in decentralized fragmentation lies protection. The conferencing court is better suited for coherent systematic leadership and, particularly, for innovation. Which of these two is the better vehicle for the judicial junction depends on what you think judges ought to be doing.'[39]

As McCormick warns, there are trade-offs. Certain types of decision-making might be likely to produce certain outcomes, whether stability and rigour or innovation and fresh perspective. A related issue is where one sits on a scale of what the best form of decision making is: impersonal groups ('collective clarity') or aggregated individuals ('individual paths to truth'). If judges pull in different directions, having a single judgment as a harness might give a single direction; though none of them might be happy with that aggregate direction. It is also possible that a single statement which commands respect might be too vague or fail to resolve the underlying tension and leave too few clues for the future. As is commonly said of contracts (and treaties), that they are 'disagreements reduced to writing', there is clearly a risk in thinking agreement answers all relevant questions. Lawyers might also think that, by losing the individual judgment, they are losing a guide to what persuaded individual judges and what might persuade them in the future. By contrast, working in teams can function in impressive

37 For a recent look, see E Macfarlane, 'Consensus and Unanimity at the Supreme Court of Canada' (2010) 52 SCLR (2d) 379.

38 E Macfarlane, *Governing from the Bench: The Supreme Court of Canada and the Judicial Role* (Vancouver and Toronto, UBC Press, 2013) 102 and ch 4 generally.

39 P McCormick, *Supreme at Last: The Evolution of the Supreme Court of Canada* (Toronto, James Lorimer & Co, 2000) 64. McCormick goes on to suggest that individual judges made themselves the centre of the Court, writing more judgments themselves and giving fewer dissents and concurrences, giving (Ronald) Martin J and (Patrick) Kerwin J as prime examples: ibid 66.

ways, and not only within the judiciary. In France, the almost priestly role of academics, carefully explaining terse *Cour de cassation* judgments, has grown up over many years as a close relationship between specialised groups at the bench and in academia. It is not, as some foreigners think, simply a necessary evil. At least to many in France, while it is not perfect, it is a partnership where the different actors carry out different tasks but pursuing a common goal.[40]

IV. CONCLUSION

The key question must be how judges reach their decisions and what the differences are when they do so as a group. Issues of what task they are performing, who they are, and how group decisions are made, are three important factors. Some individual perceptions, grounded in the practices of one judiciary and legal system, might need refining before their full value can be realised. For instance, it is overly simplistic to see a rule-based decision-making process with strict time limits as inherently better than an informal one. Similarly, single composite judgments do not necessarily show more clarity, multiple independent minds assessing evidence do not necessarily produce better answers, and deciding a very large number of cases does not necessarily make the decision-maker into a bureaucrat. By the same token, models of working, whether as scientists or humanities scholars, vary across universities and countries, as across government departments and ranks. We need to move past individual examples and generalisations: build a conceptual structure of decision-making, populate it with good examples, and test the explanations we generate. Specific anecdotes need not be seen as synecdoche. They can be unpacked and slotted into a wider conceptual structure of decision-making. With enough honest examples we can test what comparisons and explanations our structure generates. We must avoid the risk that in trying to probe judicial decision-making, we might impede it. Having judicial discussions public rather than private might reduce the openness of ideas and discussion. Perhaps instituting a tradition of valedictory despatches from the bench, thus importing the diplomatic tradition in a new setting, might be enlightening. They could be sealed from the public for 30 years to help generate honest, if not necessarily perfect, perspectives on judicial decisions. The only difficulty would be making sure no academics got their hands on them first.

[40] See particularly M de SOl'E Lasser, *Judicial Deliberations: A Comparative Analysis of Judicial Transparency and Legitimacy* (Oxford, Oxford University Press, 2004).

CHAPTER 20
CONCLUDING REMARKS

Wolfgang ERNST, Beate GSELL, Birke HÄCKER and Thomas RÜFNER*

When we first conceived the conference documented in this volume, we started with quite a narrow focus. We wanted to compare 'group choice' mechanisms employed by a selection of important courts around the world. We thereby hoped to learn more about voting processes and their formal frameworks, and possibly to explore the equivalent in judiciaries where such processes are not a formal part of the collegiate decision-making process. In short, we were primarily after the 'rules of voting' in collegiate courts. We did indeed learn much about such processes. Yet the most enlightening product of the conference was arguably a broadening of our perspective: We began to understand better the interconnectedness of a range of different elements, all of which impact the quality of collegiate decision-making in a much more direct or significant way than we had anticipated.

The size of the collegiate body, for instance, appears to be a decisive factor within the decision-making process, in that it is liable either to encourage or to inhibit a free exchange of views. The larger the number of judges involved, the more formal their contributions tend to become. Very large benches also tend to emphasise the role of the presiding judge and the *rapporteur*, right up to a point where all other members of the panel risk losing the chance to influence the decision-making process effectively. Though a smaller body does not necessarily guarantee a free exchange of arguments, it seems to us that

* The authors jointly organised the 'Collective Judging' conference. Wolfgang Ernst is the Regius Professor of Civil Law, University of Oxford, and a Fellow of All Souls College. Beate Gsell is Professor of Private Law, Civil Procedure and European Private Law and Procedure at Ludwig-Maximilians-Universität (LMU) München as well as a Judge at the Higher Regional Court of Appeal in Munich (*OLG München*). Birke Häcker is the Professor of Comparative Law, the Director of the Institute of European and Comparative Law, University of Oxford, and a Fellow of Brasenose College. Thomas Rüfner is Professor of Private Law, Roman Law, Legal History and Civil Procedure at the University of Trier as well as a Judge at the Higher Regional Court of Appeal in Koblenz (*OLG Koblenz*).

'going big' is almost certainly detrimental to a culture of substantive debate. The practice of some judiciaries to compose larger benches for cases deemed to be a greater 'importance' than others may therefore actually have an adverse effect on the quality of intra-court exchanges.

One feature of collegiate decision-making which we had thitherto not sufficiently appreciated was the fact that 'trilaterality' of proceedings can make for intellectually highly productive interactions: The judges of a bench interact not only with one another, but also with both of the parties. When one compares appellate and supreme courts of various jurisdictions, one finds a striking difference regarding the involvement of parties and their lawyers in the exchange of legal arguments which set the stage for the ultimate decision-making. Moreover, there seems to be insufficient awareness that advocates' contributions are a 'design element' which could be employed to incentivise the discussion among judges, too. A lively oral hearing with the parties' lawyers provides an especially fertile ground for debate, by comparison with courts where the parties' input takes the form of written briefs to be discussed by the judges *in camera*. An oral hearing in which judges engage with the parties' advocates may also incentivise the active participation of judges who are neither presiding nor reporting. It is a ubiquitous risk of collegiate decision-making that members who ought actively to contribute to the process 'tune out' unless positively challenged.

We further gained a better appreciation of the role of judicial assistants. Their role is not necessarily confined to supporting the judges to whom they are assigned. Insofar as they are allowed or encouraged to interact among themselves, they will create a parallel 'group choice' environment, which may to some extent predetermine the discussion among the members of the court. A 'design element' which has not yet been sufficiently tested, as we see it, is the incorporation of judicial assistants into the formal decision-making process, by way of giving them a say – if not a vote – in the decisive post-trial hearing or even at an earlier stage.

An element of some importance is the order in which courts sequence the input from a *rapporteur*, the judges' conference(s), and a hearing with the parties. It seems desirable to prevent prospective decisions emerging prematurely, so as to avoid turning all subsequent steps of the procedure into a mere formality. On a seemingly profane level, a tight case-management keeping all the judges in the loop and pushing for a short and intense throughput may also encourage individual judges to participate more intensely.

Most importantly in our view, the conference identified a 'soft' factor which seems indispensable for the successful working of a collegiate court. It is the team spirit, the *esprit de corps*: all members of the court must act on the conviction that producing a good judgment (or, where appropriate, a good set of judgements in the common law tradition) is a truly joint exercise. This team spirit is not an element that can be 'switched on' at will. However, we suspect there are factors which indirectly contribute to the all-important team spirit, most notably judicial career patterns.

We realised at the conference just how important the judges' election or appointment processes were for a well-functioning collegiate court, or – in a wider sense – the typical career patterns leading to an appeal or supreme court position. If judges share a common background, such as at the Inns of Court in London, members of a bench will already know one another well when sitting together for the first time. While the resulting uniformity may also have considerable downsides, of course, it can assist in building and nurturing the spirit of a shared task and a shared methodology as to how one should proceed. Electing judges from quite diverse backgrounds is highly attractive from a number of perspectives, yet it may at the same time increase the difficulties of building the spirit of a team unified by a common task. This realisation is important as it underscores the need to pay particular attention to 'team building' in more diversely constituted courts.

Supra- and international courts face the additional challenge of building collegiate teams from lawyers originating in different judiciaries and legal traditions. That challenge may be met more readily where a court, by virtue of its subject-matter and remit, brings together experts from the same field of law who may already be familiar with each other. Nonetheless, extra impediments can arise when these experts have no previous experience of collective judicial decision-making, as will for instance be the case with legal academics who have tended to work 'in freedom and loneliness' before joining the judiciary. Unfortunately, the conference *rapporteur* for arbitration whom we had invited to speak was prevented from contributing to the event. It would have been interesting to learn to what degree arbitrators, who tend to come from a fairly close-knit pool of lawyers, feel the need to acquaint themselves with each other when coming together to hear a new case.

In systems where career judges 'advance' through their national judiciary, which they have entered not long after graduating, they will typically have gained experience in collective judging over the years by the time they reach the appeal or supreme court level. They will thus have a sound idea of how collegiate interaction works. These experiences, however, need not be solely positive or consist only of active contributions. A young judge who realises that the presiding judge 'calls the shots' may well take this to be the normal state of affairs. Advancement in career judiciaries may, moreover, depend on the shown ability to 'blend in' within a collegiate setting. While this may be seen as a contribution to swift and efficient operation in the higher echelons of the judiciary, there is also a real risk of predominantly promoting yea-sayers.

Mixed responses were triggered by the idea, championed by Ernst, that collegiate decision-making processes within many judiciaries need to become more transparent, both for the parties concerned and for the public at large. We learned that courts nowadays make increasing efforts to let the public access paperwork produced in the course of proceedings, by putting briefs, minutes of hearings, etc online, if possible in a speedy, sometimes almost real-time manner. In addition, intensive debate about streaming oral hearings appears to be on-foot. While the respective benefits and downsides – greater transparency *versus* lawyers and judges 'playing to the gallery' – are still being weighed up, there seems to be a distinct trend in favour of giving the public easier and broader access to hearings. There was, however, also a clear and almost unanimous signal that judges remained in need of an intellectual 'shelter' where they can test ideas and arguments in an open and unrecorded exchange, trying to see which way a majority (if required or desired) might be found. The strong sentiment voiced at the conference was that such exchanges needed secrecy to remain frank and intellectually fruitful.

A difference of approach and opinion emerged regarding the post-decision position of individual judges, which may have an (indirect) impact on the collegiate decision-making process, and the post-decision spirit required of members of a bench. Are judges at liberty to comment publicly on the collegiate decision to which they have contributed? This is less of a problem for courts in the common law tradition, where judges can always choose to give, in full court, an individual opinion setting out their own views without the need to compromise as part of a group. However, judges who do not have this option and perhaps lack the valve of a publishable dissenting opinion, if outvoted, may wish to distance themselves by way of a critical case note or the like. This, in turn, may harm the spirit of the team exercise. Comparing courts and judiciaries, considerable differences emerged as to the appropriateness – or even the legality – of such post-decision publications.

In summary, we came away from the conference with the conclusion that many and diverse factors impact on the collegiate process: the size of the collegiate body; the biographical background of the judges (both in terms of collegiate work experience and in terms of homogeneity *versus* diversity); the recruitment/selection process for appeal and supreme courts; the role of judicial assistants; case management procedures; the secrecy or transparency of intra-court debates; supplementary outlets for dissenting votes and public *ex post facto* comments by individual judges. All these elements deserve attention and scrutiny in and of themselves, but even more so in their interconnectedness.

ABOUT THE EDITORS

Wolfgang Ernst is the 29th Regius Professor of Civil Law in the University of Oxford and a Fellow of All Souls College. His main areas of research and teaching are Roman law and the Roman law based doctrinal history of civil law. Recent research topics include monetary legal history and the legal history of 'social choice', including the history of collective judging. He also contributes to contemporary private law issues, with a main focus on contract law, personal property (including art restitution issues), and monetary law.

Birke Häcker is Professor of Comparative Law and the Director of the Institute of European and Comparative Law at the University of Oxford; she is also a Fellow of Brasenose College. Educated in both English and German law, her work has for many years spanned different legal systems. Her main areas of research and teaching lie in comparative private law and comparative legal history. Besides bridging the traditional common law/civil law divide, she has a specific interest in the emerging 'comparative common law' phenomenon.

www.ingramcontent.com/pod-product-compliance
Ingram Content Group UK Ltd.
Pitfield, Milton Keynes, MK11 3LW, UK
UKHW051846100926
8556IPUK00005B/486

9 781780 6862